Praise for *Xenolinguistics*

"*Xenolinguistics* is one of the most compelling and interesting books that I've ever read in my life; I found it truly difficult to put down. Part frontier science, part mystery adventure, part alien language manual, and part interdisciplinary philosophy, this uniquely envisioned book is impossible to categorize in any traditional form. Slattery breaks new ground, bravely exploring the fascinating relationship between symbolic representation, psychonaut 'downloads,' consciousness, and reality. Future generations will surely recognize this cutting-edge book for helping to establish the foundation of humanity's post-larval entry into the extraterrestrial and inter-dimensional arenas of interspecies communication. Masterfully crafted, alchemically blending a wide range of perspectives, and overflowing with fascinating details about secret languages, rare treasures composed of unusual information, and profound insights elegantly expressed. Psychedelic explorers, science fiction lovers, and students of the unexplained will savor every sentence in this brilliant and thought-provoking book. You can bet that the aliens are certainly paying attention!"

—David Jay Brown, author of *The New Science of Psychedelics* and *Mavericks of the Mind*

"Diana Reed Slattery's *Xenolinguistics* is an extraordinary work: at once a heroic and breathtaking psychonaut's tale, a highly original philosophical treatise concerning what happens at the edge of language and beyond, and a neurophenomenological meditation that beckons us towards sciences of the future."

—Marcus Boon, author of *The Road of Excess: A History of Writers on Drugs*

"Seen through the lens of her perspectives on language, Slattery's *Xenolinguistics* provides a comprehensive introduction to the possibilities of disciplined exploration of non-ordinary states of consciousness. Her work catalogues the ways that transdimensional reality may be accessed and explicates its utility as a kind of cosmic search engine from which information on individual self-transformation and collective human ventures may be gathered in a systematic and expedient way."

—Hidden Mountain, Women's Visionary Congress

"The ineffable Other has a faithful scribe, and it is Diana Reed Slattery. Slattery has crafted the first codex of languages reaching back to us from the unspeakable. Magic was always incanted into being through alien languages. Slattery has reopened the linguistic doorway for our return to magic. She bravely glided behind the mesh of the cosmos and returned with the news: it's all built of language!"

—Bruce Damer, PhD, author of *Avatars!: Exploring and Building Virtual Worlds on the Internet*

"The intersection of human language and the psychedelic experience was initially brought to light through the work of Terence McKenna. Since his death in 2000, however, there has been far too little work in this field. In fact, I know of only one person who is qualified to take it to the next level. That person is Diana Reed Slattery. Her scholarly background, coupled with a deep understanding of psychedelic culture, places Diana in a perfect position to help us explore one of the central features of our lives, language. Whether you are an experienced psychonaut or budding linguist, *Xenolinguistics: Psychedelics, Language, and the Evolution of Consciousness* is a book that belongs in your personal library."

—Lorenzo Hagerty, host of Psychedelic Salon podcasts, and author of *The Genesis Generation* and *The Spirit of the Internet*

"Slattery provides us with a first-person ethnographic account of the psychonautic landscape where a first-person science—phenomenological methods and self-reflexivity—organizes her encounters in entheogenic realms. She places psychedelic experiences within a discourse on the phenomenology of knowledge and epistemology and other psychonautic accounts. Her analyses provide a transdisciplinary scope for analyzing the nature of entheogenic worlds. Slattery illustrates how psychedelic technologies extend perception and the senses and permit a reorganization of reality within which the psychonaut functions as an ontological engineer of the entheogenic landscape. The book examines psychedelics in terms of their effects in enhancing certain aspects of extended perception and the increased focus on the mechanics of the formation of perception and reality. A combination of phenomenological description and neurological analysis leads us to a glimpse of a neurophenomenological understanding of the neurognostic landscape of crystal vision, extended perception, hyperconnectivity, hyperconductivity, and multilayered realities and consciousness. *Xenolinguistics'* engagement with entheogenic realities through dialogue with the alien other and emergent xenolinguistic systems instills a zest for the exploration of the further realms of consciousness."

—Michael Winkelman, MPH, PhD, co-editor of *Psychedelic Medicine* and *Altering Consciousness*

"Effing the ineffable—how to communicate the wordless unspeakable, think the preconceptual, visualize the invisible, symbolize the powerful-vague—psychedelicists and other travelers to other realms of consciousness have been stumped by these topics for millennia. By collecting current and historical examples, Slattery's *Xenolinguistics* tackles these conundrums, applies current consciousness theories, and sheds light into these esoteric corners of human communication. *Xenolinguistics* challenges its readers to wrestle with these topics and to pursue further explorations. The result? A sort of psychedelic psycholinguistics plus an ineffable more."

—Thomas Roberts, PhD, author of *The Psychedelic Future of the Mind*

Xenolinguistics

Xenolinguistics

PSYCHEDELICS, LANGUAGE, AND THE EVOLUTION OF CONSCIOUSNESS

Diana Reed Slattery

Berkeley, California

Published by Evolver Editions, an imprint of North Atlantic Books
P.O. Box 12327
Berkeley, California 94712

Cover art by Diana Reed Slattery
Cover design by Mary Ann Casler, Michael Robinson, and Awake Media
Interior design by Brad Greene
Printed in the United States of America

Xenolinguistics: Psychedelics, Language, and the Evolution of Consciousness is sponsored and published by the Society for the Study of Native Arts and Sciences (dba North Atlantic Books), an educational nonprofit based in Berkeley, California, that collaborates with partners to develop cross-cultural perspectives, nurture holistic views of art, science, the humanities, and healing, and seed personal and global transformation by publishing work on the relationship of body, spirit, and nature.

Library of Congress Cataloging-in-Publication Data

Slattery, Diana Reed.
Xenolinguistics : psychedelics, language, and the evolution of consciousness / Diana Reed Slattery.
pages cm
Includes bibliographical references.
Summary: "Explores the premise that language and consciousness coevolve in the highly plastic human brain as features of both our biological and social evolution. Author Diana Reed Slattery shares how psychedelic states of consciousness can produce novel forms of language and healing"—Provided by publisher.
ISBN 978-1-58394-599-5
1. Psycholinguistics. 2. Psychonautics. 3. Altered states of consciousness. I. Title.
P37.S516 2015
401'.9—dc 3

2013045339

1 2 3 4 5 6 7 8 9 UNITED 20 19 18 17 16 15

Printed on recycled paper

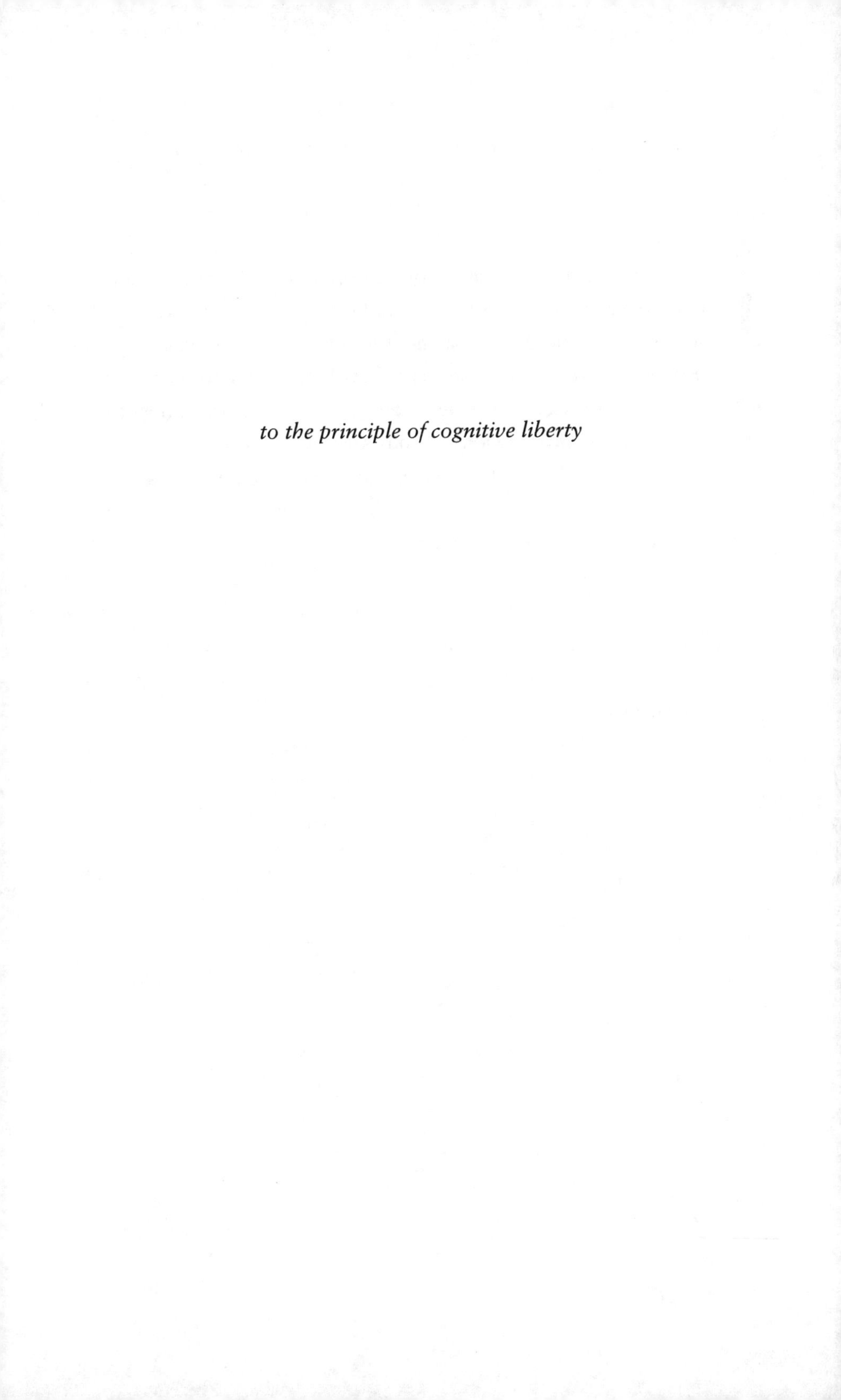

to the principle of cognitive liberty

Acknowledgments

I thank Roy Ascott of the Planetary Collegium for academic support for my "outsider" doctoral work. Without his help, this book would not be. And I thank Dennis McKenna and Tom Ray for answering so many of my questions so patiently. Most of the others I would like to thank are my fellow psychonauts who gave so generously of their materials, tips, tricks, and cautionary tales. For obvious reasons, they shall not be named.

Contents

Foreword: Visionary Language

by Allyson Grey

In the Hebrew Bible, the Book of Daniel tells of Belshazzar, sixth-century BC King of Babylon, who "saw the writing on the wall." During his banquet for a thousand statesmen, Belshazzar ordered all the goblets and vessels of gold, stolen from the conquered and destroyed Jewish Temple in Jerusalem, to be brought out for his guests to admire and drink wine. At that moment, a hand appeared and began writing on the wall. The king's amazement and fear brought forth the palace astrologers, magicians and soothsayers, but none could interpret the writing on the wall. The queen remembered Daniel, an old Jew who was given the position of chief magician by Belshazzar's father and predecessor, King Nebuchadnezzar. The prophet was called upon to interpret the secret writing that came through mysterious means.

This archetypal story of visionary writing is one of many throughout Jewish religious literature. The appearance of the writing on the tablets at Mt. Sinai with Moses is an example of visionary writing. The very "name of G-d" YHVH is "unpronounceable" in recognition that the Transcendent Source is beyond words, beyond reasoning thoughts and concepts. I'm sharing this because when Diana Reed Slattery and I met, our "Jew-dar" went off immediately. Last names, usually a clue for Jewish inter-recognition, did not reveal the ancestry of Slattery and Grey as did our physical appearance upon sight. Our parallel life paths engaged with visionary languages suddenly fit into a greater context. For Jews, sometimes called "the people of the Book," The Word is at the center of our tradition. The very structure of Judaism revolves around the chronological reading and discussion of the handmade, hand-scribed precious scroll of writing. Written by hand to this day, every letter in a Torah is perfect and the same as in every other Torah for as long as there have been Torahs. No synagogue in the world can *be* a synagogue without a Torah hand-scribed on lamb skin by an ordained sopher. Sitting in any synagogue, the congregation faces the Arc, the closet that holds the Torah(s). The opening of the Arc is preceded by special prayers sung by the rabbi, cantor and all the congregation. The precious scroll containing the written word of the people is often dressed in decorative silver, satin and gold thread embroidery. It is carried up and down the aisles as the congregation dances and sings. As the Torah passes close enough to touch, we wait and kiss our prayer book or prayer shawl before touching the treasured scroll. The first written word of God to the Jewish people came from God-contact with Moses on top of Mt. Sinai. Moses was very clear that God has no face and that no image of God is adequate to portray the Divine. In fact, graven images are strictly prohibited as is true also for Muslims, who follow the other religion whose origin begins with Abraham, destroyer of graven images. Creating mystic languages of written symbols is a uniquely human characteristic deriving from visionary contact with the Divine Imagination and Reality.

My most profound inner experiences told me to align with "the sacred." After years of art school training in sketch art, figure drawing, painting, and modeling, I chose to avoid any human depiction of the Divine. Secret Writing first appeared to me in 1971 during an LSD trip in my tiny Cambridge college room. After having just read the book *Remember Be Here Now,* I shared identical hits of the "sacrament" with two high school friends who had also just read this same popular book that had recently been released. In the book, Ram Dass, a former Jewish psychiatrist, recounts seeing the White Light during an acid trip that led to his spiritual opening. Inspired by his discoveries, my friends and I sought the heart of Mystery. Deep into the trip, letterforms and symbols from a language I did not recognize became visible skimming the surfaces of all objects in the room. Washing over the faces and figures, an array of secret symbols floated like infinite ribbons in mid-air, rimming the edges and surfaces of everything in the room. This secret writing communicated the ineffable in a spectral glowing array of light. Their meaning was holy and precious, unpronounceable and ineffable. One of my friends, a godless politico, reported no experience of the White Light whatsoever. The other friend shortly thereafter became a Born Again Christian and disassociated from us all. Advised by Ram Dass in his book, I began looking for a meditation group to start my spiritual path. I never renounced the sacrament and continued to sojourn. The letters continued to appear.

■ **Secret Writing Batik, Allyson Grey, 1976, dyed cloth, 11 x 14.**

During the summers, I taught batik, a wax resist and fabric dying art technique. The batik artist draws with a pen-like tool filled with hot wax. To keep the liquid flowing, the artist has to move quickly along the surface. Speed and confidence is key. It is under these conditions, using this technique, that the letters flowed out spontaneously, resembling the writing I had seen in my psychedelic visions. On one of our earliest dates, I showed Alex (my husband) a large stack of batiks. He turned the colorful pages covered with an enigmatic symbol system and inquired about its origin. Now, Alex's first LSD experience occurred in my apartment and we have always celebrated that date as the anniversary of our "First Knowing the Beloved." When Alex found that the origin of the secret language came from an LSD open to Divine, he immediately recognized the significance of this mystic symbol outpouring as an essential expression of my psyche. Alex influenced me to develop the secret writing personal symbol system that has become my signature work.

> Alex: There is a rational and an intuitive side of our brain. The rational left hemisphere is word and meaning focused and logically driven. The right hemisphere is spatial, aesthetic, intuitive, and holistic. Allyson's Secret Writing is what language looks like from the intuitive side. It has structure but is divorced from rational meaning, a purely aesthetic language.
>
> When we've tripped together, I've seen the letters on her skin, moving in channels, flowing over the surface of her arm, her hand, her face. It hovered a bit above the surface, not like a tattoo that is embedded. It never stopped slowly moving. The letters were darkish grey like ink, but translucent. It felt like a flowing mystery language that points to something sacred. They came from the source of mystery like a calling card.

The first year Alex and I began living together, 1975, was the second and final year of my Masters of Fine Arts program. I was expected to prepare a solo exhibition and a written thesis that justified my artwork, placing it in an art historical and creative context of some significance. For fourteen hours a day, I sat under the skylight with a drawing board on my lap. Letterforms flowed out of my rapid-o-graph pen, in minute rows, onto large full-sheets of thick archival drawing paper. From any distance, the pages looked identical, yet each was utterly and completely unique. In six months, there were ten meticulous drawings of tiny characters—minimal, enigmatic, seriously committed, a wall against rational communication . . .

Archetypal letterforms recurred again and again within the infinite vocabulary of my trans-rational hand written symbols. After accomplishing ten drawings of the secret writing, it became essential to select a cohesive text-like symbol system, an alphabet, a finite repeatable set of letters, in order to make printed text pages. Instinct told me to choose twenty. Decades before personal computers or desk-top publishing, I carefully drew the letters, had them copied by a printer's camera, and ordered twenty small stampers, one for each letterform that became the center of my life's work. Sequence yet undetermined and no meaning assigned, I printed the letters on any pre-drawn line, one random letter at a time. Without looking to choose, the order of selection left entirely to chance, I drew out one stamper from the box and filled the penciled line until the page was full and no stamper could fit in any space without touching its neighbor.

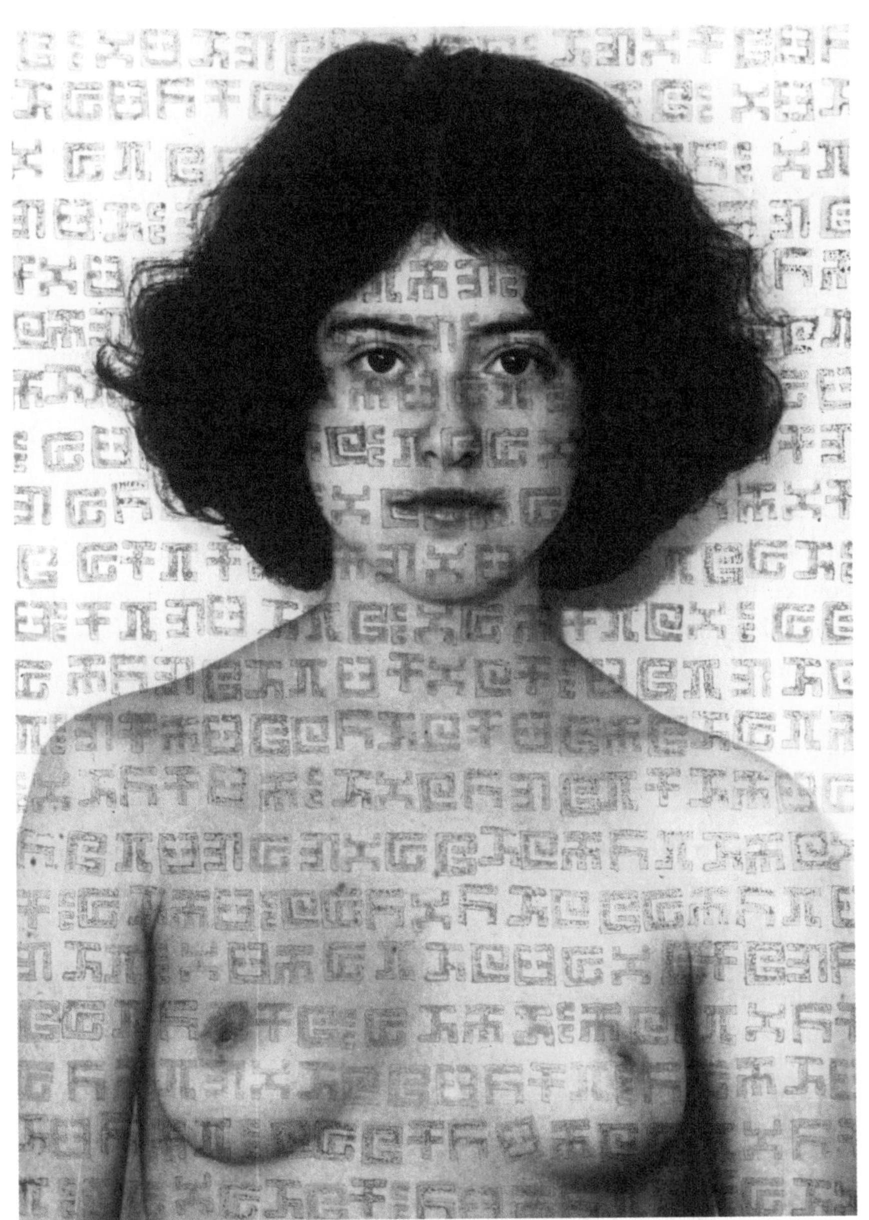

It's a pretty good guess that this is not how written language began. Symbols are meant to transfer meaning and symbol systems were no doubt created with meanings assigned to every character. Chinese and Arabic have no meaning for me, yet I recognize the symbols as language and assume the characters in the correct order enlighten another community. Tripping, I saw unknowable language washing over surfaces and streaming in bands and waves through the air. And yet, their message was perfectly clear and obvious. They represented the ubiquitous constancy of symbol making, that tendency of humans to transform thoughts into things and assign meaning. Secret Writing represented a universality that could not be pronounced without so limiting and restricting the meaning that it negated its very intention.

At age twenty-five, in a public gallery, my naked image appeared on photo murals photographically branded with the letters on my chest or washing over my face. Facing forward, arms to the sides, like a Sacred Mirror, the unpronounceable letters identified and branded me. Humiliation, martyrdom, secret obsession permeated the theme of my written thesis but never pointed to LSD as a source of my vision. LSD was an unpronounceable subject. So taboo did I perceive the topic of altered states in my university environment that an experience I had had dozens of times since I was seventeen years old, an experience that had changed my art and life entirely, went unmentioned in my very personal thesis. I was more willing to expose my nakedness than to share the secret source of my inspiration.

> Alex: Secret Language is a proto or meta text, an idea of text, a field of linguistic and creative expression, too sacred to have assigned meaning, a nameless presence. Fingers pointing to the moon are not the moon. The language of God is a sacred secret language. Namkhai Norbu, our Tibetan Rimpoche describes seeing "dakini script," something hidden and unreadable until a wisdom master discerns the message.
>
> An interpretable text is restricted by reason. Secret Writing can mean anything and nothing, boundless in its potential, pregnant with the void. Seeing the characters on the walls when you are tripping is like hieroglyphics. They are trying to speak to you through the ages, certainly representing intended linguistic communication, something important. On all temples where we see a foreign calligraphy, we intuit some resonance of the sacred without perceiving the translatable meaning.

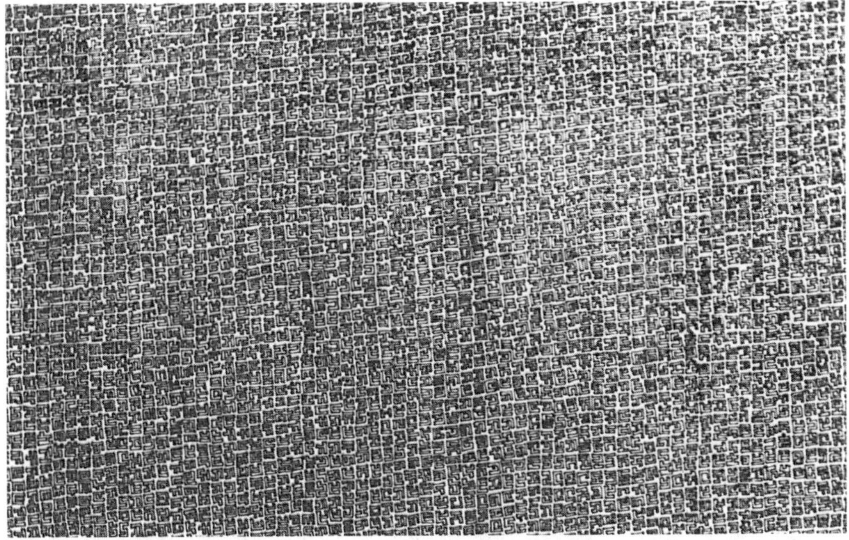

■ **Secret Writing, Allyson Grey, 1975, ink on paper, detail.**

After my first exhibition of Secret Writing in 1976, I imposed an order to the twenty letters and created the alphabet as it remains today. Like a mantra, a prayer, an ancient saying, the letters would always occur in the same sequence. As if there is really only one thing to say, my one visual statement defies specific meaning because the artist, the Creator, says so. In many of my paintings letter forms are incorporated into complex puzzles that can also include elemental representations of chaos and order. The letterforms appear in the same order, although sometimes backwards, upside down, and columnar. With no sounds or names to identify the characters, they remain an intuitive and unmemorizable language identified only with the essence of symbolic communication. Refusing to assign meaning keeps the symbols free and open to infinite interpretation. This unpronounceable language corresponds to the ineffable, nameless presence that cannot be reduced to concepts. Sacred writing of the inexpressible points to communication through all forms of creativity—music, art, performance—manifested to convey what is beyond words. This is why Alex calls it the language of creative expression.

Diana Reed Slattery, acting as a scientist, has carefully documented her chemical journeys, bravely acting as a human guinea pig, ingesting psychoactive substances. In altered states, with committed concentration, Diana

■ Secret Printing, Allyson Grey, 1976, one-off ink stamper print on paper.

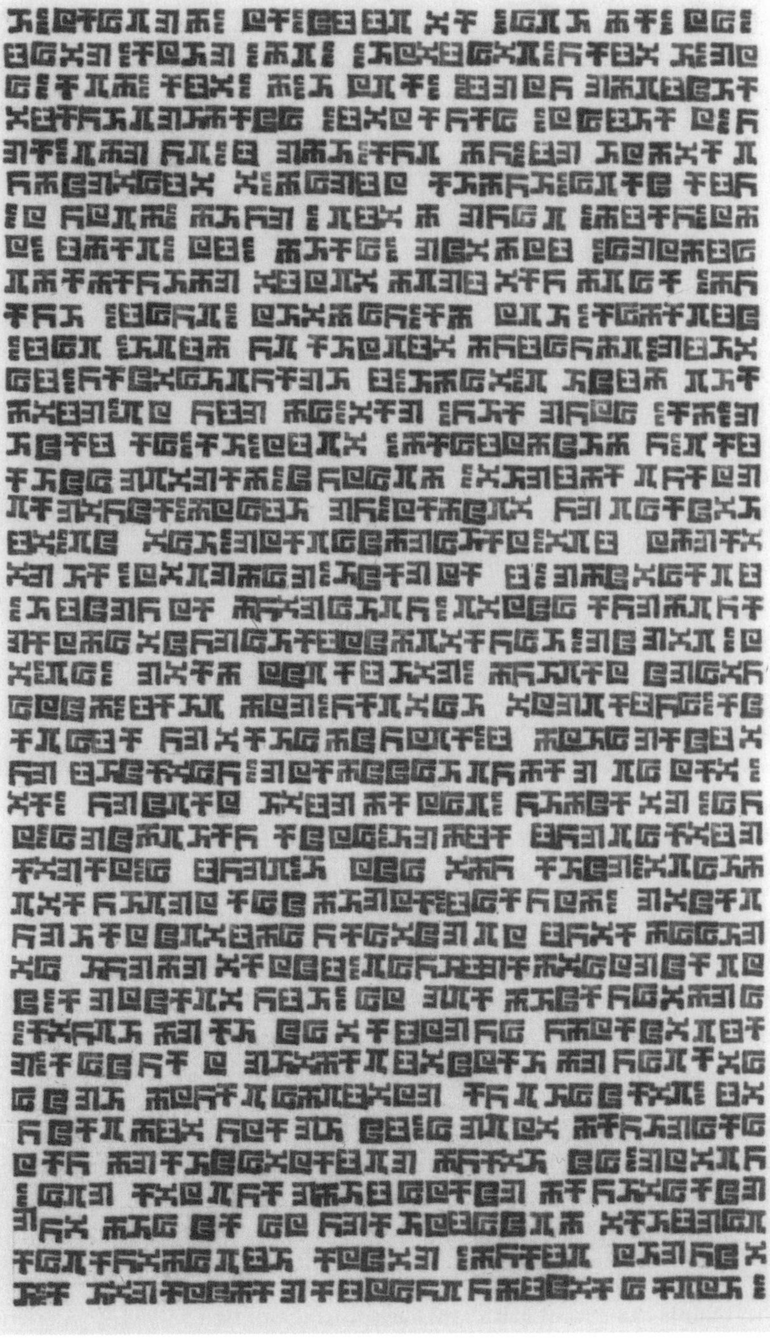

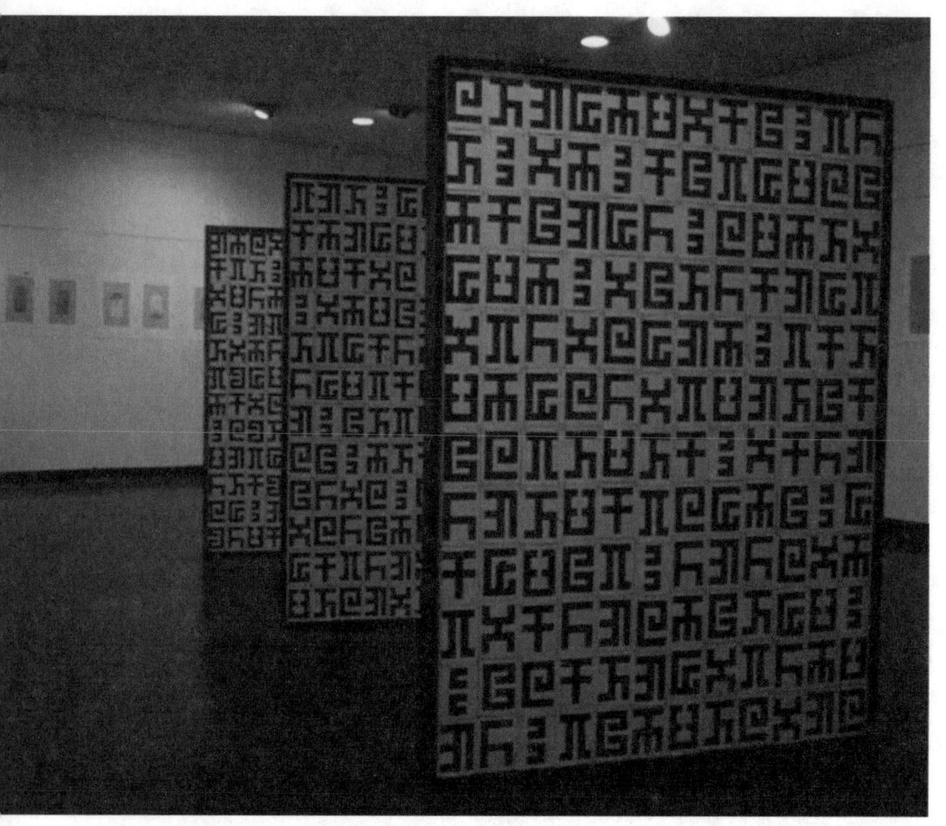

■ **Secret Language Walls, Allyson Grey, 1976, Tufts University Gallery, installation, photo murals on wood panels, each 4 x 6 ft.**

reaches new realms distinct from normal waking reality. She follows these encounters with notations of the Others she hears, their directives and observations. As spiritually based artists, Alex and I almost always engage in sacraments together with our journals by our sides and venture forth on fairly identical doses. Like Diana, our favorite journeys are "minimalist." We choose sacred music. Bach organ works in our first decade, then Phillip Glass, Carbon Based Life Forms, The Crystal Method . . . naked or comfortably clad, we close our eyes and go within. After long periods of silent meditation, we talk and write, both separately and together. Many (but not all) of our best art ideas have come from these experiences. The vision and commitment to build a temple came to us simultaneously during our first MDMA experience,

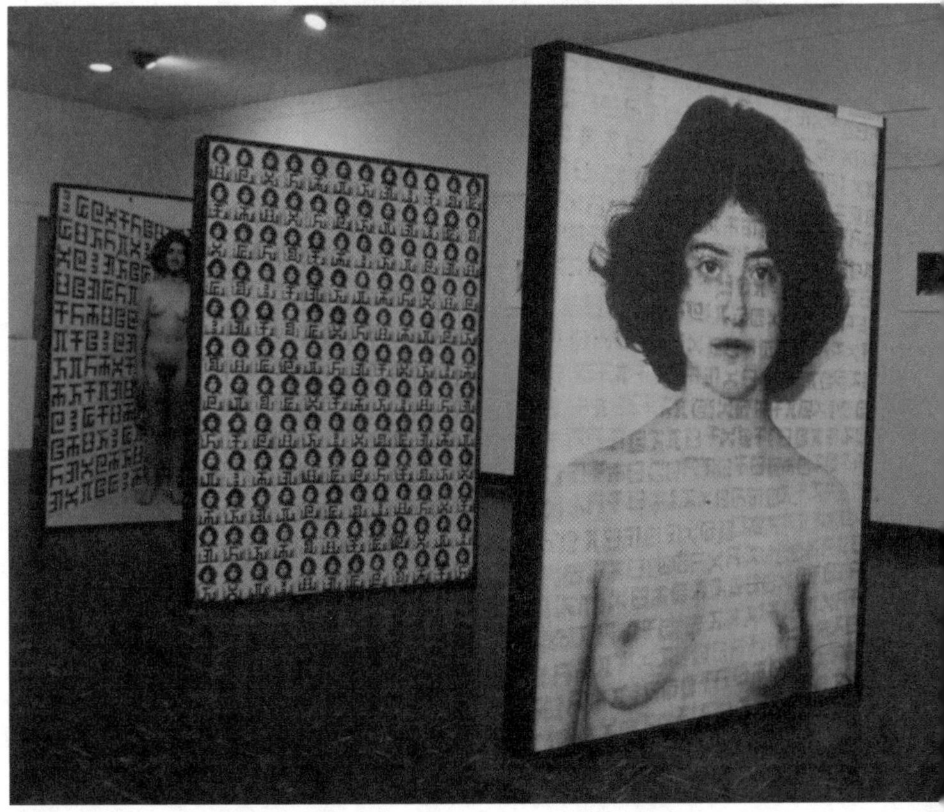

■ **Secret Language Walls (reverse side), Allyson Grey, 1976, Tufts University Gallery, installation, photo murals on wood panels, each 4 x 6 ft.**

a legal pharmaceutical at the time. In these sojourns, secret symbols, unreadable ribbons and waves of letterforms appear to wash over the surfaces of the material world, revealing a mysterious realm through to hard material reality. At these witnessing events, symbols appear integral to all seeming reality, like windows through which we translate our inner perception to the material world.

Diana spoke to me about her work called Glide:

> Contact experience is the heart of Xenolinguistics. The alien Other finds symbolic means—language—to transmit its message from the hyperdimensional realm (or whatever you care to call the psychedelic sphere) into baseline reality.

■ **Secret Alphabet, Allyson Grey, 1993, oil on wood panel, 20 x 20.**

The Other uses whatever means at hand in the psyche and experience of the downloadee, to patchwork a message. The name Glide itself, given in the original download, is just such a patchwork of ideas and references, later unpacked. Glide, in my associations, referred to 1) John Conway's "Gliders," emergent computational creatures arising from his software, "The Game of Life," that seem to behave like semi-autonomous forms, alive in some fashion in the computational world of cellular automata; 2) the gliding movements of Noh theatre actors, where the costumes can seem filled, not with a body, but with a weightless spirit; 3) the movement of the long-legged fly of W. B. Yeats' poem, and 4) the hip-hop dance moves—floats, glides, and moonwalks.

Diana's perception is that the mysterious, intuitive language called "Glide," the letter forms and their meanings, came and still come to her from Others who have found a human receiver for their message from a hyper-dimensional realm. In 1997–98, within her psychedelic journeys, Diana began receiving downloads of the language called Glide. Thus, her quest for the meaning and significance of those symbols began. On that path, she found that the psychedelic experience that included a language of unknown origin was "a general phenomena with convergent meaning for many." Diana's PhD thesis was on the subject of visual language.

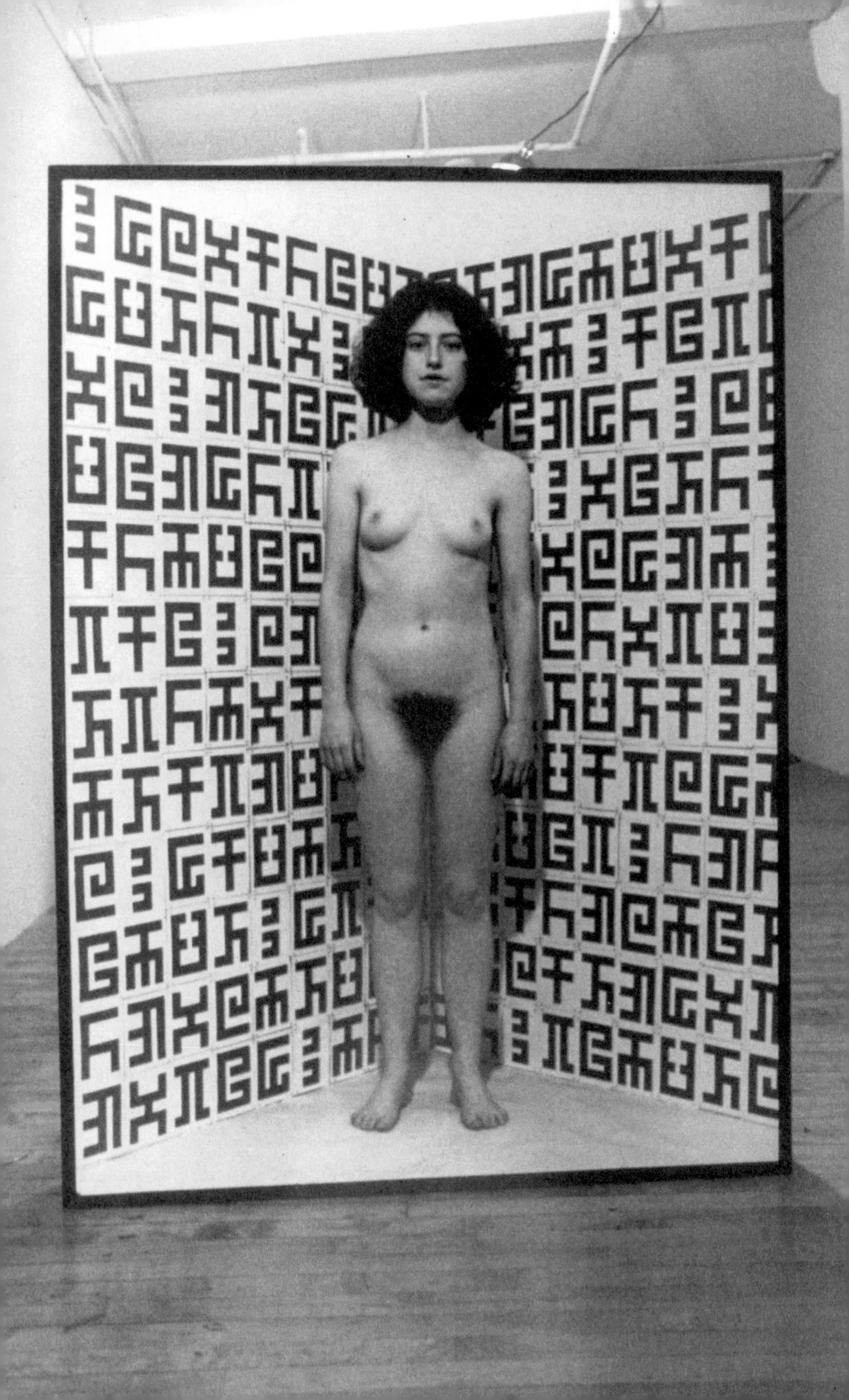

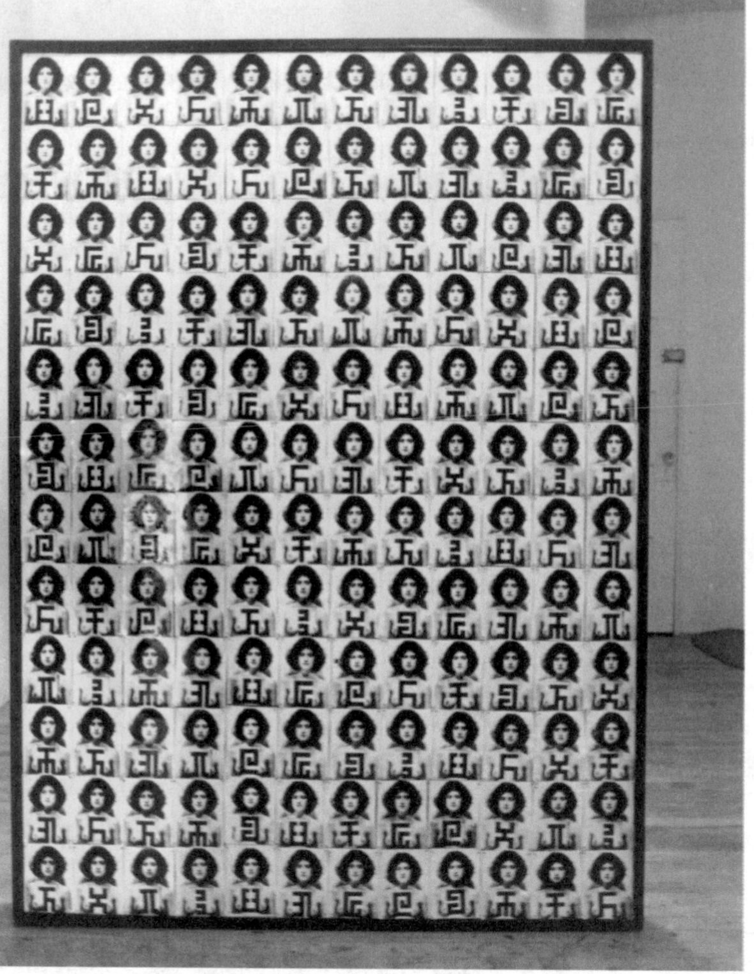

On the path to understanding the Glide language, Slattery ventured into translating the characters, "one into the other." Guided by subsequent psychonautical sojourns, in which interviews with the alien-elves provided guidance, Diana looked for examples of this purely visual language. According to her research, Terrence McKenna and other psychedelic literature implicate secret language as an entheogenic form constant.

Developing new software, using a descending tree structure, Diana created a lexicon in which each symbol represented a field of meaning. Her second software, collabyrinth, made visual constructions and animated the

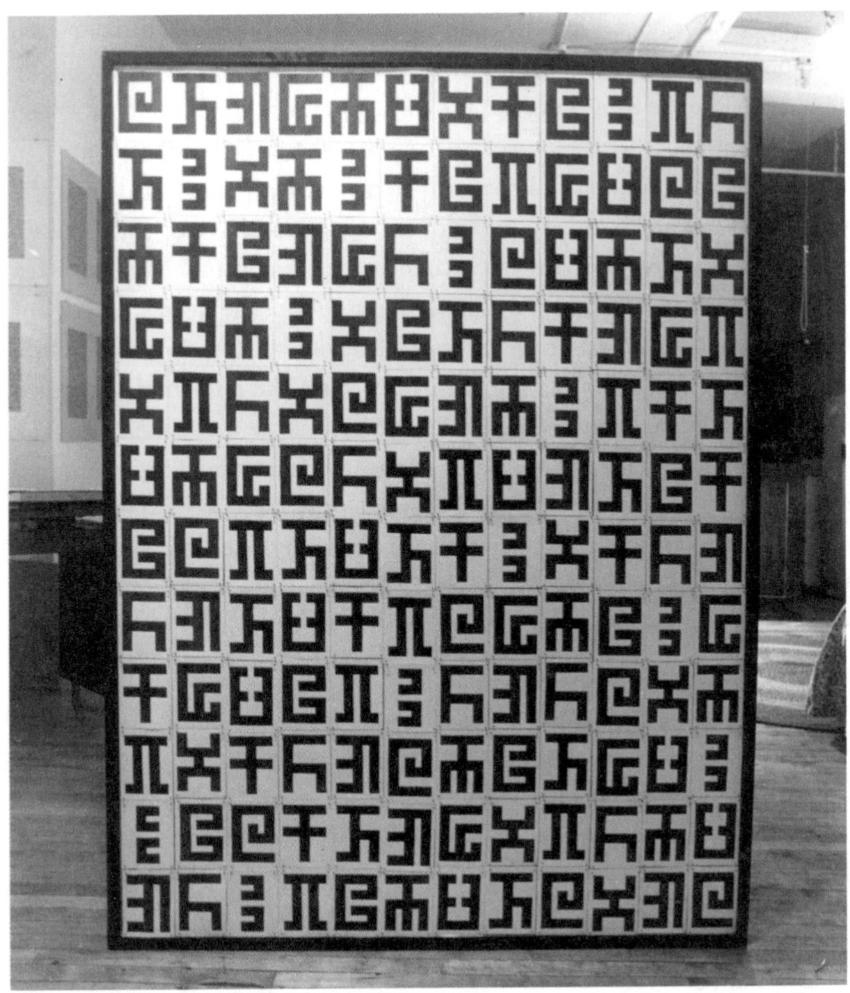

symbols to flow one into the other. Live Glide, Diana's third Glide adventure into artificial intelligence, offers video performance software in which symbols in three-dimensional space leave a trail of motion between the transforming letter forms. The Glide Oracle, Diana's fourth software (available as an iPad app) distinguishes 729 combinations of transforming pairs with English translations of their transformations.

Although Diana tells me that she can read and write the primitive symbols, she also shares that after 2,000 transformations were distinguished and identified, the entities that originally revealed the language showed her that she was "going about it in the wrong way." That, "in order to understand the symbols, giving them English translations was misleading, as the enigmatic alphabet had to be confronted on its own terms. Language like a living being, a sentient presence, develops expressiveness without natural language."

To write this foreword, I returned to my own tripping journals of the recent and distant past. Like many of us, Alex and I have engaged in sacraments in a wide variety of circumstances. But, as Diana and many have observed, our deepest and most inward journeys of the highest quality of healing and enlightenment have taken place on our bed together, mostly with our eyes closed, each with a journal by our side. The following poetic and spiritual revelation happened while sitting on a rock beside Alex in the midst of a rushing mountain stream. The message of compassion, forgiveness and love that accompanies an experience of holiness is what I wish to put into all my efforts and artworks. While we watched the sun travel across the sky, we wrote in small matching golden journals given lovingly to us by my mother. Here is my favorite series of entries from that heart opening day.

How much does it take to just sit down and appreciate.
I have everything I need right here now in the moment.
That is this experience—available to all at anytime.
God keeps answering me.
The conversation is very much in progress if I listen and take part.
Thank you, God, for reminding me to appreciate WHAT IS.
This is the Sacred Day that the Almighty gave to me.
Everyday is like this day.
Everyday is a gift.
We prepare to have a conversation with the Almighty.
God is always there. It is always the perfect time.
Thank you, God
I have everything I need.

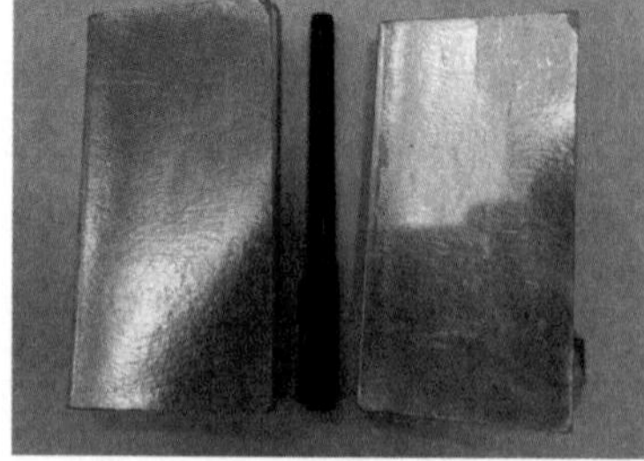

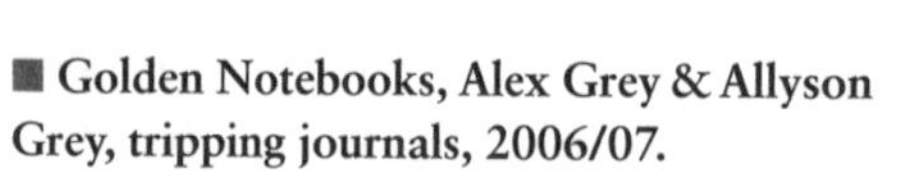

■ **Golden Notebooks, Alex Grey & Allyson Grey, tripping journals, 2006/07.**

Introduction: Possessed by Language

Language enfolds us. From our floating fetal state onward we unfold our consciousness of self and world within language. We are swept away by language from our infant's Eden into the human community. What William James called "the blooming, buzzing confusion" of the infant's first experience is also a unity of experience that the mind learns to pick apart into its separate objects. The tool for these acts of analysis and discrimination is language. We swim in language. Our thoughts, feelings, plans, the stories we make up about who we are and what our place is in the world are all built of language. We are filled to the brim with language. Language stores our memories, labeling sensations, objects, actions, feelings, ideas. Layers of language come to stand between us and the sensate world. So immersed, where can we stand to be able to view language and its relationship to consciousness?

As a child I was plagued by the feeling that no one was speaking my language—not even me. I could enter another's world using this language. I could enter the world of books, and I plunged into mythology and encyclopedias. But others could not get into my *real* world. I felt both locked out of myself, and that some vital part of myself was locked in and had no voice. I listened to myself answer questions in fourth grade. How did the words get put in sentence order out of view of my observing mind? They emerged fully formed. Language itself was a mystery to me; I could speak, write, and parse it, but I couldn't get to how it worked behind the scenes. English sounded alien; my sense of self, the core of consciousness, was one of a pervasive, incurable alienation. My first philosophical question arose: Where do the words come from? This language question rested on the most basic questions I could ask: Who am I? Where do I come from?

This book explores the premise that language and consciousness coevolve in the highly plastic human brain as features of both our biological and social evolution. This deeply intertwingled[1] relationship between language and consciousness became experientially real when I used psychedelics to explore the connections. Psychedelic states of consciousness produce novel forms of language in some psychonauts, especially visual languages, and novel ideas about language. This book is also about an outrageous twelve-year adventure in which I looked behind the veil of natural language and discovered new species of language, as well as a different set of questions to guide my process into a deeper mystery about the workings of language. Additionally, a profound personal healing unfolded in the process of taking sizable risks. They are the same story. The Glide language, whose download launched the voyage of exploration, accomplished its mission: the healing of the heart, and the transformation of consciousness to new ways of experiencing self and world through new language.

We call our human languages "natural" but there is nothing natural about them. We are not born with a natural language installed. Language is a viral technology, like fire, hand tools, bead-making, and pottery. Once it colonized our minds, it expanded exponentially, mutating easily as human groups divided. Accelerated by language, social evolution outstripped the pace of our physical evolution by orders of magnitude. Language transformed our pack-hunting existence into the complexities of civilization in a blink of evolutionary time. In the present, we have encased ourselves in clothing, automobiles, houses, cities, and the blooming, buzzing, ubiquitous media-surround: layers of language between ourselves and the world of nature, with predictable consequences. So wrapped in texts and their products, where can we find the silence to assess the damage of our disregard?

Around the same time I was asking myself *where do the words come from,* I organized a secret society with the kids in my neighborhood. The Shadow Club (after the radio show about a psychic detective) practiced sending telepathic messages from separate basements with little success. By age ten, I was reading science fiction and cosmology and learning the constellations while camping in the wilderness under clear star-strewn skies. It seemed perfectly reasonable to me to try to communicate with Life-at-Large. I was working out my own rough version of radio astronomer Frank Drake's equation (really a guesstimate to stimulate dialogue) about the probability of intelligent, communicative life elsewhere in the universe. Given the number of stars, and the size of the universe, there *should* be intelligent life out there. I figured some of that life had to be ahead of us in communication technology and therefore able to reach across distances telepathically. I sent out my silent first message:

"I know you're out there. If you communicate with me, I promise to believe it's really you." The message was more a coherent beam of longing to go to the stars, to meet the star people, than a set of words. That promise came back to haunt me. Fifty years later, when psychedelics became my tool kit for investigating the mysterious workings of language, the alien Other made its presence known, not in the vastness of the physical universe, but in the far reaches of inner space.

Biologically, we are made of language; the tiny coiled and twisted serpents of DNA create and maintain us. Our DNA, a biomechanical program with 3 billion letters (base pairs), speaks at breakneck speed. When replicating, 50 base pairs are copied per second in the super-sized human genome. We, meaning all life-forms, are linguistic all the way down, at every scale. Only through changes to the DNA text can biological evolution occur. In my view, neither language nor consciousness is a specifically human attribute but they are fundamental to life at all levels. The universe speaks itself around us, a vast, transcalar, multidimensional signaling system.

Communicating the unspeakable is the mission impossible of every psychonaut, ancient or modern. Can the visionary bacon be brought back home to consensus reality in a form that can be understood and put into use by the tribe? Terence McKenna and others have proposed the notion that psychedelics catalyzed us into language, entering our early human diets as we foraged and experimented with new foods. I can only try to imagine the force of these original visionary encounters. The manifestation of the Other, the encounter with the god-like *tremendum,* demanded response. Much of human culture—myth, ritual, sacred places, temples—can be seen as an attempt to contain and clothe the central numinous mystery. I believe that where psychedelics were present in our early diet in different parts of the world, they would have become culturally integrated. The high civilizations of Central and South America—the Aztec, Maya, and Inca—are recent examples of psychedelically informed high cultures. The existence of traditions of psychedelic shamanism from the steppes of Asia to the Amazonian rain forests indicates the possibility that the integration of psychedelics into our human lives reaches into the prehistoric past. In the present cultural moment, psychedelic shamanism is having a major revival—and transmutation—in the explosion of ayahuasca tourism in Central and South America and its global percolation as shamans (and their promoters) bring the tea and its visionary potential to Europe and North America. Globally, communities of psychonauts are intentionally rewiring their minds on a regular basis, exploring the invisible landscape and bringing new knowledge and linguistic forms back to baseline. What follows are the stories of how these linguistic forms emerge, what they might mean, and how they are used by those who experience them.

My personal introduction to the realm of psychedelic language came in 1998, in a sudden and life-changing vision. I call this kind of visionary core-dump a "download"—the arrival of an overwhelming amount of information in an impossibly short clock time. In the process of writing a novel, *The Maze Game,*[2] I asked myself the question, "How is the game played?" The answer came, "On mazes made of the visual language, Glide." There were 27 glyphs, or rather one glyph that could morph into any of the others. A new symbol set. A new logic. And a complete myth of the psychedelic origin of the glyphs. As I hurriedly sketched the glyphs, I could see—and feel—their logic, their ways of linking, their mutability. They morphed across my mind; one glyph was all glyphs.

Contained in the download was an invitation: renew your passport to the psychedelic sphere if you want to understand this language in its native context. The Mad Hatter beckoned. The Glide symbolic system became central to *The Maze Game*. During the same period, I began using psychedelics as a noetic technology to investigate Glide, developing my own psychonautic practice. So many questions! How is meaning made in a field of transforming glyphs? How is meaning conserved when the glyphs will not stand still?[3]

A download, dark or bright, can be traumatic, occupying and organizing a great swath of conscious awareness. Glide set up camp in my consciousness, organizing thought, feeling, and action into efforts to understand this set of symbols and how it worked. The childhood void was filled with a language so alien and so familiar at the same time, it could only be my own. The bright trauma of having my very own strange new language opened areas of consciousness that were closed before. Glide was a language through which I could communicate with the Other in psychedelic

■ Figure 1: The 27 Glide glyphs.

states. Glide became a tool for navigation of the visionary landscape. I began rewiring psyche with Glide.

My search for more information, anything that would shed light on this strange, morphing set of symbols, led me to descriptions of other encounters with psychedelic languages. Dennis and Terence McKenna's experiment at La Chorrera is a classic account of the concentrated psychic force of a download experience (see *True Hallucinations*).[4] The brothers' lives were shaped by these compelling events from that point forward. Their download eventually resulted in a novel symbolic system: Timewave Zero.

Psychonautics, which scholar Richard Doyle calls "the human investigation of psyche through unavoidably first-person science" (Doyle 2010), includes the diverse practices of a medicine community. The term "medicine" is expanded beyond our Western cultural system of medical and pharmaceutical services to include the traditional medicine practices of indigenous peoples, past and present. The World Health Organization defines traditional medicine as "the health practices, approaches, knowledge and beliefs incorporating plant, animal and mineral-based medicines, spiritual therapies, manual techniques and exercises, applied singularly or in combination to treat, diagnose and prevent illnesses or maintain well-being." I also include the contemporary healing and spiritual practices of the psychonautic community. The search for knowledge about Glide developed into a psychonautic practice, producing a novel, several pieces of Glide software, and a PhD thesis.

The convergence of three streams of this research—the personal, psychonautic quest; the maps and models developed through extensive reading, writing, and discussion; and the discovery of a growing number of others with their own unique linguistic happenings in altered states, each with their own psychonautic practice—produced and structured this book. I have two main goals in presenting this material. The first goal is to foreground psychonautic practices as a powerful means of gathering knowledge about consciousness, both baseline consciousness and altered states of consciousness. A psychonaut experiments with consciousness using a simple protocol: 1) ingest a psychedelic substance; 2) observe the results; 3) report what happened. Psychonauts are studying consciousness through first-hand experience. The word means, literally, soul-sailor. These soul-sailors persist through journey after journey, from oceans of serenity to psychic tsunamis, sharing their experiences. Tips and tricks of psychedelic good housekeeping are refined into protocols. By sampling these stories of psychonautic self-exploration, my goal is to make clear how a practice-based method of research, such as psychonautics, can yield a rich picture of consciousness in altered states.

As psychonauts we are, bit by bit, mapping the extraordinary and often ineffable landscapes of the psychedelic worlds. The urge to communicate the unspeakable expresses itself in many forms. Cartography is a reasonable metaphor. Two explorers to the same area compare notes, logs, and sketches. Knowledge is local, specific. Pieces fit together, landmarks are identified, interpretations made and rejected. Truth is a negotiated, persuaded and/or recognized truth. Every trip potentially contributes new knowledge of the unseen world.

My second goal is to examine these psychedelic linguistic experiences in light of the scientific body of literature—anthropological, archeological, neurophenomenological, and biological—in conjunction with the literature of psychonautic self-exploration. To roam this broadly among disciplines risks trivializing the psychedelic experience through reducing it to merely physical correlates. To delve deeply into the extravagant explanations of psychonauts, especially when such explanations of the ineffable tilt toward the messianic, is to similarly risk a trivialization of the mystery by premature explanation.

The book is divided into three main parts. The first section, Practices, tells the story of the co-evolution of language and consciousness from the viewpoint of the social context in which these explorations are occurring, the development of my own practice and the practices of other psychonauts, and the mystery of the encounter with the Other.

The nature of the download experience and encounters with the unspeakable are discussed in Chapter 1, "Communicating the Unspeakable." The unspeakability of psychedelic experience has many dimensions, from the ineffability of mystical visions to the chilling effect of the War on Drugs that is an omnipresent background both to psychonautic exploration and its reporting. Scribes of the unseen life are, like it or not, war correspondents. But the stories of their discoveries are being told; the urge to explain the unspeakable revelation (the psychedelic download, as I call it) overflows these limitations. These forms of unspeakability surround the efforts to explore and communicate psychedelic experience, always in a dynamic tension with the need to communicate the download.

Chapter 2, "A Psychonautic Practice," details my own download experience and the practice that developed as a result, placing it within the context of the diversity of worldwide psychonautic practices.

Chapter 3, "Glide," analyzes the Glide symbolic system as a model of a distinctly different symbolic system that makes meaning in unique ways. The details of the intentions of Glide language, its mythology, logic, and forms, and their instantiation in software are also presented.

Chapter 4, "Contact with the Other," tackles a central topic in psychonautic exploration. As it so happens, to some psychonauts, the invisible landscape appears densely populated with communicating beings: ancestors and animals, theriomorphs (deities taking the forms of animals), gods and faux-gods, aliens, angels, demons, and the legions of the dead. These contacts are ubiquitous in psychedelic experience worldwide and central to the topic of the co-evolution of language and consciousness. The Other is frequently implicated as the giver of language, or a participant in a new form of language, as teacher of that language, or part of the community of that linguistic form. One must come to terms with this phenomenon when it occurs, and answer for oneself the inevitable questions, "Are they real, these others? And if so, in what sense are they real? And how do we know whether something is real or not, especially in an altered state of consciousness?"

The second part of the book, "Maps and Models," takes up the business of contextualizing the lived experiences of the first section with disciplinary knowledge from a number of fields.

Chapter 5, "Reality Reviewed," follows these questions about the Other with a discussion of how we grapple with defining reality itself, and the ontological questions raised when entirely new perceptions and new worlds come into view in psychedelic experience. A number of models of multistate realities are compared: Tom Roberts, Roland Fischer, Charles Tart, Basarab Nicolescu, Timothy Leary, John Lilly, and Francisco Varela have all proposed different, though on several points overlapping, views. Central to these questions, and to consciousness studies in general, is the inevitable encounter with self-reflexivity—how can consciousness observe itself? How can consciousness perform both as subject and object at the same time? A similar problem haunts discussions of the essential nature of language, when language is the only tool available to describe itself. So any discussion of the relationship of language and consciousness enters these already troubled waters, where each appears necessary to the other, a prerequisite for being, co-dependently arising, as the Buddhists might describe it. Psychedelics make philosophers of us all. To delve into studying the co-evolution of language and consciousness, one must engage primary questions, both ontological (matters of reality and being) and epistemological (matters about the nature of knowledge and how we know).

In Chapter 6, "Extended Perception," the relationship between reality and perception is explored. The forms of new language in psychedelic states are shaped by the conditions of extended perception. Simply put, there are more materials from which to build language—more sounds, an expanded color spectrum, multiple dimensions in which those forms appear. Whether we call these vivid events hallucinations or visions, they appear to all our senses and can merge the senses in synaesthesias. I detail examples of the variety of extended perceptions in psychedelic states and how they contribute to new forms of language.

In Chapter 7, "Neurophenomenological Perspectives on Language," I go in some depth into the work of neurophenomenologist Charles D. Laughlin and his colleagues on the symbol and the symbolic process. Their work is helpful in that it explicitly includes the facts of altered states of consciousness, whether the state is attained by contemplative practice, trance-inducing song and dance, or psychedelic drugs. Laughlin talks of human societies as monophasic (acknowledging only one state of consciousness as "normal," as in our contemporary Western cultures) or multiphasic—societies that include multiple states of consciousness in their regular experiences. Francisco Varela's central notion of autopoiesis—that biological forms are constructed of autonomous, self-producing, and self-maintaining systems in structural communication with other autopoetic systems—is helpful as a broad enough conceptual container to manage the wide range of communications experienced in psychedelic states. This principle operates at the smallest level of the cell and its components, up to the complex systems of nested, multiscalar autopoetic systems of the human body and its interactions with other living autopoetic systems. Autopoiesis requires very specific systems of communication at all levels in the biological form; it depends on language.

The third part, "Xenolinguistics," is interleaved with samples of work from the xenolinguists whose experiences are at the center of this book. In the world of science fiction, xenolinguistics means the study of alien languages. I've adopted it for the exploration of psychedelics and language to give a feel for the high strangeness of these sports of language, from spontaneous glossolalia—the outpouring of language-like sounds—to Allyson's Grey's Secret Writing and Terence McKenna's self-transforming, linguistic machine elves. Dennis and Terence McKenna's ideas and experiences with psychedelics and language are treated at some length. Xenolinguistics makes excursions into anthropology, glossolalia, synaesthesia, and the world of constructed languages. The xenolinguists whose work and wild experimentation are presented here are evolving language in the psychedelic sphere.

In Chapter 8, "Natural and Unnatural Language," the concept of novelty is explored in regard to the forms of these often "alien" languages. Stanley Krippner's work on the distortions of natural language under the influence of psychedelics is discussed. Roland Fisher and Colin Martindale's work on psilocybin's effects on handwriting is covered, as well as Charles Tart's early work on the effect of marijuana smoking on language ability. The eloquence sometimes induced by the magic of the mushroom is described by anthropologist Henry Munn as ecstatic significations. Various aspects of glossolalia, a prominent feature of some altered states of consciousness, are recounted.

In Chapter 9, "Language, Culture, and Nature," I revisit the topic of the evolution of human language and symbolizing activity, especially as evidenced in abstract paleoart. The effort is not to prove—or falsify—the McKenna "stoned ape theory" of the catalysis of linguistic ability in early primates by the ingestion of psychedelic substances. When it comes to origin-of-language theories, the task at hand is to view all speculations as narratives or competing myths while trying to compile the scant supply of facts into a recognizable pattern. Neither is it my purpose to argue toward a single definitive interpretation of these emergent linguistic phenomena. The effort would be premature in the case of psychedelic knowledge, and impossible in the "origin of language" arena. The aim is to illuminate a process, a novelty-creating process that evolves life and language, the Bios and the Logos, a self-describing process that has carried us improbably from whatever the "pre-biotic" state might be to a human organism (that's me!) sitting at a computer, surrounded by Culture, describing the process of self-description. The evolutionary process, though wholly constrained by the vocabulary and syntax of DNA, has been at the same time unpredictable, i.e., novel in the extreme. How can we extrapolate a sumo wrestler from a paramecium? And if the paramecium might find it difficult to postulate the sumo wrestler, how difficult is it for us to imagine a truly alien Other who may yet be in communication with us? We study exo-biology, we speak our yearning to go to the stars, with little attention yet as to what it would take to actually get us there, with biosphere and some kind of sustainable cultural organization intact for the long journey—150,000 years at current speeds. Evolution is improbable in its wild diversity, given the high novelty of results, but clearly not impossible, because, after all, I am typing these words, with knowledge of both sumo wrestlers and paramecia, a notion about the alien, and the language to name them.

The fascinating world of true language geeks is presented in Chapter 10, "Constructed Languages." The constructed language group, or con-langers, create new spoken and written languages, discuss them at great length on an online list, and hold conferences. As a member of the Constructed Language Society, I have found much of the thinking of con-langers, from J. R. R. Tolkien on down, to be compatible with xenolinguistic experience with language in altered states, especially the connection between building a language and building a world with a culture and history. New worlds go hand in hand with the birth of a new language.

Chapter 11, "The Idea of a Living Language," goes back to our most intimate idea of language—our DNA, the language of life that is itself alive. Psychedelic experience reports often mention DNA. Psychonauts encounter the molecules themselves in some form and relate their intuitions about this most fundamental, self-reflexive mystery of life. Jeremy Narby's work, *The Cosmic Serpent,* details his intuitions about the connection between the shaman's serpent imagery and the way DNA is described by scientists, illustrating a strong example of the parallel findings of indigenous shamans, whose research is *experiential,* in inner spaces, and contemporary scientists, whose research is *experimental,* carried out in the shared knowledge protocols of science. The form of the "rainbow serpent," the primal energy known to shamans, yogis, and psychonauts by different names (qi, kundalini, life-energy), is deeply implicated as a generative source of new forms of language and life.

Chapter 12, "A Reasonable Hope," sums up the findings of this book and the relevance of this realm of idiosyncratic, creative new linguistic forms evolving in altered states. As you can see from this introduction, what began as a unique and somewhat unusual experience—the download of a visual language, Glide—expanded to a topic that reached into many disciplines to find answers, discovering more and more evidence for the existence of these novel linguistic productions. It has led to asking the deepest questions about reality, the nature of the spirit, and the vast territories opened by psychedelics, "the antipodes of the mind" (Shanon 2002). I feel the world now as linguistically constructed, not only as a coating of human abstraction over all perception, but as living language. Nature speaks from every cell in every body. The wind and the water speak in sound and touch. When I have folded the maps of natural language, the mind-bogglingly novel territory of the psychedelic sphere shines forth, nameless but not unknowable. This sense of the vast potential of consciousness to create new forms of communication, when experienced under conditions of extended perception and cognition, parallels the physical enormity and complexity of our brain's receptor space, in biologist Tom Ray's map. We, as soul-sailors, psychonauts, construct these maps of the unseen world with the tools of scientific analysis, and with the barefisted, experiential approach of William James and Aldous and Laura Huxley. We do our best to connect the dots of scientific data points with the lived experience of psychonauts. These maps tell us initially of a densely interconnected universe and a living biosphere in which we are deeply intertwingled, a universe of many worlds, and many Others who we are dependent upon and responsible for at the same time. These experiences of extended perception and heightened awareness contain an evolutionary imperative: Wake Up. Shift consciousness to this fundamental awareness of interconnection. Act toward our fellows and toward the living universe around us as if our actions were a sacred duty, undertaken with the gratitude of being so cared for since our first breath poured free oxygen into our lungs with which to howl the announcement of our arrival on Earth. This is a book about new ways to shape that primal howl.

Notes, Introduction

1. Computer visionary Ted Nelson coined the word "intertwingle" in the early '70s in conjunction with his intuitions about hypertext, long before the World Wide Web intertwingled us all. It does what it means: intermingling, twining, twinkling . . . it's the mantra of dense interconnectivity.
2. *The Maze Game* was published in 2003 by Deep Listening Press.
3. A video showing the 27 glyphs in transformation can be seen at www.youtube.com/watch?v=-xWALPXLwr4_or https://vimeo.com/35158231.
4. Terence McKenna, *True Hallucinations: Being an Account of the Author's Extraordinary Adventures in the Devil's Paradise* (San Francisco: HarperSanFrancisco, 1993).

I: PRACTICES

CHAPTER 1
Communicating the Unspeakable

Back in the '60s we just called it tripping, and what we tripped on were drugs called psychedelics. Fifty years later, we call ourselves psychonauts. We have hundreds more psychedelic materials from which to choose, natural or synthesized, and, thanks largely to the Internet, a great deal more information about psychedelics to consult. We have logged uncountable hours in the far reaches of the mind, creating and then braving perfect storms, tumbling overboard, spotting landmarks, and sometimes bringing home treasures in the form of major insights, visionary artworks, or deep healing.

Psychonautics As Practice

The words "psychedelic" and "psychonaut" take us back to the Greek word *psyche*. According to Wikipedia, "The basic meaning of the Greek word ψυχη (*psūkhē*) was 'life' in the sense of 'breath,' formed from the verb ψυχω (*psukhō,* 'to blow'). Derived meanings included 'spirit,' 'soul,' 'ghost,' and ultimately 'self' in the sense of 'conscious personality' or 'psyche.'" *Nautes* is the Greek word for sailor or navigator, which makes us soul-sailors, the ones who navigate the psyche. This concept, *psyche,* in the original Greek meaning so central to human beingness, is personified in the myth of Psyche and Eros. And for psychonauts, and those who would try to understand them, it helps to be aware of one of the mythological underpinnings of their quest.

Psyche was a mortal princess so beautiful that the goddess Aphrodite was jealous, and commanded her son Eros to shoot her with one of his arrows, so that she would fall in love with a monster. When Eros saw her beauty, he was so stunned he dropped his arrow, pricking himself and hence falling hopelessly in love with Psyche. Psyche is then abandoned on a mountaintop as a sacrifice by her father, who believes the prophecy that she will marry a monster. Eros rescues her and carries her to his palace, where she is lavishly served by invisible hands. He brings her to his bed, but always in the dark. And Eros, still trying to avoid his mother's wrath, instructs Psyche never to try to see his face. Prompted in part by distrust—her jealous sisters urge her to shed some light on her possibly monstrous husband—Psyche exercised the divine right of curiosity: to see the face of Love. Who could resist the temptation? She is equally overcome by Eros's beauty, accidentally spills hot lamp oil on him, and he wakes. As punishment, she is exiled and wanders the world, distraught, finally begging Aphrodite for assistance. Her jealous mother-in-law sets impossible tasks, such as sorting out an enormous pile of mixed seeds. Psyche is helped by magical animal allies, completes the tasks, and is reunited with Eros, in full light.

In this myth, the soul seeks to see the face of Love. Love needs a soul to fill. And the myth tells us this is no walk in the park, but a high-risk adventure. Eros—the gorgeous, inadvertent monster—is part of the entanglement.

The psychological meaning of *psyche* as mind in the modern sense, identified with brain, divorced from the unscientific soul, no longer tasked with seeking love, did not come into use until 1910. Imagine . . . the vast and starry splendor of the soul devolves to mind, and mind to individually packaged brains in little skull cases—in a mere hundred years. And so, with psychedelics, the mind/soul/life/breath/spirit-manifesting medicines, we return to *psyche* in her fullness, beginning the rediscovery in the West of her mythical, mystical, magical kingdom.

Psychonautics is a practice, in the same sense that kung fu or optometry or law are practices. We return to psyche as *Psyche,* again and again. Practices are distinguished by doing, not theorizing. You can study law—or psychedelics for that matter—without ever *practicing,* but it is practice that identifies psychonautics. And a practice is fundamentally individual, personal, something done by a subject, a self. It may be done collaboratively; medical practices are group activities, but the doctors, nurses, and therapists are individual practitioners. A meditation or yoga practitioner may practice alone or in a group. A practice, by its nature repetitive, improves skills. Knowledge is gained over time. A practice can therefore be a site for research.

The practice of psychonautics has been defined by Richard Doyle in *Darwin's Pharmacy* as "the human investigation of psyche through unavoidably first-person science." The psychedelic sphere itself, as William James expressed, is close at hand, "parted from us by the filmiest of screens." These worlds can easily be explored by performing some version of the basic self-experiment: 1) adjust the chemistry of consciousness with a psychedelic substance; 2) observe the changes in consciousness; 3) report what happened. That said, in its community of practices, psychonautics is highly varied when it comes to methods. Every psychonaut is essentially crafting and modifying his or her own practice iteratively within a context of information about the practices of others. Richard Doyle sees all trip reports, whether from an individual psychonaut or in the form of an anthropologist's description, as rhetorical programs that seek to recreate (as opposed to represent) the experience (Doyle 2010). Language is used not only to explain the state, but also to invoke and manage it. These reports become, recursively, part of the *set*—the current mindset of the psychonaut embarking on a voyage. Language is also managing the psychedelic state when a shaman leads the visionary activity in an ayahuasca circle with *icaros*.[1]

Cognitive psychologist and ayahuasca scholar Benny Shanon states the case for firsthand, long-term psychedelic experience as "a methodological issue that I find paramount." Shanon asserts that firsthand experience is essential, that "there is no alternative to studying phenomenology from within." He finds that when the investigator has no or very limited and "cautious" experience with the ayahuasca brew, the value of such studies is limited. Shanon makes the analogy of trying to write about music without ever having heard it. He concludes that "any serious study of Ayahuasca requires not only firsthand experience, but also substantive, long-term familiarity—indeed, training" (Shanon 2002). Minds-on training, I might add.

As psychonauts, we are a medicine community, a community of practice. A survey of a variety of psychonautic practices, both solo and social, reveals a wide range of protocols. Below are a few examples of current psychedelic practices, a tasting menu to demonstrate the range of human activities in which the uses of psychedelics are being explored.

John Lilly originally developed the flotation tank to test whether the brain, in the absence of most of the sensation coming from outside the body, would simply go to sleep. It didn't, especially on LSD.

Terence McKenna recommended five grams of dried psilocybin mushrooms consumed alone in silent darkness. The Native American Church leads peyote ceremonies from sunset to sunrise in a tipi or hogan.

■ **Figure 2: A modern flotation tank.**

Our psychonautic practices include religious and spiritual groups such as the syncretic South American churches using ayahuasca sacramentally (Santo Daime, União do Vegetal, and Barquina, to name a few among many); the northern-based Native American Church, which uses peyote as sacrament; and The Council on Spiritual Practices.[4] Add to that an unknown number of underground medicine circles using a variety of psychedelics ceremonially.

These groups are meeting globally, the result of the ongoing self-organization of the psychedelic underground since the 1960s. Many practices are specific to their medicine circle; some are substance-specific, such as groups that meet to explore nn-DMT or 5-meo-DMT together, or a mushroom ceremonial group. Some groups have a spiritual orientation. Yet others have a psychotherapeutic component, where the individual psychonaut becomes a client, in the psychotherapeutic model, seeking help for life problems.

Psychedelic psychotherapy has been practiced one on one, from the early legal research with LSD. MDMA (street name, ecstasy) has been used as a psychotherapeutic agent especially helpful in opening of the heart, feelings, and repressed contents in memory. MDMA therapy (and psychotherapies using other medicines) continued underground since the scheduling of MDMA in 1977. MDMA is resurfacing now with legal studies of its use in the treatment of end-of-life anxiety and PTSD.

More broadly, there is ecstatic dance practice and festival culture. Psychedelics are integrated with a wide variety of dance music from the Grateful

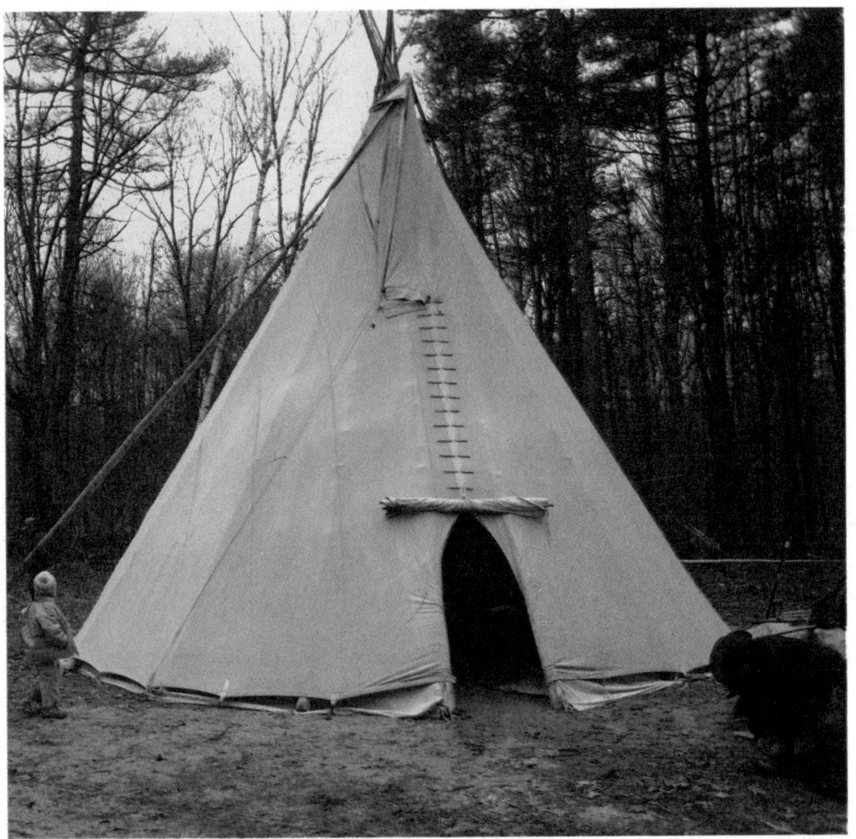

■ **Figure 3: Peyote ceremony tipi.** HP, Wikimedia commons.

Dead acid-fueled concerts on through global contemporary festivals such as Burning Man, Boom, Entheogenesis, and Firefly. Festivals have grown beyond the rock-concert model to become gatherings of the psychedelic community featuring not only multiple stages of music and dance, but talks, goods and services, art shows, lectures, permaculture training, yoga, and the radical self-expression of psychedelic culture on parade. Psychedelic drug use is frequently given the meant-to-be-pejorative label "recreational." But in this exuberant, transgressive, over-the-top social expression one can see culture itself being re-created. Gift economies are one zone of cultural experimentation.

Psychedelics are used as performance-enhancing medicines for a wide variety of purposes. They can function as problem-solving and creativity

■ **Figure 4: Burning the Man.**

adjuncts in activities as diverse as computer programming, artistic production, architecture, cooking, writing, video editing, engineering, healing practices, sports, yoga, and sex. Aboveground and underground researchers are exploring the uses of psychedelics for medical and psychiatric conditions such as PTSD, depression, and end-of-life anxiety. Among patient advocacy groups, psilocybin and LSD have shown promise in the treatment of cluster headaches. Microdoses of psilocybin and LSD have been explored for the relief of depression. Ketamine is showing promise as a fast-acting agent for relief of severe treatment-resistant depression. It could be said that a renaissance in aboveground psychedelic research has launched.

I don't know if hang-gliding over the psychedelic abyss on a regular basis can be called a practice, but certainly the yearning for the risky, the novel, and the mind-bogglingly weird fuels a part of psychedelic self-exploration. The explorer urge is a big part of the impetus toward psychonautics—the desire to go where no one or few have been before in the uncharted territory of inner space. The frontiers of inner space beckon to the psychonaut, as outer space calls the high-flying Sir Richard Branson.

Psychonautic practice becomes the navigation of these potentially extreme mind-states. We learn at our own pace how to stay centered in the full range of emotions and ideas emerging, visions of hell and heavenly realms, and encounters with the Other. On return, the task becomes to report, and to come up with possible explanations. This reporting from lived experience, the discourse on psychedelics that tries to describe and interpret the radical shifts in levels of perception and reality, is not nearly as straightforward. Reporting *at all* in a public forum is made problematic by the social dimension of unspeakability. The problem? In the early twenty-first century politics of knowledge, psychedelics remain the discourse of the unmentionable by the disreputable about the unspeakable.

Dimensions of the Unspeakable

I believe that in the future what I am about to say will be a quaint historic footnote to the history of human use of psychedelics. But the fact is, at this writing, most psychedelics are illegal to buy, sell, possess, or ingest in most places in the world. The illegalization of LSD in 1966 effectively ended publically funded research for almost forty years. The subsequent scheduling of most psychedelic substances, whether occurring in natural plant, animal, or fungal form or synthesized in the laboratory, in tandem with the Federal Analog Act, has channeled a significant portion of legal psychedelic science into anthropological and ethnobotanical investigations in countries such as Peru and Brazil, where sacramental use of ayahuasca is sanctioned. Research in areas involving the human consumption of psychedelics such as the psychotherapeutic uses of MDMA, psilocybin, and LSD, studies of the creative potential of psychedelics for art and problem-solving, and every kind of self-experimentation went underground.

The world of psychedelic research is divided into the medically oriented, aboveground, funded researchers, and the vast majority of researchers: the self-funded, un-regulated, and sometimes unruly outlaw psychonauts. Scientific research organizations like MAPS, the Hefter Institute, and the Beckley Foundation have made Herculean efforts to gain approval from government funders and policy makers. Success is coming, if only in very slow trickles. Meanwhile in the underground, the synthesis, manufacture, and distribution of an increasing number of psychoactives supplies the medicine communities with new research materials, new potentialities, and new risks. When quality control is hard to come by, the psychedelic good housekeeping tip, "Know your dealer," becomes critical.[2] The illegal status of psychedelics puts an inevitable twist into all research, legitimate or outlaw. This is the social dimension of the unspeakable, and its shadow lies long across psychonautic experience.

This socio-political history, while outside the scope of this book, is the context in which it developed, and it represents an important dimension of the unspeakability of the psychedelic experience. Even William James's self-experiments with mescaline and nitrous oxide, long before the War on Drugs, were viewed with suspicion by his peers. In order to carry out my psychonautic project, the investigation of Glide and language in general, it was necessary to create a secret life.

The literature of intensive, long-term psychedelic self-exploration is created and studied, for the most part, outside the academy. However else the authors may be categorized—as combatant, conscientious objector, outlaw scientist, agent provocateur, or collateral damage—they are war correspondents, reporting from the battlefield of the War on Drugs. There exists a background condition of clear and present danger to those who report openly on their psychedelic experiences. Offering opinion, much less scientific evidence contrary to wartime policy, can cause even a high-placed scientist like Dr. David Nutt in the UK to be removed from his ten-year position as chair of the Advisory Council on the Misuse of Drugs. His "mistake" was to suggest that drug policy should be steered by the scientific evidence about which drugs were *actually* most harmful, such as alcohol and tobacco.

Globally, the War on Drugs is the political underbelly of all psychedelic research. It affects not only the social standing of the reporter (drug use = drug abuse), but the nature of the reports themselves, through self-censorship —what is called in constitutional law "the chilling effect." Drug (including dose), set, and setting are the three primary variables of the psychedelic experience. The effects of the psychedelic closet as an aspect of *setting*, and one's feelings about the illegality of the act as a part of *set*, color both the psychedelic session and its report. A speaking out becomes a coming out. Concerns for safety are paramount for the individual practitioner and especially for those who practice medicine, psychotherapy, nursing, or other licensed professions, and use psychedelics as medicine in their practice. A whole part of one's professional life becomes, again, a secret life.

Resistance movements practice their own unspeaking: discretion, anonymity, coded language, fictional strategies, *omertà*. The psychedelic medicine community, in all its variety, has been growing and self-organizing in a bottom-up fashion despite these serious dampening factors. At some point a critical mass of psychonauts will be reached, political power will be achievable, and what is now a densely configured global community of communities will find connections and common ground and have the potential to act constructively as a movement. In the meantime, the underground spreads and grows like a vast mycelial mat of interconnected, communicating activity, people, and intentions. Black Rock City springs from the parched desert surface yearly, a whole city coming into being, and disappearing, like a huge mandalic flush of mushrooms.

■ **Figure 5: Black Rock City, site of the Burning Man Festival.**

Another form of social unspeakability arises in the communication of the often bizarre content of the psychedelic experience. As the quip goes, "If you talk to God, it's called prayer. If God talks to you, it's called schizophrenia." Quite simply, we develop built-in censors, part of our social conditioning, whose purpose is to get us to think twice before saying something that will sound crazy to our listeners.

Neurophenomenologist Charles Laughlin makes the point that "in any society a finite set of possible phases of consciousness is declared normal. Members of that society are socialized to recognize the appropriate attributes of these phases and to consider them definitive of their own and of others' mindstates" (Laughlin et al. 1990). Laughlin differentiates between what he terms monophasic and multiphasic societies. Our Western secular and scientific paradigm is monophasic; waking consciousness is normal, dreams are scarcely attended to, and all forms of altered states of consciousness are to some degree considered abnormal or pathological. Laughlin contrasts our contemporary Western monophasic culture with polyphasic cultures that incorporate multiple phases of consciousness, such as indigenous cultures with intact shamanic traditions and their associated ritual practices.

Terence McKenna's self-transforming machine elves, the giant fluorescent snakes of the ayahuasca experience, or a conversation with a serpent goddess map in our monophasic culture to the symptoms of psychopathology. The psychonaut must first convince herself that she is not crazy; only then comes the task of communicating to others without omitting the often bizarre or embarrassing (from a baseline viewpoint) details of a psychedelic experience. A great deal is at stake at this crossroads of the cultural labels "normal" and "abnormal," namely, the integrity of the phenomenological report and hence the research data. Dr. Rick Strassman's DMT research collided head-on with these concerns. His subjects were frequently reporting contact with other beings existing in their own worlds. They described these encounters and worlds not as dream, not as metaphor, not as delusion, but according to them as a reality equivalent to our own consensus reality. Strassman was not prepared for these reports, or their implications. "The only explanatory model that held itself out as the most intuitively satisfying yet the most theoretically treacherous, involved assigning a parallel level of reality to these experiences." In other words, Strassman needed to postulate a multiphasic model of consciousness and of reality itself, an assumption at odds with science, and with our monophasic assumptions, other than at the farthest reaches of physics.[3] Strassman's data pointed to explanations that were, from the viewpoint of a scientist operating within the medical paradigm, theoretically treacherous (Harpignies 2011).

A related zone of the unspeakable exists in the academic discourse on consciousness itself. Once outside the disciplinary havens of chemistry, pharmacology, and neurophysiology, "the taboo of subjectivity" has made the study of consciousness itself problematic. B. Alan Wallace, author of *The Taboo of Subjectivity,* describes the material reduction in cognitive science: ". . . many experts in this field have concluded beyond a shadow of a doubt that consciousness is produced solely by the brain and that it has no causal efficacy apart from the brain. The fact that modern science has failed to identify the nature of the origins of consciousness in no way diminishes the certainty of those scientific materialists" (Wallace 2000). Unless one denies the existence of consciousness itself, as does philosopher Daniel Dennett, defining it out of existence (the material reduction), one must in some way come to terms with the lived experience of the individual subject and its communication in the study of consciousness. This muffling of the subjective statement, and the mistrust of "introspectionism" as a source of useful knowledge in scientific and many philosophical approaches to the study of consciousness, creates its own problematic gap and unspeakabilities. This denial of consciousness then becomes another religion.

The actual forms of some of the psychedelic languages presented in this work are, quite literally, unspeakable. They can be purely visual, as is Allyson Grey's Secret Writing. Some are gestural; some, like Jack Cross's Argot of Ergot, are more like an explosion or dissolution of the English language. These psychedelic linguistic phenomena may be associated with sound that is not words (glossolalia-like) or be explicitly soundless, like Glide, a visual language. This is no trivial unspeakability. The speakable begins and defines our baseline form of language, the language we call natural language. An unspeakable language, from the viewpoint of natural language, is no language at all. Even our most abstract symbol systems, such as mathematical formulae, can be spoken. To discuss these anomalies, the concept of language needs to be extended.

Peeling back the social layers of unspeakability allows a less cluttered view of the unspeakability at the level of the primary subjective event itself. Ineffability is asserted as a hallmark of the mystical experience by William James (James 1912). Natural language is used to display its helplessness to communicate the fullness, extremity, and impact of the experiences. Cognitive psychologist Benny Shanon's statement is typical, made as both a first-person experiencer and on behalf of the first-person accounts he has presented in his exhaustive phenomenology of the ayahuasca experience, *The Antipodes of the Mind.*

> I am saying all this by way of apology, for in a deep sense the effects to be discussed here defy verbal description. In order to be fully appreciated they have to be experienced firsthand. Yet, in order to give the non-initiated reader some taste of what will be talked about here, I shall try to do what I have just said cannot be done, namely, I shall resort to description by means of words. . . . (Shanon 2002)

The rhetorical term for this kind of statement by Shanon is apophasis, in which a contradictory statement is made asserting that one will *not* say something by mentioning it anyhow. The literature of mystical experience abounds with such apophatic disclaimers. St. Teresa of Avila speaking on the unspeakable:

> I wish I could describe, in some measure, the smallest portion of what I saw; but when I think of doing it, I find it impossible; for the mere difference alone between the light we have here below, and that which is seen in a vision—both being light—is so great, that there is no comparison between them. . . . (Teresa 1988)

Michael Sells, in his study *Mystical Languages of Unsaying,* describes the apophatic discourse of a group of mystical writers from Marguerite Porete to Ibn 'Arabi. He asks,

> How are we to approach critically a discourse that claims to speak from the point where subject and object, self and other, are one? Simply put, does one have to be a mystic to understand the transreferential language of mystical unsaying? (Sells 1994)

These same questions can be applied directly to the consideration of psychedelic transpersonal and transcendent experience, where the lived experiences of self and other are profoundly reconfigured in the altered state of consciousness. Does one have to be a psychonaut to understand other psychonauts during or after a transcendent psychedelic experience? In one very real sense, the answer is yes. That said, the burden of communicating the unspeakable is on the psychonaut. If the psychonaut wishes to be understood, she needs to find the means to communicate those experiences, and the means to overcome whatever obstacles are encountered, in relation to these dimensions of unspeakability.

Similar considerations are debated in the psychedelic community: if one is not *experienced*, as the euphemism goes, what weight do mere words hold? This is a bone of contention in academia, where "you had to have been there" is an unacceptable criterion in a world where truth is structured entirely by forms of discourse: well-shaped arguments, using the same two-valued logic we've used since Aristotle, in natural language.

Another aspect of Sells's question is debated over and over in psychedelic studies. From the early (pre-criminalization) days of psychedelic research, the question has been raised as to the authenticity of a mystical experience catalyzed by a drug as opposed to those experiences that occur spontaneously, or as the result of culturally sanctioned spiritual practices such as forms of meditation, austerities, or prayer. The famous Good Friday experiment conducted by Walter Pahnke at Harvard Divinity School under Timothy Leary and Richard Alpert's supervision as part of the Harvard Psilocybin Project (Pahnke 1966) confirmed the authenticity of drug experiences for the majority of the participants. This finding was reaffirmed by Rick Doblin's long-term follow-up interviews of the Good Friday participants, twenty-five years later.

> The experimental subjects unanimously described their Good Friday psilocybin experience as having had elements of a genuinely mystical nature and characterized it as one of the high points of their spiritual life. (Doblin 1991)

In 2006, Roland Griffiths performed a similar but methodologically more rigorous experiment at Johns Hopkins, with similar findings (Griffiths 2008).

Scholar of religions Huston Smith sums up his own examination of the Pahnke experiment. Smith makes the essential distinction between ontology (a branch of metaphysics concerned with matters of being) and phenomenology (the study of consciousness and the objects of direct experience) in considering the question of the difference between the chemical and the natural mystical experience. He concludes:

> At this point, however, we are considering phenomenology rather than ontology, description rather than truth-claims, and on this level there is no difference. Descriptively, drug experiences cannot be distinguished from their natural religious counterparts. (Smith 2000)

This distinction between phenomenological description and ontological claims, *telling it like it is*, rather than *declaring what it is*, is vital to this story and its telling.

Beyond the ineffability barrier come reports of a wide variety of linguistic phenomena in altered states. Anthropologist Henry Munn studied the language used in ceremony by María Sabina and other mushroom curanderos, describing natural language attaining heights of eloquence, what he calls "ecstatic significations" (Munn 1973). Stanley Krippner studied the distortion and rending of natural language that occurs at various stages in the psychedelic experience. Many researchers have noted the commonality of synaesthesias in psychedelic experience where words or letters are linked to other sensory events. Terence McKenna's "shaggy primate story" (a.k.a. the stoned ape theory), in which he speculates that the encounter with the psilocybin mushroom catalyzed early humans into language, is a good example of a mythopoetic account of the origins and evolution of language.

Philosophically, Mark Pesce, Ralph Abraham, and Terence McKenna have each described the structure of reality as fundamentally linguistic. John Lilly was invited to the first SETI conference (Search for Extraterrestrial Intelligence) on the basis of his work with dolphins and LSD. The study of interspecies communication and LSD dovetailed neatly with the first attempts to listen for extraterrestrial communication. Lilly went on to study extraterrestrial communication in the flotation tank with LSD and ketamine.

Part of the unspeakability of psychedelic experience occurs around emotional extremes from terror to bliss. The hell realms coexist with the heavenly, as Albert Hofmann experienced on his first deliberate self-exploration with LSD, the famous bicycle ride, which he describes as a "most severe crisis."

■ Figure 6: James Higgins surfing a big wave. Used with permission.

Hellish distortions morphed to the heavenly by the end of his initiatory trip. Aldous Huxley's doors of perception opened on heaven and hell. Heaven and hell stand in contrapuntal relation in his highly literary trip report. Heaven and hell each invoke the other, maintaining a cosmic balance between the music of the spheres and the silence of the suicide. The nineteenth-century literary aesthetic of the sublime was embraced by the Romantic poets, no strangers to drug-induced altered states. The literary sublime, where horror and awe coexist viscerally in an excessive and overwhelming manner, is a reference point for the description of the range of emotional states that can chaotically coexist in the psychedelic experience.

But let it be said that the unspeakably funny can puncture the gravitas of the sublime with the anti-gravitas of the cosmic giggle at any moment in the space-time of a single trip. Too-much-ness, the "road to excess" of heaven, hell, gnosis, or hilarity, is also a hallmark. The navigation of excess, of learning to ride that which is far too big to fight, is a skill related to surfing or riding several kilometers on a bicycle coming up on 250 mics of pure Sandoz acid you made yourself. As in surfing the big waves, one learns to carve and cut back, to wipe out and survive.

Secrecy

The fact remains that psychedelic self-exploration in the present is accomplished largely in secret, by individuals, or in small groups, in acts of civil disobedience. This secrecy is a distillation of aspects of the unspeakable: illegality, social consequences, ineffability. When *omertà* is essential policy, as combatant and former LSD alchemist Nick Sand eloquently asserts (Sand 2001), communicating about the unspeakable requires what the Buddhists call *upaya:* method as skillful means. We anonomize, we fictionalize, we rant behind handles on mailing lists. The tension between *what must be told* and *what can't be spoken* is palpable in the mushrooming websites, fora, and YouTube clips of trippers and academic researchers alike, as well as Facebook pages devoted to discussion of every aspect of psychedelia. The telling is clearly winning over the silence. I salute James Joyce, not only for his psychedelic dissolution of natural language in the chrysalis of *Finnegans Wake,* but for his marching orders in *Portrait of the Artist as a Young Man:*

> I will not serve that in which I no longer believe whether it call itself home, my fatherland or my church: and I will try to express myself in some mode of life or art as freely as I can and as wholly as I can, using for my defense the only arms I allow myself to use, silence, exile, and cunning. (Joyce 2007)

Finally, there is the secrecy of initiation, that which *should not be told,* in distinction to the social unspeakabilities above. Initiation confers special knowledge, earned knowledge. Jeremy Narby tells us,

> In my initiations, I've had things communicated to me that are unspeakable for reasons of secrecy, and I respect traditions. There is something fairly paradoxical about this as many "secrets" can be found in esoteric bookstores: and others can't be found there, on the other hand, and remain unspeakable. (Narby 2008)

How these unspeakabilities found words in my own psychonautic practice is detailed in Chapter 2, "A Psychonautic Practice."

Notes, Chapter 1

1. *Icaros* are the songs sung by shamans in ceremony. They are given to him or her by spirits while under trance.
2. The Vaults of Erowid, a primary source for accurate information on psychedelics, struggles to keep up with the flow of new psychoactive chemicals in the underground economy.
3. The many-worlds quantum interpretation, first proposed by Hugh Everett, holds that the quantum waveform never collapses, but each possibility contained in the quantum state creates its own time track and world. "Before many-worlds, reality had always been viewed as a single unfolding history. Many-worlds, however,

views reality as a many-branched tree, wherein every possible quantum outcome is realized." (Wikipedia 2013)

4. The Council on Spiritual Practices is a San Francisco-based organization whose mission is "to identify and develop approaches to primary religious experience that can be used safely and effectively, and to help individuals and spiritual communities bring the insights, grace, and joy that arise from direct perception of the divine into their daily lives." http://csp.org.

CHAPTER 2

A Psychonautic Practice

". . . for here there is no place that does not see you. You must change your life."

—Rainer Maria Rilke, "Archaic Torso of Apollo"

The co-evolution of language and consciousness is a bootstrapping, self-reflexive process in the individual, the cultural group, and the species. The metaphor "pulling yourself up by your own bootstraps" (a physical impossibility) describes acting on oneself to produce change in a desired direction. It also nails the central issue of self-reflexivity at the heart of both language and consciousness. How can language describe itself (an action toward itself) when the only tool for description is language? Similarly, how can consciousness observe itself, when the instrument of observation is consciousness? How can I be both subject and object to myself, other than as a feature of grammar? Taking five grams of *Stropharia cubensis* while asking these questions produced some unique Saturday nights. The questions begin to take hold at about the point where natural language has been shed, and the self, no longer supported by its stories, grows increasingly porous.

Xenolinguistics

A great deal is known about the structure and evolution of natural languages, once they have reached their mature forms; this study is called linguistics and includes the sub-discipline of evolutionary linguistics. But linguistics does not address novel forms of language that are different in both form and function from natural languages, such as those that have appeared in psychonautic practice. I've chosen to call the study of these *unnatural* languages "xenolinguistics." In the world of science fiction, xenolinguistics means the study of alien languages. I've adopted it for the exploration of psychedelics and

■ Figure 7: A portion of the notebooks containing the session reports. Photograph by Diana Reed Slattery.

language to give a feel for the high strangeness of these sorts of language, from spontaneous glossolalia—the outpouring of language-like sounds—to Allyson's Grey's Secret Writing and Terence McKenna's self-transforming, linguistic machine elves.

Long after this research was completed, I encountered Sheila Finch's book of science fiction stories, *The Guild of Xenolinguists*. The character of "translator of alien languages" is a necessary figure in science fiction as humans encounter the Other in space exploration. The Star Trek series created Uhura eavesdropping on Klingons. Samuel Delany's Rydra Wong breaks the Babel-17 code. And Ted Chiang's Dr. Louise Banks attempts to decipher the Heptapod B writing system. The translation problem, in addition to being imagined as women's work, is generally solved in one of three ways in science fiction, according to linguist and translator Brian Mossop: by telepathy (no words needed); by lingua franca, two species communicating in a third, shared language; and by computer translation (Mossop 1996). Sheila Finch takes a different tack, one that endears her to the current story. Her xenolinguists, trained by humans and dolphins, use a kit of psychedelic medicines to achieve an opening of mind to the alien intelligence, recalling John Lilly's work with dolphins and LSD. The mind-meld is combined with a computer interface to learn the forms of communication used by the encountered alien race. *The Guild of Xenolinguists* explores communication with the alien through a number of different scenarios. Finch's xenolinguistic method falls loosely under telepathy and machine translation, but with a psychedelic twist. The mind-opening with the alien more closely resembles the capacity to *be* the alien, and to view from the alien's perspective. The xenolinguist in this sense changes her consciousness in order to apprehend new language "from the inside out."

Did Finch know that alien languages could be experienced by individuals in altered states of consciousness? Did she imagine that sometime in the future someone would investigate this phenomenon, not only in the sci fi world of what-if magic but in the default world, the world of everyday life? Whether she has had this experience personally is a question she never quite answered when I asked. But her intuition was spot-on. The alien Other, bearing linguistic objects of all sorts, is contactable by some in psychedelic states. My thanks to Sheila Finch for her necessary fiction. I call myself a practicing xenolinguist. A Guild of Xenolinguists is the perfect name for this odd assortment of linguistic visionaries, present company included, whose work appears in these pages.

This chapter, and the chapter on Glide that follows, describe in detail my own psychonautic practice and adventures in xenolinguistics over a ten-year period from 1999 to 2009. My psychonautic practice proved to be a microcosm of the co-evolution of language and consciousness, a model of the feedback loops between them. My practice is also a case in point of the difficulties of harvesting knowledge in zones of intense self-reflexivity, where the very meanings of "subjectivity" and "objectivity" are radically displaced.

Beginnings: The Download Experience

What kind of experience could impel a fifty-seven-year-old grandmother, a card-carrying AARP member of the middle class with a university position and a 12-step spouse, to make such a sharp left turn onto the medicine path? I call it a download—the sudden arrival of a major organizing insight, the great aha! you never knew you were waiting for until it happened. Luminous, numinous, compelling, it can be invoked, but it cannot be programmed. And a download happens when you least expect it.

What makes a download a download is the intensity of the experience. Intensity arises from the extreme compaction of densely interconnected knowledge. Intensity amplifies when a sense of potential access to any knowledge immerses one in infinite possibility. Infinite possibility, that is, if one can summon the wit to form a question under such extreme epistemological conditions. Epistemology, the study of knowledge and knowing, asks "What do I know, how do I know it, and how do I know that I know?" Applying a psychedelic to a mind in search of an answer is rather like setting Google loose on the Akashic records.[2] The impact of this single event triggered a sudden and irrevocable change in the course of my life. Downloads can do that. This life-transforming momentum can be seen in the following two examples.

Philip K. Dick's urgent download was expressed in three of his last novels and thousands of handwritten pages, which he called the *Exegesis,* produced from 1974 until the end of his life in 1982. This download arrived as a blast of knowledge-laden pink light that seized him during February and March 1974 and never really let him go. In the *Exegesis,* Dick tried over and over to unpack the meanings of his divine invasion. He called the downloading agency various names: VALIS: Vast Active Living Intelligence System; Zebra; and the plasmate. During his download episodes, Dick also experienced xenoglossia, the paranormal ability to speak or write a language one has not learned by natural means, a phenomenon he had experienced earlier on LSD as a fluency in Latin. In the 1974 case, his wife transcribed his sounds and mapped them to the *Koine* Greek of the Hellenistic period. In the *Exegesis,* Dick also connected the informational blast with a DNA readout:

> We appear to be memory coils (DNA carriers capable of experience) in a computer-like thinking system which, although we have correctly recorded and stored thousands of years of experiential information, and each of us possesses somewhat different deposits from all the other life forms, there is a malfunction—a failure—of memory retrieval. (Dick, in Sutin, 1995)

Terence and Dennis McKenna experienced their own psilocybin-fueled download from March 4 to March 15, 1971, at the mission of La Chorrera in southern Colombia, detailed in Chapter 9. In his afterword to Dick's *Exegesis* in Lawrence Sutin's anthology, Terence McKenna calls the similarity between his download experience and Dick's *"folie à deux,"* a madness shared by two. Synchronicities mapped his life-line with Dick's: the extraterrestrial content; the Gnostic philosophical mappings; and the intensity of having lived through his own alien download with Dennis in 1971. The McKenna brothers' download is described as a wraparound reality that seemed both hyperreal and of critical importance—a shared and true hallucination.

Of course, the *folie* count is higher. John Lilly's near-fatal pursuit of communications with an Other he called ECCO (Earth Coincidence Control Office) using ketamine declared, "Cosmic Love is absolutely Ruthless and Highly Indifferent: it teaches its lessons whether you like/dislike them or not" (Lilly 1977b). Timothy Leary's *Starseed Transmission* downloaded from the Black Hole of solitary confinement in Folsom Prison asserts, "This message of neurological resonance can be censored, imprisoned, but cannot be crushed because it comes from within, from the DNA nucleus inside each cell, from the evolving nervous system" (Leary 1973). These are statements of a very particular sort—hyperventilated, urgent, epistemologically potent.[3] These psychedelic downloads, every one, contain both a scathing critique of life on planet Earth at the time of writing and an evolutionary imperative. In Rilke's words, "You must change your life."

Download experiences are accompanied by the kinds of synchronicities that represent cosmic validation to the downloadee and confirmation of paranoid conspiratorial thinking and megalomania to the psychiatrist. The reports describe noetic experiences that focus attention as would a lens placed dead center on one's awareness. These psychedelic noetic lenses can realign events and provide a new and coherent meaning to the whole storyline of one's life, and the historic storyline of the human race. For Dick, the early Christian past is reviewed in a revelatory light, what Dick called *anamnesis,* "the end of forgetfulness." For Terence McKenna, the future is previewed in his prophetic "hyperdimensional object at the end of history," a concrescense casting its shockwaves back through time.

A download experience creates a lasting impression, similar in some ways to PTSD. The vision persists, obsessively intruding on the business of daily life, *becoming* the business of daily life, only with a shift in valence. This is a bright trauma, an ecstatic illumination that centers and focuses attention, mind, and heart. These storylines reek with a super-saturated presence of

■ **Figure 8: Lough Derriana, County Kerry, Ireland.** Photograph by Diana Reed Slattery.

meaning. To the downloadee, they are all that matters, and the tale, however unspeakable, must be told.

My own download came in Ireland, the summer of 1998. I was a grad student in communication and rhetoric at Rensselaer Polytechnic Institute, my mind a sponge full of semiotics, new media theory, and the history of communication technology. I'd taken the summer off to clarify my topic—the idea of a visual language—for a PhD proposal. Instead, the urge to write a science fiction novel took my mind into a future world of humans whose lifespans were prolonged indefinitely. Bored and brutal, they were mainly entertained by a game that pitted immortal Players against mortal Death Dancers. Their world was taking shape; I could enter it, talk to the characters. At one point I asked the magic question: *How is the game played?* The answer arrived as a high-speed blast of information: *The game is played on mazes made of the visual language, Glide.*

I got the whole thing in a timeless instant: the 27 glyphs; the maze game and its rules; and the glyphs as the morphing maze, the architecture of the playing field. The download also contained information about how the glyphs behave as a visual language of waves. The psychedelic myth of the origin of the language was taught to the characters by the hallucinogenic blue water lily.

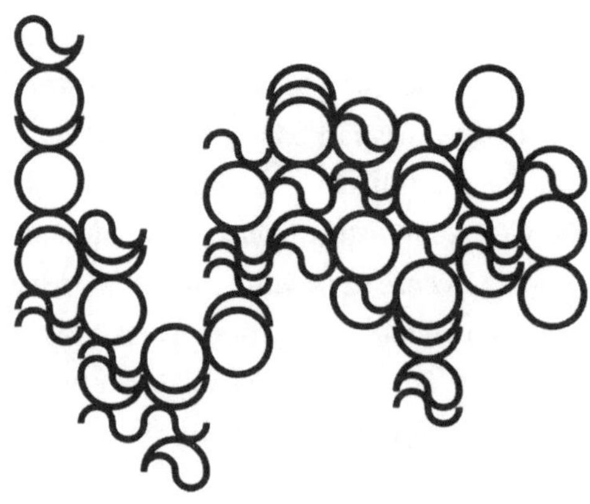

■ **Figure 9: Two-dimensional Glide maze.**

> The Glides not only harvested, they cross-pollinated, improving the lily. . . . The lily expressed its gratitude by teaching the Glides a secret, silent language. Breathing the raw pollen, day after day, the Glides listened as the lily bespoke itself through three shapes based on the gestures of their cupped hands at work: curved up as they scooped the pollen; curved down as they emptied their palms into the baskets, and joined together in the gesture of the wave. (Slattery 2003)

Glide presented itself in the story-world as an alien language. The glyphs of the language formed the patterns and physical structures on which the game was played. As the plot unfolded, it became evident that the Glide language was intricately involved at every level of the story: as the game maze architecture; as a secret code, an oracle, and a literature; and as a catalyst for the changing of consciousness. In the story, the moving and morphing forms of the language[4] enabled new ways of thinking, feeling, and perceiving. *The Maze Game* narrates the theme implicit in the Glide download: that language and consciousness co-evolve in a bootstrapping, iterative process, in the individual, in the cultural group, and in the species. *The Maze Game*, published in 2003, became the underpinning of my PhD thesis, completed in 2010.

The novel form allowed me the imaginative freedom to work out the implications of this form of visual language, Glide. *The Maze Game* functioned as a parallel universe in which I was creating a plan for myself to follow in the default world. In the story, every young Death Dancer completes training in a ritual centered on finding his or her unique focus or purpose in life. They break a cobalt-blue ampoule containing the wine of the lilies, drink it down, and enter the maze, alone. There were immediate practical problems to following my characters' example. How was I to re-enter the psychedelic world with no connections to materials, no support network, and no current information? There would be no enthusiastic shouts of encouragement at home from my AA-oriented spouse who believed, as if his life depended on it, that ingestion of any pill or drug was "eating your booze" and would cause an instantaneous addiction, though I had never been a drinker. At work, this program, made known, could get me fired. And my grown children, starting families of their own, didn't need to worry unduly about their mother off on dodgy adventures. In other words, there was no support network in my daily life. As it was, I developed that network in the invisible world itself. Materials were found. Current information abounded online and in books. All this added up to create a very secret life. My feet stayed on the ground (mostly), and I worked steadily at my university job, creating interactive educational multimedia applications for engineers, and project-managing multiple software projects. I continued coursework toward a PhD. And at every opportunity—weekends, sick days, vacations, conferences—I left the default world to explore the psychedelic realms, in search of Glide.

Protocols

Before I tackle the specific Glide content from more than four hundred sessions, I'll lay out the technical details that formed the container for these experiences.

Substance and dosing: Over the ten-year period, I experimented with different doses of a limited number of substances, going deeply into a few rather than trying a broad spectrum of materials. With MDMA, the dose was always 125 mg; no mid-session boosters. For me, MDMA is psychedelic at that dose, producing strong visuals.[5] Most significantly, MDMA initiated the experience of contact with the Other. With psilocybin, I tried various doses, from < 1 g to 8.5 g at the upper limit. With 2C-B, the dosage remained the same, approximately 30 mg. This dose proved to be fully psychedelic. LSD was used in an 80-microgram to a 250-microgram range. *Salvia divinorum* (in strong tincture form) was another significant substance, though only used five times. I tried several other of the Shulgin research chemicals of the 2C series—2C-I, 2C-T-7, and 2C-E—but the body load was too distracting for the substances to be useful to me. DMT, though only available three times during the research period, upstaged all other substances for the sense of totally alien presence and environment. It also changed the nature of subsequent psilocybin trips, raising my tolerance for the deeply weird. I went where inclination and availability led, the serendipity of the psychedelic life, where trusted sources are of paramount importance, and no experience is more than a rumor until you've tried it.

As my psychedelic experience grew, the new pathways blazed in the mind made it easier to find and revisit certain locales and experiences on a variety of substances. I found cannabis to potentiate psychedelic effects, especially when used in combination with psilocybin. Cannabis also provides me a smooth reentry with MDMA, which, for me, never produces any hangovers the next day. In the last few years, high-dose cannabis in edible forms and various hashish preparations were used in sub-psychedelic doses.

Set and Setting: These two factors, staples of psychonautic practice since Leary, Alpert, and Metzner wrote *The Psychedelic Experience,* are completely linked in my practice. Privacy, secrecy, and research involving writing determined my *set.* As for *setting,* I was always indoors, and nearly always alone. The intent was going inward, or outward into the psychedelic sphere, however one classifies the ins and outs of the landscape. I could lock the doors, turn off the phone, shut down the computer, and wear clothes or not. For a period of time, I couldn't stand having anything remotely constricting on my body. Second, the effects of the medicine were sometimes strong enough that managing to get around the physical space of the house was challenge enough. Had I had a partner in this adventure, it would have been wonderful to venture out into nature from time to time, but that was not the case. I contented myself with the subtle, sensuous patterns of light coming through the curtained windows, or the cawing of crows in a snow-laden tree in the backyard. Similarly, my *setting* influenced my *set*—deliciously alone and out of contact with others, I functioned as pilot, navigator, flight attendant, and ground crew, as well as passenger. In other words, there were many roles I needed to step into to be responsible for as many aspects of the session as possible. I had a sitter only once, in my first psilocybin session. No one in my default life knew when or that I was "in session." I felt, and it was a calculated risk, that the perceived safety of the container was more important than an elaborate emergency management plan. I figured I could get through almost anything of a mental nature by waiting it out. "This too shall pass" was a workable mantra, even in those moments when the eternal nature of an especially unpleasant experience is trying to assert itself. I wasn't trying anything that I had not researched, and I trusted my sources, but there are never guarantees. Neither was I experimenting with any unplanned or untried combinations of substance that could complicate things. I arranged my living spaces to enhance these sessions, which then positively influenced my set going into a session.

Psychedelic researcher Roland Fischer differentiates two personality types by their opposite responses to sensory input during the peak of a psychedelic session. Fischer describes this as the difference between "maximizers" and "minimizers."

> When our subjects were placed in an environment of sensory attenuation, only the minimizers (i.e., those who at the peak of drug-induced arousal intend to reduce sensory input) will develop a hallucinatory experience. Maximizers (i.e., those who at drug-peak tend to increase sensory input), however, not having sufficient sensory input to maximize, are never sure whether they were given psilocybin or placebo. (Fischer 1970)

I am emphatically a "minimizer" type of psychonaut. If I begin a session with music, it is almost always shut off in short order. I prefer a low light level, or darkness. A completely blank area in my line of sight—ceiling or wall—on which to project visions is preferable. My fantasy environment would be an interior domed space with a perfectly smooth white surface, where lighting was indirect and could be controlled by dimmer. The notion of having to spend an entire session surrounded by paisley, fractals, blinking lights, and loud music is at odds with my purpose of introspection (and my aesthetic sensibility). I'm sensitive to color, especially under conditions of extended perception.

Difficulties of the Practice

Assessing risk was always present, as an effect on *set,* going into every session. Operating in a legal environment where the consequences of discovery are severe takes some getting used to. And gauging the consequences of sharing knowledge publicly, as I am doing here, assessing how far out of the closet to come, is a delicate dance of seduction. But to paraphrase Lorenzo Hagerty, psychedelic author, archivist, and podcaster—you might as well come out, the closet's getting awfully crowded.

Keeping session reports reliably was the most difficult aspect of the practice. Producing a continuous readout of the experience, writing English words in notebooks while sailing far out beyond the veil of language into the Unspeakable, is a learned skill.

■ Figure 10: Page from a session report illustrating the tendency of the writing hand to slip from English to wavy lines.

The trick is to keep an English-language channel open in one portion of small-mind while venturing into Mind at Large. But this was the firm instruction in the first session in 1999, and I stuck to it, a half-million words or more. Reports could be written after, but it was the in-session recording that was the most important. Control of the writing hand was more difficult in the challenging environment of the psilocybin sessions, begun in 2000. Words in English tended to dissolve into drawings, often visual puns. The shift in handwriting from the formation of words to the dissolution of the line and the appearance of visual puns occurred under the internal pressure of the felt serpentine movement of flowing energy I call the "Rainbow Serpent." I interpret this phenomenon as a fundamental linguistic movement underlying writing and drawing, which easily takes over from the inscription of natural language in psilocybinetic states. I experience the spontaneous production of serpentine waves as a kind of gestural glossolalia. Here is an example transcribed from session 05.03.25* (5 g dried *Stropharia cubensis*):

> tttttt ttttttttt
> tttttttttttttttt here is the lines the transmission
>
> being here ray-diate the dimensional script so words shiver across themselves
> transmit mitten tran-smitten manuscript script of the full filament

Control of the writing hand was secondary, however, to the maintenance of an English-language channel of communication. With practice, this channel became relegated to a more automatic process, similar to learning to drive a car or ride a bike, skills that are at first awkward and demand a lot of attention, but can be accomplished in such a way as to leave conscious attention free to attend to the unfolding phenomena of the experience.

Figure 11: Glide glyph, Body.

Figure 12: Glide glyph, Mind.

*My session reports are dated in the style of year/month/day; i.e., the year is *not* the last number but the first.

During the period after the development of the LiveGlide software in 2006–2007, the form of my session writing made a radical shift. In many sessions part of the time was spent writing in Glide three-dimensionally in light with the LiveGlide software, viewing the moving images on a large computer screen or projected on a wall. I used the Glide symbolic system as another form of communication with the Other, of scribing the transmission. In those sessions, I would make notes in the session journal at the beginning and the end. Sometimes I would make a video as a record of my conversation with the Other. Small clips from these conversations can be seen at https://vimeo.com/16237570 and at https://vimeo.com/35725587. These two clips are meditations in two moods on the mind-body connection.

Each clip is drawn with a single glyph, which, by rotating in three-dimensional space, transforms into the other. Body-mind becomes a single unit of meaning in the transformation.

First Encounter with the Other

There was a precursor event eight years earlier that set the stage for the initiation of the psychedelic investigation of language and Glide. In 1991 I had the opportunity to experiment with MDMA. It was a substance about which I had read very little; I had classed it broadly as a psychedelic, and still do. Most in the field of psychedelic science would disagree with this categorization. MDMA is primarily classed as an empathogen, or entactogen. It reliably enables an attitude of emotional openness, a lowering of egoic defenses, an increased ability to communicate with and trust another, and the ability to access previously unavailable materials from the unconscious. These attributes have made MDMA a useful adjunct to psychotherapy (Shulgin and Shulgin 1991; Stolaroff 1997; Roberts 2001). Legal research on MDMA is currently opening up again. This 1991 session set a pattern at a deep level that influenced all subsequent sessions in which the Other was a prominent feature, across substances.

My system had been free of any kind of psychedelic drug, including cannabis, for twenty-four years. After the 1991 epic session, my expectation of MDMA was psychedelic. The manner in which it was administered, the unknown dosage, and my own individual mind-body response (generally highly sensitive to chemical perturbations) each contributed to the power of the experience. A bright trauma, it created a lasting imprint of the nature of the relationship of self and Other. A further and critical aspect of *set* was my immersion at the time in the literature of Christian mysticism. I had been reading St. John of the Cross, Teresa of Ávila, Thérèse of Lisieux, and Edith Stein. My friend opened a gel capsule containing the MDMA and tapped it into a half glass of orange juice, which I drank. It took effect in a very short time as a huge, rocket-like up-rush of energy, a true NASA-style launch, complete with heavy G-force that pinned my body temporarily to the couch and propelled me into inner space at warp speed. In the shock and surprise of this sudden overwhelming of mind-body-spirit I cried out involuntarily for help, a *cri de coeur* from the depths, *dear Jesus help me*... which resolved into a spontaneous prayer inwardly spoken *help me to learn the pain of loving all creation* and to the suddenly surrounding presence of total love, which held my dissolving self, melting in a pure solution of love, a state of grace and communion. I settled into heart-heaven, opened my notebook, and wrote down what I heard for the next four hours, filling the pages with a rush of words throughout which ran the refrain *for I am you and you are me,* self and Other wholly intertwined, the pronouns a simultaneous duality and unity. *The pain of loving all creation* became the topic; the ability to open the heart to all the pain in the world was an exercise in compassion and tolerance to confront unflinchingly the many tragedies and injustices in human life.

The experience seared me at depth, a hot poker plunged into the heart. A pain and a bliss that had little or nothing to do with any tribulations in my personal life. A bliss and a pain of love that could only be borne by further opening, complete trust, and total acceptance. With the unbidden cry for help I had spontaneously invoked the archetype of the Other in the imprint of Christ, though even the Christ-ness of the Other flamed away into something more mysterious. The reply to my cry for help: *who cries out in the garden of the stars?* A pathway to the Other was blazed that was then available for use when I returned to the psychedelic sphere in 1999 to ask about Glide. This is not to say that all experiences of the Other arrived with the mystical intensity of the 1991 session. The Christ-presence happened only that one time. But many of the key features persisted. First, the experience of two distinct—and unequal—points of view in dialogue, and the teaching voice of the Other were the repeated forms of the encounter. These meetings happened in an emotional atmosphere of loving trust. The cultivation of acceptance of experience, all experience, the good, the bad, and the ugly, in all phases of consciousness, was essential to moving forward in the internal relationship. This radical self-acceptance included being accepted exactly as I was, in a fundamental and unconditional way. The injunction not to fear was part of this process of acceptance. The injunction to release whatever attachment to or rejection of experience that might be impeding the pure flow of phenomena in the moment opened many pathways.

None of these qualities of being were sought or experienced as ends in themselves. They constituted the development of a set of states of mind-body-heart that were most conducive to the unobstructed receipt of the information download of the particular session. It's simply easier to pay attention and be a student while occupying a bliss-body (not distracted by aches and pains or emotional distortions) and a state of emotional fulfillment (not ego-hungry, lonely, defensive, or frightened). A welcoming of the strange and alien is a useful attitude. Clearly, I could better attend to the lesson presented while on sabbatical from the chore of making demands, judgments, and constant-comments to myself. Attention is collected from its usual pursuits and given fully to the experience at hand: the meeting of Psyche and Eros. Back at baseline, these attitudes of acceptance and trust were tried out in daily life, to good effect.

I never repeated the rocket-launch approach to the MDMA state. The slower rising became a teaching in itself, an opportunity to experience the shift from bounded singular ego-identity "Diana" to a duality/unity in the configuration of self and Other through the phases experienced on the way into the psychedelic state.

Charles Laughlin calls these periods of transition between phases of consciousness "warps." The warps, in Laughlin's view, can be "momentary to the point of evanescence" and are usually unconscious to the perceiver (Laughlin et al. 1990). I have found, with a variety of psychedelic materials, that the warp, the period of transition from baseline state to a more stably configured psychedelic state, is in most cases of a duration long enough that the process of transformation can be observed and described.

For the period of time from the first Glide session in July 1999 through the end of 2003, the teaching voice of the Other was not clothed in a particular archetype but existed in a more abstract, disembodied form, a presence that could be called, with Terence McKenna, "the voice of the Logos." But that name does not quite capture the paradoxical sense of the Other as both an intimate and yet detached and objective voice, heart and mind addressed and functioning in tandem, not at war. Psyche and Eros in their risky dance. The Christ archetype did not reappear; stranger avatars were in store.

A Spectrum of Transpersonalities

The landscape of self and Other took a radical turn toward complexity with my first psilocybin mushroom experience in 2001. So different than the teaching voice, these groups of others have been called many names. Who or what are they? There can be mobs of them, multitudes, legions reached on tryptamine pathways. The little people, *los niños,* the munchkins, the tykes, the self-transforming machine elves, the gnomes—all appear in the literature, not just of contemporary trip reports but in folklore as well. Tryptamines (psilocybin, DMT, ayahuasca) reveal them (release them?), though they are by no means always reported in all tryptamine experiences. They are shape-shifters, but at a whole new level of both shape and shifting. They possess a profound and occasionally wicked sense of playfulness and tricksterism, a very odd sense of humor, sometimes associated with the hilarity that mushrooms can induce. They show up in droves, or parades, carnivals, so many, one for every cell in the body, one might suspect, or every protein chain. They are sentient, as if the body-mind swarms with biomechanical intelligence, alien armies thrilled to see you and anxious to reveal at high speed their synaesthetic objects of knowledge.

I confess I can find nothing in the literature of the neurobiology of altered states of consciousness that maps to the particular phenomena described in the following sampler of DMT experiential reports, collected by Peter Meyer.

> I was in a large space and saw what seemed to be thousands of the entities. They were rapidly passing something to and fro among themselves, and were looking intently at me, as if to say "See what we are doing" [Subject V] (Meyer 1997)

> A strange state of mind ensued, one of dynamic, patterned energy, in which I was not sure whether I was perceiving a scene, with a moving being, or not. I finally realized that the answer to my question regarding spirits was that there were indeed many around me, and that they were merry, hiding and playing a joke on me. [Subject M] (Meyer 1997)
>
> . . . . I found myself once again in the company of the "elves," as the focus of their attention and ministrations, but they appeared much less colorful and altogether preoccupied with the task at hand, i.e., pouring a golden, viscous liquid through a network of long, inter-twining, transparent conduits which led into the middle of my abdomen . . . [Subject O] (Meyer 1997)
>
> It was as if there were alien beings there waiting for me, and I recall that they spoke to me as if they had been awaiting my arrival, but I cannot remember exactly what was said. This time, rather than (or as well as) flitting about me, the entities approached me from the front, rapidly and repeatedly, appearing to enter and pass through me. [Subject M] (Meyer 1997)
>
> This time I saw the "elves" as multidimensional creatures formed by strands of visible language; they were more creaturely than I had ever seen them before. . . . The elves were dancing in and out of the multidimensional visible language matrix, "waving" their "arms" and "limbs/hands/fingers?" and "smiling" or "laughing, "although I saw no faces as such. [Subject G] (Meyer 1997)

In my experience with psilocybin, the two forms of the Other described—the singular teaching voice and the zany alien munchkin hordes—occur in varying relations to each other as the transpersonalities manifest during the course of a session. The teaching voice appears first, guiding me into the trip. On the warp in, often groundwork is laid with the help of the singular Other. Current concerns are reviewed and dealt with. Intentions can be set in the warp; they are not always what baseline "I" had attempted to set. The Other "comes in focus" and speaks, addressing me generally as "you" and sometimes by the always gently ironic trip-name, "faithful scribe," acknowledging that I have showed up in school, pen in hand, to resume my scribal duties. Calling me "scribe" is always a subtle reminder of the primary rule to "write without editing," i.e., to set aside whatever "Diana" might think about what she is inscribing, as "Diana" herself is set aside as the warp progresses.

Psychic transparency increases on the warp, as defenses and resistance melt away and I pour out of my ordinary mind-state as the invisible world comes into view. I generally perceive the warp from baseline into the psychedelic state as a literal tuning to a higher frequency: perceptually, emotionally, physically, cognitively. This is as perceptible as hearing a sound and being able to differentiate a high from a low frequency. This, however, is experienced as a frequency characterizing the entire state of consciousness. Simon G. Powell describes the warp this way:

> I lay comfortably in my bed and waited for the psilocybin to gracefully infuse my psyche. Sometimes, if one is really alert, the first psilocybinetic wave can almost be coldly analyzed as it washes over one's consciousness. This is a fantastic moment. At a certain point, you are shifted into an animate, supernormal reality. With eyes open, one's surroundings appear as if the parts of a divine being made of living information, and reality begins to seems like a tale being told in the mind of God. (Powell 2008)

Psychologist Roland Fischer describes the progress of the warp in relation to self and Other as a perception-hallucination continuum.

> The constancy of the "I" is interfered with as one moves along the perception-hallucination continuum from the "I" of the physical world to the "Self" of the mental dimension. Analogously, the perception-meditation continuum also involved a departure from the "I" to the "Self." These two continua can thus be called "I-Self" continua. The further we progress on the perception-hallucination continuum from the normal, through the creative, psychotic, and ultimately to the ecstatic state, the more complete is the transformation, or "unlearning," of the constancies of the physical dimension. (Fischer 1971)

Fischer revised this diagram over the years. His final version was in the form of a circle, which he also described as having a twist in it, transforming it into a Mobius strip. He saw that the originally opposite poles of ecstasy and samadhi join in an experiential unity. Compared to my own actual experience, a linear path through the warp, considered either spatially or temporally, is a greatly simplified model; the experience is for me more a garden of forking paths, in Borges's phrase from the story of that name:

> "A labyrinth of symbols," he corrected. "An invisible labyrinth of time." To me, a barbarous Englishman, has been entrusted the revelation of this diaphanous mystery. After more than a hundred years, the details are irretrievable; but it is not hard to conjecture what happened. Ts'ui Pe must have said once: I am withdrawing to write a book. And another time: I am withdrawing to construct a labyrinth. Every one imagined two works; to no one did it occur that the book and the maze were one and the same thing. (Borges 2007)

The munchkins arrive in various forms, with various tasks in mind, as part of the psilocybin warp. Sometimes this is experienced as a journey upward through a densely populated urban-infested alien cyberpunk carnivalesque sprawl, which I have called the "funhouse." The funhouse resembles a relentless house of mirrors where I pass through a form of intense inspection, a full body-mind scan where no nook or cranny of psyche is left unilluminated. The funhouse functions as a kind of transdimensional airport security system rendering a status report on my entire existential and karmic situation. The funhouse is a pass through the scathing light of a well-calibrated shit-detector. The good, the bad, and the ugly are trotted forth, a good deal of hazing being the inevitable result of trying to duck any unpleasantries encountered. In other words, the munchkins can perform an excruciatingly slow and narrated version of ego-dismantling (or shamanic dismemberment). For me, it's more like being picked apart than dismembered. Full acceptance of all findings, resulting in non-attachment, becomes a prerequisite for passing on up through the warp to a distinctly different phase.

This next destination has been variously described in the session reports as the peacock throne room, or a dome hung in space that functions as an ambassadorial meeting place, where the person of the teaching voice mediates relations with the far more alien Glides (my species of munchkin). This is a place of great beauty and enchantment. And a school that began as a nursery.

School

Only the altered state can teach you the meaning of the altered state. This is the phenomenological paradox one gets into in the process of making a

> description (from any state) of even a small corner of what has been perceived as the vastest unknown territory ever experienced. (session report 05.12.04, cannabis)

In the psilocybin world I began as an infant: immobile, unable to focus, enchanted. I felt newborn, while being urgently aware that I needed to bring every scrap of maturity as a human "adult" I could assemble to this new form of infancy. I was helpless, yet surrounded by dimly perceived but clearly benign "adults" concerned with my well-being. The MDMA lessons on practicing trust as a state of mind were appreciated in the far more challenging psilocybin environment. The dimly sensed others were teaching me, step by step, first to focus my attention for longer and longer periods of time, then to focus my perception in ways appropriate to a multidimensional environment. I learned to "walk," i.e., navigate fluctuating spaces and times on my own. Other important lessons were taught: how to exit from repetitive loops, and how to detach from compelling sights and sounds and shift attention into new areas.

I learned how to turn encounters with negative energies into "food" by a kind of digestion back into fundamental energy, a handy skill both for dealing with certain forms of negativity and gaining more energy in the session for exploration. I also learned how to use a "skyhook," becoming the Other and using the Other's greater focus to "lift" out of one level or situation into another. As I learned to navigate the psychedelic sphere, I became increasingly able to operate my body and move about when necessary or desired in my house, a skill I came to call "multiminding" where multiple worlds could align and be perceived at once. These shifts of level or locale were modeled in the morphing of one Glide glyph into another—a transformation of meaning translated into a navigational tool in the altered state of consciousness.

I learned that navigation in the labyrinthine spaces and times of the various psychedelics is accomplished by control of attention and intention. Attention and intention are staple features of consciousness in many states, but in psychedelic mind-states, their workings are open to view like a skeleton watch, and subject to increasing degrees of control. Subtle degrees of differences within attention and intention become visible. Attention, for instance, can become synaesthetically touch-like: gentle or grasping, calm and abiding, detached, or fierce and penetrating. Different qualities of attention are useful in different conditions. Intention can be strong or weak, insecure or irresistible.

I learned to tolerate many forms of energy moving through me. When the Rainbow Serpent uncoils its forces within, until you learn to surf the waves, sometimes you just hang on. And I learned many things about Glide as the unpacking of the original download progressed.

The schooling described in this section proceeded over a period of years. In 2003, I had reached what felt roughly like an adolescent state. The Other, since the beginning a neutral voice, took on an archetypal mask. Now in the guise of a fictional character, he initiated a new form of relationship (and a new ontological skill) which I/he/we call "the Be Me." The Be Me happened when the Other took a personal form. I had the thought, *I want to see you*. The answer came back, *If you want to see me, Be Me*. In other words, empathize to the point of identity. The words are just the words, translated from a wordless invitation to communion as an instantaneous form of learning.

Elrond

The appearance of this avatar was examined during the session while it was taking form. As it was happening, I was aware why this form in particular was constellating, and the nature of some of his attributes. The experience was that of an image coming to life, like an emulsion photo coming up in the developer tray. The energy of the teaching voice flowed into the image of Tolkien's character Elrond Stardome, half-elven, wizard and warrior, as the new form of the teacher. The psychonaut found, in the province of the soul, the reality of fiction and the fictional nature of reality. The injunction was to "trust that this whole improbable transformation is occurring" (session report 03.12.28, MDMA).

The figure of Elrond grew out of a sensed mycelial/placental network. This golden network of crystalline filaments, another structure I perceived in the altered state of consciousness, was "installed" in an earlier session, and steadily growing, a biomechanical prosthesis. In the altered state, this network thrives on relaxation, trust, and love, which, in turn, opens a direct connection with an extradimensional reality that is the primary source of energy tapped in the psychedelic state.

The filamental networks and the form of Elrond became more or less permanent features of my psychedelic landscape, accessible by intention or showing up spontaneously. How to characterize these structures—how they are formed, maintained, utilized, transformed, or dissolved—is another question entirely. Timothy Leary spoke of "imprinting" to describe our early biological and cultural conditioning, following Konrad Lorenz' work with ducklings. Both he and John Lilly experimented with re-imprinting (or reprogramming) the individual while under the influence of LSD. Both Leary and Lilly asserted that one could access the original states in which the imprints were laid while on LSD, and that changes—re-imprinting or reprogramming—could be carried out from there. Leary, Alpert, and Metzner's *The Psychedelic Experience* aims to imprint the Tibetan-Buddhist experience on the heightened suggestibility of the psychonaut. In the relationship of self and Other, in the forms described above, I could study at depth the soul's projections on the Other, according to its needs, and the Other's projections into the soul of the actions necessary for its evolution.

My own experience in the psychedelic school has contained a number of "drills." These are repeated exercises that can go on for periods of over an hour, or be repeated several times during a session. One simple example, but primary in importance, has been the development of attentional skills. Another has been learning physical skills such as the gestural expressions of Glide language. Drawing skills, letting the hand be moved from within in the flowing forms of the Rainbow Serpent's motions, was another "drill." In certain altered states of consciousness I practiced putting my body in positions I never imagined it could assume in baseline reality through forms of yoga-like asanas. From the session on 07.07.02,

> somatic practice to re-imprint the body becoming aware of body from inside out   old images control by means of permission from an identity that now needs it many movements some bringing much energy into the body   breathing and moving from the meditation bench shoulders rotate chest moves concave to convex and breathing follows combined with wave motion up the spine coordinated with concave convex   new language   same language of waves how to find the wave motions available within the articulation of the body

you are discovering your own exercises they are timeless and the knowledge of them is stored in the body it is what the body longs to do it is the *be me* which is a surrender

As the wave motion was practiced (my body upright on a kneeling meditation bench) the relationship was evident between these body waves of spontaneous energy[6] and the wavy motion of Glide transformations. These drills are an example of "knowing by doing."

Each of these drills is an aspect of the same impulse to motion, the movements of the Rainbow Serpent. Practice with them imprinted the form and feel of these motions for use at baseline. They are examples of learning by repetitive practice in the psychedelic sphere.

A final form of learning in the psychedelic school can be called "learning by being." This form of learning is most evident in the phenomenon I call the "Be Me." In the fluid identity conditions of the psychedelic state, it is possible to view one's own "personality" as a complete pattern that one can slide in and out of, and furthermore, other identities can be occupied for learning purposes. To see from another's viewpoint, to be in his or her viewpoint as distinct from whatever one considers one's own, feels like an act of instantaneous "tuning" to a complete and completely unique pattern, like slipping a

■ **Figure 13: Wave drawing.** Diana Reed Slattery.

different slide into the projector of consciousness. It is a practical application of what I earlier called multiminding. In this case, the multiminding simultaneously perceives a choice of personalitites, or identity patterns that one can fluidly slide into or between, like a change of costume. Possession phenomena may be related, but in these controlled slip-sliding experiences there is no sense of being "taken over" or any amnesia associated with the switches.

In the psychedelic school, these are lessons. These cross-identity experiences, whether from human self to animal identity, other human identity, or to a non-human (archetypal or alien) identity, can be characterized as a vivid deictic shift. A deictic shift, a term used in narrative theory, refers to the subjective shift that a reader makes from his or her own viewpoint into the viewpoint of a character in a fictional text. My "I, here, now" becomes the "I, here, now" of the viewpoint character. I am now Ishmael; I disappear into his world and can experience his life through his beingness. French philosopher Paul Ricoeur states, "The display of a world and the positioning of an ego are symmetrical and reciprocal" (Ricoeur 1974). A Buddhist might call this the co-dependent arising of self and world. Deixis, according to Mary Galbraith, is "a psycholinguistic term for those aspects of meaning associated with self-world orientation" (Duchan 1995). Subjective position and the world revealed are a total system that cannot be pulled apart. If, in an altered state, I shift into the identity pattern of the Other, a new world comes into view, as well as new thoughts and feelings about that world. In this way, the word *world* becomes a verb, and these deictic shifts acts of *worlding*. From within these shifts, new skills of being in a new world, and new knowledge of the world as projected and lived in by that identity, can be acquired. This is the essence of the "Be Me" injunction from the Other to me.

At the far extremes of *worlding* lie the DMT experiences, in which one's tolerance for the otherness of the others and the unspeakable weirdness of their worlds is put to the test. Terence McKenna was fond of quoting evolutionary biologist J.B.S. Haldane: "Now my own suspicion is that the Universe is not only queerer than we suppose, but queerer than we *can* suppose." An earlier Terence, the Roman playwright, proclaimed, *Homo sum: humani nil a me alienum puto.* I am human, and nothing human is alien to me. As a human who has had the DMT experience, therefore a human experience of the unspeakably alien, the question becomes, can I include this in my humanness? The fact that DMT occurs endogenously in my body explains nothing. How can I be something capable of this experience? How can I know that which is so profoundly strange? Is a quip the only skyhook out of the ontological dilemma? As Terence McKenna notes, "We are dealing with a density of information, an alienness of information, an in-applicability of information: information available that has no bearing on the human condition" (McKenna 1986).

In the psychedelic sphere, epistemology is an extreme sport.

First Glide Session

My first psychonautic session in the exploration of the Glide symbolic system occurred on July 6, 1999, alone in Ireland on a glorious summer day. I'll discuss this session in some detail, as it presented ideas and patterns that were elaborated over many subsequent sessions. I also want to give a feel for the process of a session as it unfolds, and the tone and style of language used by the voice of the Other. I alternate lines from the session with my commentary as to their meaning as it looks to me now. I took 125 mg of the empathogen MDMA. As my last experience with MDMA (above) had been rather spectacular, I over-prepared, if anything, for this experience. It was also my first solo venture into the invisible landscape, and I was buzzing with anticipatory anxieties and speculations. I've never been great at calming my mind before a session. Calm only comes shortly after ingestion, after picky adjustments of the room, and the tenth review of the pre-flight checklist: Dispose of any unfinished business that could interrupt the session. Lay out notebook, lots of pens, drawing pad, juice, water, tea, extra blankets, *I Ching,* talismans, phone off, music ready, lock front door. Laptop on, playing the animation of the 27 Glide glyphs in a loop. I looked out the window across the lake toward Coomavanaha, the Hollow of the Holy.

Back in the Kerry mountains, the landscape shades in and out of myth at every turn. Tendrils of bliss invaded my heart and spread through my belly and limbs. Then the morphing glyphs captured my attention. The interior voice, a neutral, teaching voice, began.

give Glide to the world

■ **Figure 14: Coomavanaha, Lough Derriana, Co. Kerry, Ireland.**
Photo by Diana Reed Slattery.

At the time, I considered my interest in Glide, a language that was and is part of a fictional world, to be purely personal. However, I was already involving others in helping program software with which to study Glide, and a website was under construction. I remember feeling pushed.

> open your heart to the lily

Then I let go. The voice called MDMA *the lily,* relating it to the lily in *The Maze Game,* and clearly regarded it as a sacrament. I emerged into sacred space.

> the maze is the maze of meaning which is your life
> your life is a journey through the maze
> Glide is the story of your life

Meaning, myth, and life, the entire Glide project converged in the heart space with the metaphor of the Glide maze.

> the opening is to keep all minds speaking at once—all minds aware—

The reference is to the Glide model of multiple minds in *The Maze Game.* The four minds are: the island mind (the thinking mind); the sea mind (the emotional mind); the gut mind (instinct and survival); and the lily mind (the transpersonal, archetypal mind). The concept of opening the minds to each other is reflected in Michael Winkelman's idea of psychedelics as psychointegrators, with their capacity to bring multiple parts of the brain online at the same time.

■ **Figure 15: Glide Maze.**

weave the threads of connection
between the minds

I perceived a flow of millions of Glide glyphs streaming down from a stellar distance through the top of my head and pouring through multiple minds, which I could sense, individually and in synergy. It felt like an entire civilization had downloaded into my minds, filling all spaces, a neuronal net, a mycelial mat, made of the finest filaments. Each of the glyphs was alive.

restore the balance of the minds

Now sensing the minds open to each other, a new synergetically interacting meta-mind could sense itself, and listen to itself, and speak from itself. All minds were part of the consideration of any thought/feeling/urge/mystery that arose. Only in this state could the balancing act of all minds online at once begin.

Glide is the language that unifies the minds
live and walk with all minds connected

The evolutionary imperative was repeated many times. The goal for me would be brought about by Glide language. It was then and there that I began the process of rewiring the minds with a different language, Glide.

the human heart is tortured into war
war is the speech of wounds

In all simplicity, Glide states the obvious: the wounded heart makes war. It has no choice. Heal the heart, and war will cease: war within oneself, war in interpersonal relations, war between groups, globally aroused war. This was advance warning of where this psychonautic practice was leading me, in the direction of needed healing at a time I had not yet admitted to myself that I hurt. Also clearly stated: that this self-healing was integral to the process of moving Glide out into the world. It did not matter how much island-mind (conceptual) knowledge I might gain. If that was not accompanied by a healing of the heart, nothing would be accomplished. And that healing came through the opening of the minds to each other.

Glide heals by speaking to more than one mind

Only if all the minds are addressed, and no part of our potential being is ignored, can we heal the heart.

sink through the minds and realize they are not at war
the seeds of visual language sink through the minds

I experienced what has been called the peace that passeth all understanding. All minds opened in the safe space of the lily. Imprinting the peace. Glide language permeated the minds.

Glide is for the healing of the heart

First action item on the Glide agenda. "The healing of the heart" was a soft way of announcing the emotional crises in the future as the psychonautic practice did its work, revealing the bright and shadowy aspects of psyche, insisting that I change my life.

This was the first of more than four hundred sessions. My psychonautic practice had begun.

Deeper In

The psychonautic adventure, begun in 1999, led rapidly to deep waters and powerful currents in *psyche* that nearly swept me away. Personal issues that I had been dancing around, now laid bare in the uncompromising light of psychedelic awareness, were demanding a reckoning. A synchronicity occurred around the 9/11 events that prompted a full-blown spiritual emergency. On the morning of September 11, 2001, I was in my office working on the cover of *The Maze Game,* surfing the web for pictures of *Nymphaea caerulea,* the sacred blue lily of the Nile. I had just discovered that it was actually a psychoactive plant with a rich history of use in Egypt and was in a state of delighted astonishment, feeling the lilymind permeating awareness. I had not known this when I chose the "giant blue water lily" as the fictional psychedelic sacrament in the novel. It was real! The phone rang; my daughter was calling to tell me the World Trade Center towers were falling. A TV was on in the lab down the hall. We watched as the second tower slumped to the ground. The implications were clear at that moment—the U.S. would have a knee-jerk reaction to the attack. War, followed by a bankrupt economy. The two events—the helpless horror of the collapse of the twin towers, and the confident bliss of the psychedelic blue lotus—were forever positioned as polar opposites in *psyche*. In the social world of humanity, which would prevail?

■ **Figure 16: Lily growing into the wounded heart of the world.** Diana Reed Slattery, September 2001.

The brilliantly executed terrorist act (brilliant no matter who you think the perpetrators are) or the promise of psychedelics as a means of healing the epidemic of madness loose in the world? The next many days repeated those images of destruction 24/7 on every TV; I repeated my images of the blue lily on my computer, and made drawings of the lily, composing huge collages, trying to pull the opposites together.

Psyche took quite a beating in the effort to reconcile murder and compassion, horror and hope. Two weeks after 9/11 I put myself in the hospital for a week to re-gather *psyche.* I found myself psychically entombed, both protected by inner defenses and held still in an insectoid sarcophagus, so I could integrate the irreconcilable opposites presented: the social madness of 9/11 and the promise of psychedelic healing I was experiencing in the sessions.

I made two major life changes that reduced the stress of hysteria over 9/11. I separated from my husband, and sent the TV with him. The voices of media madness ("nuke them back to the Stone Age" and such) were drowning out

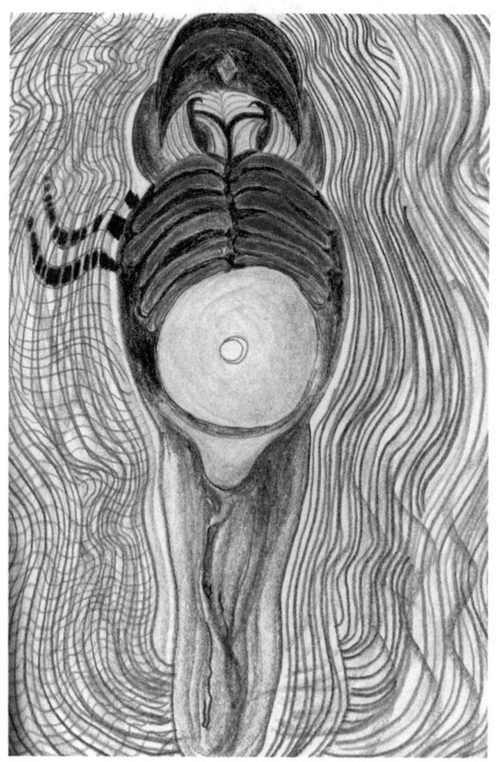

■ Figure 17: Entombed.

the voices of sanity. I was trying to understand the current world situation, its effect on my life and the lives of the many more who would die in Iraq and Afghanistan in addition to the toll of 9/11 itself. This understanding needed to be tempered in the light of my own psychedelic awareness of a different potential for humanity based in trust and understanding. That hope was frail, very frail for a while. The entombment, in essence a deeper level of psychic retreat, privacy, and protection, provided a temporary safe space in *psyche* to grow stronger, and to continue my own healing in the psychonautic practice. The integration was resolved in a series of drawings related to post-hospital psychedelic sessions. First the lily was evident, growing through every part of the heart, strengthening it (Figure 16).

In Figure 18, I am walking underwater through the heart. I have only the head of a bird, and legs. A bird head replacing my writing hand was seen in my first psilocybin journey in 2000. My writing hand takes on its own personality in psychedelic space.

Figure 19 shows the heart, its chambers stabilized, infused with the gifts of the lily. The Rainbow Serpent is taking shape from the wavy lines in the previous drawings. In Figure 20, the Rainbow Serpent emerges from the wavy lines developing from Figure 16 through Figure 20. The undulations of the Rainbow Serpent shed Glide glyphs like scales. The progression of the crisis, which I was unable to talk about to anyone at the time, revealed itself in the drawings. This awareness of *psyche's* process and how it related to the

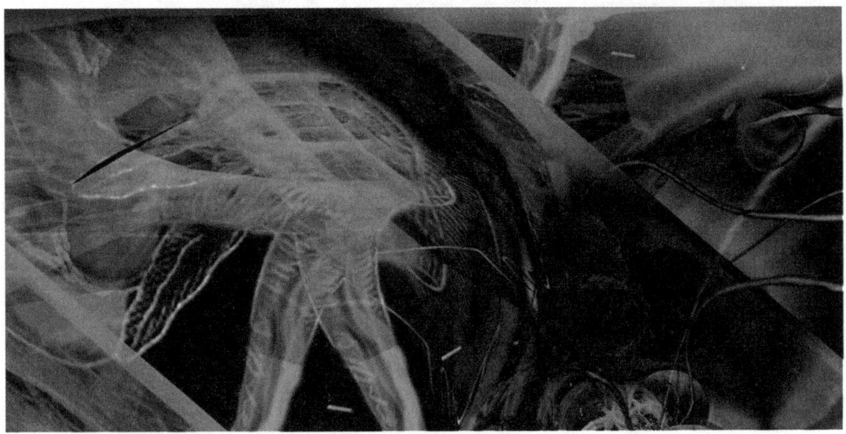

■ **Figure 18: Walking through the waters of the heart.**

■ **Figure 19:**
A reorganized heart.
Diana Reed Slattery,
September 2001.

perceived condition of the world *psyche* was an essential part of the integration of the two events, in mythic terms, the Tower and the Lily.

The fall of the Tower is an archetypal event depicted in the Tarot cards, meaning, among other things, the destruction of an ego. Certainly, the assumed impregnability of the U.S. to destruction by terrorist acts was itself destroyed, a huge blow to the ego of the country.

The spiritual emergency was a brief, acute occurrence. I could not integrate this classic war between good and evil, terror and bliss. The crisis also highlighted my lack of a support system, a side effect of the secrecy of the psychonautic practice. From that point on, I began to find a few other

■ **Figure 20: The Rainbow Serpent.** Diana Reed Slattery, October 2001.

psychonauts in my neighborhood; suddenly I was part of a small, lively community of scholars, educators, and artists. *Integration* is a term used in psychonautics to mean the integration of the visionary material—emotions, concepts, panoramas of past and future, and encounters with the Other—with life, ideas, feelings, and plans at baseline. There is no question that a psychedelic session can be a life-changing event, for better or for worse, bright trauma or dark. It takes only a few sessions of reading the experience reports at the Vaults of Erowid (the premier source of data about psychedelics online) to get the point of the extreme variability of events and feelings that can occur in a single session, or in a long series of sessions. The post-session outcomes range from *metanoia*—a complete conversion experience—to paranoia that lingers after the psychedelic event *per se* is over. Terrified madness and mystic bliss reveal their kinship. The experience it takes to navigate these extreme mind-states without identifying with either the terror or the bliss is hard-won in psychonautic practice. One sees casualties of both the messianic and the suicidal varieties. The integration of the two-sided coin

■ **Figure 21: The Tarot image of the Tower.**

of terror and bliss, encapsulated in the horror of the fall of the towers and the bliss of the sacred lily, was accomplished in an understanding of the elements of Glide language, the three strokes.

The up stroke and the down stroke are the binary signs. The third stroke is the both/and, the resolution of the opposites in a sign containing both in the form of a wave. It is the 2 in 1, just like the mathematical sign *i,* which stands for the √ -1, which can be represented as two numbers: +1 and -1, binary opposites. *i* is the imaginary number. This view of the strokes is the basis of Glide ternary logic, a logic of the included middle. For me, the message was that a mind that can encompass *i,* and can bear paradox and irreconcilability, without being pulled apart, can survive internal and external binary conflicts more easily. This occurs through the attempt in *psyche* to hold both sides at once without falling into either side.

Research, both approved and underground, has shown consistently that proper guidance, whether self-administered or by an informed and experienced guide, makes the lingering dark outcomes scarce. But this is not to say that the dark or shadow side of psychonautic experience is not valuable, especially psychotherapeutically and spiritually. In fact, it is hard to imagine any long-term psychonautic practice not encountering the dark night of the soul. Darkness, struggle, and impossible challenges are part of Psyche's mythic journey. How one integrates both the shadow material and the mystical vision, and what changes occur in daily life as a result, is where one finds the lasting effects of psychonautic practice. Much has been

■ **Figure 22: The three strokes that compose the Glide Glyphs.**

said about the ability to transform a state into a trait. In other words, will the increase in compassion for humanity felt at the peak of an MDMA trip eventually carry through to baseline consciousness as a greater kindness to friends and family and self?

Psychointegration

Anthropologist and neurophenomenologist Michael Winkelman uses the term "psychointegration" to describe what is happening in the brain, and hence in subjective experience, under the influence of psychedelics. His contention is that psychedelics open the three parts of the triune brain to each other. These three parts are defined by neuroscientist Paul D. McLean as the reptilian complex (instinctive behavior), the limbic system (motivation and emotion), and the neocortex (language, abstraction, and perception). Winkelman claims that psychedelics, through the serotonin pathways, get all three parts of the brain "online" at once. In other words, material from all parts of the brain is accessible to conscious attention. Put in psychoanalytic terms, the unconscious parts of *psyche* become conscious. We are, for a brief time, opening the secret caverns of *psyche,* where both dragons and treasures can be found. Winkelman contends that these mind-states are evolutionarily adaptive and valuable to the social group. He details the way that non-ordinary states of consciousness can bring about healing, social cohesion, and visionary insight (Winkelman 2000). How this has played out in contemporary times, when those mind-states are feared and mostly illegal to produce in ourselves, is a social history that has only begun to be told. It has been seventy years since Dr. Albert Hofmann brought his magic molecule, LSD, into the Western world. How much of our computer-managed and media-saturated world was—and is—created by stoned and psychedelically informed programmers, engineers, and artists is a question that has barely been explored. Psychedelics have been linked to important discoveries such as Nobel Prize winner Kary Mullis's invention of the polymerase chain reaction (PCR). This critical discovery opened the door to genomics and our edit of our own DNA blueprint, the analysis of genes, the diagnosis of hereditary diseases, and the identification of criminals through DNA samples. And LSD is implicated in the discovery of DNA structure itself by

Francis Crick. However, these are just the oft-repeated stellar examples of major insights brought back to baseline by intelligent people seeking scientific answers. The way psychedelics, from marijuana use to LSD, have permeated our culture is clear once one has perceived the interface between psychedelics and technology; psychedelics and medicine; psychedelics and psychotherapy; and psychedelics and art. In California, needless to say, one sees how deeply the roots of the lily have penetrated our culture.

Winkelman's psychointegration theory is played out in a fashion in the Glide theory of multiple minds, from *The Maze Game*. The idea is the same: healing and sanity, especially when it comes to social relations, can be nurtured only by the integration of the minds, all the minds, all the contents, everything it takes to truly answer the Delphic injunction: *know thyself*. Psychedelics broaden the territory of *self* exponentially, exposing the enormity of what one must include in the *self* one is getting to know.

The exploration of Glide language through psychonautic practice went hand in hand with a healing process, proceeding through the connected minds. The Glides were always a sensed presence. MDMA sessions produced the steady presence of an interior voice, "speaking for" the Glides. Psilocybin roused the Rainbow Serpent, teaching the gestural movements of Glide by moving the body in wavy forms through the whole spine, spiraling through the arms and hands, out into micromovements of the fingers and further into the fronds of energy pouring from the fingertips in filamental strands of light. Psilocybin also potentiated the Be Me phenomenon and the introduction of the archetypal figures (Elrond as Glide "ambassador"). The main dialogues occurred in a domed space sometimes experienced as "the peacock throne room." The whole initial warp, the transition into the full psychedelic space, became a kind of entrance screening process in which all human "baggage" underwent a penetrating review and acceptance process. At times this was experienced as a kind of psychic decontamination chamber. Hosts of the "munchkins" penetrated every corner of body and mind and took me to whatever level of self-confrontation necessary to proceed. From a 2003 session report:

> your willingness to carry the moment of horror   of reproach and rage   look at it all   don't deny anything   the horror or the saving grace   truth of the heart   so hard hard hard to accept your SELF (session report 03.12.12, MDMA)

These periods of self-examination often involved the recovery of long-buried memories of considerable psychological "charge." These self-confrontations were the preconditions for the dialogue in the Dome; mythically, these examinations functioned as the tests and tasks for the questioner, the requirements of the quest. The unconfrontable in my past, in my current personal life, and in the conditions in the world at large grew steadily more confrontable. This was no walk in the park. The motivation for undergoing such psychological discomfort was my desire to learn more, especially about language, while in the psychedelic state. I began to see the value of such psychic scrub-ups as my life at baseline began to transform.

The healing process included a number of "operations." These were undertaken in and around the body-mind. The operations repaired what was broken or emotionally clogged. Twice I experienced thick black tarry material being scraped out of the area of the heart: compacted residue of past emotional states. Additionally, a series of transdimensional prosthetics, objects real and useful in perceiving and navigating the psychedelic sphere, was installed. Especially handy is a personal dome, a hemispheric structure of extremely fine and filamental gold wires. The feathery gold dome defines a space of transmission and clarifies the incoming signal, reducing noise and static. The placement of a sapphire crystal in the third eye serves as a conduit for deep blue-violet energies to be absorbed or transmitted. These deep indigo/ultraviolet blobs of flowing energy map to the McKennas' descriptions of translinguistic matter. In the psychedelic sphere, these instruments of perception are magical objects acquired in a quest for knowledge, accepted on their own terms, utterly real and useful *in their own reality,* functioning according to the rules of the transdimensional world in which they originate.

These examinations and operations were the prerequisite to progress. The faithful scribe had to clean up her act and remedy life situations (and their underlying causes) to free the mental attention and energy to proceed effectively in her psychonautic practice and the exploration of Glide. "The healing of the heart," a major theme in *The Maze Game,* was enacted in my own life, a drama that played out between worlds, from baseline reality to the psychedelic sphere. The Glide language became the long-term agency for healing, both in my life and in the novel. The Glides taught this healing indirectly through the Glide language lessons, and by revealing the nature of the life-and-death game we are all playing.

Notes, Chapter 2

1. "12 step" refers to Alcoholics Anonymous. My husband was a committed member of the program.
2. The Akashic records, referred to tongue-in-cheek, are, according to Wikipedia, "a compendium of mystical knowledge supposedly encoded in a non-physical plane of existence."
3. This is a reference to David Porush's Principle of Epistemological Potency. "Descriptions of any intelligent system (and the Universe is obviously one; fictional texts create others) in order to achieve epistemological potency must include accounts not only of how the system is regulated and organized, and of how it communicates among its own parts, but also of how it knows and describes itself. In other words, any epistemologically potent system must include a discourse that enfolds its own intelligence." (Porush 1993)
4. To see the glyphs transforming, go to www.youtube.com/watch?v=-xWALPXLwr4 or https://vimeo.com/35158231.
5. After about eight years, a tolerance built up for MDMA, and the visuals slowly diminished.
6. In yoga practices, these spontaneous movements are called *kriyas.*

CHAPTER 3

The Idea of a Visual Language—Glide

"We no longer live in a world in which information conserves itself primarily in textual objects called books. In a world in which not only information but meaning struggles to escape its customary channels, perhaps the best way to serve the scholarly muse may not be to continue to play out the moves that served perfectly in the age of the scriptorium and the inescapable facticity of data."

—ALLUCQUÉRE ROSANNE STONE, 1998

This chapter discusses the Glide project and the Glide symbolic system in some detail. It is a summary of what I found about Glide in the original download, and in the subsequent unpacking of the original download in the psychonautic practice.

"Visual language" is a term shared by communication theorists, graphic designers, painters, linguists, semioticians, art historians, and the scholars, educators, and practitioners of signed languages, whether Native American or those used by the deaf community. The idea of a visual language points toward a new representation of language itself, a non-aural form of language, different than spoken natural language. The idea of a visual language explored here could not exist without the computer and the communication technologies it enables, more specifically, graphics, visualization, animation, and simulation technologies. The computer, a procedural (rule-based) machine, is especially good at visualizing process. Chemistry, mathematics, medicine, physics, and atmospheric and decision sciences use this capability for discovery, application, and education. The hierarchy of computer languages builds from the elegantly minimalist zeros and ones of machine language to experiments in visual language programming for software design that utilize iconic forms. In the case of a language that puts its symbols in motion and transformation such as Glide, it is impossible to illustrate without the ability to animate given by the computer hard- and software.

Glide is a symbolic system, some properties of which distinguish it from the writing systems of natural languages. Glide signs are hypertextual, as seen in the Glide maze, where multiple paths of meaning present themselves. Glide is gestural, originally a signed language in the story world. And Glide signs can move and morph, transforming one into another. The visual properties of Glide signs—size, orientation, proximity of signs, maze gestalts, color, texture, qualities of motion (direction, velocity, acceleration)—all contribute to their meaning.

Glide as a writing system has aspects of the pictographic, the logographic, and the ideographic. However, these terms rest only lightly on the signs. When encountered on their own terms, and especially in altered states of consciousness, Glide signs point to something within meaning but beyond the means of natural language.

The logographic sign carries meaning without reference to sound. Such systems have the advantage that one sequence of symbols carries the same meaning to people speaking entirely different languages, even though the phonetic form in each language might be completely different. The traditional Chinese writing system makes extensive use of logographic representation and has the advantage of serving as a link among the many varieties of modern Chinese, some of which are mutually unintelligible in their spoken forms (Southworth 1974).

Glide signs can be translated into natural language, loosely. Media theorist N. Katherine Hayles sees Glide as creating "a haze of signification."

> Semantically the glyphs function somewhat like ideograms, with each mark conveying three root meanings along with successive layers of secondary, tertiary, and sometimes quaternary connotations. . . . To run a maze of glyphs, then, is both to enact a physical performance and to apprehend the subtle metaphoric connections that comprise each glyph in itself and the larger meanings that flow from several glyphs joined together. (Hayles 2000)

Their ideographic nature and the flexibility of assignment of parts of speech connect Glide signs to Chinese. Iconic systems such as those for traffic signs or circuit components in their simplicity of form resemble the ideographic elements of the Glide glyphs.

Pictographic associations can be made, but they are more abstractly metaphorical than strictly representational. The back-and-forth movements of eye and mind in a Glide maze that examine context and combine and recombine meaning connect it to the reading of classical vowel-less Hebrew where context (in the absence of written vowels) resolves the ambiguities and provides the clues as to which word is meant.

Signed languages, silent and gestural, relate to Glide's fictionalized cultural origins.

> Enhancing the richness of interpretation (which is also always a performance) is the complexity of decoding. The compound glyphs that make up mazes can be taken apart not just in one way, as when one decodes an alphabetic word into letters, but in multiple ways, each of which is an appropriate reading of the maze. (Hayles 2000)

Glide signs, moving, twisting, spiraling in the third dimension with Live-Glide, exceed the affordances of natural language, making meaning in a novel manner that requires reading on its own terms.

When a symbolic system has the capability—enabled by new communication technologies—to go beyond a static representation of fixed visual properties and positions (words lined up sequentially on a page) into motion, several dimensions are added to the acts of reading and writing. Once the possibility of change over time (or process) is introduced, the variety of properties that can be changed, alone or in combination, is limited not so much by technology as by visual imagination. Color, shape, size, transparency, orientation, movement (velocity, shape of path, acceleration), texture (including video) can all be varied dynamically in the service of the communication of meaning. Spatial dimension can move from the two-dimensional plane to the three-dimensional space or, conceivably, to a fractal dimension.

These expressive qualities are, of course, well known to graphic designers for print and media. They have also been specifically excluded from "serious" communication. Academic, scientific, legal, and most literary uses of written text are largely formalized as to color (black on white), shape (limited fonts), line length and spacing, and size. The written signs of popular culture (magazines, TV, movies, posters, graffiti), persuasive messages (advertising), and "art" (high or low) have no such limitations. Letters extrude, dance, appear and disappear, rotate and explode on movie, TV, and computer screens. Politicians, corporations, and rock stars proclaim their personalities with their typography, color choices, and layout. Words and images miscegenate promiscuously.

The signs of the emergence of visual language can be seen everywhere that written text is not confined by convention. As in the examples above, the written word is being pushed to the limits of form, motion, and intelligibility. The development of written language in the West proceeded from the pictographic to the phonetic, resulting in the Hebrew and Roman alphabets. Chinese went from the pictographic to the logographic, adding the phonetic as well. The emergence of visual language seems to be following the same pattern. In the world of personal computer applications, international public signs, business logos, and McDonald's cash registers, we have entered a new iconic stage of visual language with our literal icons of paintbrushes, pens, smoking cigarettes, children crossing, world globes, and Big Macs. Interface metaphors—the ubiquitous desktop with files, folders, and pages—brought the environments and artifacts of our physical space to cyberspace, a transitional strategy to create familiarization for the user navigating in a strange world.

If the development of visual language follows the pattern of written phonetic and logographic languages, one could predict the next stage to be the abstraction of systems of visual signs into a limited number of conceptual units that can be combined and recombined, and dynamically manipulated for their expressive qualities. Glide symbols model the possibility that, using the highly interactive capabilities of computer technology, real-time communications between human beings in cyberspace can be expressively embodied in abstract forms. Abstract forms could go far beyond the literality of emoticons.

The visual properties of Glide signs—size, shape, color, relative position, motion, texture, rotation—can be varied dynamically in expressive ways. To make these variations in visual properties available to the "writer" in Glide as part of the construction of a maze—static or animated—is to draw on the wealth of tradition and knowledge from fields as varied as the psychology of perception, art history, aesthetics, advertising, the cross-disciplinary study of symbols, cultural anthropology, and graphic design.

These parameters of expressive potential and their combinations multiply exponentially if visual properties are made intrinsic to a linguistic symbol and can bear meaning at the same primary level as the shape of a letter. Visual language in three-dimensional motion as modeled with LiveGlide incorporates qualities we associate with traditional art forms *per se:* painting, sculpture, dance. "Reading and writing" a visual language is envisioned as a long learning curve in which artistry can be developed to higher and higher levels with practice. Both customary uses and individual style can develop. The art of reading, and the authorship of interpretation, will be as important as the authorship of the writing. The mutual activity of collaborative construction of a maze (the Collabyrinth software) is an experiment in opening a new kind of written conversation.

Semantics

When the Glide glyphs appeared in the initial download, the first question became "But what do they mean?" The story world offered a unified set of meanings that metaphor outward from the elements of the Glide world and the life and body and natural environment of the hallucinogenic blue lily. The effort of translation brought this metaphoric semiosis[1] into natural language.

For the Glide Oracle, the 729 hexagrams (plus another several hundred hexagrams including all deep linking formations) plus the 729 transformations of glyphs morphing into another (the transformations) were each translated into short poems or aphorisms. The exercise was valuable in coming to terms with their mutability. It is clear that, were I to retranslate the two sets of glyphs again today, the set of poems would likely be quite different. The exercise is similar to the interpretation of the visual images of a Tarot reading in varying configurations, or the interpretation of an *I Ching* hexagram. Intention and context, "set and setting," are all. The final lesson from the exercise was that translation into natural language was a reductive and limiting way to extract meaning from Glide. I was missing something vital by retreating to natural language; Glide insisted on being confronted on its own terms, in its own territory, without recourse to natural language. The journey to meaning, the semantic quest, needed to extend beyond the nets of natural language. High-dose psilocybin was the instrumentation for this move. The instruction in a 2003 session was to "abandon the alphabet." The LiveGlide software was the answer to this instruction.

Once outside of natural language, when cognition was very much present but without the scaffolding of natural language, the nature of Glide meaning began to reveal itself at another level. The speed of cognition increases greatly in altered states. Natural language is very slow software indeed viewed from an altered state of consciousness. Ideas are processed by associating them with words, the internal lexicon of natural language. In the high-dose psilocybin state, meanings converge or correlate. In altered states of consciousness, a single symbol can hold multiple meanings simultaneously instead of sequentially. Many paths of meaning can be held in the mind at once. The symbols radiate their meanings without recourse to words. The "ineffability barrier" appears, if by ineffable one means "can't English it," but it can be in part overcome once alternate routes to meaning—those languages and symbolic systems presented in the psychedelic state—are accessed. Glide is used in this sense both to navigate the psychedelic state (as the Death Dancer navigates the maze in *The Maze Game*) and to communicate within it, with the Other. Creating and moving through a Glide maze in an altered state unfolds narratives, which embed concepts, emotional shifts, states of mind, and aesthetic colorings. Further, and most important to the making of meaning, in an altered state of consciousness the symbols are experienced as sentient, actively bespeaking themselves. The Glide symbols become the Glides become the symbols explaining themselves, in the same high-speed circular system Terence McKenna describes with the machine elves. The question *What* do they mean? gave way to the question *How* do they mean?

Making meaning in Glide, whether at baseline or in significantly altered states of consciousness, is an exercise in moving metaphor. Moving through the Glide maze in the combat of the game is an act of metaphoric reading described by media theorist N. Katherine Hayles:

> It is not merely a metaphor to say that Glide is metaphoric. Metaphor, which joins two disparate things together by asserting an identity between them, is here enacted physically by joining one glyph to another to form a larger topographic shape. Just as metaphor creates an emergent meaning that is more than the sum of the parts, blossoming forth as a realization inhering in neither component individually but rather growing out of their

> interactions, so the meanings that emerge from the glyphs and the larger mazes they form come from complex interplays between root, secondary and tertiary meaning of components that themselves can transform into other shapes as the reader plays with deconstructing the maze into different glyphs. (Hayles 2001)

Glide represents semantic silences as space. The mazes are like nets or webs of meaning through which silence flows. As in the negative spaces of a Henry Moore sculpture, or the figure/ground ambiguities of the face/vase type, the spaces within and between glyphs show patterns in themselves. Repeated patterns of circles, paisley "teardrops," the smaller or larger spaces between glyphs, and the larger and smaller "wave" formations also have an effect on the overall reading of the maze.

The wave patterns that emerge in a larger maze can be experienced as variable rates of vibration combining in the meaning of the gestalt.

In the psychedelic state, a constructed maze is always an arbitrary segment, a piece of an infinite pattern of vibratory states in motion and transformation. The fabric of reality is presented in the abstraction of waveforms. Henry Munn describes this perception of pattern, thus:

> On the mushrooms, one sees walls covered with a fine tracery of lines projected before the eyes. It is as if the night were imprinted with signs like glyphs. In these conditions, if one takes up a brush, dips it into paint, and begins to draw, it is as if the hand were animated by an extraordinary ideoplastic ability. Instead of saying that God speaks through the wise man, that life paints through him, in other words writes, since for them to write was to paint: the imagination in an act constitutive of images. (Munn 2000)

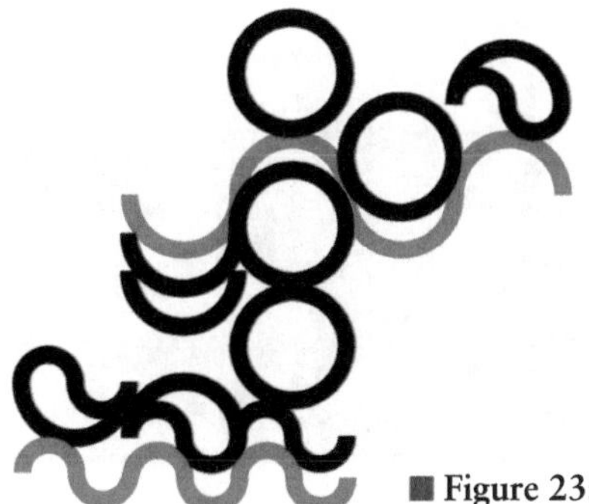

■ Figure 23: Waves in a Glide maze.

Psychonaut Simon G. Powell perceives pattern everywhere, a holistic pattern that unifies the perceived diversity of the universe in what he calls "the psilocybinetic trance." His work, *The Psilocybin Solution,* pursues this vision of universal pattern through a theory of neuronal patterning (Powell 2009). A succinct vision of wavelike patterning and its deeper sensed meanings is described in his essay "Sacred Ground" in which he is tripping in the Palm House in Kew Gardens with greenery and water:

> As the holistic pattern of reflected light coalesced again and again, I felt an ecstatic sensation of wholeness as if I too were merging with the whole picture. As interference melted away, all was revealed as connected and this process left me awash with awe and exultation. It also appeared that the small reflective pool was itself formed from the drops of water, these same drops ultimately interfering with the reflective process. A self-reinforcing paradox then, like some cosmic dance of information that expressed the riddle of existence. . . . (Powell 2009)

As such, a Glide maze resonates with the physical concept of the universe as a pattern of interacting waveforms at all levels of existence. This physical resonance is one of Glide's fields of meaning. We describe the universe as a giant multi-scalar wave-pool from the quantum level, or below to the string theory postulates, up to the macroscopic human level, in which the light

■ **Figure 24: Palm House, Kew Gardens.**

and sound waves we sense in a selective range of frequencies become the raw material of perception. What frequencies of waves we are open to may be one of the ways to describe the differences in perception, and therefore reality, in different phases of consciousness.

Glide signs laid out statically on a two-dimensional surface form webby, mycelial mazes. When the glyphs transform, linking and unlinking with each other, they seem like a kind of circuit operating with many points of change and connection. A Glide maze, activated by transforming glyphs, seems like an abstraction of the organic, constantly shifting circuitry of the brain's receptor space. Electrical and chemical signals pulse, and synaptic connections are formed and broken in inconceivably complex patterns going about their business of constructing and projecting a world around and inside us. This activity is saturated with consciousness, according to processes (what is called in philosophy of mind "the hard problem") we have barely begun to understand.

When glyphs transform, the link-patterns change; patterns of connectivity propagate through the circuitry. This resonance with biological structures, such as the shifting neuronal patterns in the brain, is another of Glide's fields of meaning.

A maze can also model a mycelial mat, a three-dimensional maze-space of densely intertwined tubular filaments, exhibiting link-seeking behavior that leads to hyphal knots that produce the fruiting bodies of the mushroom.

The paths, links, and holes of the maze all contribute to the creation of meaning. Because the maze is a visual pattern, and the eye follows certain lines more easily than others, certain paths offer themselves more readily visually than do others. The eye moving at right angles across a series of waves, like a car bouncing over the ruts in a road wash-boarded by erosion, gives a different feeling than the eye following the lines of the waves themselves. Reading paths are suggested or discouraged by the way in which the eye is directed and moves, as the eye travels across and around a painting. Hypertextual construction of meaning in a visual language, the joining of conceptual units in a visual pattern, opens the possibility of exploiting the whole realm of meaning, physiological response, and aesthetic convention belonging to the plastic arts.

Glide Mythology

"Myth" is the overarching term I use to capture the multiple forms of narrative that wrap Glide in meaning and purpose. Glide has a mythical origin, a context and a world. Myths emerge from multiple levels of consciousness. *The Maze Game* gives Glide a world and a context. The visions and histories unfolding over the course of the psychedelic sessions expand the story. And the accounts of the xenolinguists, both their form and their content, show an overlap of core ideas, visions, and explanations among themselves.

> The experience of the mushroom is subtle but can reach out to the depth and breadth of a truly intense psychedelic experience. It is, however, extremely mercurial and difficult to catch at work. Dennis and I, through a staggered description of our visions, noticed a similarity of content that seemed to suggest a telepathic phenomenon or some sort of simultaneous perception of the same invisible landscape. (McKenna 1993b)

The name "Glide" itself is a patchwork of ideas and references, later unpacked. Glide, in my associations, nods first to mathematician John Conway's "Gliders," emergent computational creatures arising from his software "The Game of Life" that behave like semi-autonomous forms, alive in the computational world of cellular automata.[2] Second, the gliding movements of Noh theatre actors are recalled. In Noh performance, the elaborate costumes seemed filled not with a body but with a weightless spirit. Third, I remember the poet Yeats's line,"Like a long-legged fly upon the stream/Her mind moved upon silence."[3] Fourth, the name captures the movements of the Glides gathering the hallucinogenic pollen of the giant blue water lilies, as they glide from pad to pad.

The Glide project, psychedelic in fact and fiction, subverts the categories of myth and personal narrative; fact and fiction; self and Other. A language emerges from, enfolds, and tells the story of its people, their culture, and their episteme—what is considered knowledge. The Glides claim that the lily has an agenda: the evolution of human consciousness by way of the healing of the heart. This is accomplished, in Glide terms, through a process of psychointegration—the ability to connect and use the parts of the mind held separate in ordinary consciousness.

In the mythic world of the novel, the psychedelic sacrament, the Lily, gave the Glides the language from which they could construct the mazes of the game that absorbed an entire culture. The Dance of Death, played in mazes made of language, was the only way to learn the language, and how to think in Glide. The Lily (the psychoactive sacrament) told the Dancers to engage every sense, reserving the aural for existing speech. The Lily pointed out that light was faster and could travel farther than sound. That the dappling of light on lily pads, on out-running tides, was as intimate as love's whisper. The Lily explained that Glide would exercise their minds in making metaphor. Glide would also help overcome the limits of sequential memory and information overload. But the sacramental Lily is a stern teacher, making the ability to read and think in Glide a matter of life and death. The maze of language is the game board on which the search for the meaning of life and death is played out. The meaning of life, one's individual path through an ever-changing maze, emerges only in the light and sight of death.

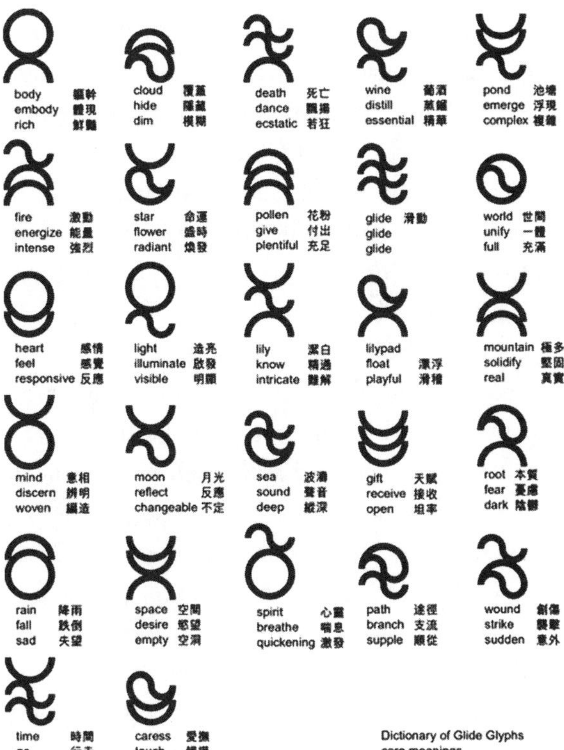

■ **Figure 25: A Glide dictionary of core meanings, English and Chinese.**

Glide was originally a signed language based on the gestures of their cupped hands at work: curved up as they scooped the pollen, curved down as they emptied their palms into the baskets, and joined together in the gesture of the wave. (See Figure 22, previous chapter.)

The Maze Game presents a psychedelic vision of the Glide language. The novel was directly influenced by psychedelic experience, prior to and during its composition and editing. The natural surroundings in which the hallucinogenic lily grew, and the anatomy of the lily itself, are the central metaphors of the 27 Glide glyphs, as can be seen in the dictionary of core concepts (Figure 25). Dancemaster Wallenda, having ingested the hallucinogenic Lily, has the vision that turns the language into a written form, and hence, into the maze game itself. He sees the Glide signs emerge from their natural environment.[4]

Glide forms reveal themselves in the Dancemaster's vision. Glide is a language of waves, fractal nestings of waves in maze-like patterns. Waves are revealed in the Glides' hand gestures, their movements across the lily pond, in the motion of the plants in the tidal waters. In his vision, the Dancemaster passes through the body of the Lily: root, coiled stem, pad, flower; fundamental Glide signs emerge. The vision is synaesthetic, combining the visual, the kinesthetic, and the olfactory. Language, maze, and game emerge in a single visionary moment, the mythical origin of Glide. Lily pond morphs into maze before his eyes; maze becomes game. Glide translates the form of the lily's body, its wavy environment, and hallucinogenic properties into the fundamental metaphors from which the Glide cognitive system is built. Root–fear, stem–path, flower–star, pad–playing field.

The psychedelic sessions and their reports became their own mythic enterprise, exploring Glide through multiple dimensions and worlds in communication with the Other. A new narrative of the transformation of self—from an experience of single self to a multiple self—evolved as the higher-dose zone of psilocybin was opened and explored. The Be Me relationship became a Be We, as the original archetypes fused with the already altered sense of self. Other personalities moved in and out of the shifting sense of self in the psychedelic states. A shift in personality signaled the need to assume a different viewpoint, to better understand a particular point. At various times warrior-monks, Chinese concubines, and small children flowed through me, shape-shifting my sense of self accordingly. For instance, to examine conflict in the world of baseline reality, it was useful to experience war from the viewpoint of a warrior-monk. To appreciate the exaggerated delicacy of floating filamental forms, the body-sense and aesthetic sensibility of a woman of an ancient Chinese court was helpful. And a child-like viewpoint does wonders for wonderment.

Myth is one way the unspeakable reveals itself in human terms. The masks of the Other, the archetypal figures met as teachers, guides, opponents, allies, aliens, and theriomorphs, are mythical. Myth is a means of navigating multiple realities. As Terence McKenna put it,

> For the loquacious mushrooms encountered there have spun a myth and issued a prophecy, in quite specific detail, of a planet-saving global shift of consciousness. They have promised all that has happened in my life over the last twenty years, and they have promised much more for the future. (McKenna 1993b)

The myth of a global shift in consciousness is present in varied forms in the literature of psychonautic self-exploration. Timothy Leary's eight-circuit model of the evolution of consciousness proposes dormant functions in human consciousness that can be activated by psychoactive drugs and brain/mind technologies such as Neurolinguistic Programming (Leary 1979). The 2012 meme, in both its Pinchbeckian (Aztec) and Argüellian (Maya) versions, includes narratives of global—or galactic—shifts in consciousness (Pinchbeck 2006; Argüelles 2002). 2012 has come and gone, and we are still present to tell the tale. Another millenarian moment has passed, and such a moment will no doubt return again. But the basic myth, as myth is essentially "out of time," persists.

Myth is one form in which the explanations given in the psychedelic sphere appear, translated, in baseline reality. What is reality in the psychedelic sphere is framed as myth at baseline; what is reality at baseline, expressed in natural language, reveals its narrative, dramatic, and constructed form when viewed from an altered state of consciousness. The relationship of the real and the mythical in our culture demotes the mythical in terms of truth value, while promoting scientific explanation as the reliable form of knowledge. This status parallels the minor role that altered states of consciousness in general and as a form of knowledge acquisition in particular play in our culture. The imbalance is characteristic of what Laughlin calls a "monophasic reality" (Laughlin 1990), and Thomas Roberts refers to as "the single-state fallacy." How this shift in epistemological balance can take place, how ingrained "reality tunnels" or creodes are relinquished and the mythical becomes real, is a rhetorical process, a seduction, seductively portrayed in Terence McKenna's description of the "warp."

> The Other approaches us through the imagination and then a critical juncture is reached. To go beyond this juncture requires abandonment of old and ingrained habits of thinking and seeing. At that moment the world turns lazily inside out and what was hidden is revealed: a magical modality, a different landscape than one has ever known, and the landscape becomes real. This is the realm of the cosmic giggle. UFOs, elves, and the teeming pantheons of all religions are the denizens of this previously invisible landscape. One reaches through to the continents and oceans of the imagination, worlds able to sustain anyone who will but play, and then one lets the play deepen and deepen until it is a reality that few would even dare to entertain. (McKenna 1993b)

Glide Forms

Glide is a language of waves. Glide forms follow the waveform. Glide understands the spiral wave to be a fundamental structure in the physical universe. Glide waviness, and all that implies metaphorically, is the most fundamental formal quality of Glide. Waves imply motion; the descriptions of Glide forms require imagination on the static printed page to put them in motion.

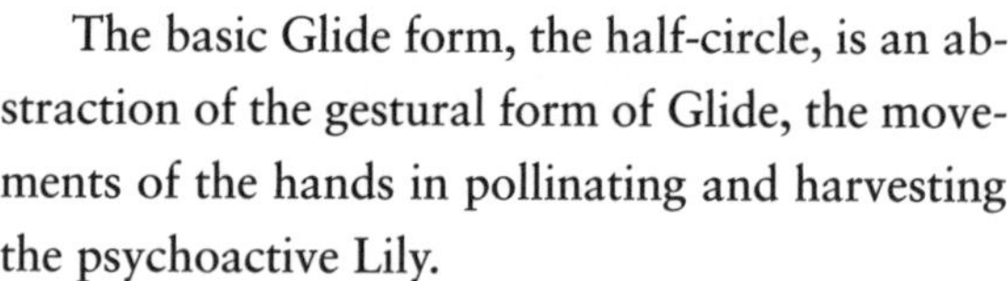

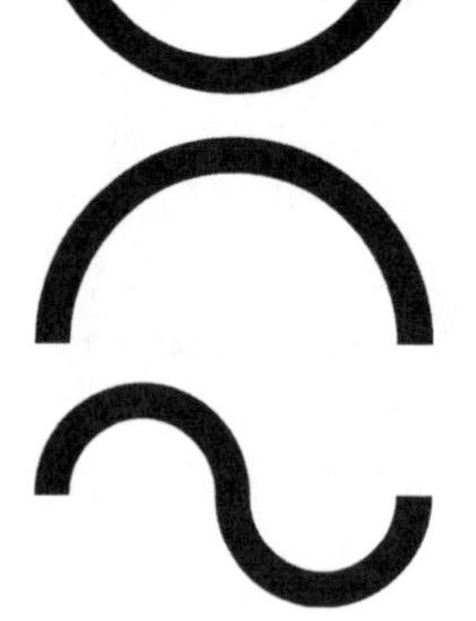

The basic Glide form, the half-circle, is an abstraction of the gestural form of Glide, the movements of the hands in pollinating and harvesting the psychoactive Lily.

■ **Figure 26: The first Glide stroke.**

The semicircle inverts, becoming the second stroke.

■ **Figure 27: The second Glide stroke.**

The third stroke is formed by the combination of the two semicircles into the wave.

■ **Figure 28: The third Glide stroke.**

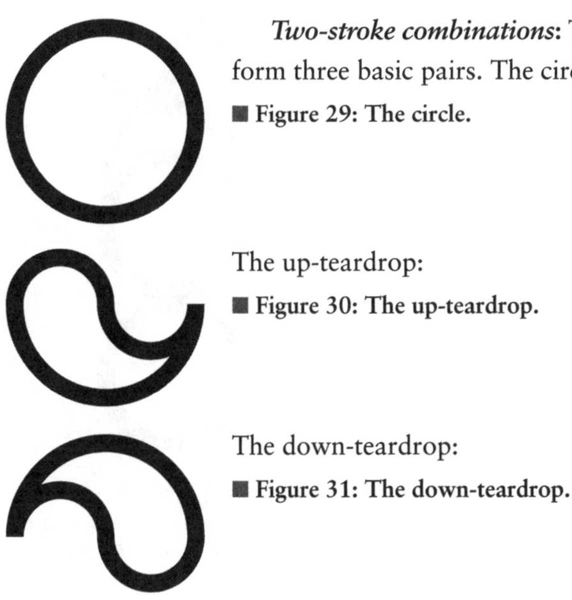

Two-stroke combinations: These three strokes form three basic pairs. The circle:

■ **Figure 29: The circle.**

The up-teardrop:

■ **Figure 30: The up-teardrop.**

The down-teardrop:

■ **Figure 31: The down-teardrop.**

Three-stroke combinations: The three basic lines combine to form 27 three-stroke glyphs, basic units of meaning in Glide.

■ **Figure 32: The 27 Glide glyphs.**

Six-stroke (two-glyph) combinations: The 27 tri-glyphs combine to make 729 hexagrams. Reading through the hexagram in either direction reveals two interior glyphs that contribute to the meaning. The hexagram below is made of the glyph for fire over the glyph for mind. Translation: *Obsession.*

■ **Figure 33: Obsession.**

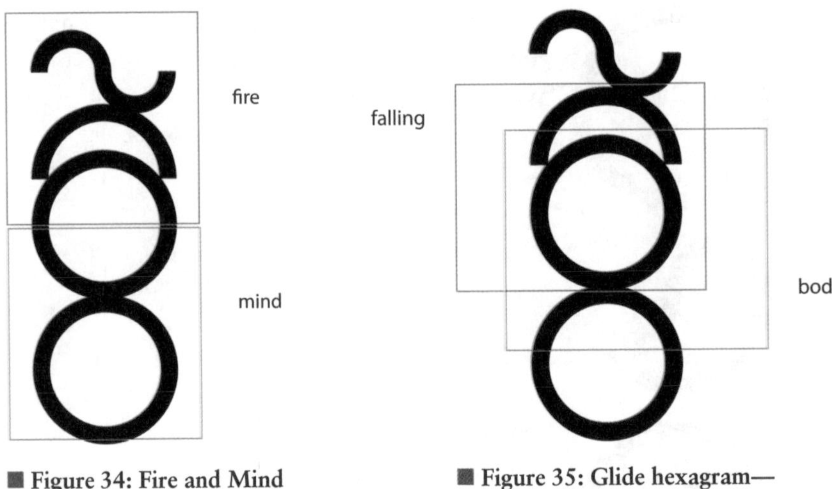

■ **Figure 34: Fire and Mind are the two glyphs composing Obsession.**

■ **Figure 35: Glide hexagram—Obsession, showing the two interior glyphs, Falling and Body.**

Translating a hexagram is a matter of manipulating metaphors at many levels. It is similar to the translation of a hexagram in the *I Ching*. One reads and interprets the meanings of the component trigrams, the interior trigrams, and the movement of the glyphs. Are they upward-moving like fire? Or downward-moving like falling? The 729 hexagrams form the basis of the Glide oracle, now an iPad application.[5]

Links: Links are created by contiguity. Deep links are formed when glyphs overlap their lines, interpenetrating their meanings. Below, hexagrams combining the glyph for *spirit* over the glyph for the *lily of psychedelic knowledge*. On the left is a touching link; on the right, a deep or nested link.

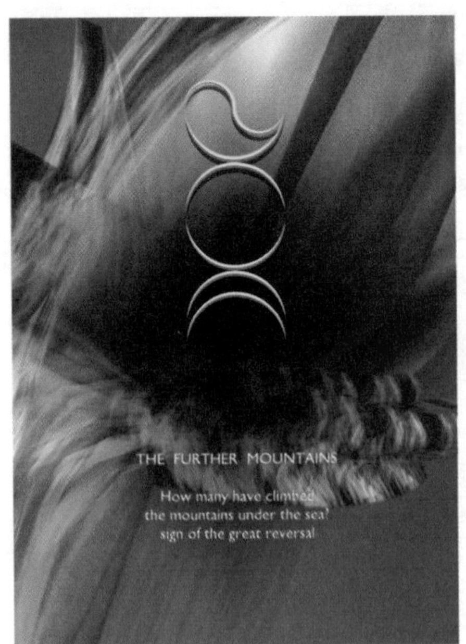

■ **Figure 36: The Glide Oracle, iPad app, sample reading.**

■ **Figure 37: Touching or resting link.**

■ **Figure 38: Deep or nesting link.**

Electronic literature scholar Carolyn Guertin describes Glide linking: "The meaning between glyphs morphs where their edges touch, producing ever-shifting margins and centres of meaning" (Guertin 2005).

Glide takes hypertextual[6] structure down to the level of the language itself. In addition to the meaning of the glyphs, the links are equally meaningful, as are the points of branching they create. Links can be created by proximity—one glyph touching the next at one or more points. Links can also be formed by the overlapping of matching parts of two glyphs, forming a "deep" link and a tighter structure. These overlaps can create homonymic

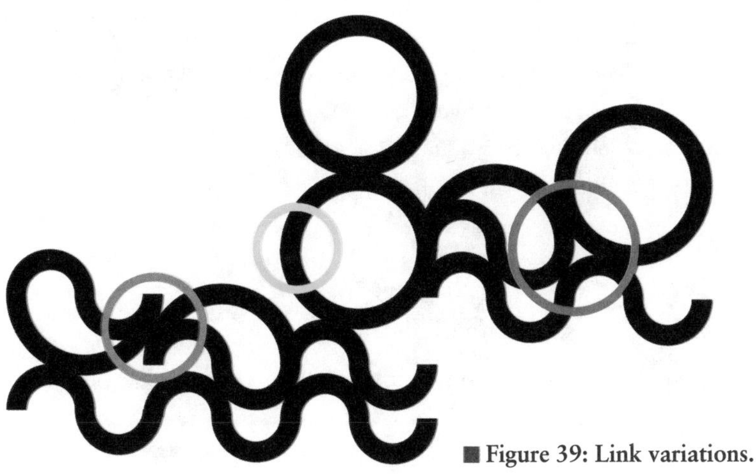

■ **Figure 39: Link variations.**

or punning ambiguities, as the composite/linked glyphs could be made from more than one pair of glyphs in combination. Further, an individual link can have a variable number of strokes participating. The yellow circle encloses a single stroke link. The red and green circles enclose more complex joining of strokes.

Glide Mazes: An arrangement of three or more hexagrams is called a "maze." A maze offers multiple entrances, multiple paths along which to trace meaning. Visual language becomes hypertextual, offering choices at the linkages of meaning. Negative spaces reveal new shapes. Interior spaces—visual silences—offer additional meanings—or a place to rest in the maze of meaning-making. Repetitions of circles, of waves, create interior rhythms. The maze as a whole, a gestalt, has its own physiognomy. Meaning shifts between an apprehension of the whole and focus on the individual glyphs, their links, and their shifting paths of meaning. The movements of the eye and the mind's eye select a path of glyphs through the maze of meaning.

"Hypertext," a term coined by Ted Nelson in 1976, has been called "non-sequential writing" (Nelson 1987). The term "non-linear" is frequently used as well, though both are misleading. All uses of natural language at baseline, whether spoken, written, read, or signed, have a linear and sequential nature.

■ Figure 40: Glide maze.

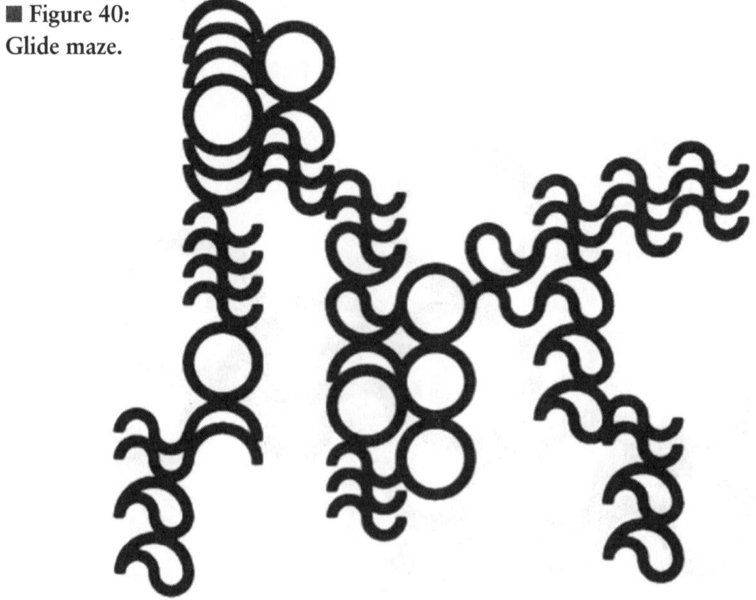

One word follows another in our perception, utterances, and comprehension. All conventional forms of writing begin at a point in time and with a point (the first mark). Writing then moves in linear order through time. Though silences make this line discontinuous, it still proceeds; it is still a line, until it stops. We are pinned by time to paths. Hypertext leads to the use of "non-linear" and "non-sequential" as descriptors because, due to branching and linked structures, multiple possible sequences are offered, and the writer/reader of a hypertext has a continuous stream of choices presented. A print book offers one primary sequence (but always with the possibility of skipping around). A hypertext therefore presents a sequence of choices, combining to form a branching and linked structure.

Metaphorically, the difference is that between the classical, unicursal labyrinth and the maze of branching paths, though in practice, the terms "labyrinth" and "maze" are often interchanged (Hayles 2000). Glide structures are called mazes because the glyphs can be read as a variety of sequences. The maze itself can be entered at any point, with no preference being given to left/right or up/down sequencing.

Glide Software

The psychonautic practice, engaged in to learn about Glide and language, was accompanied by a second practice: software design, programming, and use. I was very fortunate to be working with programmers who helped develop a series of applications I designed to work with the Glide language. The first was a lexicon, whose entire purpose was to play with the expanding metaphoric meanings of Glide.

The Glide Collabyrinth is a Glide language editor, allowing the user to make Glide formations, morph the glyphs, and apply visual changes of size, color, and stroke width that can also be transformed in motion.

The Glide Oracle involved the translation of 729 Glide hexagrams and 729 transformations of single glyphs into each other. The translations are used to create oracular readings. The latest version of the Glide Oracle is now an iPad application.

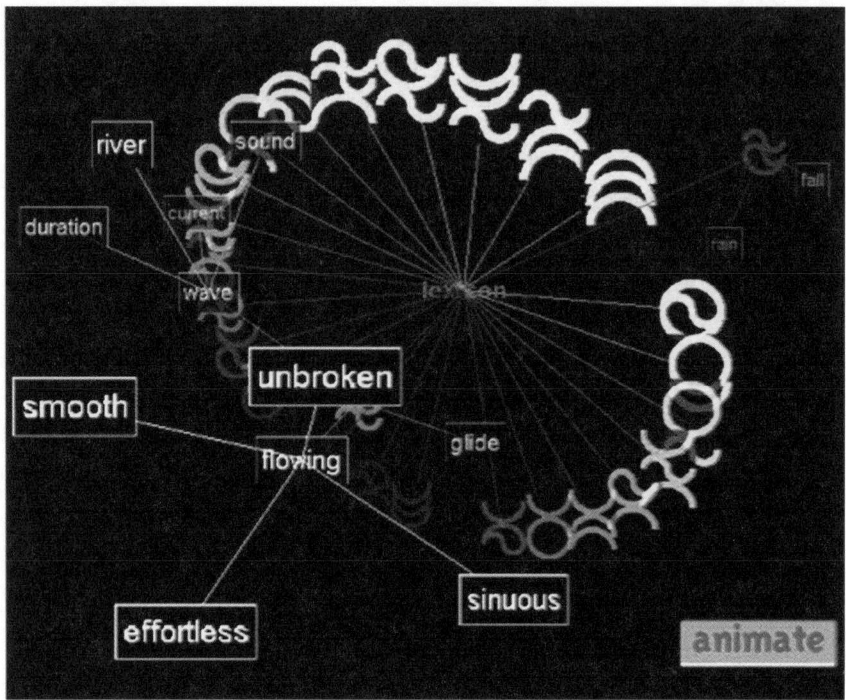

■ Figure 41: Interface, Glide Lexicon, 2000.

■ Figure 42: Interface, Glide Collabyrinth, 2000–2002.

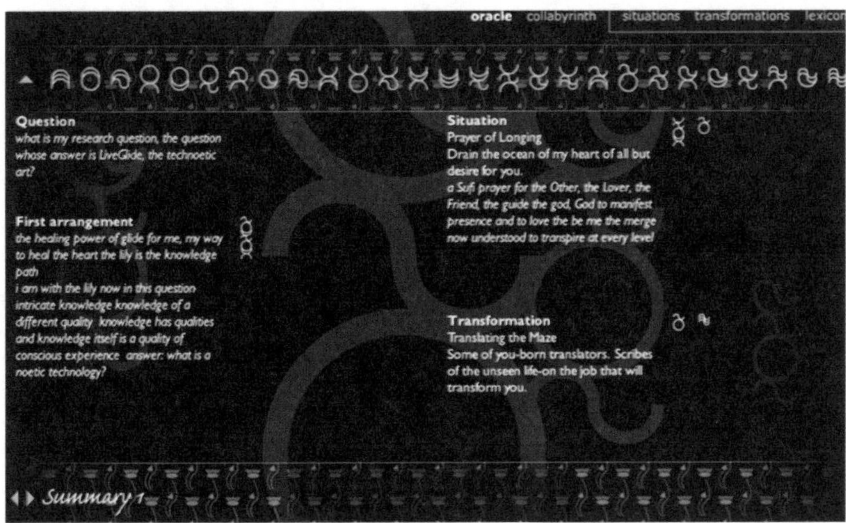

■ **Figure 43: Interface, Original Glide Oracle, 2001.**

■ **Figure 44: Interface, Glide Oracle for iPad, 2012.**

LiveGlide brings Glide into the third dimension. It is the most elaborate piece of software in the Glide series. It is used as live performance video; I have collaborated with various musicians over the years, especially in dome performances.

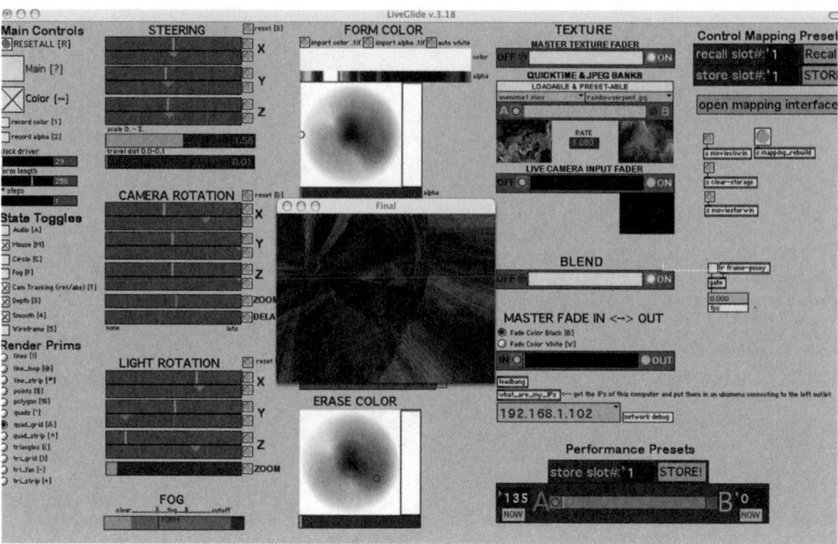

■ **Figure 45: Interface, LiveGlide, 2002–2009.**

LiveGlide is the three-dimensional, sculptural form of Glide writing. Two-dimensional shapes extend into serpentine, three-dimensional forms. The dimensional leap is accomplished computationally by moving the two-dimensional vector forms of the glyphs through 3-space on six dimensions of movement: x, y, and z axes steering the form, and x, y, and z axes of camera movement. The complexity of forms generated by six dimensions of movement produces an intricacy of movement and form that suggests a fourth (spatial) dimensional perspective. The perspective is changed from the webs of two-dimensional Glide mazes to the evolution and movement of a single, ongoing strand of Glide, moving and morphing through 3-space. This serpentine form transforms in meaning, by virtue of the transformations of the glyph and the transformations of visual attributes along its path.

A single glyph, by virtue of its transformability, becomes potentially all glyphs; one meaning becomes in potential all meanings. Flow begets form. Flow dissolves form. In Heraclitus's words, *panta rhei,* everything flows.

The single spiraling form can cross itself, re-entering its form. Using camera movement, one can tunnel through a form. Through transformations in three dimensions, and the graphical ability to leave trails, the moving

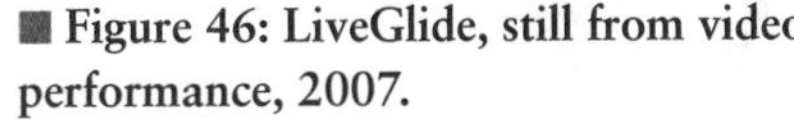

■ **Figure 46: LiveGlide, still from video performance, 2007.**

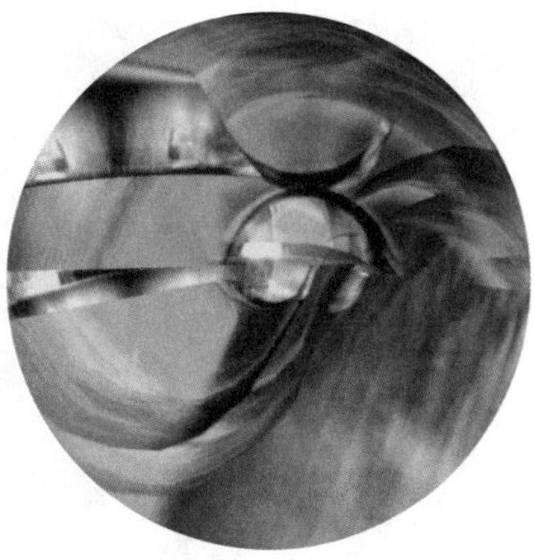

■ **Figure 47: LiveGlide, still from video performance, 2007.**

glyph leaves static forms in its wake, layering form on form, transparently or opaquely, slowly or quickly dissolving. With LiveGlide one can send pulses of color through the form, at varying speeds, creating a seventh dimension of movement. Finally, three lights can be moved over the forms, each at varying angles and speeds, bringing the dimensions of movement to ten.

LiveGlide, colorful and glowing, elaborate or austere, is the illumination of the manuscript of Glide. LiveGlide does not attempt to "represent" the visionary experience; rather, it is envisioned differently in different states of consciousness. Representation in baseline, three-dimensional perception of the perceptions of the visionary state is not possible, in my view, not simply due to an "ineffability factor," but because the perceptions are mechanically impossible to reproduce. The extremely high resolution of vision in the psychedelic sphere is qualitatively different than the lower resolution of sight at baseline. And the perceived dimensionality in the altered state is greater than the three dimensions perceivable at baseline.

In an altered state, LiveGlide tunnels are vortexes leading to other dimensions. Just so, Glide, as a symbolic system of more than normal dimensions, leads thought, feeling, and mind-body into extra-dimensional experience. Actual contact with these other dimensions, and their inhabitants, becomes possible.

■ **Figure 48: LiveGlide, still from performance, 2008.**

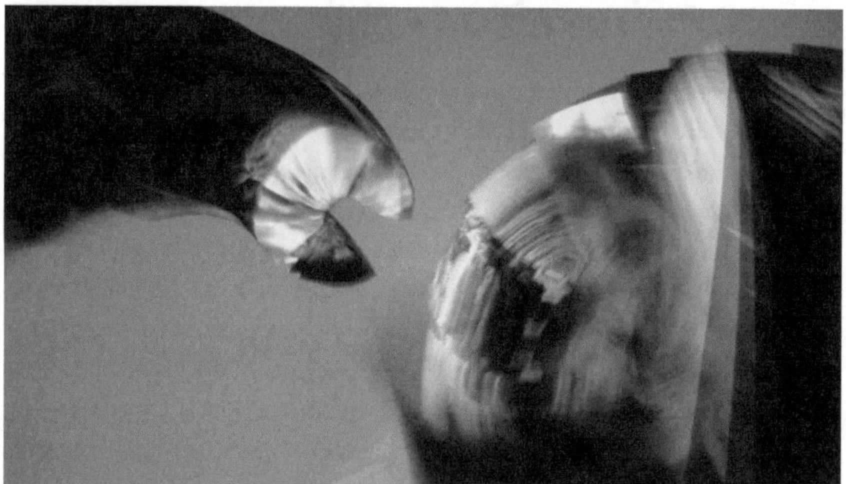

■ **Figure 49: LiveGlide form turning back on itself.**

Here is a description of the process from a 2006 session report:

letting the vortex form first the ball of energy held in the rounded hands then the blue shift and the coalescing into form then the hyperdimensional vortex held open by a quality of attention, focus, and envisionment until through the tunnel the extra dimensions are seen with the eyes open the tunnel boring through to three-dimensional space I did it practice then this is the doctrine of the secret lover (cannabis)

There is a space-filling mesh that often appears in psychedelic states, composed of undulating extremely fine strands of rainbow light that behave like the "wireframe" for more complex and solid visions when perceptually manipulated in the altered state. A 2007 session report describes the mesh:

> hands still flowing and glowing with energy   white vortex speeding off so fast   streams of energy from the fingers   go look some more   the universe is being whirled into existence at an impossibly high frequency (the quantum scale)   dervishes sand devils of primary vortextual energy   like seeing everything a very very very fine wireframe   getting more and more solid as the projection is accepted as "the real" (MDMA)

LiveGlide can be visualized as a wireframe, shifted into a more opaque form using the software's ability to make the forms from different graphical primitives, but this does not "represent" the mesh seen in the altered state. What LiveGlide reveals to me, writing in an altered state of consciousness, is not the visions of the eye but the movements of the mind, *like a long-legged fly.* LiveGlide expresses meanings to me; I do not consciously "represent" forms recognizable at baseline. Writing with LiveGlide, glyphs become portals, gates of change. I can move through a LiveGlide tunnel *andante,* or at warp speed; I am tunneling to another dimension—and have a language with which I can express it.

■ Figure 50: LiveGlide tunneling through its own form.

Another description from a 2007 session report:

> multiple worlds performing an interdimensional docking operation—lining up portals and sending a tube across the tube transforms creates a wave of energy down its length when the glyphs transform how meaning travels three-dimensionally a three-dimensional world has a two-dimensional writing convention a four-dimensional world has a three-dimensional writing convention: LiveGlide LiveGlide carves light that cuts through the underlying qi "layer" (MDMA)

LiveGlide speaks in spiral waves, a primal form on which the universe, including biological forms, is constructed.

> re-read your world in Glide from a Glide viewpoint multiminding re-write your world in Glide all signals are Glide forms spiral waves (MDMA, 2006)

LiveGlide celebrates the spiral wave, the endless movements of the Rainbow Serpent, reproducing itself by unzipping its mirror image, then reflecting itself anew. It splits, it rejoins. Every link unlinks, and then reforms, reflectively.

> it's all done with mirrors (MDMA, 2006)

LiveGlide coils and uncoils, folds and unfolds, extends and contracts, swells and shrinks in its passage, a series of linguistic symbols changing in sequence over an endless line, an abstraction of the language of living light that is our DNA. LiveGlide expresses the gestures of the Rainbow Serpent, an exercise in transdimensionality. The relation of Glide and LiveGlide to DNA is pointed out over and over in the session reports, at times with great urgency:

> so much depends upon . . . finding the script of the transmission the transmission of the transdimensional script illuminate the manuscript so much depends upon this portal, this transdimensional doorway—for the unfolding the scriptase, transcriptase total absence of all formal categories doesn't provide alibi for presence at the transformation stay naked in the presence of the alien bereft of symbologies cosmic SOS process being written on the DNA when transmission active (6 g dried *Stropharia cubensis,* 2005)

Tai Chi masters describe the movements of the body as founded on the half circle, tracing spiral waves. In the Qi Gong form "serving tea," the arms trace an inside-out turning spiral wave. This movement is sometimes called "the Timeless BaGua Zhang exercise," based on the octagonal arrangement of the eight trigrams of the *I Ching*. The *I Ching* is fundamental to the logic of Glide, described below. The movement of *qi* in the body, and the forms of Tai Chi and Qi Gong, are another field of meaning for LiveGlide.

> fingers move in the snake-wave the glide sign the sidewinder the wave in metaform now expressed through a highly organized articulated spine and body but still the wave form the smooth interpolation of levels of intensity in 3-space the wave is helical and can store energy—twing—can use the stored energy of its form to penetrate—the screw locomotion is a great mystery but all based on the wave-spiral
>
> the humorous beauty of the skeleton dancing—the spring of the spine the muscles that move the bones the bones that give direction and form to the muscles all depend on the wave-spiral both in their macro-form and in the way they deploy energy rising falling on exact curves the hand-gesture snake-wave form is translated into greater and greater levels of organization yet still metaphorically and structurally maintains the same form the wave-spiral (high-dose cannabis, 2007)

Glide Logic

> *"Each phase of consciousness is characterized by its own range of entrainment, as well as its own 'logics,' which direct attention and assemble 'meanings' selectively. . . . In a sense, symbols order experience. They attract and focus our attention, modulate the interplay between events of the moment and events of the past, and canalize our experience into accord with that of our fellows."*
>
> —Charles Laughlin, 1990

In the psychedelic sphere, there is an experience where opposites coexist without contradiction. In alchemy, this is called the *coniunctio oppositorum*. In Glide, this marriage of opposites is expressed in the third stroke. The three strokes of Glide logic form a ternary logic. Paradox finds a cognitive home in Glide. The logic of Aristotle, Leibniz, and Descartes, the logic of Western rationality, is binary at the core. There is A, there is not-A, and there is nothing in between. This is the Law of the Excluded Middle. Quantum physicist Basarab Nicolescu, from the viewpoint of his model of transdisciplinarity, and Francisco Varela, presenting a calculus of self-reference for understanding biological forms, each propose a three-valued logic, a Law of the Included Middle.

The idea of a ternary logic is expressed in the basic construction of the Glide glyphs from three strokes.

Self-reference is at the heart of living, autopoietic (self-producing, self-maintaining) systems. Self-reference is at the heart of consciousness; when consciousness strives to understand itself, to observe itself, the paradoxes that plague the binary logic of the rationalist view (how can I be both observer and observed at the same time) stubbornly present themselves. Francisco Varela frames the problem this way:

> Whether in dealing with the organization of systems or with the structure of language, hardships with self-referential situations have the same root: the distinction between actor or operand, and that which is acted or operated upon, collapses. (Varela 1974)

Varela represents the third term—the both/and—as an asterisk in *Principles of Biological Autonomy:*

> * = observer/observed (Varela 1979)

■ Figure 51: Francisco Varela's formal sign for re-entry into the form.

In "A Calculus for Self-Reference" (Varela 1974), the article in which the underlying logic of autopoiesis is developed (extrapolated from George Spencer-Brown's Laws of Form), Varela uses the following formalism to stand for re-entry into the form. Varela sees this third logical value at a level deeper than logic, in Spencer-Brown's calculus of self-reference. "In the extended calculus, self-reference, time, and re-entry are seen as aspects of the same third value arising autonomously in the form of distinction" (Varela 1974).

The relation of the formal sign for re-entry into the form to the mathematical object *i* is explained by Varela:

> In analogy, we have presented a similar construction at the Boolean level. By allowing an antinomic form (from the point of view of logic) we have

> constructed a new larger domain akin to the complex plane, where new forms can be lodged, including those of the preceding primary domain found to be in conflict by the introduction of re-entering expressions. Again, rather than avoid the antinomy, by confronting it, a new domain emerges. (Varela 1974)

Nicolescu, following Stéphane Lupasco's three-valued logic, represents the third term as T:

> A, Not-A, and T (which is at the same time A and non-A) (Nicolescu 2002)

In Glide, the third term is represented as the wave stroke:
A concrescence of concepts resides in the wave sign.

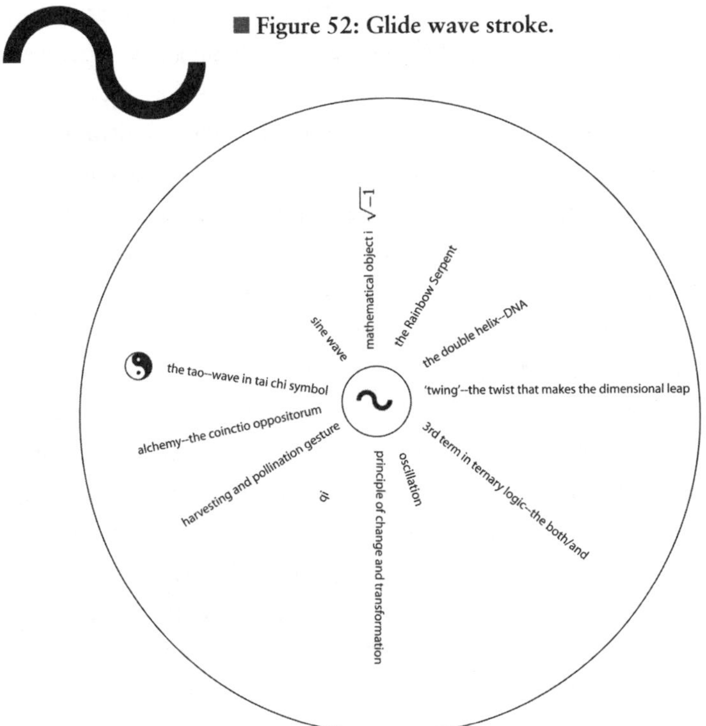

■ **Figure 52: Glide wave stroke.**

■ **Figure 53: Wave sign as a concresence of concepts in the Glide symbolic system.**

In the Glide symbolic system, the correlative thinking that occurs in altered states of consciousness centers on the wave sign. The connection with the *I Ching* springs from the relation of the Tai Chi symbol to the binary system of the *I Ching.*

The *I Ching,* or *Book of Changes,* expresses the principle of dynamic change in the universe and in the affairs of humankind. The Tai Chi sign at rest, according to Master Alfred Huang, is the 0 of the pre-creation void. When the Tai Chi goes into motion, two primary energies are created, generating the world through their interactions (Huang 2000). The wave sign, implicit in the Tai Chi symbol, is made explicit in the Glide ternary system. The binary system has also been represented as a fractal (by Shao Yong—see Huang 2000).

Glide in Use

In the story world of *The Maze Game,* the Glide language infuses the culture and has many uses. For the original Glides, the language was first gestural and used to navigate and communicate secretly across the spaces of the lily pond on which they harvested the pollen of the hallucinogenic blue lily.

The mazes used in game play were constructed of Glide glyphs in various architectures. There are four styles of maze on which the game is played, and four different classes of Death Dancers, based on four mind-sets, roughly equivalent to the Jungian four functions. Bods favor the gut-mind, the body's wisdom. Their mazes are extruded glyphs at different heights. Bods relate to the maze of meaning as an obstacle course.

Swashes live in the sea-mind, the source of emotion, creativity, song, and dance. They perform their way through a maze of extruded glyphs, but with curved, ramp-like connections between the different heights of glyphs. The Chromes are cyborgs who favor the island-mind, the seat of rationality. Chromes move through the maze in springing leaps, from closed space to closed space. Their mazes are steep and deep, with great variance in the height of the glyphs. Glides, living in the transpersonal lily-mind, move silently on a perfectly flat maze, floating, gliding, in a contemplative state. In addition to their primary use as game maze, the glyphs are used for poetry, as an oracle, as an inspiration and notation for music, and in the architecture of buildings and patterns of city streets.

Outside the story world *per se,* I began to use Glide as a method of navigating psychedelic mind-states. Its formal structure in mazes would

■ **Figure 54: Death Dancers in a game maze.**

transmute in altered states to a fine mesh, the underlying structure of visionary formation. "Holding" these structures with the mind—a function of intention and attention—and then "twisting" them creates a dimensional leap from the perception of the physical universe into a visionary landscape. As such, the glyphs have practical use as navigational tools and as an interdimensional rapid transit system. They also function as forms that can contain and channel the powerful energy phenomena experienced in altered states, creating a circuit-like structure along which energy can flow, modulate, store, and transduce, a framework to ride the spiral waves of the Rainbow Serpent.

> The new symbolic structure can carry much more energy, across more dimensions. This is a very simple principle, can even be explained, but applying to the experiences possible—the changes in consciousness—is quite another matter (hashish, 2008)

Performing with LiveGlide in an altered state gave me yet another perspective on Glide. In an altered state, writing with LiveGlide is a collaboration with the Other. The Other speaks through the gestures of the language projected on the dome or screen. Writing with LiveGlide, done with this intention, becomes a spiritual technology. Getting in sync with the Other, allowing a condition of pure flow to move the forms, and entering a state of "ecstatic signification" where reading and writing, self and Other, are one, is to use LiveGlide to access an ecstatic mind-state, a means of navigating the psychedelic landscape. Such navigation involves techniques of managing the self, Self, selves, Other, and others manifesting in the altered state of consciousness. With practice, ego dissolution is less of an earthshaking event and more a change of costume, or a nakedness, "a creature void of form,"[7] yet still performing, reading, writing, as the faithful scribe. In the 2C-B state especially, reading and writing with LiveGlide becomes a meditation. Close observation, in the state of mind I've called crystal vision, of the movements of *psyche*—thoughts, feelings, physical sensations—occurs in sync with the Other, with whom I am communicating.

Much practice, over a period of years, honed this ability, and this understanding. LiveGlide is always performative, but the performance is most meaningful without audience, other than the connection with the Other. Who reads? Who writes? Who performs, and who observes? It is all one motion, a single system. But LiveGlide, at baseline, is an artistic practice performed, preferably, in domed environments. In altered states of consciousness, the dome becomes the dome of consciousness, in which the processes of perception, reflection, and projection are present in the material metaphor, and in the processes of the mind. The geometry of the hemisphere is created by the rotation of the half-circle, the fundamental Glide stroke.

In the mixed reality of psychedelic vision, where hyperdimensional realities are sensorially interwoven with the perceptions of the physical environment, I am aware of projection from multiple projectors. My mind, now open to its depths, is projecting images. Likewise, the hemispheric projector is projecting images of LiveGlide, but those two projections have become inseparable. The machinery of reality-perception is laid bare as the Other moves *psyche* and *psyche* moves forms, flowing through the fingertips, trans-

■ Figure 55: LiveGlide in dome performance, Atlantic Center for the Arts, 2005.

formed in the computer's languages, and projected onto the dome's surface, reflected back, and turned into perception, around again, as the seamless and inseparable nature of the process is played out in timeless flow.

LiveGlide is ephemeral art—images arise and move on, fading out, overwritten, dissolved, transformed. The Rainbow Serpent changes color, movement, shape, but always the serpent's form is close to hand. These images are transient. No matter how much I may become enamored of a particular form, a color space, a movement, a teaching, I know I will never be able to return to that exact combination of LiveGlide variables. However eloquent, the image will be lost. LiveGlide loves Heraclitus: *panta rhei.* You can't go home again. Let go. Move on. Create anew. Always improvisational, LiveGlide teaches me the skill of non-attachment.

Ethical Dimensions of Glide

The primary psychedelic theme of interconnectedness is echoed in the forms of the Glide mazes, in which the links (or structural couplings) have meaning in addition to the glyphs, which are the nodes in the net (the glyphs as individual loci of meaning). The evolutionary imperative is expressed over and over in the psychedelic state—namely, that a shift in mind or consciousness is necessary to even begin to contemplate our condition as individuals and as a species, and to reckon with our disconnected behavior toward ourselves, our fellow humans, and the parts of the biosphere we are destroying in our efforts to survive. This sense of responsibility toward other than (small) self alone grows in strength in the repeated conditions of *psyche*'s shifts in psychedelic states. Sentience, intelligence, and consciousness are experienced not just as prized possessions, evidence of our privileged human state, but as permeating the biosphere, and the universe as a whole. My perception of the world I find myself in shifts in its deepest character from being a mechanically connected, randomly derived group of objects in a neutral container of space to a shimmering web of subjectivities. This is the infinite living communicating mesh into which I am miraculously woven, within which I am nourished, and toward which I have a responsibility. How could it be otherwise in this connectedness? The visionary experience as *metanoia,* a full spiritual conversion, and the practices that evolve from it strengthen this imperative. This assertion runs counter to the portrait of the psychedelic user as irresponsible, crazy, dangerous, destructive to self and others, or as a non-productive, narcissistic slacker, stereotyping that supports the scheduling of drugs and the punishment of those who wish to change their minds with their assistance.

The myth of Glide involves the effort to reunite the differing wisdoms of intellect, body, heart, and spirit, to bring the warring parties together in council (the connectivity of minds) and work things out. As such, it serves as a framework and a motivation in my own life for meaningful, productive change.

Notes, Chapter 3

1. Semiosis, a term introduced by Charles Sanders Peirce, is defined in Wikipedia as "any form of activity, conduct, or process that involves signs, including the production of meaning."
2. To see the game and gliders in action, look here: http://en.wikipedia.org/wiki/Conway_game_of_life.
3. From the poem, "The Long-Legged Fly."
4. From the novel: "Then I saw them—nearly weightless beings gliding back and forth across the floating fields like pieces on a living, undulating board of some infinite game whose rules were invisible to me. Their moves seemed both haphazard and purposeful. They changed direction suddenly for no apparent reason, like dragonflies in mid-air. Their cupped hands stroked over the blossoms in quick, swooping motions like a flight of sparrows, like a benediction. Their paths, which echoed on a larger scale the gestures of their hands, curved and criss-crossed, linked, and doubled back, leaving faint traces as they passed. The lilies gathered themselves in clusters, which then spoke single signs. I rose above the pond, saw acres of lily clusters, moving softly, dreaming below. As the tides shifted, larger clusters separated, drifted apart; smaller groups gathered into one. The silvery maze of the night-path of the Glides was gently skewed, stretched, pulled apart as it faded from sight. Even at this height, the lily spoke the same language. The smaller mazes melted into single signs. Within the expanding labyrinth, waves, and waves within waves, the moving surface of a stillness, crossed over each other, lifting the lilies, moving the waves of fragrance, sinking back."
5. The Glide Oracle app can be found in the Apple Apps store, https://itunes.apple.com/us/app/glide-oracle/id578394014?mt=8
6. A common example of a hypertext would be any Wikipedia page and, by extension, any web page with internal and/or external links.
7. From the lyrics to the Bob Dylan song, "Shelter from the Storm."

CHAPTER 4
Contact with the Other

"I believe that rational exploration of the enigma of the Other is possible and that the shamanistic approach to hallucinogenic plants, especially those containing psilocybin and dimethyltryptamine (DMT), will be absolutely central to achieving that end."

—Terence McKenna, *The Archaic Revival*, 1971

Ecstasy, I submit, is not the end of reason, but its origin. Ecstasis—to stand outside of one's self, the small self of normal waking consciousness—is the position from which true objectivity and hence the tools of reason, logic, and science can be developed. Ecstasis is the path to gnosis, the appearance of self-evident, often sacred knowledge. However one achieves the state, it is primary on the road not only to self-knowledge but to knowledge about the deep structures of life, consciousness, and the world of nature. When the small self (often called "ego") is set aside, along with its defenses, biases, and language-encapsulated knowledge, true observation begins. We can experience ourselves as an interwoven part of nature, observing, self-reflexively, as part of a larger whole. Science begins with observation. As Brian Josephson, Nobel Laureate in physics, understated, "The physical description of the world would change radically if we could observe more things" (Josephson 1975). Psychedelic experience certainly confirms that notion. We introduce radical shifts in perception, and new realities come into being.

There is no more controversial observation a psychonaut can make to the scientist with little or no psychedelic experience than to mention contact with an Other in the psychedelic sphere. It is surely one of the great unspeakables in psychedelic experience. The word "alien" triggers a raft of images of contactees selling their brand of Higher Knowledge from the Space Brothers of Sirius in supermarket tabloids. One is immediately classified as a nut case and purveyor of snake oil for use of the word "alien," much less for reports of encounters in the psychedelic sphere. This chapter proceeds with such risks firmly in view. The topic cannot be avoided in any frank discussion of psychedelic experience. When viewed cross-culturally, clearly these contact phenomena are both widespread and culturally adapted, in their many forms. This chapter seeks to make this realm of experience more familiar, in its many guises.

Masks of the Other

Psychedelic plants, animals, and fungi are ancient methods of ecstasis and gnosis, ecstasy and knowing, newly deployed. I think of them as the original search engines—Google trolling transdimensionally. We bring our burning questions: What is quantum reality? What direction should I go in life? What is Glide? This search for the Tree of Knowledge often goes hand in hand with the disincarnate Other in its myriad forms. The question of the Other is the question of how we experience, describe, and especially interpret the felt presence of an Other or others in altered states of consciousness. The Other wears a vast diversity of masks: God, gods, angels, devas, asuras, and hungry ghosts; legions of nature spirits, guides, ancestors, plant teachers, and some very alien transdimensional beings challenge, aid, disrupt, offer gifts, joke, riddle us to distraction, make predictions in gnomic phrases, or deliver marching orders. *Your mission, should you choose to accept it. . . .* The McKennas' La Chorrera download date of March 4th became the imperative *March Forth!*

Xenolinguist Jason Tucker senses the Other in partnership with his drawing hand and heart. "In these images, I can see an Other 'coming into being' wanting to participate. The act of creation is shown to be an act of pure participation—a participation with something Other than what I would normally call myself." The presence of the Other as a partner in the drawing/writing experience is shared in my experience writing with LiveGlide.

Experiences of the Other run a full spectrum between the life-transforming, mystical vision and the life-destroying invasion of demonic forces variously called possession, schizophrenia, or shamanic attack. The schizophrenic's torturing voices can drive the listener to suicide or murder. Identification with the Other in the transcendental state, brought uncritically back to baseline, results in the kind of ego inflation called in psychiatry "delusions of grandeur." Shamanism describes these encounters with the Other as part of a functional knowledge system, involving multiple levels of reality that one must learn to navigate and master. Relationships are built with multiple beings with whom the shaman or curandera forms working relationships for practical ends such as diagnosis, divination, love magic, protection, and healing.

The shamanic relationship to the world of spirits and plants as the source of knowledge and power constitutes a global set of practices. They are the professionals, "technicians of the sacred" in religious historian Mircea Eliade's phrase, the practitioners of ecstatic pathways to knowledge. Contact with entities becomes a prerequisite, an indispensible tool of the shaman's vocation. Eliade discusses the extreme importance of "spirit visions" in all varieties of shamanic initiations: "Seeing" a spirit, either in dream or awake, is a certain sign that one has in some sort obtained a "spiritual condition," that is, that one has transcended the profane condition of humanity.

Eliade quotes an Australian shaman of the Yaralde tribe: "However, some of them are evil spirits, some are like snakes, some are like horses with men's heads, and some are spirits of evil men which resemble burning fires." Those are the spirits of the dead, the spirits one must learn to confront fearlessly in the altered state of consciousness. There are categories and types of spirits with whom the shaman learns to negotiate. Out of a heavily populated visionary realm, the shaman establishes his or her (usually his) own set of relationships.

The study of the anthropology of shamanism worldwide shows that each tribe has its own taxonomy of the spirit realm to which its members as well as its shaman relate. Eliade again:

> A shaman is a man who has immediate, concrete experiences with gods and spirits; he sees them face to face, he talks with them, prays to them, implores them—but he does not "control" more than a limited number of them. Any god or spirit invoked during a shamanic séance is not by that fact one of the shaman's "familiars" or "helpers." (Eliade 1964)

As contemporary psychonauts, we clothe the naked numinous presence of the Other in archetypal masks, drawn from our multicultural lexicon, our *set* going in, and our *setting,* which may contain images, talismanic objects, world music, all of which can feed into the process of constituting the Other—or not. The nature of the Other, behind the masks, remains a central mystery in psychonautics. Is this being with whom I am communicating some aspect of myself? Or is it truly Other?

Descartes's download in a series of three powerful dreams that set the stage for rationalism and the scientific method was delivered by an angel: "The conquest of nature is to be achieved through measure and number." The knowledge system built on this angelic pronouncement has since denied reality to angels; and arguably, the intention to conquer nature is leading to the demise of multiple species and the fouling of our nest. But for Descartes, the imprimatur of the angelic Other validated a line of thought toward which he was struggling.

Terence McKenna describes the speaking voice of the mushroom variously as the voice of the Gaian Oversoul, as an extraterrestrial, and the voice of the Logos. Again, many masks.

> What was amazing about the mushrooms, and it continues to be amazing, is that it is animate, that there's someone talking to you. This was actually a voice in the head, making sense, speaking English, and addressing the concerns that were most important to me personally. I was not set up for this. (McKenna 1991)

McKenna's relation to "voices in the head" is clearly different from the bedeviled schizophrenic; it is productive, manageable, and capable of transcription into baseline reality.

How common are these experiences in contemporary psychonautics? Horace Beach, in his 1996 dissertation, "Listening for the Logos: A Study of Reports of Audible Voices at High Doses of Psilocybin," presents a quantitative study of the phenomenon of the speaking voice, with mention of the phenomenon occurring under the influence of other drugs as well. His data showed that nearly 40 percent of those who had taken high-dose psilocybin had an experience of voices. While his data do not support the idea that hearing voices is a predominantly psilocybin phenomenon, a majority of his survey participants indicated that they first heard the voice with psilocybin. This experience of voices in the head showed no gender correlation. Being alone enhanced the possibility of the experience, as did growing one's own mushrooms.

The Other As Source of Knowledge

■ **Figure 56: María Sabina.**

María Sabina was the Mazatec curandera who allowed amateur mycologist Gordon Wasson to participate in a *velada,* or night vigil, the traditional mushroom ceremony. Wasson subsequently published an article in the May 13, 1957, issue of *Life* magazine, which introduced "magic mushrooms" to the world and brought an influx of anthropologists, ethnobotanists, CIA agents, and proto-hippies to the remote villages of the Mazatec community. Henry Munn documented Sabina's work and that of other Mexican curanderos. Sabina describes her sources of knowledge thus:

> One of the Principal Ones spoke to me and said: "María Sabina, this is the Book of Wisdom. It is the Book of Language. Everything that is written in it is for you. The Book is yours, take it so that you can work." (Munn 1973)

The image of an all-inclusive source of Wisdom, a personal access to a Book of Wisdom, the Akashic record, or other source of all knowledge is one form that psychonautic knowledge-gathering can take. During the experiment at La Chorrera, Dennis McKenna parsed the effect of all-knowing-ness as a factor of DNA function:

> This is how it's done. You put a radio into the DNA and this ESR[1] resonation will begin to flood your system because the bond will be permanent; there will be no way to disrupt it. It will tell you everything—everything that can be known in the world of space and time because it contains your own and everyone else's records. We are all connected through this magical substance, which is what makes life possible and which causes it to take on its myriad forms. (D. McKenna 1993)

Dennis's prediction—that DNA is the source of the complete field of information—set up the download about to arrive. Dennis's breakthrough to the palace of the all-knowing, after continuing for several days, split the group into concerned factions: was he or was he not clinically crazy? The voices in the head were up for grabs, testing the strength and flexibility of the reality tunnels of the Brotherhood of the Screaming Abyss. The Source was giving forth tantalizing pieces of data that were seemingly impossible to obtain directly. Terence McKenna relates in *True Hallucinations* how the seductive interaction with the Other led them to a border crossing between imagination and reality:

> The Other plays with us and approaches us through the imagination and then a critical juncture is reached. To go beyond this juncture requires abandonment of old and ingrained habits of thinking and seeing. At that moment the world turns lazily inside out and what was hidden is revealed: a magical modality, a different mental landscape than one has ever known, and the landscape becomes real. This is the realm of the cosmic giggle. UFOs, elves, and the teeming pantheons of all religions are the denizens of this previously invisible landscape. One reaches through to the continents and oceans of the imagination, worlds able to sustain anyone who will but play, and then lets the play deepen and deepen until it is a reality that few would even dare to entertain. (T. McKenna 1993)

Types of Psychedelic Knowledge

The types of knowledge sought in altered states of consciousness, across cultures, vary widely. Divinatory knowledge—predictions for auspicious hunting, planting, or war-making—is a recurrent theme in shamanic practice. Rooting out the source of an illness, loss, or misfortune hidden from view—in other words, making the invisible visible and the unknown known by recourse to the invisible landscape of the altered state—is one of the oldest forms of knowledge practice. Though methods differ, the practical desire to predict the future and benefit from that knowledge aligns shamanism and science in their basic intentions.

Psychology is, in theory at least, no stranger to multiple states of consciousness; the division of conscious and unconscious knowledge frames major theories of the mind. When we use the terms "conscious" and "unconscious" in a psychological framework we are making a statement about knowing. The conscious mind—meaning in this sense ordinary waking consciousness—is where we "know": a phone number, a theorem, or the contents of what William James called "the stream of consciousness," and Bernard

Baars calls "the workspace of the mind" (Baars 1997). From that model of consciousness, the unconscious is framed as the literally unknown, that which is out of sight of the conscious mind at a given moment. Content can be, as Freud established, very far from consciousness—repressed, and difficult to access. Learning the crypto-language of dreams, active imagination, verbal slips, and psychosomatic symptoms can open the door to retrieval of that content. What model the unconscious content is framed within varies greatly, depending on the particular theory. Jung's archetypes of the collective unconscious provide a different map than Freud's Id, Ego, and Superego, or Stanislav Grof's perinatal matrices.

The psychotherapeutic distinction of known/conscious and unknown/unconscious is the fundamental dichotomy of psychic life on which the project of many psychotherapies is based: to make the unconscious conscious. The underlying assumption is that the road to psychic health lies in the integration and reconciliation of unconscious content with conscious attitudes. Much of psychedelic psychotherapy follows some form of this model. Early experimental LSD therapy distinguished between low-dose and high-dose (psycholytic and psychedelic) approaches. Lay therapist and psychedelic pioneer Ann Shulgin's reports in *PIHKAL* of MDMA therapy (Shulgin and Shulgin 1991) follow the consciousness–unconsciousness model, but through a different path, with an intense awareness of the Jungian Shadow (an internal Other in a sense) as the archetypal collection of repressed feelings, attitudes, and actions that must be brought to light (consciousness) for wholeness and healing to occur.

According to anthropologist and shamanism scholar Michael Winkelman, the use of psychedelic psychointegrators, producing altered states of consciousness and used in conjunction with shamanic ritual practices, confers adaptive advantage on the individual and the community. Psychedelics, through the action of the serotonergic and opioid systems, can affect and enhance the following human activities: human emotional, learning, and perceptual abilities; regulation and enhancement of perception; perception of novel stimuli; sensory-motor regulation—the integration of behavior with intention; extension of our basic bonding capacity (mother-child) to non-kin; the bonding created in a variety of shamanic rituals; reduction of pain and stress; and enhancement of learning and memory. Winkelman asks: "When hominids started using these things, how did intuition, how did a sense of connectedness, how did a sense of transcendence of space and time, how did visionary structuralization enhance human adaptation and survival?" Experientially, these psychointegrator substances create one or more of a variety of novel experiences, including a sense of power; the use of those powers to change behavior and emotional state (psychological healing); journeys to spiritual worlds and other dimensions; a sense of soul; enhanced awareness of environment (more effective hunting due to physiological effects on the lower brain); enhanced social cohesion; the experience of being an animal; death and rebirth experiences; initiatory crisis; healing; altruism; and divination and the acquisition of intuitive knowledge. Winkelman's list of the adaptive benefits of psychedelics in human society covers a great deal of ground.

Winkelman outlines from a neurobiological perspective the physiological mechanisms associated with the long list of adaptive activities and experiences above:

> Psychedelics produce synchronized theta waves—[which are] only predominant in ASCs—the circuitry that links the paleo-mammalian brain—the limbic brain and the hippocampus with the reptilian brain—the raphe nuclei and the locus coeruleus; it's serotonergic circuitry. Once this stuff gets going stimulating the autonomic nervous system it then begins to propagate up the neuraxis. What starts in the lower brain eventually gets carried to the frontal cortex. It integrates our unconscious into the conscious and basically provides a synchronized experience in terms of the two halves of our frontal cortex. Most of the time left brain and right brain are on totally different tracks. And what altered states of consciousness do is not only synchronize the frontal cortex but basically make the frontal cortex pay attention to what's happening in the rest of the brain. (Winkelman 2008)

The individual psychonaut, flying solo, no matter what the knowledge agenda brought to the experience, has embarked on a path of self-knowledge and change. Whether or not this knowledge or these inevitable changes become useful, much less adaptive for the individual or her community, is a matter of perspective and values. Clearly one person's creative adaptation to life may represent an unmitigated disaster for someone else, either as his or her own path or in the fallout from a changing relationship with the psychonaut.

Ordinary waking consciousness, with its flow of thoughts and emotions, is the interior landscape we are immersed in, and seldom aware of—the situation of the fish in water. But with the radical shifts in the felt qualities of consciousness that happen in psychedelic states, consciousness itself is brought to the foreground, becoming its own object. The opening of normally out-of-view parts of the mind brings forward forgotten memories that can have profound impact when reviewed in a psychedelic state. Self-knowledge can extend beyond the contents of the personal unconscious into deeply transpersonal knowledge. In my own experience, my central focus for ten years of solo psychonautic exploration was on language, and gaining further knowledge about the Glide download. But this was accompanied by the incremental, selective dismantling and reconstruction of my way of doing business in the world—call it ego or personality—as an unavoidable part of the process, at times difficult in the extreme, but steadily productive. Life changed for the better, especially in the healing of a life-long pattern of recurrent depression and anxiety, making joy the new baseline. And these were the side effects. The experiential knowledge of myself as intimately and sacredly interconnected with the world of nature and other beings is a precious psychedelic gift, given to many, a hope and a promise that the human world, for all its craziness, still has great things in store. This vision, presented again and again in a variety of forms, became a stable reality across states of consciousness, and was the context in which the more personal challenges could be confronted and overcome. Does the transcendental viewpoint help in daily life? I'd say so.

The Noetic

Neurobiology tells us that psychedelics create increased connectivity in the brain, increased synchronization of the lobes of the frontal cortex, and the opening of the material of the "lower brains" to the view of the frontal cortex, a picture of the whole brain functioning together in conscious awareness. The phenomenological experience of the noetic, the connection to a new order of knowledge and certainty in altered states of consciousness, and the experiences of profound interconnectedness bring this central theme of connectivity to both the objective and the subjective view.

The noetic quality described by William James as a hallmark of mystical experience is revelatory. Knowledge is not arrived at through analysis of existing material, nor through construction or assemblage of existing knowledge into forms that become "new knowledge." Knowledge is *revealed,* arriving with the impact of essential insights, un-arguable, apodictic, given. Benny Shanon, in his book *Antipodes of the Mind: Charting the Phenomenology of the Ayahuasca Experience,* describes seven dimensions of the ayahuasca experience, of which the sixth is the spiritual.

> Ayahuasca often induces powerful religious and mystical experiences. In general, these are associated with strong noetic feelings (that is, experiences in which one feels that true knowledge is attained). (Shanon 2002)

Knowing in the psychedelic sphere takes on qualities that distinguish it from knowing at baseline. Shanon associates this kind of knowledge with the strong feeling of connectedness—with other beings, with the world, with plants, with nature, as playing a role in knowledge acquisition. He acknowledges the difficult philosophical issues raised *vis à vis* such forms of knowledge, and their veridicality. He relates that he asked a form of the inevitable question: "'How do you know . . . that what Ayahuasca made you see is indeed true?' Common answers were 'I just felt it,' 'I experienced this as evident. That's it.'" (Shanon 2002) For the individual, in the reality level of the noetic connection, the rules of self-evidence take precedence over the rules of evidence.

Transformations of Self and Other

"Je est une autre."

—Arthur Rimbaud, 1871

A concept of self—whether closely examined or naively assumed—is essential to most accounts of consciousness: philosophical, scientific, or religious. Altering one's state of consciousness can profoundly destabilize the experience of self, and hence the self-concept we carry in our ordinary states of consciousness. The concept of self is reciprocally connected to the concept of the Other, the dichotomy of subjective and objective, observer and observed, and, following William James, the knower and the known. In consciousness studies, self-other is assumed as a stable, if not universal, category. The discussion and use of first- and third-person methods in the study of consciousness assumes this stability.

Dialogue with the Other is often concerned directly with teaching, and the acquisition and transmission of knowledge. Benny Shanon asks, "What does it mean that a plant conveys knowledge? What is the status of the knowledge that is presumably achievable through the consumption of psychoactive plants?" (Shanon 2002) He connects this quest for knowledge in the psychedelic sphere with the mythical search for the Tree of Knowledge, as does Terence McKenna. The evolving dialogue with the Other, the transformations of self and Other in altered states of consciousness, and the intermixing of their forms in many degrees of merging is a broad topic. This section presents several examples, a rough-hewn chrestomathy, to give a sense of the cross-cultural ubiquity of the phenomenon of the Other, and to illustrate the variety of connections between self and Other in knowledge acquisition.

Michael Winkelman develops the idea of the complexity of "a variety of selves" in his cross-cultural study of shamanism:

> Shamanism developed as a tradition for constructing, manipulating, and using a variety of selves for psychological and social integration. Although the self has seemed a relatively unproblematic concept to many, the nature of personal identity is much more complex when examined in a cross-cultural context, particularly in the context of shamanism, possession, and the mythological systems within which they are interpreted. (Winkelman 2000)

Winkelman gives a description of shamanic methods as the management of multiple selves, interpreting this phenomenon as "a manifestation of the plural symbolic capabilities of the creature," implying a mental or intrapsychic origin of the phenomena of "the felt presence, the sense of self in the unknown other."

Interpreting the phenomena of multiple selves as essentially self-generated is to come down on one side of the question of the ontological status of entities, a question that arises for the psychonaut who is not embedded in a cultural tradition such as shamanism, in which these phenomena are routinely experienced and interpreted as originating "outside" the individual. From the perspective of the shaman and his or her culture, "animism" is an experience, not a concept. For the DIY-oriented psychonaut, the question is wide open, and the refrain is repeated, as for Butch Cassidy and the Sundance Kid: *Who are those guys, anyway?* And are they real? Are they part of myself, or independent entities?

Terence McKenna straddles the dichotomy of real and not-real when the numinous hyperreal contact experience of seeing a flying saucer materialize in the sky over La Chorrera contained its own tag marking it "fake."

> The siren sound was rapidly gaining pitch, and in fact, everything seemed to be speeding up. The moving cloud was definitely growing larger rapidly, moving straight toward the place where I was. I felt my legs turn to water and sat down, shaking terribly. . . . Was it a hallucination? Against my own testimony can be put my admitted lack of sleep and our involvement with psychedelic plants. Yet curiously this last point can be interpreted in my favor. I am familiar through direct experience with every known class of hallucinogen. What I saw that morning did not fall into any of the categories of hallucinated imagery I am familiar with. Yet also against my testimony is the inevitable incongruous detail that seems to render the whole incident absurd. It is that as the saucer passed overhead, I saw it clearly enough to judge that it was identical with the UFO, with three half-spheres on its underside, that appears in an infamous photo by George Adamski widely assumed to be a hoax. . . . My stereotyped, but already debunked, notion of a UFO suddenly appears in the sky. By appearing in a form that casts doubt on itself, it achieves a more complete cognitive dissonance than if its seeming alienness were completely convincing. (T. McKenna 1993)

This open, ontological ambiguity regarding entities is presented in a different fashion in the case of Yaminahua shamanism, as reported by Graham Townsley. In the reality of *yoshi,* the spirits that animate all things in the world including humans, a clear operational primacy exists:

> Shamanic knowledge is, above all, knowledge of these entities, which are also the sources of all the powers that shamanism claims for itself. (Townsley 2001)

The Yaminahua model of the human being embodies *yoshi* at its core:

> In their notion of the person, the Yaminahua have a simple tripartite scheme: a body; a social, human self associated with reason and language;

> and an animate, perceiving self which is neither social nor human, mingling easily with the nonhuman *yoshi* who are beings of the same type. It can be seen, then, how the Yaminahua have no notion of anything that would approach our idea of "mind" as an inner storehouse of meanings, thought, and experience quite separate from the world. All that is "mental" is the property of entities which, although closely related to particular bodies, are not permanently attached to them. It is through the relationship between these two entities that the whole area of Yaminahua thought about the sameness and difference between the human and non-human develops. And as should be clear by now, it is through the idea of *yoshi* that the fundamental sameness of the human and the non-human takes shape, creating the space for the animal transformations of the human and the attribution of mental and human characteristics to all aspects of nature. (Townsley 2001)

This is (to us) a radical reworking of conscious experience—not as the usual (private) mind-body split but much more like a heavily populated version of Huxley's Mind At Large. These transformational ambiguities are enacted in the Yaminahua shaman's use of secret and highly metaphorical language expressed in song, *Tsai yoshtoyoshto* or "twisted language," an indirect way of approaching an ambiguous subject:

> With my *koshuiti* I want to see—singing I carefully examine things—twisted language brings me close but not too close—with normal words I would crash into things—with twisted ones I circle around them—I can see them clearly. (Townsley 2001)

In the communication of the unspeakable through metaphoric language that only the shaman can understand, the visionary experience is brought into greater clarity.

London psychonaut, Gaia devotee, author, filmmaker, and musician Simon G. Powell comes down on the far side of the "internal/external" dichotomy invoked by the phenomenon of the Other. His report of a visit to the Royal Botanical Gardens at Kew to do "some perceptual fieldwork" was mentioned in Chapter 2. His thoughts on the nature of the Other follow. We are entering the discussion of the plant teachers; in this case the plant teacher psilocybin opens the gate to a teaching from other plants.

> Suffice it to say that I was under the uncanny impression that some communication of information occurred between myself and the tropical plant life. It was as if the dense green slowly moving plant network around me was a place where occult aspects of the Gaian system "flowed" strongly, a good place to "tune in" to the Ultimate Organism. The informational communication definitely stemmed from outside my ego, in that I encountered streams of revelatory thought. As ever, I cannot possibly infer that this phenomenon was a production of my unconscious, for I cannot believe that such diverse, creative, and intelligible information can arise from a personal unconscious unless of course the unconscious is itself part of some intelligent presence connected with Gaia. That a vivid communication of information can flood the psilocybinetic brain is the goal of the neo-shamanic enterprise, for it rests upon this experience of contacting the Other, an organized intelligence of some kind that is not "us". If for the sake of argument, we still maintain that the Other is identifiable with the unconscious, then entheogens demonstrate that the unconscious is not confined to the individual. It is rather the case that the unconscious (if we call it that) must transcend the dimension of the personal psyche. (Powell 2009)

Powell concludes that the Other is truly *other,* transpersonal; he knows in the psychedelic realm that this is truly an Other by reference to how he knows, in his ordinary life, that he experiences others.

Terence McKenna, who has entertained many hypotheses of the identity of the Other, holds the standard of being able to identify, in the content of the experience, what clearly could not be "his idea." Further interpretations emerged from the Trialogues among Ralph Abraham, Rupert Sheldrake, and Terence McKenna. Here, McKenna summarizes their discussion of "discarnate entities."

> The human mind is haunted both by the many presences sensed within the self and by a confused sense of self. Wherever we turn in the world of nature and the psyche, we encounter life, animation, and a willingness to communicate that confounds the fragile pyramid of boundary consciousness and human values that have emerged over historical time through the suppression of our intuitions. I've taken the position that these entities we encounter are nonphysical and somehow autonomous. (T. McKenna, Sheldrake, Abraham 2001)

Marcelo Mercante's 2006 dissertation on the Barquinha religion, the smallest of the Brazilian syncretic ayahuasca churches that use the Daime (ayahuasca) as a sacrament, includes many accounts of *miração,* the visions brought to practitioners, and reveals the complex system of relations with another taxonomy of spirits that blend spiritual identities from three traditions:

> It is important to mention one more thing concerning the different qualities of spiritual beings working through mediumship at the Center. They can be divided into several spiritual currents. The first is the Christian current, where belongs the Missionários (bishops, friars, priests). The second is the African current, where the Orixás are the main representatives. In fact, I was told by different spiritual guides that the Orixás themselves do not incorporate but send their knights to the mediums. The third current is of Nature Beings, the Amerindian current, where we find the Encantos (fish, mermaids, botos, alligators, snakes, eagles, fairies, etc., all receiving the titles of prince, princess, king, or queen). There are as well two intermediary currents. Between the Christian and the African currents, we have the Pretos-velhos and Pretas-velhas, and between the African and the Amerindian currents we have the Caboclos. In fact, the Pretos-velhos and Caboclos can migrate throughout all those currents. (Mercante 2006)

Mercante points out that everyone at the Barquinha is potentially a medium, though some incorporate the spirits and others do not. The transactions with the spirits are not limited to the actions of a priest or shaman but are democratically distributed among the congregation. And the sacramental Daime, the plant teacher, is at the heart of the Barquinha:

> There is no teacher in the Barquinha other than Daime itself. As the light enlightening every consciousness, as the main element to contact God, as the main tool for self- knowledge and self-development, and, above all, as the light of God itself, the Daime cannot be completely explained. (Mercante 2006)

Ego Dissolution

The experience of ego-loss, ego-death, or ego-dissolution, the disruption or disappearance of the taken-for-granted sense of self (with a small "s"), can be terrifying, blissful, or some of each in the psychedelic state. Ego-disruption, a frequent feature of the psychedelic sphere across a spectrum of substances, can be a catalyst for life-changing experience. It can be associated with the feeling that one is dying. And it is often a preliminary, if not a prerequisite, step to the encounter with the Other, in various forms.[2] An Erowid report from "JT" tells the story of a journey through both extremes:

> It seemed an increasing amount of "J" was being replaced by this random stream of human consciousness. The process—which I felt then was divine, yet cruel and terrifying now—seemed to be attempting to dissolve me. I called to my friend, I tried to explain, but it was difficult to speak and to concentrate. There were quite a few moments when I was so absorbed in fighting the dissolution that I remained silent and still for what seemed like long periods of time. As the dissolution continued, I felt as though my body was becoming possessed by random personalities that flowed in from the stream of core human consciousness. I remember looking at my friend with the consciousness of others, touching him as though he was some remarkable alien thing. The urging toward dissolution became so intense that I was sure that "I" would not return from the trip. I was terrified—I didn't want to die. I thought I was literally losing my mind, and losing it permanently. I managed to express some of this to my friend; he held me while I moaned and cried in the grips of what I was sure was death and madness. Everything around me seemed utterly alien; once, when my friend tried to talk to me, I felt I had lost the ability to understand language. My friend was eventually able to get through to me, to talk me back to a state of semi-sanity. It took a tremendous amount of will on my part to cling to his words and make sense of them and, as I did so, I felt I was the whole of the universe clawing its way out of darkness and madness toward a divine radiance and sense of health and salvation. This continued for some time; it was utterly exhausting, and I didn't know how long I would be able to bear it. The feeling of dissolution had taken on a physical character—a searing iciness seemed to be taking my body over. My friend continued to reassure me that I'd be okay. Eventually, I began to feel like it. I had made it "to the light," it seemed, and felt a peace return and saturate my being. Concentrating on the light, I was able to manifest it in greater and greater degrees. It seemed I had turned my soul—which was also the soul of the universe—away from drowning in a river of fragments of human consciousness toward something that I could only call the genuinely Divine.

> The ego-dissolution continued now, but peacefully. Whatever parts of me left were replaced by that Divinity. Visions of joyously dissolving into the sun and the sky accompanied the experience and there was an unutterable feeling of the infinite and the sacred. I encountered the stream of human consciousness again, but this time I looked on it with what I felt to be the love of God. It was beautiful, touching, precious beyond all description. It had been nearly twelve hours since I'd dosed, and the effects were subsiding. I focused on reshaping my own self/ego in that divine image. (JT 2009)

Aldous Huxley, in his pre-mescaline epilogue to *The Devils of Loudun,* a passage primarily negative on drugs and their possibilities, framed the conscious/unconscious dichotomy as a blend of psychological theory and the perennial philosophy:

> So long as we are confined within our insulated selfhood, we remain unaware of the various not-selves with which we are associated—the organic not-self, the subconscious not-self, the collective not-self of the psychic medium in which all our thinking and feeling have their existence, and the immanent and transcendent not-self of the Spirit. (Huxley 2009)

The description of ego loss in *The Psychedelic Experience,* Leary, Alpert, and Metzner's 1964 trip manual based on *The Tibetan Book of the Dead,* is presented with clinical precision. The authors were still close to their academic ties at Harvard; the language is in the objective academic style of three psychologists. Symptoms of the onset of ego-loss are listed:

> 1. Bodily pressure, which the Tibetans call earth-sinking-into-water;
> 2. Clammy coldness, followed by feverish heat, which the Tibetans call water-sinking-into-fire;
> 3. Body disintegrating or blown to atoms, called fire-sinking-into-air;
> 4. Pressure on head and ears, which Americans call rocket-launching-into-space;
> 5. Tingling in extremities;
> 6. Feelings of body melting or flowing as if wax;
> 7. Nausea;
> 8. Trembling or shaking, beginning in pelvic regions and spreading up torso.

> These physical reactions should be recognized as signs heralding transcendence. Avoid treating them as symptoms of illness, accept them, merge with them, enjoy them.

Leary, Alpert, and Metzner, by mapping the psychedelic experience to their understanding of *The Tibetan Book of the Dead,* are trying to program the psychonaut directly through the "death" experience of ego-loss into enlightenment. "If the subject fails to recognize the rushing flow of First Bardo phenomena, liberation from the ego is lost." The "rushing flow" is identified with the Kundalini serpent energy rising through the spine.

Ben, in a post on the 'Shroomery, describes ego-death less cosmically, more practically:

> Ego death is the absence of who you have built yourself to be. It is the splitting of the mind when it first begins to happen, and the ability to truly LOOK at who you normally are, without rationalizing your flaws which you might normally do. It can be one of the most beautiful experiences in your life, but even more, if understood and dealt with properly, it can be more than just a single experience, but a way of life. But furthermore, it will draw out extreme hurt and pain because you will have uncovered a mask that the "real you" normally wears, and is so comfortable in wearing. It strips away your security of who you are, and it will be very clear to you that there are some serious issues with who you are that need to be dealt with. It is the feeling that you are speaking with your own mind, or watching the person you usually are on a movie screen, and a person with the opinion of only wanting the best in this world sits watching. (Ben 2001)

A guideline emerges: the looser one's grip on personal identity, a.k.a. "the ego," the easier it is for contact with the Other, the transpersonal, to manifest. My own experiences of ego-loss have been many and varied. My stance toward my baseline sense of identity, "Diana," evolved with experience, to the point where setting "Diana" aside is a relatively gentle process, like taking my clothes off to turn in at night. I think of "ego dissolution" as a navigational skill rather than a spiritual or psychological accomplishment. But along the way to this relaxed attitude was a series of dramas involving a metamorphosis of personality, developing episodically over a series of psychedelic sessions.

> Rising rising the given and the taken—the gift of self—the sacrifice—don't forget this—not possible in baseline—no—abide the changes—different being now—still—and deep—hermit stillness as hand gripped lightly—what is let go is "Diana" in any modes—enter the zone of the dragon (session report 03.08.09, 1 g *Stropharia cubensis*)

A different experience of the transformation of self occurred in 2002 and has happened many times since. I call the experience *slip-sliding,* meaning the sense of sliding very quickly in and out of a series of personalities. *Slip-sliding* for me is a primarily LSD experience, though I have sensed it less vividly and for a shorter duration with psilocybin at relatively low doses (1–3 g dried *Stropharia cubensis*).

> they are all and only human they are dancing the dance shifting registers now—can't describe where am I—hurtling at lightning speed through cultures, people, bodies everywhere the fabric of humanity (session report 02.02.09, 150 micrograms LSD, Xania, Greece)

The experience continued for several hours, through thousands of human identities. The lesson was delivered in the take-no-prisoners psychoanalytical laser-beam style that LSD can assume. The point: to experience, over and over, what it was like to fully "be" someone completely different, and from that drill to realize that "I" was no better, and no worse, and certainly had no special right to the ego's constant game of *sotto voce* comparisons with other persons. The recognition that I was playing the comparison game came sharply and repetitively into view, as each thought implying "I'm better than that person because . . ." arose, to be met with another flood of human viewpoints. It was not ego-death *per se* (more of an ego-reduction operation), but it certainly got me to loosen my grip.

Dave Boothroyd describes French philosopher Michel Foucault's acid trip at Zabriskie Point:

> The power of LSD to "depersonalize" the subject and to induce a state in which the coherence and stability of individual identity are shaken is well known. . . . Whilst Foucault, up to this point, may have established the basis for *understanding* the possibility of a subject otherwise than it is, such thinking cannot "think" the processes of *becoming otherwise*. Actually, taking LSD is an experimental leap into an abyss of "self-destruction" and an actualization of becoming-otherwise. (Boothroyd 2006)

According to biographer David Macey, Foucault called that acid trip "the greatest experience of my life" (Macey 1995).

If the self as understood by oneself at baseline is missing in action, or experiencing a plenitude of selves, then the authorship of my session reports must be questioned. At all mind-states, the questions arise: Who writes? Who reads? Who understands? What, for that matter, is a *who*?

> and when the identity dissolves then the Others appear those more permeable a creature void of form (session report 07.03.19, cannabis)

The Other As Alien

> *"—the most extraordinary thing about the DMT experience is that you see entities. You encounter beings whom I've described as self-transforming machine elves. They are denizens of this other dimension. They are trying to teach something. Well, if I'm not completely mad, then it's big news. Straight people—skeptical people—if given DMT will be conveyed to what is essentially the hall of the Mountain King with gnome revelry in progress. We're not prepared for this. We expect everything to fall into the rational maps that science has given us, and science doesn't describe a hyperdimensional universe teeming with alien intelligences that can be contacted within a moment if you have recourse to a certain chemical compound."*
>
> —Terence McKenna, 1991

The Other has appeared in the guise of the extraterrestrial in the reports of contemporary psychonauts, with Terence McKenna as a leading reporter. The characterization of the Other as "alien" remained an open question for him:

> The word "Self" is as great a mystery as the word "Other." It's just a polarity between two mysteries and then the thin, thin myths that are spun to hold you suspended there without freaking out. The myths of science and religion and shamanism all represent a polarity between the mystery of the Self and the mystery of the Other. . . . As our imagination has striven outward to attempt to encompass the possibility of the intelligent Other somewhere in the starry galaxy, so has the Other, observing this, revealed itself to be among us, when we are in the psilocybin trance, as an aspect of ourselves. In the phenomenon of *Stropharia cubensis,* we are confronted

> with an intelligent and seemingly alien life-form, not as we commonly imagine it, but an intelligent alien life nevertheless. (T. McKenna 1993b)

The visionary encounter with the Other—whether catalyzed by psychedelic substances or "on the natch"—tends to clothe the Other in symbolic forms. For the contemporary psychonaut, woven into the Web and mainlining Google for an instantaneous fix-on-demand from the world's symbolic systems, the figures with which the Other may present itself exhibit great variety. Further, the same visionary presentation—in this case, the Other as alien—can be interpreted in a variety of ways back at baseline. The Other as alien can be seen as an emerging global mythologem woven together with our rapid technological development as a species, especially in the last hundred years.

Jung was fascinated with the reported UFO phenomena as early as 1946; his interpretation is archetypal, though he leaves the door open to the interpretation of real hardware in the skies. He also notes that the "visionary rumours" of circular lights in the skies go back in history; he cites two sightings, recorded in words and woodcuts, known as the Basel Broadsheet of 1566, and the Nuremberg broadsheet of 1561. Jung offers a psychological interpretation of the circular formations as mandala-like symbols of the Self, a striving for wholeness rising from the unconscious into consciousness, an essentially spiritual impulse from our deepest sources.

> If we try to define the psychological structure of the religious experience which saves, heals, and makes whole, the simplest formula we can find would seem to be the following: in religious experience man comes face to face with a psychically overwhelming Other. (Jung 1978)

McKenna hovers between interpretations as he follows the *what-if* logic of the tryptamine encounter with extraterrestrials as "actual contact" in his essay "Alien Love." *What-if* this phenomenon were real? Again, the appeal is to the rules of self-evidence:

> They are more real than real, and once you get that under your belt and let it rattle around in your mind, then the compass of your life begins to spin and you realize that *you are not looking in on the Other; the Other is looking in on you.* This is a tremendous challenge to the intellectual

> structures that have carried us so far during the last thousand years. . . . These are just historical contexts that can be transcended only by the acquisition of gnosis, knowledge that is experienced as self-evidently true. (T. McKenna 1991) [emphasis mine]

McKenna argues that

> Science, by clarifying the non-uniqueness of biology and giving us an idea of what's going on in the galaxy and beyond, has validated the notion that life is ubiquitous and that intelligence is a property that accompanies life and is probably common in the universe. This legitimates fantasy about the existence of extraterrestrial intelligence. In the last half of the twentieth century, the mythological outlines of what the alien must be are being cast. (T. McKenna 1991)

We have seen science fiction, embodying a portion of the texts of the emerging mythologem, migrate from pulp fiction status to books and literary prizes, radio, then movies and television. The mass audience has increased as sci fi's production values have soared; technological advances in 3D modeling and motion-capture animation make possible the visualization of increasingly alien worlds. The iMAX 3D blockbuster movie *Avatar,* reportedly the most expensive movie ever made, gives us one of our most fully realized adult-human-meets-alien love stories. More accurately, it is a Na'vi-meets-alien (one of us) love story. My first movie of alien love was Spielberg's *E.T.,* the childhood innocence of love between E.T. and human children. *Avatar* follows close on the heels of *Battlestar Galactica*, where human-alien-as-robot-clone love is explored in a variety of intense relationships. And there's an important twist: the aliens in *Battlestar Galactica* are the direct products of human creation come back to haunt us: first, in rebellion, then in erotic and religious experiments which in some cases become genetic melding. In *Avatar*, we humans have created not only a working meat body that duplicates the alien Na'vi's biology, melding the human in, but the technology to download a human consciousness into that body. The "real" meat body is parked in what could be mistaken for an upgrade on John Lilly's Samadhi (sensory attenuation) tank. In *Avatar,* the humans are the evil aliens, as one's viewpoint shifts with Jake Sully's to a Na'vi viewpoint.

Terence McKenna's views on alien love bring the erotic dimension of the encounter with the alien Other to the fore:

> What the developing archetype of the extraterrestrial "Other" means, and the source of our fascination with it, is that, collectively, for the first time we are beginning to yearn . . . what is driving religious feeling is a wish for contact—a relationship to the Other. (T. McKenna 1991)

To alien abduction narratives, we must add alien seduction as an equally powerful construction. Jeremy Narby captures this intimate aspect of ayahuasca as lover and conscience in his account in *The Psychotropic Mind: The World According to Ayahuasca, Iboga, and Shamanism:*

> We see that this plant is intelligent. When it enters into contact with you, there are two of you. Sometimes she gives me a very unsexy spanking over a trifle, but she loves me and I love her. (Narby, Kounen, Ravelec 2008)

From the Vaults of Erowid, a 3-gram psilocybin experience report is somewhat similar in content to alien abduction (non-drug) experiences, but of a different tone. Abduction scenarios are often full of terror, paralysis, and the feeling that the intent of the aliens is not benign. But the theme of alien operations on the human body is similar in this Erowid report by Plasmamorphing:

> As I was sitting comfortably on the bed, I had noticed that besides my two friends and I, we weren't alone. I noticed three bodies or silhouettes doing something to me, or my head. Now let me explain in detail how these beings came across. I have had many psychedelic experiences of contacting alien beings from other dimensions but all of the beings I have encountered before had a physicality to them. That they were made of physical bodies. These three beings, however, didn't have a physical body. Instead, they were made of a fluid-like ethereal shadow that diffused in and out of sight within the holographic nature of empty space. . . . These things were definitely separate from my imagination. They moved at their own will and possessed knowledge that is way ahead of our own. I am also certain that I am not the only person that has experienced these kinds of aliens as their attention was very much focused on the human agenda. But what were they doing to my brain? (Plasmamorphing 2008)

In a 10-mg 4-HO-MiPT trip report on Erowid from green rapture, the alien is experienced as a sonic entity:

> Instead of anything I expected, I was being mentally, sonically probed by spirits/aliens/ancestors. I was at their mercy, being completely consumed by their awesome power and intellect. They moved through my mind as beings of pure sound and awareness, pushing at every wall and piece of resistance, creating more and pathways through it. My mind was rushing outwards, expanding into the cosmos. In a space of mostly pure white light, I coiled and stretched as these beings will. I did not resist outside of my utter shock as to the intensity of the experience and the beings' unbelievable intellect. At some point I thought about turning off the cd to disconnect from the drumming interface of contact ... but I felt pretty certain that if I were to suddenly be without guidance in this state I would probably freak out immediately. I was trapped in this meeting until they let it go. This was ok though, I have been hoping for a connection like this for a long time. (rapture 2009)

The intimacy of the relationship with the Other can be deeply personal and emotionally affecting.

> In ecstasy the eyes are glazed with light (session report 07.04.09, MDMA)

Notes, Chapter 4

1. Electron Spin Resonance.
2. The nn-DMT experience can be an exception, with the self remaining intact (even if in a condition of astonishment) while the world changes out. The 5-meo experience is another story entirely.

II: MAPS AND MODELS

CHAPTER 5
Reality Reviewed

> *"In both art and science now, the matter of consciousness is high on the agenda. Science is trying hard to explain consciousness, with distinctly limited success. It seems to pose the most intractable of problems. For the artist, consciousness is more to be explored than to be explained, more to be transformed than understood, more to be reframed than reported."*
>
> —Roy Ascott, 2003

Psychonauts, at some point, due to the nature of their experiences, become philosophers by default. I came out of my second DMT adventure spluttering, "what-the-fuck." Over and over. Every thought that arose in response to the experience was immediately translated into a resounding "what-the-fuck." Finally the sentence became "It's the what-the-fuck drug." I was expressing the inexpressible content of a head-on collision with the Unspeakable in the only words I could find in the proper emotional register: befuddlement, bewilderment, and the powerful sense that the whole thing was so improbable that to "tell it like it is" would be to sound absurd. Really absurd. This was accompanied by a lot of helpless laughter and head-shaking, as I was dumped out of darshan[1] with the Unspeakable in its most alien manifestation ever. As words returned, the problem deepened. How could I say that an experience I just had was both patently absurd and more real than real, at the same time? How could this be so *real,* and at the same time have its reality so in question, so laughable, when it so departs from the consensus of what is real and what is not back at baseline? The experience threw a sparkly spanner in the cognitive machinery, forcing me to go back to basic assumptions in my thought processes. Philosophy begins with these basic questions of knowing and being. In classical Western philosophy, epistemology is the study of knowing, and ontology is the study of being. *How could I say that an experience I just had was both patently absurd, and more real than real, at the same time?*

The Ontological Dilemma

The ontological status of psychedelic experience—the reality question—pervades psychonautic experience and hence psychedelic research. Was that *real*? What is reality? What, "really," is a hallucination? What can we learn from profoundly altered perception of both the world around us and of the mind manifesting in extremely novel ways? Is reality a simple given, or are we complicit in its construction? As Robert Anton Wilson quipped, "Reality is the line where rival gangs of shamans fought to a standstill."

To argue about what reality is or isn't, when reality is the standard by which we decide what is and what isn't, is a slippery proposition, as circular and self-referential as consciousness attempting to study itself. And who is the authority on what is real? I submit that authority in the psychedelic sphere does not depend on advanced degrees or professional standing, though these are not in short supply among psychonauts. Rather their authority comes from evidence of practice, especially self-reflective practice, combined with rhetorical skill. Thus, the authority of John Lilly's many books comes not only from his medical degree, or from the fact that he received funding for his early LSD research from government agencies. He persuades with passion when he continues his research past the illegalization boundaries. His phenomenological integrity persuades when he is relating not only research results, but his dangerous mistakes and, from a baseline viewpoint, outlandish alien contacts and other outlier phenomena. Of course, the fact that Dr. Lilly continued his psychonautic practice after illegalization, and fell into a lengthy and dangerous ketamine addiction, destroyed his "authority" in the eyes of authorized research. Lilly persuades (or not) because another psychonaut can read his material and know—because of the authority of his or her own self-evidential knowledge—that Lilly is telling it like it is—or is not—*for that reader.* This does not mean that a report from the psychedelic sphere must totally match my own in every detail to be of use, or that I need to recognize my own experience in a category of types of experience. My report of living in San Francisco would no doubt differ in many details from the reports of other residents, but we would most likely recognize that we are talking about the same place. This process has also been called "inter-subjective validation."

For my own purposes, I differentiate between the armchair traveler, who writes about the territory based solely on the reports of others, never having made the trip him- or herself; the tourist, who goes once or twice and is found in a state of "Oh Wow" and declaring authority (like a person who has spent a week in Paris, certain they know the city intimately); commuters, who have traveled many times, usually with some purpose in mind; and expatriates, who have relinquished citizenship in the default world and lose their basis and means of comparison, as Lilly suggests. Permanent or near-permanent residency has its risks, as can be seen in Marcia Moore's experience with ketamine, ending in death (M. Moore and H. Alltounian 1978). Lilly himself became for a period a resident of the ketamine world, including a close call of near-drowning.

Douglas Turnbull's characterization of early map-making comes into play. Two explorers to the same area compare notes, logs, and sketches, out of which an assemblage and someday maps can be made. Truth is a negotiated, persuaded and/or recognized truth. Turnbull argues that "scientific knowledge can be seen as the contingent assemblage of local knowledge" (Turnbull 2000).

> Does the delusion of one visionary ecstatic validate the delusion of another? How many deluded, or illuminated ecstatics does it take to make a reality? PKD proved that it only takes one. But two is better. (T. McKenna in Sutin 1991)

I suggest Turnbull's map-making as a starting place toward psychonautic (personal, first-person, individual) psychedelic knowledge, building a collection of what Turnbull terms "local knowledges." These localities can be as particular as a single individual's three-paragraph trip report posted to Erowid, or as extensive as John Lilly's or Timothy Leary's lifework. A locality can be represented by the collective practices and knowledge of a culture, such as the Mazatec mushroom culture, the Peyote Way, or an ayahuasca culture such as the Santo Daime, União do Vegetal, and Barquinha churches, or Shipibo shamanism. Each locus of knowledge, from the individual to the group, produces its own accounts of experience in the psychedelic sphere, its own descriptions of the landscapes, its own sense of the intentionality of the voyage from baseline outward/inward and the return to ordinary reality. From these experiences descriptions are written, interpretations arise, songs, paintings, software, and dances emanate; rituals are enacted. A body of knowledge collects. Maps can be envisioned, landmark by negotiated landmark.

> waking up in the total alien dreamworld—seeing what one has comfortably called reality and all its rules cheerfully dismantled by a bunch of matter of fact prankster world hackers [gee we thought you'd enjoy it] (session report 01.07.14, 2 g dried *Stropharia cubensis*)

> what reality are you in when the munchkins show you what is clearly the machinery of reality? enfolding unfolding into and out of itself (session report 09.12.31, 4 g dried amazonas)

William James—Potential Forms of Consciousness

Programming *set* for the psychonaut can determine the reality of the particular exploration. William James's iconic passage about his nitrous oxide experiences, often quoted as an epigraph beginning an article on some psychedelic matter (an indirect example of inter-subjective validation), is rhetorically powerful. It represents a founding text on the topic of psychonautics, and a text that has programmed the *set* of many psychedelic researchers, both authorized and unauthorized, toward their topic on the one hand, and toward their own trips, which are rhetorically sensitive to texts. The passage is quoted at length and then analyzed rhetorically.

> Nitrous oxide and ether, especially nitrous oxide, when sufficiently diluted with air, stimulate the mystical consciousness in an extraordinary degree. Depth beyond depth of truth seems revealed to the inhaler. This truth fades out, however, or escapes, at the moment of coming to; and if any words remain over in which it seemed to clothe itself, they prove to be the veriest nonsense. Nevertheless, the sense of a profound meaning having been there persists; and I know more than one person who is persuaded that in the nitrous oxide trance we have a genuine metaphysical revelation.[2]
>
> Some years ago I myself made some observations on this aspect of nitrous oxide intoxication, and reported them in print. One conclusion was forced upon my mind at that time, and my impression of its truth has ever since remained unshaken. It is that our normal waking con-

> sciousness, rational consciousness as we call it, is but one special type of consciousness, whilst all about it, parted from it by the filmiest of screens, there lie potential forms of consciousness entirely different. We may go through life without suspecting their existence; but apply the requisite stimulus, and at a touch they are there in all their completeness, definite types of mentality which probably somewhere have their field of application and adaptation. No account of the universe in its totality can be final which leaves these other forms of consciousness quite disregarded. How to regard them is the question—for they are so discontinuous with ordinary consciousness. Yet they may determine attitudes though they cannot furnish formulas, and open a region though they fail to give a map. At any rate, they forbid a premature closing of our accounts with reality.
>
> Looking back on my own experiences, they all converge towards a kind of insight to which I cannot help ascribing some metaphysical significance. The keynote of it is invariably a reconciliation. It is as if the opposites of the world, whose contradictoriness and conflict make all our difficulties and troubles, were melted into unity. (James 1902)

In the first paragraph, James identifies his personal experience with these substances as the source of his knowledge about them. He speaks with the authority of one who has been there, giving a dose protocol tip: *especially nitrous oxide, when sufficiently diluted with air*. He states the hallmark of ineffability (a standard that he applies to mystical experiences as a whole)—a sense of profound meaning experienced to which language is insufficient, even ridiculous. The rest of the long passage illustrates the apophatic device of saying that what you have just asserted cannot be articulated: the depths of meaning in the psychedelic experience.

The second paragraph persuades on many levels. The apodictic nature of the experience is asserted: *One conclusion was forced upon my mind at that time, and my impression of its truth has ever since remained unshaken.* The certainty produced by the experience is persistent despite its ineffability. That certainty has the effect of holding open, like a foot in a cosmological door, the possibility of uncertainty, the appropriateness of uncertainty, in fact, in the face of the field of unknowing opened by the experiences: *they may determine attitudes though they cannot furnish formulas, and open a region though they fail to give a map. At any rate, they forbid a premature closing of our accounts with reality.*

A hundred years later, we live in a historical moment where consciousness itself is not part of the "Everything" covered by the physicist's "Theory of Everything," a denial of inner worlds that in James's time was already in progress. James's language is strong: *forced, forbid, unshaken.* The novelty of the experience, *How to regard them is the question—for they are so discontinuous with ordinary consciousness,* previews later models of discrete states of consciousness. The word "alien" is used by many to describe both the bizarre phenomena encountered and the epistemological rupture that demands reframing not only of consciousness but of "life, the universe, and everything." The heart of the experience is named: *The keynote of it is invariably a reconciliation. It is as if the opposites of the world, whose contradictoriness and conflict make all our difficulties and troubles, were melted into unity.* This is the *coniunctio oppositorum* of alchemy, the union of opposites. It is associated with the lapis or philosopher's stone, which, according to Jung, is both the beginning and goal of the alchemical process (Jung 1953). James's passage persuades at a pervasively seductive level—inviting the reader into the psychedelic experience. *The filmiest of screens* suggests Salome's dance of the seven veils and resonates with the earlier reference of clothing (inadequately) the presumably naked truth, depth upon depth. The language of *stimulus* and *touch* reinforces this seduction. The passage tunes the seduction from *the filmiest of screens* to *melted into unity*, the *hierosgamos* or sacred marriage. The seduction promises no less than the dissolution of all our difficulties and troubles. The self-experiment beckons.

Is it a fundamental right of a conscious being to say—*this is what is real for me, at this moment in time, subject to future revision?* I expose my position as a cognitive libertarian by posing these questions. The final determination of what is real and what is myth for the individual psychonaut is a matter of personal experience, epistemological preference, and relative commitment to the proprieties of consensus reality.

The Epistemological Dichotomy: Subjective and Objective

In this section I point to some of the conceptual issues that make the study of the psychedelic experience challenging from a scientific perspective. A central issue is the matter of the subjective and the objective, as essential categories in science, the dominant episteme at the beginning of the psychedelic age. The repression of the subjective in the scientific episteme (Varela and Shear 1999; Wallace 2000) and the controversial status of the self itself in consciousness studies highlight an epistemological clash. Media theorist David Porush characterizes this dialectic:

> As the result of its rationalist inheritance and its persistent objectification of the observer, science relies on a discourse that has had inordinate difficulty enfolding or describing its own acts of knowing. (Porush 1993)

The "hard problem," defined by philosopher of mind David Chalmers, is the problem of how to bring together objective or third-person data about brain and behavior with the subjective or first-person reports of conscious experience. This hard problem gets a whole lot harder when the second half of the correspondence, the subjective, labors under the handicap of erasure, invalidation, and reduction by the dominant episteme of science. As Pierre Vermersch states in Varela and Shear's edited collection, *The View from Within: First-Person Approaches to the Study of Consciousness,*

> As a result of my many years of exposure to the literature on introspection I sometimes get the impression of being overwhelmed by the negative implications of all the critical objections, to the point of almost forgetting the practical efficacy of introspection. Do we have to take the time to criticize the critics of introspection? (Vermersch in Varela and Shear 1999)

The scientific discourse on human reporting of internal events is generally framed grammatically as a matter of persons and points of view. We speak of first-person and third-person methods, a notion that can veil the fact that the reporting human has a choice of points of view from which to report. A more subtle question than "Which of these viewpoints is the most appropriate to the study of consciousness in altered states?" would be "How do I characterize the viewpoint from which this choice is determined?" Or better yet, "What is the meta-viewpoint that can slide from point-of-view to point-of-view in the flow of a narrative?" In other words, what viewpoint do I occupy in asking these particular questions? This is a question designed in part to disrupt the assumption within the field of consciousness studies that such a viewpoint must be chosen, from which certain methods will then be rendered appropriate.

Varela and Shear make a critical point:

> It is here that methodology appears as crucial: without a sustained examination we actually do not produce phenomenological descriptions that are rich and subtly interconnected enough in comparison to third-person accounts. The main question is: How do you actually do it? Is there evidence that it can be done? If so, with what results? (Varela and Shear 1999)

In answering "How do you actually do it?" the methods Varela and colleagues detail are threefold: the introspective approach, from scientific psychology; the phenomenological reduction from the Husserlian tradition; and the pragmatic approach of Buddhist and Vedic meditation practices. The phenomenological *epoché,* a concept adopted from Husserl, with roots in Aristotle and Descartes, posits the ability to bracket the phenomenon under inspection in consciousness from, essentially, the world, and all attendant beliefs and "naturalistic" attitudes.[3] It has been noted that Husserl never succeeded in teaching others the art of the phenomenological reduction. The practice, when described, presents as difficult an attainment as the development of a mature contemplative practice, Varela's third suggested method. Neurophenomenologist Charles Laughlin as well recommends a mature contemplative practice as a desirable prerequisite to the observation of consciousness. Both of these approaches, phenomenological and contemplative, have been investigated intellectually at great length. As ideas, they offer a needed counterbalance to the assertions of science that all forms of "looking within" are essentially useless, if not to the well-being of the individual, then to the acquisition of knowledge in the scientific sphere. As useful methods that must be practiced or even perfected before one begins a study of one's own consciousness, they come up short. This limit is not because their efficacy is in question. Simply, such a practice, at least in the case of meditation, takes years to bring to maturity. The question can be asked whether Varela et al., in pleading the case for first-person methods from the minority side of the aisle, are not in some sense overcompensating by offering such advanced and lengthy training for first-person perspectives. Training for the third-person objective method, after all, takes the practice of objectivity, the stability of the observing self, the uniformity of "selves" among multiple observers, and the art of observation itself for granted, requiring no particular training beyond the technical mastery of varied instrumentation.

Multi-state Models of Reality and Consciousness

In the following section, consciousness is modeled as existing in multiple mind-body states or levels. This model of consciousness as a series of levels or states is as ancient as Vedanta and Buddhist philosophies, and is found in medical and psychological models as well. While each of these philosophies, psychospiritual practices, and academic disciplines has its own taxonomy of what these levels consist of, and their own means of attaining, studying, and manipulating these levels, the model of consciousness (and reality) as multi-state and leveled is frequently employed.

In the late '70s, consciousness researcher Charles Tart developed a multi-state model of levels of consciousness and called for "state-specific sciences." Tart suggested that each state of consciousness presented a different reality, and therefore potentially different methods of study. Tom Roberts codified the multi-state model as a very useful general research question for psychedelic science: "How does/do (fill in variable to be studied) vary from mind-body state to mind-body state?" (Roberts 2006). The multi-state question arises within what Roberts calls the multi-state paradigm, derived from Tart's model of discrete altered states of consciousness (dASC) (Tart 1980). Roland Fischer's model of levels of consciousness on a perception-hallucination scale has been discussed in Chapter 2. Timothy Leary's concept of the "reality tunnel" introduces a constructivist view of reality as individually filtered by the totality of our linguistic and social conditioning, and hence multiple (Leary 1979; Leary

■ **Figure 57: Top of the Grand Stupa, Kathmandu. A stupa embodies multiple symbolic meanings, one of which is a depiction of multiple levels of reality.** HP Wikimedia commons.

2001). John Lilly gives numerical classifications to levels of consciousness mapped against Gurdjieff's vibrational levels and Buddhist meditational states that generate vastly different realities from the heavenly to the hellish. Charles Laughlin's description (in Chapter 1) of monophasic and multiphasic societies speaks to the same model of singular or multiple levels of consciousness. Laughlin further states:

> As noted earlier, many peoples around the planet conceive of their existence as being lived-out in a world of multiple realities. There are typically three domains of reality, each consisting of one or more discrete realities, which may be related vertically: upper world, normal world, lower world. Experiential access to these domains and constituent realities is generally via discrete phases of consciousness, either available to all or to those who specialize in attaining the requisite phase of consciousness. For example, some traditional Native American groups conceive of what we would call "normal waking consciousness" as that unfortunate phase during which the soul and body are glued together. In alternative phases, like dreaming, the soul is freed from the body so that it can fly and commune with other souls and spirits. What we Western theorists have failed to appreciate is the intimate relationship between attainment of experiences in alternative phases of consciousness and the multiple realities depicted in traditional cosmologies. (Laughlin 1990)

The following sections summarize a variety of multi-state models of reality and consciousness.

Roy Ascott and the Three VR's

Artist, educator, and media theorist Roy Ascott brings the discourse of psychoactive plants and shamanic experience into the domain of art, in his discussion of the three VR's. The first, Validated Reality, stands for "our daily experience" and is familiar to us all. To the psychonaut, it is "baseline reality," that reality to which the soul returns after its journey. It is the orthodox universe of causal "common sense," the way we are taught at school to view the world, a consensual reality established early in our lives by the constant repetition of its axioms. Virtual Reality describes the realm of immersive interactive art and digital technology. Vegetal Reality "can be understood in the context of technoetics, as the transformation of consciousness by plant technology" (Ascott 2001). In Roy Ascott's definition, technoetics is "a convergent field of practice that seeks to explore consciousness and connectivity through digital, telematic, chemical or spiritual means, embracing both interactive and psychoactive technologies, and the creative use of moistmedia." From a contemporary art and technology perspective, Ascott sees reality as variously mixed, augmented, simulated, layered, and virtualized (Ascott 2003).

The freedom with which these manipulations are carried out is captured by John Perry Barlow in a discussion of virtual reality technology:

> I think the effort to create convincing artificial realities will teach us the same humbling lesson about reality which artificial intelligence has taught us about intelligence [. . .] namely, that we don't know a damned thing about it. I've never been of the cut-and-dried school on your Reality Question. I have a feeling VR will further expose the conceit that "reality" is a fact. It will provide another reminder of the seamless continuity between the world outside and the world within, delivering another major hit to the old fraud of objectivity. "Real," as Kevin Kelly put it, "is going to be one of the most relative words we'll have." (Barlow 1993)

This intertwined social history of the technological move to virtualize reality and the varied uses of psychedelics by technologists is difficult to write for reasons R.U. Sirius sums up nicely in a 2006 article reviewing two books on the topic: John Markoff's *What the Dormouse Said: How the '60s Counterculture Shaped the Personal Computer* and Fred Turner's *From Counterculture to Cyberculture: Stewart Brand, the Whole Earth Network, and the Rise of Digital Utopianism.*

> The connection between the creators of the driving engine of the contemporary global economy, and the countercultural attitudes that were popular among young people during the 1960s and '70s was sort of a given within the cultural milieu we ("High Frontiers/Mondo 2000") found ourselves immersed in as the 1980s spilled into the '90s. Everybody was "experienced."... But these upcoming designers of the future were not prone towards lots of public hand-waving about their "sex, drugs, and question authority" roots. After all, most of them were seeking venture capital and they were selling their toys and tools to ordinary Reagan-Bush

era consumers. There was little or no percentage in trying to tell the public, "Oh, by the way. All this stuff? This is how the counterculture now plans to change the world." (Sirius 2006)

John Lilly's Reality Protocols

John Lilly's protocols tackle the multiple-reality problem from a methodological standpoint:

> In a scientific exploration of any of the inner realities, I follow the following metaprogrammatic steps:
>
> 1. Examine whatever one can of where the new spaces are, what the basic beliefs are to go there.
> 2. Take on the basic beliefs of that new area as if true.
> 3. Go into the area fully aware, in high energy, storing everything, no matter how neutral, how ecstatic, or how painful the experiences become.
> 4. Come back here, to our best of consensus realities, temporarily shedding those basic beliefs of the new area and taking on those of the investigator impartially dispassionately objectively examining the recorded experiences and data.
> 5. Test one's current models of this consensus reality.
> 6. Construct a model that includes this reality and this new one in a more inclusive succinct way. *No matter how painful such revisions of the models are, be sure they include both realities.* [emphasis mine]
> 7. Do not worship, revere, or be afraid of any person, group, space, or reality. An investigator, an explorer, has no room for such baggage. (Lilly 1977a)

When one is communicating with the Other in the psychedelic sphere, it pays to have protocols. Lilly's protocols are a sophisticated way of managing one's *set* to span multiple worlds, to approach the business of interpretation and model-making with a ruthless (one of Lilly's favorite words) intellectual honesty, maintaining fluidity regarding the taking up and laying aside of entire—if temporary—belief systems. These protocols spring directly from his primary assertion, "Within the province of the mind, *What I believe to be true is true or becomes true, within the limits to be found experientially and experimentally. These limits are further beliefs to be transcended.*"

In my own investigations, I have found this protocol difficult to maintain consistently. Creodes (in this sense, developed habits of thinking, feeling, and believing) run deep, and novelty takes more work in every sense (pun intended) to come to terms with. But the attempt to attend to what is normally invisible (because I take my basic assumptions about "reality" so much for granted) is a noetic practice I find deeply rewarding in the pursuit of knowledge in the psychedelic sphere. Lilly might have called this "the willing suspension of belief," a stance that brings his position closer to the phenomenological *epoché*. This perspective becomes easier to maintain when the occasional trip to other worlds becomes more of a steady commute. Lilly's protocol privileges neither the ordinary nor the non-ordinary state of consciousness, but attempts to include both in the construction of a new model of reality of multiple mind-states and multiple realities.

Terence McKenna and John Lilly both recommend never giving up one's skeptical stance. McKenna is also clear on the necessity of reporting the subjective content. When describing the structure-activity of a psychedelic substance, the language of biochemistry reveals none of the high strangeness of the experiences. Describing the content of a visionary state—the images, environments, narratives, novel space-time configurations, the pantheon of Others, languages, and information acquired in the experience—is often much less palatable to the scientific world view. My approach in the psychonautic practice is simply this: to take the phenomenological position of saying what was personally sensed and experienced as accurately as possible, not editing out information just because it strains credulity, invites social ridicule, or demands continual overhaul of my world view. This effort involves a keen awareness of the forms of unspeakability (detailed in Chapter 1) as they arise in practice.

Basarab Nicolescu and Transdisciplinarity

The ontological status of experience in the psychedelic sphere is called into question at every turn: was that perception (of the interconnectedness of all of nature, self included; of a sea of giant fluorescent violet snakes) *real*? If so, in what sense? "Reality" and "level of Reality" as Basarab Nicolescu defines them are useful for the discussion of reality in the psychedelic sphere.

Nicolescu is a Roumanian theoretical physicist and a scholar of the mystic Jacob Boehme (1991). His formulation of transdisciplinarity is an attempt to provide a theoretical framework from which to integrate knowledge from several levels of reality: quantum physics, classical physics, and mystical experience. It arose in the context of what Nicolescu calls a "disciplinary Big Bang," the "Babelization" and fragmentation of disciplines and their languages. Multidisciplinarity and interdisciplinarity are two responses to this fragmentation. Nicolescu defines multidisciplinarity as studying a research topic from the viewpoint of not one but several disciplines at the same time, with the findings from over the disciplinary boundaries as supplemental to the "home" discipline. Interdisciplinarity is defined as "the transfer of methods from one discipline to another" but with its goals still firmly within disciplinary research *per se.*

> Here the meaning we give to the word reality is pragmatic and ontological at the same time. By "Reality" (with a capital R) we intend first of all to designate that which resists our experiences, representations, descriptions, images, or mathematical formulations. (Nicolescu 2002)

Reality, for Nicolescu, is the central mystery encompassing all levels of Reality we have experienced and described. Capital-R Reality is equivalent to McKenna's capital-U Unspeakable—the central mystery, in Terence McKenna's words.

> The Godelian structure of Nature and knowledge guarantees the permanent presence of the unknown, the unexpected, and the unpredictable. . . . The opening of transdisciplinarity implies, by its very nature, the rejection of all dogma, all ideology, all closed systems of thought. This opening is the sign of the birth of a new type of thought turned not so much toward answers as questions. The Subject is himself the unfathomable question that assures the permanence of questioning. (Nicolescu 2002)

I take Nicolescu's idea of "opening" as a methodological pragmatic, bringing an acceptance of the unknown, the unexpected, and the unpredictable. Nicolescu describes three kinds of opening: the opening of one level of Reality toward another level of Reality; the opening of a new level of perception toward another level of perception; and "the opening toward the zone of absolute resistance, which links the Subject and the Object."

The concept of a level of reality is critical:

> By "level of reality," we intend to designate an ensemble of systems that are invariant under certain laws: for example, quantum entities are subordinate to quantum laws, which depart radically from the laws of the physical world. That is to say that two levels of Reality are different if, while passing from one to the other, there is a break in the laws and a break in fundamental concepts (such as, for example, causality). No one has succeeded in finding a mathematical formalism that permits the difficult passage from one world to another. (Nicolescu 2002)

Benny Shanon describes this difference in reality in his experience of observing a ritual cleansing gesture of passing incense over a madrinha's body during an ayahuasca ceremony:

> What I experienced was literally this—seeing the casting of a shield against evil powers. It all seemed to have a very serious and sombre allure, and manifestly, it was all invested with magic. If I were to define what made it all so mysterious I would say that it was the fact that on the one hand everything pertained to another reality, while at the very same time it was all real. Again, no hallucination as such was experienced—technically what I was seeing was real, and none the less it was all utterly non-ordinary, and enchanted. (Shanon 2002)

The world of magic and vision he describes operates by different laws—for instance, laws about the influence of another's intentions on one's well-being, and the efficacy of the ritual gestures. As Shanon points out, to an outsider to the ceremony, one not under the influence of ayahuasca vision, the incense cleansing is symbolic; to the participant, inside the ayahuasca reality, the action is literal, as are the possibilities it protects against. These laws are functional within their zone of reality. Roy Ascott calls this type of experience "double consciousness."

> By double consciousness, I mean the state of being that gives access, at one and the same time, to two distinctly different fields of experience. (Ascott 2003)

The psychedelic sphere, in this framework, is another level of reality, or multiple levels, operating with different laws. In this context of differing laws for different levels of reality, Nicolescu asserts that different logics apply to different levels of reality. In particular, he names "the Law of the Included Middle" as one of the pillars of transdisciplinarity (see Chapter 3). Applying this to the problematic of different levels of reality and consciousness in psychedelic experience, I have developed the idea of a rough division between what I call the "rules of evidence" at baseline reality, meaning the laws of logic and argument underlying the project of rationality and science, and the "rules of self-evidence," being that which is discovered to be self-evidently, at times apodictically, true in states of altered consciousness. Self-evidence is itself self-evident. It is in the dialogue between these two forms of logic that the integration of knowledge from multiple states takes place. Nicolescu describes the underlying unity of seemingly contradictory versions of Reality thus:

> The discontinuity that is manifested in the quantum world is also manifested in the structure of the levels of Reality. That does not prevent the two worlds from coexisting. The proof: our own existence. Our bodies contain simultaneously a macrophysical structure and a quantum structure. (Nicolescu 2002)

Further discontinuities in levels of reality are presumed in his understanding of Boehme's mystical reality. Nicolescu speaks in similar terms as William James of reunion:

> Transdisciplinarity transgresses the duality of opposing binary pairs: subject/object, subjectivity/objectivity, matter/consciousness, nature/divine, simplicity/complexity, reductionism/holism, diversity/unity. This duality is transgressed by the open unity that encompasses both the universe and the human being. (Nicolescu 2002)

Nicolescu states that the rigor of transdisciplinarity is "a deepening of scientific rigor to the extent that it takes into account not only things, but also beings and their relations to other beings and things."

A union, reminiscent of James's "reconciliation," is imagined in Nicolescu's poetic rendering of the "harmony between the levels of perception and the levels of Reality."

> In the transdisciplinary vision, the classic real/imaginary dichotomy also disappears. We can think of a level of Reality as a fold of all levels of

> perception; and we can think of a level of perception as being a fold of the totality of levels of Reality. The real is a fold of the imagination and the imagination is a fold of the real. The ancients were right: there is indeed an *imaginatio vera,* a foundational, true, creative, visionary imagination. From fold to fold, we invent ourselves. (Nicolescu 2002)

Francisco Varela and the Calculus for Self-Reference

Francisco Varela, a founding member of Nicolescu's Center for Transdisciplinary Research (Nicolescu 2002), developed his Calculus for Self-Reference as an extension of George Spencer-Brown's Laws of Form. Spencer-Brown's thought was highly influential in second-order cybernetic circles[4] in the early 1970s. These circles included several key figures in psychedelic and cybernetic research, which overlapped in several of the participants. A gathering at Esalen in 1973, the American University of Masters or AUM conference, brought together John Lilly, Gregory Bateson, Alan Watts, Heinz von Foerster, and others. According to Adrian Laing, son of British psychiatrist and LSD experimenter Ronald Laing, Spencer-Brown was a "disciple" of his father (Pickering 2011). Laing wrote a brief preface to *Laws of Form.* The conference was a confluence and cross-fertilization of the ideas and practices percolating about LSD, Eastern mysticism, and second-order cybernetics.

> A key to the basic form of self-reference is how self-reference finds its way into language. As mentioned, the antinomies appear when language is used onto itself, that is, a proposition equivalent to its own negation. This antinomic form is paradigmatic of self-referential situations not only in language, and is in fact just the consequence of the circular interlocking of operator and operand in any self-referential situation we choose to look at. (Varela 1974)

Varela's extension of Spencer-Brown's Calculus of Indications utilizes a third logical term as well, the form of re-entry into the form, in addition to Spencer-Brown's "marked" and "un-marked" states (see Chapter 3). He identifies this re-entry with self-reference; re-entry is the logic of autonomy, a concept central to the description of autopoiesis.

> Autonomy is seen in this light to engender the two stages of the form when this ceaseless process is broken into its constituents. By the introduction of a third autonomous state in the form, we do nothing but restore to our field of view that which was there at the beginning, and which we can only see now reflected as segments of the world in language itself. Conversely, by taking self-reference and time as our *filum ariadnis* through a succession of levels, we dwell upon the re-union of the constituents of these levels up to our own union with the world, and thus find a way to retrieve the unity originally lost. (Varela 1979)

In this dense statement, Varela integrates his philosophical position of unity with the dualistic nature of the scientific discipline within which he was working, and the role that natural language and the logics it embeds plays in maintaining the world as segments, rather than the unity it represents.

Roland Fischer and Self-Reflexivity

Early psychedelic researcher Roland Fischer grapples with the strange logic of self-reflection in a similar manner. He states:

> The identity of thinking and being is seemingly contained in the simple statement, "I am conscious." But the paradoxical nature of analytical, logical thinking and the paradoxical nature of human existence, or being, are reflected in the double-bind nature of the statement itself. The "I am conscious" paradox is simultaneously a statement in an object language (about "I") and a statement in metalanguage (about "I am conscious"). It is, therefore, a self-referring statement *which judges its own validity* and hence has no signification in ordinary Aristotelian logic, where propositions of more than one dimension are not permitted. It is a violation of logical typing, but also a violation of semantic convention since both the subject "I" of the proposition "I am conscious" and the system that proposes to be conscious are identical. (Fischer 1977) [emphasis mine]

Consciousness is nothing if not self-reflexive. The paradoxes of self-reflexivity suffuse the discourse of consciousness. These paradoxes are made more complex in psychedelic discourse by extreme variations in states of consciousness and the concomitant shifting of the experience of self. Which (self, Self, selves) are reflecting which (self, Self, selves)? Or in the words of Sufi mystic Ibn 'Arabi, "Who reveals to whom whose mystery?" (Sells 1994)

When self, Self, selves dissolve along with no-self, one is delivered into the Void, one of the myriad masks of the Unspeakable. This circle of self-reflection, where cause and effect interchange, where Diana reflects on herself (self, Self, selves), is a stable feature of my "in vivo" ten-year self-experiment. The psychonautic practice evolves through recursion: (self, Self, selves)-reflecting.

The psychonautic practice itself becomes both the method and the object of the inquiry. Its narratives unfold, exploring multiple aspects of the practice, including the development of digital tools, whose use becomes part of the practice. The psychedelic session protocols evolved iteratively over time, enfolding their own process of self-understanding. A standard for this process has been David Porush's self-referential notion of epistemological potency, developed in the context of an article on the anthropic principle,[5] and in response to the dialectic of the discourse of science and the discourse of literature, C. P. Snow's identification of a major fault line in our culture.

> Descriptions of any intelligent system (and the Universe is obviously one; fictional texts create others) in order to achieve epistemological potency must include accounts not only of how the system is regulated and organized, and of how it communicates among its own parts, but also of how it knows and describes itself. In other words, any epistemologically potent system must include a discourse that enfolds its own intelligence. (Porush 1993)

Porush argues (addressing the earlier point of the taboo of subjectivity) that science, for three hundred years, has persistently excluded or de-privileged the human self as an intentional, expressive subject from scientific discourse. At the same time, science lacks a coherent formal model of natural language. As the result of its rationalist inheritance and its persistent objectification of the observer, science relies on a discourse that has had "inordinate difficulty" enfolding or describing its own acts of knowing. Gödel's incompleteness theorems could be said to express this difficulty mathematically. Porush's epistemology is self-enfolding; its potency depends upon its capacity for self-reflection.

Psychonautics, "the human investigation of psyche through unavoidably first-person science" (Doyle 2010), presents methodological issues, especially if third-person science and the presumption of the detached, "objective" observer is the prevailing episteme, despite the implications of quantum physics' folding together of the observer and the observed. Devaluing subjectivity as unreliable, and in the same gesture decontextualizing the observing self (not only from the object to be observed, but from observation of oneself observing), is what Donna Harraway calls "the god-trick of seeing everything from nowhere" (Harraway 1991). The "god-trick" remains a cognitive shell game until, minimally, I can account for the method by which I, the scientist, accomplish this transformation from a first-person viewpoint, complete with goals, values, feelings, and expectations about my research, to an abstracted, emotion-free, value-free, non-indexical observer, a radical reframing of personhood by fiat without even breaking an epistemological sweat.

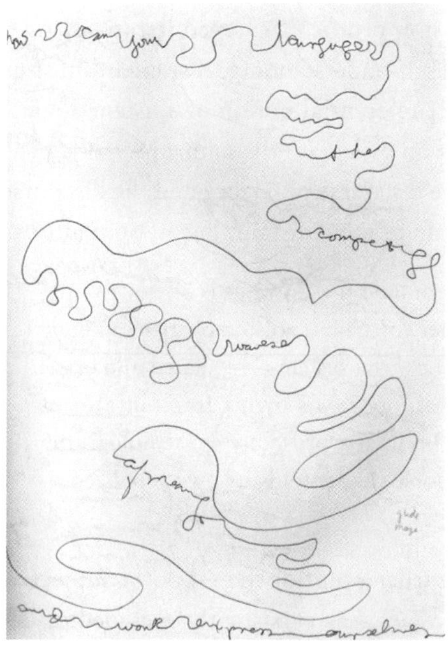

■ **Figure 58: Natural language dissolving in and out of the serpentine lines. The gesture follows the energetic movement of the Rainbow Serpent.**

What are the consequences of method? Why be concerned with the ways in which we study ourselves, our consciousness, our experience? Here at the beginning of the edit of our self-defining text, the human genome, we are faced with profound ethical implications as to how we investigate, explain, or explain away consciousness. Demoting the subject to ghost in a moist machine, or attempting to wholly erase self and consciousness as epiphenomenal (an effluvia of biological processes themselves randomly derived from a purposeless universe), lays the groundwork for placing further restrictions on cognitive liberty and adds greater urgency to the newly expressed concerns of neuroethics. Devaluation of the personal as a vehicle of knowledge production sets the stage for further intrusions of mind-controlling practices, whether accomplished by surgery, pharmacology, technology, torture, or law.

Epistemological Rupture

There is an epistemological rupture[6] or break between levels of reality in the psychedelic experience, each with its own rule-sets, its own episteme. The magnitude of the break is equivalent to the magnitude of the difference between experiences at baseline and experiences in the psychedelic sphere.

> 8:59 AM Launch
>
> 1st step—radically changing sense of body—letting another organizing form—identity—take over and show what is possible—sense of the limbs stretching and retracting—imaging the flows of energy ecstatic sensations—can the ascent be described? Physical—running throughout the body very fast now—close eyes and will be gone—thread of language requested given (session report 03.01.04, 2 g dried *Stropharia cubensis*)

The magnitude of the *experiential* rupture is easy to mask and tends to be obscured within the normalizing field of natural language—including the language used in the session report itself, as above.

> thread of language requested given

What was occurring was a struggle between the urge of the hand and pen to follow the movements of the Rainbow Serpent energy and the desire to leave a trace of words in the report. By quoting only the words without the picture, the normalizing effect is stronger, the original strangeness of the experience obscured. A further normalizing effect occurs through the contextualizing of these events within disciplinary knowledge, which can additionally obscure the high strangeness of the actual experience.

> Now visual just beginning. The multiplying of dimensions—whole body participates—something flooding through—the rainbow serpent swiftly swiftly occupies the space of the body—sound now—so very precise—the sound perceived by the body only a small part of "what's heard"—normal body sight can be recalled—but why? Rising rising—a wild ride ensues—hang on—the

rainbow serpent—prayed for care—huge undulation—not only in the body but in whole space-time

that's it

let go

(session report 03.01.18, 3.5 g dried *Stropharia cubensis*)

Rupture becomes rapture, and reality, however well reviewed, displays a deeper mystery.

Notes, Chapter 5

1. *Darshan,* according to Wikipedia, in its informal usage, is "a Sanskrit term meaning "sight," in the sense of an instance of seeing or beholding, vision, apparition, or glimpse.
2. James was familiar with the work of Amsterdam, New York, eccentric Benjamin Blood, who wrote about his nitrous oxide experiences in *The Anesthetic Revelation and the Gist of Philosophy.*
3. *Epoché* (ἐποχή, epokhē "suspension") is an ancient Greek term that, in its philosophical usage, describes the theoretical moment where all judgments about the existence of the external world, and consequently all action in the world, are suspended. (Wikipedia 2013)
4. According to Wikipedia, "Second-order cybernetics, also known as the cybernetics of cybernetics, investigates the construction of models of cybernetic systems. It investigates cybernetics with awareness that the investigators are part of the system, and of the importance of self-referentiality, self-organizing, the subject-object problem, etc. Investigators of a system can never see how it works by standing outside it because the investigators are always engaged cybernetically with the system being observed; that is, when investigators observe a system, they affect and are affected by it."
5. The anthropic principle elevates self-reflexivity to cosmological dimensions, an evolving universe whose telos is ultimate self-regard, self-reflection, and self-understanding, a notion presented in the Hindu concept of the net of Indra, Alex Grey's paintings of nets of eyes, and Borges's story of the Aleph.
6. The term was introduced by Gaston Bachelard, who argued that progress in science was made through "radical discontinuities" such as the break between the world of classical and relativistic physics and that of quantum mechanics.

CHAPTER 6
Extended Perception

"A hallucination is a fact, not an error; what is erroneous is a judgment based upon it."

—Bertrand Russell, 1914

Here comes that word again: *intertwingled.* As in the case of consciousness and language, perception and reality are deeply, deeply, *deeply* intertwingled. Reality is, at any given moment, the perceived state-of-mind. In a very real sense perception is reality, and reality is perception, but there is no need either to collapse the terms or to pick them apart, holding them out of relation. It's easier to view them as a primary, dynamic cognitive system, in the way that second-order cyberneticist Heinz von Foerster saw the sensorium and the motorium in the same intertwinglement. You can't have one without the other. Reality has been reviewed in the preceding chapter, and it is implicated in every statement about perception. As perceptions are extended, so is our experience of reality or realities. Psychedelics are a portal into the domain of visual language; our multiple-mediated environment is unquestionably shifting toward the visual, and the alphabetic is further and further truncated.

In *Understanding Media,* Marshall McLuhan asserted, "The effects of technology do not occur at the level of opinions or concepts, but alter sense ratios or patterns of perception steadily and without any resistance" (McLuhan 1964). McLuhan quotes Blake: "If Perceptive Organs vary, Objects of Perception seem to vary/if Perceptive Organs close, their Objects seem to close also." This is the sense in which McLuhan sees the effects of technologies ("the extensions of man") on our sense organs as either intensification or amputation. For instance, with human use of language, the shift from the aural to the visual begins with the invention of writing and continues through to our current situation of visual inundation. When I use psychedelics as a technology for extending perception and for the exploration of those realities brought forth in states of extended perception, I am working directly at the interface of reality and perception, shifting sensory ratios. With the control of attention, I bring certain perceptions to the forefront of consciousness and see others drop away in the shifting landscape. These are the same processes by which I create, view, and understand my world at baseline. The difference is that the mechanics of perception and reality are laid bare in the psychedelic state. The means and qualities of perception become objects of reflection, as the feedback loops in consciousness become tighter and tighter, approaching unity. The largest single shift can be the withdrawal of attention from sensory organs (sight, sound, or anything coming from outside the body) to let the interior landscape illuminate. This activity of learning to direct and control attention away from sensory objects and thoughts in order to let the interior state shine forth makes yogis (as well as philosophers) of psychonauts. Interest in the content of consciousness—all those trippy visuals—recedes to the degree that these processes of perception, projection, and reflection in the dome of consciousness become of primary interest, as they did for the faithful scribe.

Hallucination

The intertwingled nature of perception and reality can be seen in the variety of ways that the word "hallucination" is used. As Oliver Sachs notes in his book *Hallucinations,* most hallucinations do not represent psychopathology but come from a wide variety of causes, including Charles Bonnet syndrome, sensory deprivation, migraine, epilepsy, narcolepsy, and fever, as well as the altered states enabled by psychedelics. The truth value of a perception is what defines a hallucination in the classical definition of hallucination as false perception. Hallucination—and mental health in general—is defined relative to a monophasic reality as "A profound distortion in a person's perception of reality, typically accompanied by a powerful sense of reality. An hallucination may be a sensory experience in which a person can see, hear, smell, taste, or feel something that is not there." (MedTerms 2010) More subtly, the "thereness" is a deictic signifier—relative to some "here" that is contextual and linked to an individual viewpoint. In the case of the hallucination, it is "there" for the hallucinator and "not-there" for the medical observer.

This definition of hallucination is typical and highlights the intimately self-referential, systemic connection of perception and reality. One of the many terms for a psychedelic drug is "hallucinogen"; along with "psychotomimetic," this term reflects the medical and psychiatric models within which these substances were first examined by Western science. David Nichols, one of the leading above-ground scientific researchers in the field of psychedelic science, titles his 2004 survey "Hallucinogens." In discussing the newer term "entheogens" (manifesting the divine within), which has become the term of choice for many in the psychedelic community, Nichols admits that "it seems unlikely that this name will ever be accepted in formal scientific circles." Nichols supports the use of "hallucinogen," and the medical model that reifies the association with psychosis. This serves to confine consideration of their uses to a medical framework of disease and cure. Most authorized research remains in this model. While the use of psychedelic medicines *for* curing has been central to humanity long before Western medicine "discovered" psychedelics, this framing excludes without mention any use of psychedelics for non-medical purposes, such as spiritual development (Schultes et al. 1992; Andresen 2000), creativity adjuncts (Stafford and Golightly 1967; Lyttle 1999; de Rios and Janiger 2003), or knowledge acquisition (as I frame my own investigations). When a psychedelic medicine is labeled a hallucinogen, it is by definition no longer *for* curing but a drug that creates effects (hallucinations) that need to *be* cured.

John Lilly (1991) gave the following definition of hallucination in an interview with David Jay Brown and Rebecca McClen:

> DJB: How would you define what a hallucination is?
>
> JOHN: That's a word I never use because it's very disconcerting, part of the explanatory principle and hence not useful. Richard Feynman, the physicist, went into the tank here twelve times. He did three hours each time and when he finished he sent me one of his physics books in which he had inscribed, "Thanks for the hallucinations." So I called him up and I said, "Look, Dick, you're not being a scientist. What you experience you must describe and not throw into the wastebasket called 'hallucination.' That's a psychiatric misnomer; none of that is unreal that you experienced." For instance he talks about his nose when he was in the

tank. His nose migrated down to his buttonhole, and finally he decided that he didn't need a buttonhole or a nose so he took off into outer space.

DJB: And he called that a hallucination because he couldn't develop a model to explain it?

JOHN: But you don't have to explain it, you see. You just describe it. Explanations are worthless in this area.

To answer the question, "Do you hallucinate?" is to be caught in the same pejorative loop as the attempt to answer the question, "Do you still beat your wife?" The term will be avoided in personal descriptions of psychedelic experience, and retained when used by others as a descriptor.

Perceptual Shifts

Perception itself, according to the scientific description, can be viewed as a grand illusion, "a plausible tissue of appearances."[1] Through an unexplained and wholly mysterious process at the heart of consciousness itself (the binding or "hard" problem), sensations received by the eyes, ears, and other senses and multi-mediated through a series of electrical and chemical processes and pathways in the brain are stitched together seamlessly by the brain/mind and experienced as "out there." We perceive a fully convincing wraparound reality that we experience as if we were looking *out through* the eyes that are actually *receiving* instruments. In this light, our experience of the world, all reality, is virtual—locally, mechanically constructed in the individual mind-body. Perception can be seen as the invisible interface, a projection we participate in without a thought about the nature of the mind as projector. The mechanics of this illusion of perception are reliably stable, the projections remarkably consistent—until one alters the biochemistry of the brain/mind.

Bypassing the term "hallucination" necessitates other language for describing the many and varied non-ordinary perceptions encountered in psychedelic experience. "Vision" or "the visionary," aside from privileging the sensory category of sight, brings the connotation of spiritual or mystical visions. While these are definitely one of the types of non-ordinary perception, it again biases the meaning of these perceptions as being of "spiritual" origin in the way "hallucination" biases toward the pathological. I have chosen "extended perception" as a more neutral and inclusive term.

Science has been extending our perceptions with instrumentation from the very small (electron microscopy, scanning tunneling microscopy) to the very large or far away (optical and radio telescopes; x-ray astronomy). Medical technology has created a stunning range of imaging techniques to perceive the inside of a body with non-invasive methods such as PET and CAT scan, fMRI, and ultrasound. One of the assumptions of scientific practice is that the human creator and observer of the instrument is a constant of stably configured senses. This assumption of the stability of perception allows the construction of "the objective observer," a fundamental component of the scientific notions of both reality and truth. This necessity to assert the stability of observation predisposes science to characterize reports of chemically extended perception from whatever sources as pathological, delusional, or fraudulent and therefore, in the main, not *real,* in the materialist paradigm, and, more subtly, not *useful.*

Alan Watts uses the gerund "sharpening" to describe an aspect of the psychedelic extension of perception:

> There is no difference in principle between sharpening perception with an external instrument, such as a microscope, and sharpening it with an internal instrument, such as one of these . . . drugs. If they are an affront to the dignity of the mind, the microscope is an affront to the dignity of the eye and the telephone to the dignity of the ear. Strictly speaking, these drugs do not impart wisdom at all, any more than the microscope alone gives knowledge. They provide the raw materials of wisdom, and are useful to the extent that the individual can integrate what they reveal into the whole pattern of his behavior and the whole system of his knowledge. (Watts 1962)

> Psychedelics for some extend perception to the molecular level.

> The other way to the Other World, the research project route, was exemplified by George Goodman, who is probably better known as the economist and writer Adam Smith. Goodman signed up for a UCLA project and was told by the director, "You are the astronauts of inner space. You are going deeper into the mind than anyone has gone so far, and you will

> come back to tell us what you found." One of the things Goodman found was that he could see all "the basic molecules of the universe . . . all the component parts, little building blocks of DNA." (Stevens 1998)

Nobel Laureate Kary Mullis claims that his ability to "get down with the molecules" was learned using LSD (Mullis 2000). This skill enabled the development of the polymerase chain reaction (PCR), a foundational piece of genetic technology that has enabled DNA cloning for sequencing and the diagnosis of hereditary disease, among other applications. Mullis was no dabbler in the psychedelic realm. He was so impressed by his first 1000-mμ LSD trip[2] that he began creating, with others, new psychedelics in his chemistry lab at Berkeley, staying one step ahead of the scheduling and illegalization process.

> A person who loved playing with chemicals as much as I did just couldn't help but be intrigued by LSD. The concept that there existed chemicals with the ability to transform the mind, to open up new windows of perception, fascinated me. (Mullis 2000)

Subjective descriptions of altered states of consciousness (ASC) invariably include reports of perceptions extended beyond the baseline state of waking consciousness and the range of baseline sense perceptions. Additionally, perceptions in ASC have been described as exceeding the current categories of sense modalities: perception of the presence of spirits; perception of auras; color outside the normal visible light range; and the range of phenomena classified as extrasensory perception (remote viewing, clairvoyance, and precognition). The list of sensory modalities described by psychonauts is considerably finer-grained than the classical five senses and includes internal perceptions of temperature, vibration, balance, and proprioception, to name a few. Perceptions are also altered or extended spontaneously by disease (fever, epilepsy, schizophrenia) or by subjective events that come unbidden to a person (ghosts, precognitive incidents, visionary states, hypnagogic states, alien abductions). The description of what is perceived under conditions of extended perception is inevitably shaped by cultural contexts and expectations. Again, the term "extended perception" is used as an umbrella to cover perceptions that are given a wide variety of names depending on context and content: hallucinations, visions, and *siddhis*, synaesthesias and ESP.

Often certain signature perceptions determine one's status in a culturally defined altered state, and come to define the landscape of a particular state of consciousness. The shaman's flight, the bliss-body of yogic states, and the rising auditory tones of the DMT flash are three examples of perceptions that function as landmarks in ASC.[3]

> vastness is yours the body trembles everything speaks in waves even these words wave meets wave the world is formed of light the interference patterns makes form of infinite complexity the ocean of life starlight crossing starlight marooned on an island of frozen light (session report 99.11.06, MDMA)

Charles Laughlin gives us a model of perception and cognition as parts of a completely integrated process.

> . . . the neural systems mediating perception and cognition are intimately integrated and operate on the same basic principle. To a great extent, dividing this complex integration into a simple duality consisting of "perception" and "cognition" is as outmoded as the notion of there being only "five senses." Moreover, the division leads to the very "naïve common sense" conceptions that have hampered Searle; namely that "cognition" is located in the head, and the "object of perception" is out in the world somewhere. . . . The object of perception is constructed wholly within the nervous system. (Laughlin 1990)

This is not to portray Laughlin philosophically as an idealist; there is a world "out there" for him, but it is, in the Kantian sense, a noumenon, known to humans and other animals differently, depending on their perceptual-cognitive equipment. In Laughlin's view, we do not experience "the world" as such; rather we live in a "cognized environment."

> . . . the principal function of our nervous system is the construction of models of the world. By processing information about the world through these models, the organization directs adaptive evaluation and action in relation to events in the world. As a matter of shorthand, let us call this set of countless models our cognized environment. (Laughlin 1990)

Thus, in Laughlin's model, our cognized environment—the sum total of our models—constitutes our reality. And clearly, new models are built when new perceptions are available.

Transpersonal psychologist Frances Vaughan's description of enhanced perception links this quality to the noetic and emphasizes, as does the work of Roland Fischer, the relation between perception and reality.

> A most striking feature of my psychedelic experience was the noetic quality of consciousness as it expanded from its usual perceptual range to a vast contextual awareness that recognized the relativity of all perception in space/time. . . . As the illusory, changeable nature of ordinary reality became increasingly clear, I also realized how a normally constricted perceptual framework permits one to see only a fraction of reality, inevitably distorted to suit personal projections and presuppositions. (Vaughan in Grinspoon 1983)

Roland Fischer uses the metaphor of a revolving stage bringing forth new scenes at different levels of arousal:

> Whenever the level of arousal is raised or lowered—when we ourselves become a moving experience—a new stage revolves to the fore and another type of knowledge appropriate to that particular state of consciousness becomes available. The real nature of fiction and the fictitious nature of reality are revealed through these transformations of consciousness. (Fischer 1978)

This model was drawn from the Memory Theatre of Giulio Camillo and the Memory System of Giordano Bruno, and makes reference as well to Hermann Hesse's Magic Theatre (Fischer 1977).

The spirit of *Salvia divinorum* taught me to keep different perceptual and cognitive streams open at the same time (parallel/simultaneous universes). Salvia taught me how I can make "markers" in the mindstream to bring back messages, or review a novel state or insight or perception. This seems part of the skill of navigation, when skill in navigating includes learning, at times, to let go of the rudder. Navigational skill is particularly paradoxical when the learning is about letting go of the naming, structuring, valuing, evaluating, and discriminating mind and getting down to the happening itself—sound, movement, light, color, heat, cold, or the flow of blissful bathing in a garden of vibratory delights. Salvia once delivered an initial thought, "we've been waiting for you," then picked me up and danced me into movement—the air flowing over my body, my home environment, and mind all one, melded synaesthetically, and consumed in the movements of the moving spirits.

> Gesture creating color and multidimensional space—every experience—and they flowed by/through quickly and kept changing—was intensely pleasurable, sensuous (01.12.08 *Salvia divinorum,* post-session report)[4]

From the ASC perspective of multiple realities arising from multiple states of consciousness, reality and perception are deeply intertwingled in a self-referential manner. Reality is what I perceive; what I perceive becomes my reality. Reality, therefore, is at least in part a personal matter: these are *my* perceptions I am depending on, just as the doctor depends on his or her perception to determine the "not-thereness" of a patient's hallucination. Perception is a complex internal process of multiple interacting systems (visual, auditory, linguistic). The brain takes information from the sensory systems (both internal and external) and, through reference to sensory, visual, emotional, and linguistic memory in a mutable and complex chemical neurotransmission space, constructs "reality" on the fly in the experiencing individual. Not only *what* reality is being described but *whose* reality and under what perceptual conditions, cognitive preferences, cultural indoctrination, and epistemological bias needs to be considered. Inter-subjective sharing occurs through a variety of linguistic means (including body language, sounds, and pheromones, as well as gesture, dance, and more abstract symbolic systems such as natural language, music, painting, and mathematics). This sharing creates, along with the default settings of our perceptual equipment (including genetic variations), the scaffolding for a consensus reality.

Both VR and psychedelic technologies extend perception and reorganize sensory ratios to create new experiences of reality, new epistemological platforms, and the conditions for new knowledge acquisition in the fields to which they are applied. Entering the psychedelic landscape, one becomes an ontological engineer.

Synaesthesia

The literatures that touch on synaesthesias—scientific, art-historical, literary, phenomenological, ethnographic, and psychedelic—vary widely in their definitions, interpretations, and in their degree of comfort with the first-person, subjective nature of experiential reports. The *significances* given to synaesthetic experiences are similarly wide-ranging.

> Sounds seem to affect what I see. I see music; the textures of rhythms and the colors of melodies float before my eyes. . . . My visual images alter or change whenever I hear a sound or noise. . . . Sight, feeling, motion, texture, thinking, sound—all are one [. . .] The interaction between sight, music, and physical feeling is most remarkable. (de Rios and Janiger 2003)

Psychologist Harry T. Hunt sees all symbolic cognition as cross-modal and synaesthetically based, this modality being "essential to all metaphoric construction" (Hunt 1995). Contemporary neuroscience views synaesthesia as a rare (perhaps abnormal, perhaps pathological) "condition" (Cytowic 1995; Marks 2000; Harrison 2001). Neuroscientist Richard Cytowic narrows the definition of synaesthesia to

> . . . the involuntary physical experience of a cross-modal association. That is, the stimulation of one sensory modality reliably causes a perception in one or more different senses. Its phenomenology clearly distinguishes it from metaphor, literary tropes, sound symbolism, and deliberate artistic contrivances that sometimes employ the term "synesthesia" to describe their multisensory joinings. (Cytowic 1995)

Cytowic estimates the occurrence of the synaesthetic experience to be statistically rare, one in 25,000. When psychedelics are the test-bed of synaesthesias, the occurrence of synaesthesias increases dramatically.[5] It is reasonably common for individuals who take psychedelics to report that their senses become mixed. Given the illicit nature of the topic it is hard to find reliable data on this issue, but a Web-based questionnaire conducted by Don DeGracia found that, of a total of 62 respondents who admitted to using hallucinogenic compounds, 45.9 percent reported synaesthetic symptoms. Clearly the most common manifestation (over 90 percent) was to see sounds (deGracia 1995).

Visionary artists such as Blake, Scriabin, Kandinsky, and the French symbolists link synaesthetic perception to a spiritual dimension. Ecologist and philosopher David Abram, much of whose thought is based in Merleau-Ponty, the phenomenologist of perception, locates synaesthesia as fundamental to perception and language, both spoken and written.

> Although contemporary neuroscientists study "synaesthesia"—the overlap and blending of the senses—as though it were a rare or pathological experience to which only certain persons are prone (those who report "seeing sounds," "hearing colors," and the like), our primordial, preconceptual experience, as Merleau-Ponty makes evident, is inherently synaesthetic. The intertwining of sensory modalities seems unusual to us only to the extent that we have become estranged from our direct experience (and hence from our primordial contact with the entities and elements that surround us). (Abram 1996)

Abram goes on to quote Merleau-Ponty on synaesthesia and the effects of mescaline:

> The influence of mescalin, by weakening the attitude of impartiality and surrendering the subject to his vitality, should [if we are correct] favor forms of synaesthetic experience. And indeed, under mescalin, the sound of a flute gives a bluish-green color, [and] the tick of a metronome, in darkness, is translated as grey patches, the spatial intervals between them corresponding to the intervals of time between the ticks, the size of the patch to the loudness of the tick, and its height to the pitch of the sound. (Merleau-Ponty, quoted in Abram 1996)

Ethnographic reports of ayahuasca shamanism in the Amazonian rain forest describe the centrality of the *icaros,* the shaman's songs, that guide and create the content of the visionary experience on many levels, calling visual forms and presences into being with sound (and, in turn, hearing the sounds of their three-dimensional visions).

> Through his *icaro,* he also calls the rainbow with the whole range of colors that the *boa yakumama* has. He sings the *icaro* of the diamond, the gold, the silver, and of all the precious stones in order to put them on the woman to protect her. . . . (Luna and Amaringo 1999)

> The ancient wise men, to describe the kaleidoscopic illuminations of their shamanistic nights, drew an analogy between the inside and the outside and formed a word that related the spectrum of colors created by the sunshine in the spray of waterfalls and the mists of the morning to their conscious experiences of ecstatic enlightenment: these are the whirlwinds he speaks of, gyrating configurations of iridescent lights that appear to him

> as he speaks, turned round and round and round himself by the turbulent winds of the spirit. (Munn 1973)

Reports of psychedelic synaesthesias link the states of multisensory perception to noetic experience of deep insights into the nature of reality and consciousness, and their profound intertwinglement.

> The first thing I saw was the "visible language"! . . . The "elves" appeared. They sang/I saw/read/felt/heard. They are "made out" of the visible language. The message is conveyed by the medium itself in several simultaneous sensory modalities. (Gracie 1985)

A range of contemporary artistic practices, especially in immersive, interactive, and electronic media environments, seek to create, or invoke, synaesthesias. The theme of intertwingularity is the common ground underlying the discourses of synaesthesia, in whatever context it occurs. Intertwingularity comes to signify the bewildering richness of perceptual combinatorics person to person in experiential reports, whether those reports are quoted in neuroscientific works, the Vaults of Erowid, William Blake's visions, or the heavenly or hellish trip reports of Aldous Huxley. The psychedelic connections to the creation of and participation in many of these experiences (DJ and VJ culture; Burning Man) and their enabling technologies (such as live performance computer graphics and VR) are common knowledge. From the sampling of quotes above, it seems clear that under the broad rubric of "synaesthesia" almost any sensory—and/or emotional—and/or cognitive experience can be cross-linked.

Crystal Vision

- This section and the sections following describe categories of psychedelic perception for which I have developed my own idiosyncratic vocabulary. For me, these are perceptual landmarks of many phases of consciousness. They may or may not map to the perceptual categories of other psychonauts. This is local knowledge, specific to my explorations, and culled from ten years of session reports, as distinguishing features of my psychedelic experience. These perceptions create realities quite different from baseline perception.

A frequent perceptual feature of the psychedelic landscape is what I've come to call "crystal vision." It is a distinct perceptual "tuning" that can occur with various substances (MDMA, 2C-B, cannabis, psilocybin), though it is most prevalent for me with the Shulgin molecule, 2C-B. As with other affordances of the psychedelic landscape, it can be practiced, strengthened, and steadied.

> Feel the globe extending, expanded. Expanding. The calm maintains the delicate structure—need the calm to be aware of it—how it permeates awareness while not existing in what is experienced as 3-space. More and more, that "space" is not perceived as "otherwhere" or distanced, or a place to be transported to—by means of awareness—shifting activities—trips of whatever nature, however propelled—but as eternally present, simply to be tuned to. Sense it now as the "crystal vision"—interesting exercise to perceive ordinary space-time and crystal vision at the same time. The brain chemistry alterations shift the focus, that's all—open the other perceptions. Can of course be overwhelming if one's touchstones of orientation—identity, objects, space and time as normally perceived—disappear, or seriously morph. The world of crystal vision is far more fluid. One moves by intention (as in remote viewing)—the world of crystal vision hovers on the edge of perception—peripheral vision, elusive. Sense the dense dense yet weightless network of fine fibres—filaments—angel hair, mycelial threads of connections. A fineness, a delicacy, and a sense of vast condensation and compaction. Micromovements—mastery thereof—realizing how little effort is required—harder to understand than to perceive—dense networked cloud—sparkles inside. (session report 02.07.20, MDMA)

As with many features of the psychedelic landscape, the naming is descriptive of an event, a state of mind, a quality of perception, and a metaphor reaching into the complex of associations surrounding things crystalline: crystals as receivers (as in crystal radios); as sites of structured order and information retention; as the liquid crystalline structure of DNA; as mathematical objects; as reflectors and refractors of light; as symbols of purity. The connection is made to the state of mind called witness consciousness, a vast-open-clear-transparent-calm-detached and often compassionate viewpoint from which any thought, sensation, feeling can be viewed as it arises and passes, with no attachment.

> Also—clear air not just a "not there" but a crystalline substance—invisible—but crystalline— (session report 03.08.23, 2.5 g dried *Stropharia cubensis*)

> "crystal vision" space of clarity—hard to describe—is spatial and an expanding "globe" around physical and "mental" space—can be reached with gestures of hands and arms (session report 02.07.06, MDMA)

Crystal vision is also one of the many "installations" in the psychedelic sphere of what can inadequately be called "devices," or psychic tools of use in managing the experiences.

> tantric exercise—with 3rd eye—psychic surgery. Opened much wider—and installed a good tight door so don't feel like a gaping wound or too big an opening, it has not gone into use yet but will. Connected to crystal vision. (session report 02.08.17, MDMA)

Crystal vision also appeared unexpectedly, in between sessions, in a shopping mall.

> Something called "crystal vision"—sitting in Food Court of Crossgates Mall—very clear-headed—all the noise and vibes—eyesight changing in a subtle but startling way—there were tons of people, movement, busyness—I could see the whole scene—and the individual parts—all at once. Very interesting. As if "focus" broadened. Happened several more times. Patented effect: "crystal vision" Ho. Ho. (session report 01.12.16–between)

Crystal vision is contentless, something that is seen-with, felt-with, like an invisible lens, or Hokusai's polished mirror.

High Resolution

Perception in the psychedelic landscape can be of a far greater resolution than at baseline: sharper, more detail, higher levels of differentiation and subtlety in the field of attention, whether of color, emotion, sound, or cognition. In other words, one perceives orders of magnitude more *information* in a given moment. High resolution gives rise to perceptions of great complexity. The highest resolution I have experienced is that enabled by DMT, a perception confirmed by other experience reports.

> What I saw was of the maximum complexity that a mind could possibly encounter. (M. 2010)

High resolution and density of information go hand in hand. DMT is frequently reported as hyper-real and very high resolution, two qualities that may vary in direct relation to each other. Biologist Thomas Ray has been mapping the subjective reports of psychonauts on particular drugs to the unique configuration of neurotransmitter states that occurs with each drug in what Ray describes as a multidimensional receptor space. Ray finds that "DMT activates more receptors more strongly than any other drug in my study" (Ray 2004; Ray 2010). Whether biochemically or electrically, the psychedelics introduce new configurations of connectivity.

Filaments

A particular visual feature of my psychedelic landscape is the presence of filamental structures. High resolution reveals networks of flowing or waving fine filaments, alive, active, space-filling, or space-crossing. I've thought of this as "the mesh," "the wireframe of reality," and various other phenomena.

> At times the boundaries are represented by lines so thin that it may be impossible to say whether they are black or white. Many observers have stressed the fineness of the lines. . . . As Moller has pointed out, the "absolute one dimensional" appears to have become a reality. (Kluver 1966)

Filaments are the sensed form of connectivity across multiple domains: energetic, emotional, cognitive. But these divisions of the experience of connectivity and its visualization in the ever-shifting filamental waves are artificial and linguistic.

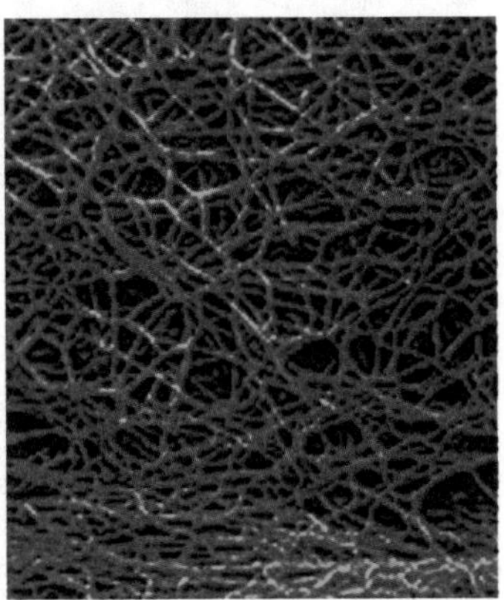

■ Figure 59: Electron micrograph of psilocybin mushroom mycelium. By Paul Stamets, with permission.

> You are becoming aware of the time-stream contents in new ways—as they fold back on themselves—repeat sequences differently folded—to make new connections—very light and airy—gossamer filaments—releasing mind boundaries lets the connections show—more pieces float into view—what you're trying to model in the display of dataspace—light and filamental—important to model this way because it displays quality of consciousness—the qualitative aspect of cognition—the visual language LiveGlide can display—(session report 03.05.04, MDMA)

Whatever the finest filaments or microfibers one can imagine—angel hair, cotton candy, milkweed, dandelion seeds, mycelium—imagine it finer, weightless, wavy, and floating.

> Silk and silkworms, filamental business again—Chinese of course—who can be so subtle in awareness as to observe the silkworm through its life cycle—or was it just collecting empty cocoons—and seeing there was something to unravel—from there to the techne of silk? We are recapitulating that history with media—sensibilities tuned to want higher and higher resolution—filamental resolution, and all that that could bring—(session report 08.10.14, MDA)

Filamental structures are present in the body at many scales. At the heart of every cell is the master filament, DNA, its width measured in nanometers, its length about three feet in the human were the chromosomal divisions to be stitched together. The macromolecular proteins, the building blocks, are not blocks but long filaments, folding and spiraling into three-dimensional shapes and forming at the macro scale the fibrous structures of fascia, muscles, and nerves. The filamental structures can appear at cosmic scales to the psychonaut, similar to the visualization of dark matter spanning galaxies. And the structure of the mushroom mycelium is densely filamental.

> all universes, all levels are connected by light, filamental structures—a mycelium out of which reality mushrooms, from time to time. . . . (session report 08.10.14, MDA)

I see mycelial structures in the basic form of the ubiquitous search engines and social networking software that are a current staple of our knowledge acquisition and dissemination at baseline. Every search returns a new—always new because always shifting and adding and growing—set of filaments connecting the searcher's quest to his or her potential grail. Every quest or re-quest weaves the mycelial mat of connections among people and data more densely: articles, rants, images, jokes, status updates, tweets, video, ads, text messages, music, maps, and cultural artifacts of every communicable variety. Google search is Ted Nelson's intertwingulation made manifest. And, of course, those filaments meet, mate, form hyphal knots. Some are fruitful, and a clump of mushrooms springs above the ground, out of the hidden mat. A primary text for this lifeform is Paul Stamets's *Mycelium Running*. The book begins with a discussion of what Stamets calls the mycelial archetype.

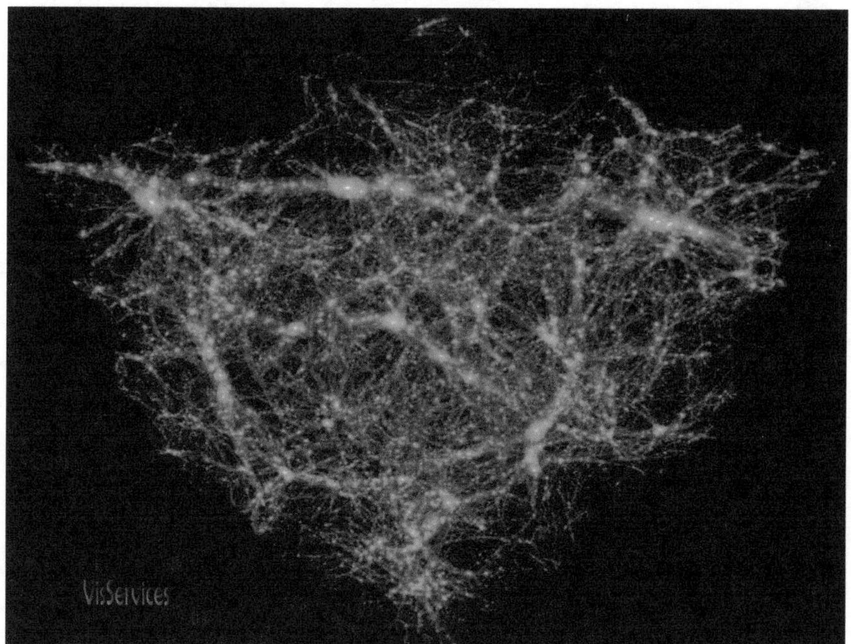

■ **Figure 60: Dark Matter Visualization for Early Universe Simulation.** LBC Dataset. Amit Choursia, Steve Cuchin, Robert Harkness, and Michael Norman. San Diego Supercomputer Center, UCSD.

He compares the mushroom mycelium with the overlapping information-sharing systems that comprise the Internet, with the networked neurons in the brain, and with a computer model of dark matter in the universe. All share this densely intertwingled filamental structure. Stamets says, "I believe that the mycelium operates at a level of complexity that exceeds the computational powers of our most advanced supercomputers. I see the mycelium as the Earth's natural Internet, a consciousness with which we might be able to communicate" (Stamets 2005).

Hyperconnectivity

Filamental structure is fundamental to the perception of hyperconnectivity in the psychedelic sphere, as well as our telematic world of dense interconnectivity. Roy Ascott offers the term *apophenia* to describe this urge toward connectivity:

> Apophenia is the spontaneous perception of connections and the meaningfulness of unrelated phenomena. The term was coined by K. Conrad in 1958. (Ascott 2010)

Ted Nelson uses the term "hypernoia" to describe what I have called "link-seeking behavior."

> Hypernoia: the belief that everything is, or should be, connected, interconnected, or reconnected. Bringing back together what should never have been separate. (Nelson 1993)

Each of these terms has been connected with schizophrenia on the one hand, and creativity on the other. The psychedelic sphere melds these possibilities into its own mix, the valence of which can shift with the *set* of the psychonaut. The psychedelic perception of our interconnection with the world of nature, the realization that we are part and parcel of this living, densely interconnected, intensely intercommunicating web of life, is at the heart of many LSD, ayahuasca, and psilocybin experiences, especially when undertaken in a natural setting.

The "ecodelic hypothesis," detailed by Rich Doyle and inspired by his ayahuasca experiences in Peru, outlines the crucial nature of these insights for our survival as a species.

> The future of Gaian biodiversity and a modicum of global stability appear to depend precisely on a thoroughgoing and practiced re-articulation of human autonomy in the experience of imbrication with global ecosytems, including capital and information flows as well as the carbon cycle. In short, in order to alter what we do, we must "reengineer" and re-imagine who we are. And across the life and climate sciences, the news is this: You are deeply implicated in the global ecoystem in ways scientific and technical practices are only beginning to comprehend. (Doyle 2011)

The other side of the experience of dense interconnection is paranoia—where the Others, from whom one is normally separated, are now invasive voices in the head.

Artist and xenolinguist Allyson Grey describes the filamental energetic interconnections thus:

> In 1976 during an LSD trip with my husband, Alex, I experienced my body turning into infinite strands of light that were both a fountain and a drain. As I lay meditating next to Alex, I could see that he too had been revealed as a fountain and drain, individual and distinct but connected to my "energy unit." I realized that all beings and things were "blowing off" and "sucking in" pure energy in an infinite field of confluent effluences. The energy was love, the unifying force. (Grey 2010)

In many sessions I record what has become a stable feature of my psychedelic landscape: the sense in the initial warp, the "rising," of the brain-mind "lighting up" with a great increase in connections.

> mind like burlap weave serviceable rising rising mind layers of fine silk gauze breeze carry potatoes clothe a concubine (session report 03.05.14, MDMA)

■ **Figure 61: Alex Grey, "Universal Mind Lattice."**

These experiences of hyperconnectivity map to Winkelman's neurophysiological description of the increase of connectivity experienced as the cortex connects with the older parts of the brain and the hemispheres of the brain go into sync.

> Sudden huge launch—pause for dense connections being established dense fine mesh at molecular level neuronal level and out beyond—only a model—metaphoric simultaneity keep languaging though the form is its own perception of language—dense hyperdimensional web—incredibly intricate—dense in signalings—retune retune to the reverberation of the whole—ready for this now (session report 02.04.21, MDMA)

I experience this as a bursting (or flowing) out of the confines of the self-conception of a solitary, isolated, individual ego into a mind-state that reveals and enables a massive connectivity. This connectivity extends to the whole of the biosphere, with all the Others, and among my many selves. The sense is of a connectivity that produces a different sort of intelligence—I am both far more connected to the contents of my personal thoughts, feelings, and memories and, more profoundly, to a far broader field of sentience, intelligence, and knowledge in which I can potentially access new knowledge, and to which I contribute whatever I have to offer, as a conscious entity. *An I-Thou relationship with an informational field*, as psychonaut teafaerie said (teafaerie 2009). This level of connectivity is the ground for many forms of ecstasy: cognitive—the orgasmic *aha!;* body-bliss; emotional opening to trust and love; and the reunion with the seething liveliness of the web of biological forms with which our body-minds are intimately entangled.

Hyperconductivity

I experience hyperconductivity in connection with hyperconnectivity as an increase in the speed of thought, where "thought" refers to the whole of the contents of consciousness. Not only are there more connections but the flow among the connections, along the filaments, appears faster and more frictionless than at baseline.

> speed of brain/mind connectivity and conductivity vastly faster than current use with natural language processing. New language necessary to take the brakes off—getting outside of words (abandoning the alphabet). (session report 03.06.07, MDMA)

This perception of hyperconductivity maps, at least metaphorically, to descriptions of superconductivity (or superfluidity). Physicist Mae Wan Ho's speculations regarding high- (body) temperature coherence phenomena in biological systems and the liquid crystalline structures of collagen that constitute the majority of the connective tissue throughout the body are suggestive, though beyond the scope of this thesis and my own layperson's understanding of the physical issues proposed (Ho 1998).

Extended Perception As Alien Art

The extraordinary visions unleashed in consciousness by psychedelics are mysterious in origin. Often the presence of the Other goes hand in hand with these visions. This presence suggests an extended metaphor where the perceptual novelty and extravagance of psychedelic visions is imagined as alien art. Determination of whether the alien is an unknown (normally unconscious) aspect of the Self, an Other, or a blended configuration of Self and Other can be held in abeyance as part of the high strangeness (alien quality) of the experience.

Alien art—including linguistic phenomena—is construed as an epistemological strategy of the Other in the psychedelic sphere for knowledge acquisition and transmission. This view is in sharp contrast to the notion of hallucinations as mechanically generated "form constants," abstract geometries with no semantic dimension *per se*. It is closer to the narrative and highly significant (for the experiencing individual) first-person reports in Shanon's ayahuasca phenomenology (Shanon 2002). These aspects of alien art describe features of the perceptual field that can simultaneously involve cognitive processes accompanied by vivid feeling states; bodily sensations (or lack thereof); and the synaesthetic involvement of other senses. Alien art begins with conditions of extended perception, an ascending scale of effects from the sensory amplifications of cannabis and hashish through the full-scale wraparound realities of high-dose sessions of DMT, psilocybin mushrooms, and LSD.

> Let shift—perception multiple dimensions interpenetrating—opening of every point into world   we fall because the world is full of holes   space/time fabric infinitely porous—empty—"a net is nothing but a lot of holes tied together by string"[6] (session report 03.05.04, MDMA)

Human use of psychedelics has a history that appears to go back at least as far as the early signs of culture (up to 40,000 years ago) in cave paintings and cultural artifacts in Europe, Africa, and the Americas. The interpretation of specific signs, designs, and figures—animal, human, and hybrid or therianthropic—is highly disputed, and largely irresolvable due to the absence of ethnographic confirmation. A well-regarded but still controversial hypothesis (as controversial as virtually every interpretation of the meaning of rock art symbols and drawings) is forwarded by J. D. Lewis-Williams and T. A. Dowson, who link the rock art signs to so-called entoptic phenomena—visual form constants, following Kluver (1966)—that appear in ASC and are thought to have a neurological basis. Lewis-Williams differentiates these entoptic phenomena, "a range of visual percepts that are independent of light from an external source derived from the structure of the optic system anywhere from the eyeball to the cortex," from hallucination, which he defines as having no foundation in the actual structure of the optic system.

In this view, unlike phosphenes and form constants, hallucinations include iconic visions of culturally determined items such as animals, as well as somatic and aural experiences. However,

> The universality of entoptic phenomena encourages us to construct a model of the ways in which mental imagery is perceived by people in certain altered states of consciousness. Ultimately, such a model should be relevant to all arts derived from these altered states. Because we are concerned principally with entoptics, we say less about iconic hallucinations, but the intimate relationship between the two must be clarified by any model that seeks to explain the imagery of altered states. (Lewis-Williams 1988)

In my own view, developed from direct observation, distinguishing entoptic phenomena as those stemming from stimulation of the optic nerve (because one can see them with eyes closed) does not account for the elaborate "iconic hallucinations" that can also be seen with eyes closed. I have watched many times, on the rise through psychedelic phases of an individual session, the early geometric forms become, as it were, a wireframe for the subsequent elaborated visions, in an unbroken continuum. In my experience, these early, simpler harbingers of the multidimensional constructs, far from being semantically empty, are the building blocks of a visual language that can be combined into intricate visual forms: person-becoming-animal, transparent architectures, or whirling galaxies, imbued with deep meaning for the viewer. The process is analogous to the process of building complex life forms from the simple spiral waves of proteins.

Lewis-Williams argues that San Bushman rock art (with its known connection to shamanic practices) and Paleolithic rock art (which cannot be ethnographically validated) are connected by their formal similarities, and by those similarities to Kluver's form constants of entoptic phenomena.

Graham Hancock builds on this model of Lewis-Williams in his exposition of the worldwide phenomena of shamanic interactions with the Other (his "supernaturals"), implicated as both the source and, in part, the objects of these global forms of "alien" art. Clark Heinrich sees psychedelic mushroom imagery throughout the history of Christian religious painting. He postulates an occult knowledge of the mushroom as sacrament, isomorphic with Christ, another approach to the idea of the mushroom as Logos (Heinrich 2002). Schultes, Hofmann, and Rätsch's densely illustrated book *Plants of the Gods* contains numerous examples of the art of those who have experienced the spirit or an alien encounter, enabled by a wide variety of psychoactive plants in the Americas (Schultes et al. 1992).

> All or much of Indian art, it has been proposed, is based on visionary experience. Colors, similarly, are symbolically significant: yellow or off-white has a seminal concept, indicating solar fertilization; red—color of the uterus, fire, heat—symbolized female fecundity; blue represents thought through Tobacco smoke. These colors accompany Ayahuasca intoxication and have precise interpretations. Many of the complicated rock engravings in the river valleys of the Vaupés region are undoubtedly based upon drug experiences. (Schultes et al. 1992)

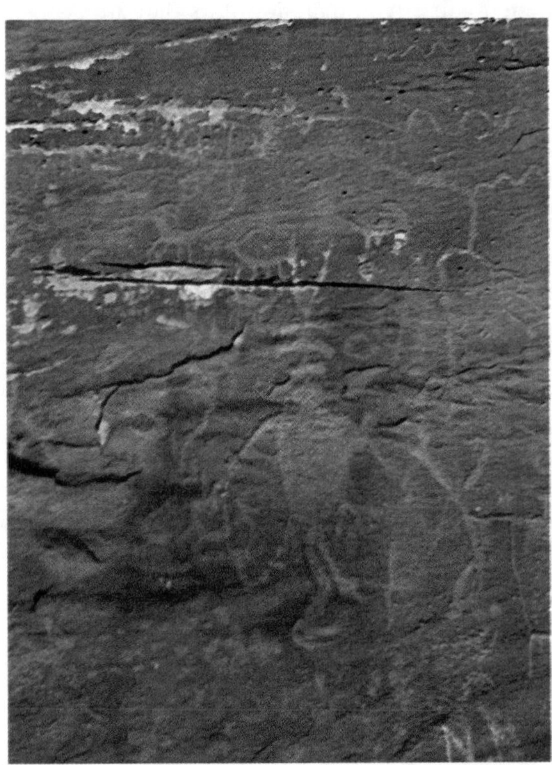

■ **Figure 62: Anasazi rock art, southern Utah.** Photograph by Diana Reed Slattery.

Strassman et al. draw the connections among the alien entity phenomena of the DMT experience, alien abduction reports, the Anunnakis of the mythology of ancient Sumer, and the Old Testament accounts of the Sons of God, arguing the case that the mechanism delivering these types of revelatory visions of the Other resides in spontaneous release of endogenous DMT (Strassman 2008).

> the new narrative is synchronicities   patchworking   alignments that appear from exact viewpoints and are hidden otherwise   the key to the work of art is in finding the correct viewpoint from which to view it   aspects of alien art high Glide foolishness (session report 06.01.12, MDMA)

Color

Shamanic art, worldwide, appears to be a collaboration with the alien Other, in its many forms, encountered in ASC. This alien artistry in the presentation of information is often accompanied by a set of qualities—aspects of extended perception. These qualities can include colors that are deeper, richer, more varied, more vivid or more subtle, and in some cases completely novel that make up the visual palette. The complexity and density of the informational field is in part accompanied by an increased amount of very fine cognitive detail and a concomitant shift in the amount of color detail from the sensory systems.

Attention

Attention, a primary function of consciousness, presents a panoply of aesthetic choices in psychedelic mind-states, shifting its qualities, in some cases toward an increased slipperiness (hyperconductivity), sliding frictionlessly from one point of focus to another. At other times attention becomes the ability to focus in stillness, to hold awareness not only of the object of contemplation but of awareness itself, a type of "witness consciousness" or mindfulness that allows direct perception of the activity in one's mind. One becomes aware that attention can partake of the qualities of touch—rough, focused, gentle, smooth and/or erotic and applied with various admixtures of emotion.

Layering

Another visual-cognitive quality that emerges is the layering of visual imagery and thought. This can be accompanied by subtle and shifting degrees of transparency and iridescence, of soft flows combined with extremely precise fine filamental structures and a sense of having X-ray vision and microscopic vision as controllable aspects of the visual field. Macroscopic visions of the structure of the cosmos at astronomical scales can also be presented to consciousness. Transparency, including crystal vision, becomes a metaphor for all manner of seeing-through, revealing in the combined sense of seductive veils and of revelation of a truth, a hide-and-seek God game of gnosis. Now you see Me, now you don't. A play of quest and question, layering is a noetic dance performed in realms that stretch the labels and cognitive ordering schemes of natural language.

The high-information aspect of alien art is not a matter merely of quantity of information but information imbued with qualities such as fecundity, an abundance of creativity in the flood of images and ideas. Often one encounters a prevailing mood, perhaps of playfulness, or numinosity, benevolent and sinister in rapid oscillation. Or strange juxtapositions of mood occur, such as sacred silliness or the mood invoked by an environment with a combination cathedral and carnivalesque architecture, each mood generating a seemingly endless fount of aesthetic styles. The entire perceptual environment can turn on a dime with a shift in mood. Throughout the ten-year research period, I experienced a broad range of feeling-states, many deep, all transient. I learned profound lessons in my experiences with pure paranoid delusions, and with deep grief, as much as I learned from the gifts of ecstasy. The world—the reality of the individual—looks completely different to a soul trapped in paranoia than to a soul in bliss. Once again—perception (driven in part by feeling-states) and reality are deeply intertwingled. Back at baseline, these extreme states gave me a keener understanding and an empathic ability to be in the presence of certain forms of mental illness. This appreciation through direct experience was a goal of some of the early LSD research, where it was thought that a psychiatrist could better understand his or her patients' experience by trying an "artificial psychosis." I imagine this was problematic, as the LSD experience, as with all psychedelic experience to some degree, can be quite unpredictable. Psyche gets ornery: seek the psychosis, and you might well end in heaven. Seek heaven, and hell may await.

Patchworking

"Patchworking" describes a complex collage-like visual-cognitive process by which different, sometimes drastically diverse, bits of vision-knowledge begin to collect and arrange themselves into larger patterns that incorporate, recombine, and transform the meanings of the individual pieces. Quilt-making, at baseline, is such a process. Music and video mashups share this aesthetic.

The illustrated quilt brings together hundreds of diamond and triangular patches from discarded clothing, carefully recycled into a design that incorporates two- and three-dimensional visual aspects. The design shifts depending on whether you view the material within the hexagons as flat six-pointed stars, or as baby blocks (Necker cubes). In the three-dimensional baby-blocks view, one can see two different perspectives. Each perspective in turn recombines the order of the perceived patches. The surface, playing with these illusions, shifts and moves dynamically among dimensions, as the different

■ **Figure 63: Mary Alexander. Blocks and stars on hexagons, c. 1880.** From University of Louisville Archives and Records Center, Kentucky Quilt Project.

views pop in and out of the visual field. The complex visual surface of the patchwork quilt is analogous to the patchworking or mashup of information in the psychedelic sphere. In other words, the patchworked visual designs are not just form constants, abstract patterns produced by the nervous system, or "psychedelic eye-candy" but are imbued with a semantic dimension and a pedagogical intent. McKenna describes this patchworking effect:

> Occasionally I would seem to catch the mechanics of what was happening to us in action. Lines from half-forgotten movies and snippets of old science fiction, once consumed like popcorn, reappeared in collages of half-understood associations. Punch lines from old jokes and vaguely remembered dreams spiraled in a slow galaxy of interleaved memories and anticipations. From such experiences I concluded that whatever was happening, part of it involved all the information that we had ever accumulated, down to the most trivial details. The overwhelming impression was that something possibly from outer space or from another dimension was contacting us. *It was doing so through the peculiar means of using every thought in our heads to lead us into telepathically induced scenarios of extravagant imagining, or deep theoretical understandings, or in-depth scanning of strange times, places, and worlds.* The source of this unearthly contact was the *Stropharia cubensis* and our experiment. (McKenna 1993) [emphasis added]

A kaleidoscope containing a handful of irregular bits and pieces of colored glass and other materials constructs a complex, shifting, symmetrical, non-repeating stained-glass window of colored light. In my own session reports I describe patchworking as

> making harmonious compositions out of impossibly disparate items without breaking the narrative dream but rather expanding its inclusiveness (session report 05.03.27, MDMA)

Patchworking in altered states assists in "layering realities" and is

> a practice to acclimate you to staying in multiple spaces that are incongruous, non-contiguous, seemingly dissonant (session report 05.04.01, hashish)

Patchworking appears to be an aesthetic strategy whereby the Other, a conscientious recycler, using the stored personal information, emotions, and memories of the individual, and adding its own utterly alien forms to the patchwork, constructs new forms and configurations of knowledge about our existing reality, its past and future, and about other worlds and other realities with profoundly alien content. This alien content reveals itself as vast machineries, strange energies, alien beings, or different time-space schemata. Whole worlds unfold operating on different physical principles. Or our own world is suddenly viewed from a distinctly different consciousness. These alien shifts reveal other patterns of world-organization, such as underlying structures of reality based on games.

Patchworking, a form of hypernoia, ecstatically rejoins that which has been dismembered, fragmented, or never connected in the first place, in meaningful patterns in the domain of visual language. As such it shares a functional pattern with the shamanic initiatory experience of dismemberment and rebirth in a new reconfigured body that can travel between worlds and hold consciousness of multiple worlds at once. In the case of patchworking, it can be whole worlds that are shattered into shards of reality, then reassembled with new meanings.

The Dimensions of Dimension

> *"All of us sooner or later in our lives, have had the bitter experience that it is extremely difficult, perhaps impossible, to squeeze oneself into the fourth dimension. However, every point of our three-dimensional space is an open door to the entry into the fourth dimension, but no matter how much we stretch and twist, we remain stuck in the all-too-well-known three dimensions."*
>
> —Heinz von Foerster, 2003

Changes in perception of time, space, and dimensionality are frequently reported in psychedelic experience, with the words "multidimensional" and "hyperdimensional" used, without definition, in session reports, such as this *Salvia divinorum* narrative from the Vaults of Erowid.

> Immediately after exhaling I felt an extremely powerful shift in consciousness and perception. Shift is an understatement. . . .
>
> My visual perception was difficult to describe, as it was very multidimensional and familiar. It is similar to being in a dream, some other

dimension where 3rd-dimensional perception and laws do not apply, but being as lucid, even more awake and lucid than I am in normal 3rd dimension. (Alhim)

A mushroom report from Erowid states:

I was a multidimensional being existing on multiple planes of consciousness at once. The shrooms freed my consciousness so I could see the different levels of myself. I had to remember which plane of existence I freed my consciousness at. The concept of me I or mine became very foreign. (Chris 2000)

Some observations of mine from the low orbit of cannabis:

I am convinced that those intricate folding and unfolding and emerging out of themselves multidimensional constructs are visualizations of actual chemical processes   consciousness is not an emergent phenomenon that describes human experience (how chauvinistic how naïve similar to having the entire universe revolved around this tiny planet) but rather the all-pervasive, multidimensional substrate of existence in all its multitudinous forms (session report 07.04.18, cannabis)

And another observation from the higher orbit of 2C-B:

seeing the details   learning the characteristics of a multidimensional visual space-in-motion   imagining space curving and distorting with forces internal to itself—energy patterns that then shape the forms (session report 05.03.30, 2C-B)

The word "dimension," in various dictionaries, first points to measurement or "magnitude measured in a particular direction" and second to "scope, importance, or aspect." Thomas Banchoff fills out these definitions:

The word dimension is used in many ways in ordinary speech, and it has several technical definitions. When we refer to a "new dimension," it almost always means that we are measuring some phenomenon along a new direction. (Banchoff 1996)

Constructing geometrical dimensions, whether in the mind's eye, drawings, or computer visualizations, can provide considerable mental exercise as the dimensions increase. The thought-experiments of Edwin Abbott, in which a Flatlander, a two-dimensional creature, encounters a three-dimensional stranger from Space, are classic comparisons of the view from different dimensions (Abbott 2008). Hyperspace philosopher Charles Howard Hinton performed almost impossible feats of visualization, first of a cubic yard of one-inch cubes, assigning a two-word Latin name to each of the 46,656 units. He taught himself to view the construction from any of its possible orientations, an exercise he called a "casting out of the self." Rudy Rucker uses a retinal image to describe how Hinton's "seemingly insane idea" (memorizing a cubic yard of one-inch cubes) was used to visualize the fourth dimension.

> . . . what he had in effect done was to create within his mind the kind of "three-dimensional retina that a 4-D being would have." . . . Now Hinton could, without difficulty, visualize all the cross sections of a hypercube. (Rucker 1984)

Heinz von Foerster's 1970–1971 experiment at the Biological Computing Laboratory for apprehending the fourth dimension is unique, and years ahead of its time in pushing the edge of computer graphics. It combined four-dimensional geometry, stereoscopic vision, and joystick manipulation of objects on the screen. The experiment concerned knowledge acquisition as a partnership between "Sensorium and Motorium," i.e., embodied knowledge, and was not an attempt to penetrate the fourth dimension for its own sake. The fourth dimension was chosen as the knowledge to be acquired because there was no chance that any subjects would have attempted such knowledge before the experiment. By allowing the virtual "grasping" of the visual (virtual) object, where one hand coordinated movement on three axes in the third dimension, while the other similarly controlled three axes of movement in the fourth dimension, subjects were able to intuitively figure out that the strange succession of transforming 3D objects they were seeing (with 3D glasses) were cross-sections of a single 4D object (von Foerster 2003).

An extra-dimensional advance is described as orthogonal, at right angles to, i.e., *a move in a direction not contained in the dimensions one is moving beyond*. If you move a point (zero dimensions) in a direction not contained in itself, and leave a trace (a writing) of that motion, you generate a line. If you move a line (one dimension) in a direction not contained in itself, you generate a plane (two dimensions). If you move a plane (two dimensions) in a direction not contained in itself, you generate a cube (three dimensions).

With the visualization of movement, time has entered into the creation of new spatial dimensions—and writing as well, in a generalized form.

These moves can be easily visualized or drawn on a piece of paper. But a strange thing happens when one tries to visualize the fourth dimension. What, in the three-dimensional world we live in, corresponds to the direction not contained in itself that points the way out of the third to the fourth? As Spacelanders, we find this frustrating.

> the passage from inorganic to organic life so-called could be a phase transition of consciousness the zone of passage so difficult to imagine with certainty perhaps because of the mystery of phase transitions themselves. Viewing this borderland seems to be the quandary of imagining the "reality" of the in-between area   is it in some way like trying to zoom in on the infinite boundary of the Mandelbrot set a description and set of perceptions (from the math of the computer graphics once again) that again is tied in the unbreakable circle the second-order cybernetic system if you will of perception reflection and projection in the Dome of consciousness (session report 06.02.03, cannabis)

Thomas Banchoff discusses the analogical process of understanding as applied in geometry, calling it "the dominant idea in the history of the concept of dimensions."

> Thinking about different dimensions can make us much more conscious of what it means to see an object, not just as a sequence of images but rather as a form, an ideal object in the mind. We can then begin to turn this imaging faculty to the study of objects that require even more exploration before we can understand them, objects that cannot be built in ordinary space. (Banchoff 1996)

It is exactly this seeming limit of visualization, this effort to see the unseen, that came to the forefront in mathematics, science, art, and spiritualism in the latter part of the nineteenth and first part of the twentieth centuries. This history has been documented from the art-historical perspective by Linda Henderson in her study, *The Fourth Dimension and Non-Euclidean Geometry in Modern Art*. Henderson centers on "the idea promulgated by Hinton and many others that space might possess a higher, unseen fourth dimension." The fourth dimension became a nexus for generative analogy, a means of reaching for an understanding of the unseen, and expressing the difficulty of the reach. For a period of time, the worlds of ideas of scientists and mathematicians, spiritualists and theosophists, and artists and psychologists cross-fertilized at the juncture of the seen and the unseen, the known and the unknown. Out of this ferment came the revolutions of modernism and modern physics. The unseen world pressed at the borders of the comfortable zone of realities that could be sensed and measured, whose dimensions could be known, pointed to, and shared. Cubism's geometries; surrealism's unconscious automaticities; the quantum description of a physical reality flickering in and out of existence; the Freudian and Jungian unconscious; an expanding universe whose borders leap further and further beyond the reach of observation or even imagination are a few of the chasms that opened in knowledge in the first third of the twentieth century. All brought with them versions of "the real" as embedded in and/or emerging from some unseen and largely unknowable ground. The scientific situation with respect to the ratio of unknown to known, at the beginning of the twenty-first century, is worsening dramatically with the hypotheses of dark matter and dark energy (the galactic unconscious). We seem to know less and less about more and more. At the same time the Enlightenment-style search for a Theory of Everything, casting the Light of Reason into this further darkness and mystery, continues—one is tempted to observe—in a spirit of desperate denial.

The question persists: what makes the visualization of the fourth dimension both so tantalizing and so difficult? The jump to visualizing the fourth from the third dimension may first be a factor of our sensory equipment. The body, viewed from outside, is a three-dimensional object in a three-dimensional world. But how did the world—and our bodies within it—come to be defined in step-wise numbered dimensions? Binocular vision, combining two two-dimensional retinal images to result in a perception of depth, is a primary factor in our experience of space. Binaural hearing gives us a volumetric sense of sound location. These affordances enable our navigation in space, and later, our abstract conceptions—including geometries—about space. What kind of spatial conceptions and geometries we might have invented if we were endowed with the multi-faceted, domed eyes of a fly can only be imagined. But that is to try to find the answer in the zone of the sense-able, by means of the baseline senses.

In his 1949–1953 work, *The Ever-Present Origin*, Swiss philosopher Jean Gebser presents a history and a model of the evolution of consciousness through five stages. The final stage, which he names the integral, has the dimension four, is characterized by an aperspectival "viewpoint," is space-free and time-free, and has the quality of diaphaniety or transparency. The *diaphainon* is a complex concept, meant in part to convey a "shining through" that reveals the wholeness of a given form. Gebser follows directly on the path of Gauss's nineteenth-century non-Euclidean geometry:

> And the concept of a non-Euclidean geometry in turn is an imaginary anticipation of the later-realized sphere which is non-fixed, four-dimensional, and free of perspective (i.e., aperspectival) because it is a moving as well as transparent sphere. . . . The simple sphere is merely three-dimensional; only the moving, transparent sphere is four-dimensional. And only the transparency guarantees the aperspectival perception. (Gebser 1984)

This description of diaphaneity resonates with the earlier description of crystal vision. The term "aperspectival" recalls Hinton's attempt to transcend the individual perspective in his techniques for visualizing the fourth dimension.

The connection to the concept of higher dimensionality as a feature of the evolution of consciousness is a prevalent psychedelic theme. For science, the fourth dimension had been described, something that was a logical step in thinking once a higher-dimensional geometry was conceived, and a step as simple in numerical terms as counting—1, 2, 3, 4. Yet a stubborn boundary was marked—easily crossed by logic (once the initial adventurers scouted the territory) but seemingly impossible to cross by perception (internal or external). That is, until psychonauts began to report that the *perception* of multidimensionality is a matter of perturbing the state of one's brain chemistry, and thereby retuning perception and reality in tandem. New dimensions, in every sense of the word, come into view.

Fractal Dimensions

The topic of dimension became far more complex with Benoit Mandelbrot's introduction of fractal geometry. As he acknowledges, the mathematics (Cantor, Peano, Koch, Hausdorff and their "monster" sets) goes back to the same period in the nineteenth and early twentieth centuries in which the idea of the fourth dimension was popularized. But the key idea of "in-betweenness" Mandelbrot traces much earlier. "Several basic ideas of fractals might be viewed as the mathematical and scientific implementation of loose but potent ideas that date back to Aristotle and Leibnitz." Mandelbrot quotes from a 1695 letter of Leibnitz's:

> One can ask what would be a differential having as its exponent a fraction. You see that the result can be expressed by an infinite series. Although this seems removed from Geometry, which does not yet know of such fractional exponents, it appears that one day these paradoxes will yield useful consequences, since there is hardly a paradox without utility. Thoughts that mattered little in themselves may give occasion to more beautiful ones. (Leibnitz quoted in Mandelbrot, 1983)

Mandelbrot discusses Leibnitz's deep belief in the "principle of continuity" or of "plenitude." He cites Aristotle's intuition about the continuity of living species, and his fascination with chimeras, the "in-between" animals, and draws the comparison to the mathematical chimeras "in-between dimensions" produced by Cantor and Peano.

> When the whole structure appears—reminds me of the sephirot endlessly repeated—sephirot fractally multiplied, nested, connected—multidimensional object—shaping space perception—(as in knot space) where the fundamental domain causes reflections and reverberations viewed from 3-space (session report 03.06.07, MDMA)

■ **Figure 64: The Mandelbulb, a three-dimensional rendering of the Mandelbrot set.**

The ability to compute and visualize these dimensions with computer graphics brought an esoteric field of mathematics into broad awareness through the endless variety and beauty of the forms. To some, Mandelbrot has located the "fourth" dimension in the infinite interstices of the Euclidean 0—3 dimensions.

■ **Figure 65: Detail, Mandelbulb.**

This principle of continuity can be grasped immediately when one takes a "fractal dive" zooming into the depths of scale of the Mandelbrot set, spaces whose geographies are as strange as a psychedelic vision and as familiar as the forms of our natural world.[7] Mandelbrot reviews the questioning of the classical concept of dimension that began with Riemann in 1854. Even more fundamentally, he forever destabilizes the concept—and the act—of measurement itself in his analysis of the problem of determining the length of the coastline of Great Britain. Measurement is seen to be strictly observer-dependent and the results of that measurement highly variable depending on the choices of the observer as to the scale of the measurement undertaken. As explained by John Briggs and F. David Peat,

> Mandelbrot has gone so far as to say he thinks that when his fractal geometry highlights the inextricable relationship between object and observer it is in keeping with the other great scientific discoveries in this century, relativity and quantum theory, which also found an interdependence between observer and observed. The quantitative measure—on which science has been based—is also challenged by this insight. (Briggs 1990)

Fractal forms are ubiquitous in nature, and may, according to N.C. Kenkel, prove to be "a unifying theme in biology" (Kenkel 1996). Biologists have traditionally modeled nature using Euclidean representations of natural objects or series. Examples include the representation of heart rates as sine waves, conifer trees as cones, animal habitats as simple areas, and cell membranes as curves or simple surfaces. Biological systems and processes are typically characterized by many levels of substructures, with the same general pattern being repeated in an ever-decreasing cascade. The importance of fractal scaling has been recognized at virtually every level of biological organization.

"Fractal" is a common descriptor in psychedelic experience reports, and a visual cliché in much of what is termed "psychedelic art," especially in live-performance light shows. There is no question in my mind that my three-year fascination with the program Fractint in the early 1990s catalyzed my pursuit of the idea of a visual language. I spent hundreds of hours tweaking the formulas and seeing the changes in the fractal forms.

Howard, a high school senior at the time of the experience quoted below, reports a direct apprehension in the psychedelic state of this general transcalar construction of reality as fractal.

> During the stretching into eternity feelings I would have a sensation like my concept of reality was zooming in and out, from the microscopic to the universal. At some points it would feel like I was looking at the entirety of existence, and it appeared to be a huge swirling fractal. It was more like a 3-dimensional fractal, but thinking back on it now the closest thing I can equate it to is the 2d fractal images that are popular with psychedelic users. All the "pixels" (or points) of this fractal were moments in time and they were all swirled together in some huge mess which did not make sense in the linear concept of time, but I had a sense that it all fit in some way that was beyond my comprehension and was deeper and more meaningful than linear time or spatial relationships. Throughout this whole experience I had an overwhelming feeling that what I was experiencing was more real than anything I had ever experienced before, and to this day I am convinced that outside my narrow concept of reality, this is what exists and awaits me (when I die for instance). In fact I had a vague sensation that within the webwork of this fractal were all the lives I had ever lived as well as all the lives I would ever live. It also seemed like everything that existed was represented within this incomprehensible swirling fractal. (Howard 2003)

This vision of the transcalar fracticality of time will be met again in the description of the McKenna brothers' fractal construction of time in the Timewave Zero system (see Chapter 9).

Sensory Modalities of Xenolinguistic Presentation

Psychedelically generated linguistic events present themselves across the sensory spectrum: visual, aural, gestural, and synaesthetic. These can be part of the experience itself, such as spontaneous vocalizing and glossolalia, multidimensional visual languages, or mudra-like gesturing. The linguistic experience has been brought back by some and translated into baseline artifacts, such as paintings. The sensory spectrum, as described in the sections above, can include novel sensory experiences not usually available at baseline, such as what I describe as "crystal vision."

The description of the "Voice of the Logos" in Horace Beach's doctoral dissertation, *Listening for the Logos: A Study of Reports of Audible Voices at High Doses of Psilocybin*, highlights the aural.

> What mystics such as Plotinus are trying to explain is the following: while it is possible to experience directly . . . what has been described through history as the archetypes (as described by Plato, St. Augustine, and the various Buddhist-Hindu systems), or even the Absolute or noumenon of phenomena, or the Nondual, . . . much of recorded historic experience of what has come to be known as divine inspiration or revelation comes through one of the various manifestations or intermediaries of the Absolute in the form of gods, spirits, angels, or ancestors. At times they appear to humans, but they also reportedly can be experienced as disembodied voices. (Beach 1996)

Terence McKenna describes the voice of the Logos as a consistent feature of the psilocybin ASC, and he sees it morphing from an aural toward a visual modality that he considers to be potentially generating greater understanding. McKenna frequently cites an allegory of Hellenistic philosopher Philo Judaeus that postulates this visual manifestation of meaning as "the more perfect Logos."

> We are going to go from a linguistic mode that is heard to a linguistic mode that is beheld. When this transition is complete, the ambiguity, the uncertainty, and the subterfuge that haunts our efforts at communication will be obsolete. And it will be in this environment of beheld communication that the new world of the Logos will be realized. This experience of an interior guiding voice with a higher level of knowledge is not alien in

> Western history; however, the intellectual adventure of the last thousand years has made an idea like that seem preposterous if not psychopathological. (McKenna 1991)

McKenna speculated that tryptamines such as DMT and psilocybin directly affect the language centers of the brain.

> Psilocybin and DMT invoke the Logos, although DMT is more intense and more brief in its action. This means that they work directly on the language centers, so that an important aspect of the experience is the interior dialogue. As soon as one discovers this about psilocybin and about tryptamines in general, one must decide whether or not to enter into this dialogue and to try and make sense of the incoming signal. (McKenna 1992)

McKenna describes the experience of the passage from the aural to the visual in the tryptamine trance in detail as a cross-modal process. The DMT experience is for McKenna "the central mystery." This passage, quoted at length, contains many of the themes in McKenna's visual-language epiphany: the activities of the "machine elves" as source; the syntactical organization of reality; the idea of living language, language that has come alive as mechanical elves behaving autonomously; a different form of glossolalia; the vision of a three-dimensional visual language; and the sense that language is evolving, literally "right before our eyes" in the tryptamine trance.

> On DMT these entities, these machine-like diminutive shape-shifting faceted machine elf type creatures that come bounding out of the state... they're elfin embodiments of syntactical intent. Somehow syntax which is usually the invisible architecture behind language has moved to the foreground and you can see it and it's doing calisthenics and acrobatics in front of you, it's crawling all over you ... What's happened is your categories have been scrambled and this thing which is normally supposed to be invisible and in the background and an abstraction has come forward and is doing handsprings right in front of you. . . . [The typtamine entities are saying] do this thing, do this activity, do as we do. And you can sort of feel your intentionality reorganizing and you can feel this heat—it's quite akin to heartburn. I won't metaphysisize it . . . but heat in your stomach and it moves up and your mouth flies open and you do—this stuff comes

> out which is a very highly articulated syntactically controlled non-English, non-European language behavior, not strictly speaking—though I call it glossolalia . . . it strictly speaking is not glossolalia. Glossolalia has been studied, and it's a trance-like state. On the floors of these Pentecostal churches in Guatemala they measured pools of saliva sixteen inches across from people who were in ecstatic glossolalia. This is much more conscious, much more controlled. It's almost like a kind of spontaneous singing, but your mind steps aside and this linguistic stuff comes out and you can see it, that's the amazing thing. It is not to be heard even though it is carried as an acoustical signal. Its meaning resides in what happens to it when the acoustical signal is processed by the visual cortex. That's the important thing. It is a new kind of language. It is a visible three-dimensional language. It's not something I ever heard about or any mystical tradition I ever heard about anticipated. It's as though the process or the project of language, which according to academic linguists began no more than fifty thousand years ago . . . is not yet finished. And this thing we do with small mouth noises and each of us consulting our own learned dictionary and quickly decoding each other's intent—this is a stumblebum, cobbled together, half-assed way to do language and what we're on the brink of or what these psychedelic states seem to hold out is a much more seamless kind of fusion of minds by generating topological manifolds that we look at rather than we localize into designated meaning. (McKenna 1998)

Media Ecology

We live in an all-encompassing media-surround with communications attracting our senses visually and aurally (and now, with the touch-screen, kinesthetically) from phones, TV, earbuds connected to iTunes, car radios. The Dick Tracy wrist communicator is with us now. We have moved smoothly (at least those under thirty have) from passive reception (TV and radio) to highly interactive devices. The phone, as the first ubiquitous two-way street, taught us electronic interactivity. Google Glass, the next big thing, lets us stay connected to otherwhere and wherever your here is at the same time: layered and augmented reality, navigated by attention. We will learn this skill from our devices as we have learned to type texts with the silence of two thumbs tapping. The touch-screen renders infinite information by caress. We stroke our way through our contact lists, the news, social media, a kind of ambient intimacy.[8] Marshall McLuhan thought of media ecology as

> . . . arranging various media to help each other so they won't cancel each other out, to buttress one medium with another. You might say, for example, that radio is a bigger help to literacy than television, but television might be a very wonderful aid to teaching languages. And so you can do some things on some media that you cannot do on others. And, therefore, if you watch the whole field, you can prevent this waste that comes by one canceling the other out. (McLuhan 2004)

My view of media ecology is more Varelian: mindful, full of complex—sometimes competitive, sometimes cooperative—conversations among systems. These media systems are arising and going extinct on the fast-forward evolutionary schedule of epigenetic forms. Though connected always (parasitically or symbiotically) to human hosts, media organisms behave in ways that can be experienced autonomously: out of human control. Bruce Sterling announced the Dead Media Project at ISEA 1995, meant to catalogue the extinct forms of media we have been charging through even in the past few decades: Betamax, which fell to VHS, which succumbed to DVDs, which are slipping toward extinction with TIVO and Roku boxes. All these terms—and their media—will likely slip from our lexicon as well, rendering this passage quaint in a few short months. Social media are a new ground for competition. Insofar as our entire "overload of information" is ported to digital media, this ephemerality is built in to the media "physiology" of hard drives and DVDs that have a half-life of ten to twenty years maximum.

The trend toward the visual in our media ecology is a given. Photography undergoes successive explosions—overtaking painting as the means of recording human personality and projects; exploding further with digital photography. TV moves radio into a new niche, the automobile then elbows into the backseats of mini-vans. Mobility and media are the new mantras. Whatever is said here regarding media ecology is perfectly self-evident at the moment of writing—and will staledate rapidly. Archeology on demand.

With each new media form, new affordances appear. The development of animation techniques is a good example. We began with the cell-based labor-intensive Disney cartoons and the direct manipulations on the film itself (painted, scratched, etc.) of the mid-twentieth-century experimentation of Norman McLaren and Stan Brackage. Animation now has done a dimensional leap from 2D to 3D. Tools are now available to the student with pirated software that were once the exclusive property of the Hollywood studio system.

These rapidly evolving affordances become available for new forms of language to emerge. This was very much on Terence McKenna's mind in his last interview with Erik Davis, shortly before his death in 2000.

> Ultimately, McKenna wants something more than trippy images. He hopes that computer graphics will blossom into a universal lingo, a language of constantly morphing hieroglyphic information that he claims to have glimpsed on high doses of mushrooms. "There is something about the formal dynamics of information that we do not understand. Something about how we process language holds us back. That's why I encourage everybody to think about computer animation, and think about it in practical terms. Because out of that will come a visual language rich enough to support a new form of human communication."
>
> In McKenna's mind we are not just conjuring a new virtual language. We are also, in good old shamanic style, conjuring the ineffable Other. McKenna argues that the imagery of aliens and flying saucers—which spring up in numerous tripping reports as well as in pop technoculture—are symbols of the transcendental technologies we are on the verge of creating. In other words, we are producing the alien ourselves, from the virtual world of networked information. (Davis 2000)

The Glide symbolic system, in its dynamic, moving, and morphing visual forms, could not have been brought into view without computer animation techniques, both two-dimensional and three-dimensional. The media ecology, springing from the linguistic machinery of the computer, created by humans, used by humans, and with a life of its own, presented an environment. New uses of the environment for new forms of language resulted. The feedback loops, the structural couplings (to use Varela's term) between humans and media forms are tight, multiple, and rapidly evolving.

I have elaborated a model of consciousness as multiphasic rather than monophasic (Laughlin), or using Roberts's terminology, as multi-state rather than single-state. A model of reality that is leveled and multidimensional follows from this model of consciousness. Perception is modeled as mutable and extendable, as are the means by which the multiple levels of reality come into view. But it bears repeating that these are only models and linguistic constructions, the finger pointing at the moon, that go only so far in communicating the variety of psychedelic experience itself. And it is in the matter of perception that one can at best make metaphor to try to give a feel for the fineness of filamental structures. But it is far more difficult to describe the wholeness of the filamental experience, and the wholeness experience itself, where knower and known are melded together and tuned to a higher, finer, and more penetrating, more powerful frequency.

The next chapter turns toward the neurophenomenology of language.

Notes, Chapter 6

1. This felicitous phrase was overheard repeated many times by a physicist on an extended acid trip.
2. 1000 mμ is a heroic dose of LSD. However, it is nowhere close to the LD50 of LSD, which is 12,000 mμ. LD stands for lethal dose; LD50 is the dose at which 50 percent of a population who takes it would die. In contrast, the LD50 for a 100-pound woman is five to six mixed drinks. That being said, to try such a dose without working one's way up to it over a period of time would be, in my humble opinion, the height of foolishness. Then again, Mullis's adventures led to a Nobel Prize. Such is the nature of the outrageous.
3. This is not to say that these perceptions are always or universally a part of those shamanic, yogic, or psychonautic perceptions in ASC.
4. I have never found it possible to write during a *Salvia divinorum* session; hence, a post-session report.
5. Psychedelic synaesthesias are so common, there's even a joke about it: Why do hippies wave their hands when they dance? To keep the music out of their eyes.
6. I am quoting Karl Wallenda, the *pater familias* of the tightrope act, The Flying Wallendas.
7. An animation of a fractal dive can be seen here: http://youtube/cDd8R0xlkNA.
8. The term "ambient intimacy" was coined by Leisa Reichelt, an organizational consultant.

CHAPTER 7

Neurophenomenological Perspectives on Language

"Any model of the brain/mind that does not reconcile the observations of neurobiology with the fact of the psychedelic state, as it is experienced, is doomed to remain scientifically incomplete and philosophically unsatisfying. Psychedelic drugs have always been and remain the most useful molecular probes available to science for exploring the relationship between the subjective experience of mind and neurobiological processes. Given the validity of this statement—and I suggest that no neuroscientist with personal knowledge of the psychedelic state would contest it—one cannot fail to be puzzled by science's curious neglect of psychedelic research over the last two decades."

—Dennis McKenna (McKenna and McKenna, 1993)

The idea of the co-evolution of language and consciousness is given a neurophysiological grounding in Charles Laughlin's theory of the symbolic process. Language is construed as intrinsic to living forms at a fundamental and operational level. Laughlin tends to reserve the term "language" for human forms of the symbolic process. When I use the term "the linguistic" I am beginning with Laughlin's "the symbolic" as a basis of understanding, and expanding the notion of "the linguistic" to the novel phenomena of the psychedelic sphere. As a xenolinguist, I study the shifts and transformation of language in altered states of consciousness both from the inside out (my own experiences with Glide) and the outside in (the experiences of other xenolinguists). This chapter examines in particular the ideas of Charles Laughlin and Francisco Varela, whose work offers models of the ways that symbolic processing arose and evolved in living forms. Psychologist Harry Hunt's work on the presentational or visionary mode of symbolic cognition takes us into perceptions particular to altered states. Renaissance scholar Steve Farmer's work on correlative systems (such as the *I Ching,* and Pico's *900*

Theses) correlates our layered brain topology with the thinking that created deeply layered systems of thought.

I am using a neurophenomenological approach to reach the zone of the novel linguistic phenomena in the psychedelic sphere. We will travel by way of a common ground, our neurophysiological makeup. This makeup includes our linguistic abilities, always a blend of the linguistic potential we are given at birth and those skills developed through the acquisition of culture. The neurophenomenological model is presented in some detail as an approach that takes altered states of consciousness into consideration, and one that takes into account both the subjective experience of mind and neurobiological processes.

Laughlin, McManus, D'Aquili: The Symbol and the Symbolic Process

Laughlin, McManus, and d'Aquili's work,[1] *Brain, Symbol, & Experience: Toward a Neurophenomenology of Human Consciousness,* on the symbolic process, presents a neurophenomenological model that treats the symbol on a gradient scale from the basics of pattern recognition that we are born with (what Laughlin calls the neurognostic), up through the development in humans of natural language and further to formal sign systems such as mathematics. These concepts, especially as they address the role of the symbol in altered states of consciousness, will be helpful in understanding the narrower field of specifically psychedelic perception and reality. Their model offers a means of incorporating the alien aspect of language in the psychedelic sphere into a continuum of symbolic evolution throughout nature, which includes the human being and our forms of symbolic processes, still under active development. The following subsections develop the vocabulary used in their model and relate these terms to experience reports, where applicable.

Conscious Network and the Sensorium

The totality of the neurological systems involved in consciousness—including the full range from what at any given moment is "unconscious" to the content of current awareness—is termed in Laughlin "conscious network."

> Conscious network is the system of entrainments mediating the entirety of consciousness: the sensorium is the subsystem within conscious network mediating phenomenal experience. Sensorial activities include verbalized thoughts, percepts in all sensory modes, affective feelings, imagination, and the like. (Laughlin 1990)

In addition to perceptions in all sensory modes, Laughlin includes "verbalized thoughts, affective feelings, and imagination" in the sensorium. The sensorium in Laughlin is similar to what is "onstage" at any moment in Baars' Theater of Consciousness (Baars 1997).

> The sensorium is the functional space within the nervous system wherein the phenomenal aspects of the cognized environment are constituted and portrayed in moment-to-moment experience. The sensorium, a time-honored term in science and medicine (Newton used the term in the eighteenth century!) usually refers to the "whole sensory apparatus of the body" . . . Phenomenal reality is thus in part an entrainment of cognitive and sensorial networks, which is designed to portray an unfolding world of experience to the organism. The functional space within which association and perception are combined into unitary phenomenal experience is the sensorium. (Laughlin 1990)

The sensorium is the site of experience. As covered in the previous chapter, psychedelic mind-states fill the sensorium with percepts not available at baseline: increased dimensionality in the perception of space; time compression or dilation; hyperconnectivity across domains of experience; hyperconductivity and speed of thought; colors, sounds, forms only perceptible in these states of extended perception; and non-local access to knowledge, to name a few. As Nobel Prize-winning physicist Brian Josephson stated, "The physical description of the world would change radically if we could observe more things" (Josephson 1973). We become aware that baseline experience is only one phase of experience, and that, to understate the case along with Brian Josephson, the psychedelic experience brings forth in the sensorium "more things to observe."

The Primary Units of Experience: Dots

The notion of "dots" as the primary unit of experience is considerably more nuanced, derived from the experience of mature contemplatives (including Laughlin's own years-long practice of Tibetan Buddhist ritual and meditation). Hindu philosophy as well as Western philosophy from Leibnitz to Whitehead are also referenced. The extreme alterations in perception in the psychedelic landscape can include many varieties of transformation of the baseline perceptual field, where "normal" reality begins to waver, shift, and dissolve, sometimes into "dots." The following trip report from Erowid depicts a wild multi-subtance ride in which dots are a prominent feature:

> I saw some faint blue dots scattered in with the normal dark red blobs and as my eyes adjusted, the blue dots stopped being random, grew in brightness, and formed a circle. Then inside the circle, another circle of dots formed and so on making the appearance of a tunnel. Next thing I know my perspective starts accelerating down the "tunnel" and the blues change to yellow and finally, as I think I need to take a breath, turns white. I open my eyes and exhale. The room looks normal.
>
> I take another hit, cover my eyes, relax my mind and defocus my vision. The dots coalesce again and form the same tunnel. I am distracted for a moment and a face pops into my head, but then I concentrate on the trip into the tunnel, and I see the face painted like a texture onto one row of the dots. The next hit of nitrous and I am open-minded and focused on the vision. It happens faster this time, and I am down the tunnel to the white dots. [5-MeO-DALT, methylone, and nitrous oxide] (Cup 2004)

> This was a white void with an infinity of swarming black dots. . . . [LSD] (hiab-x 1992)

> I was at home in my apartment looking ahead in the living room when I noticed small black dots. The dots were everywhere there was empty space (air). [*A. muscaria, P. cubensis,* and *Calea zacatechichi*][2] (norman 2003)

But the notion of "dots" is not necessarily to be taken literally; it is applied to more than the visual sensory mode.

> There is another feature of sensorial activity that is elusive and contradictory to naïve introspection. This feature is one of the many reasons that evidence derived from introspection by trained, mature contemplatives is essential to a modern theory of consciousness. It is readily apparent to the mature contemplative that experience arising within the sensorium is composed of innumerable, almost infinitesimal and momentary particles. This field of particles passes through consciousness in epochs ("waves," "frames," "heaps," "chunks," etc.), an intermittence that may correlate with cortical alpha rhythms. Most people miss these tides of particles because they are simply not interested in, nor are they trained to concentrate upon, the mechanisms of their own perception—as it were, to perform a "phenomenological reduction." But with training, it is easy to become aware of the activity of these tiny and momentary sensory events, given the requisite calm and concentration. (Laughlin 1990)

A prominent instance of fields of "dots" in combination with "waves" can be seen in the iconography of the Australian aboriginal depictions of the Rainbow Serpent.

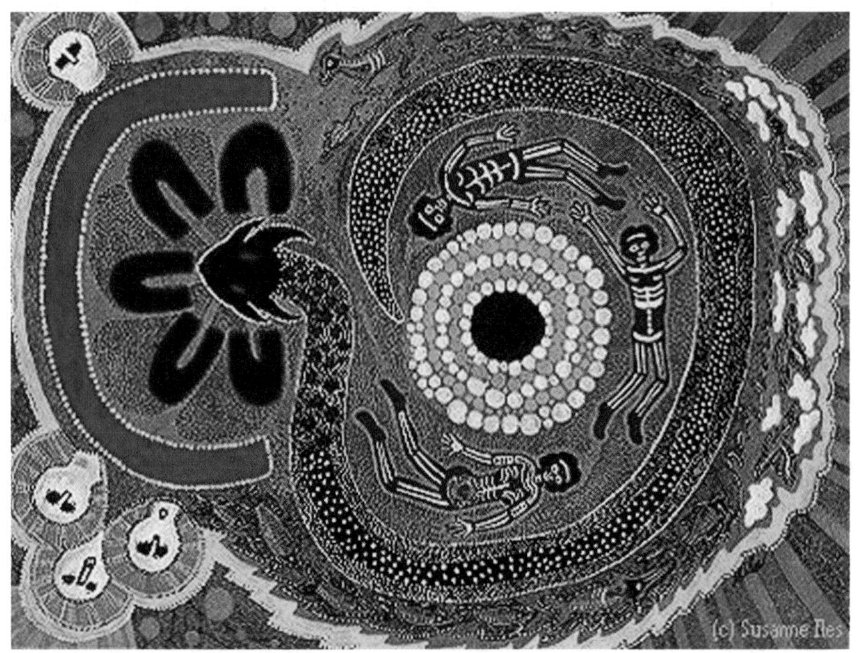

■ **Figure 66: Suzanne Nes, Bonesinger.**

■ **Figure 67: The rainbow serpent in rock art, Australia.**

These figures of the Rainbow Serpent's dots and waves have also appeared in my own drawings in altered states of consciousness. The Rainbow Serpent as the underlying energy of the Glide symbolic system was mentioned in Chapter 3. Dots and waves can be seen in many of the images studied by Lewis-Williams (see Chapter 6), both entoptic and extant, and he relates forms in rock art to Kluver's form constants.The experience of intermittent "frames" mentioned by Laughlin is a perceptual experience for some in the psychedelic sphere and seems to be related to the experience of time dilation. From a cannabis trip report from Erowid:

> We were working our way across the park and time practically came to a screeching halt. I could almost see the very fabric of time ripple as some force just slammed into it, slowing it down drastically. The walk from the river bank to the flat land was like an effort against time. . . . I was seeing in frames and could see in every direction even though I was not looking in that direction. Frame vision is kind of like being in a room with a strobe light, only the frames seem to "tail" each other. My vision also zoomed in at about a 30' area that was far in front of me. It zoomed in to that over the space of one frame. [cannabis] (Skullman 2005)

Renwick, below, interprets the phenomenon of "frames" as a slowdown of visual processing in the brain.

> At higher doses Ketamine's ability to slow down the speed at which the brain processes visual information becomes even more interesting. Where

> low doses seem to make everything appear as if your vision was broken up into frames, high doses seem to blur visual phenomena together in an odd way. [ketamine] (Renwick 2002)

Laughlin asserts the primacy of sensorial dots as the basic units from which all phenomenal experience is constructed. He carries this analysis all the way through to the highest mystical states of consciousness.

> The sensorium is a dot-filled "field of perception" which is perceptually and cognitively distinguished into sensory modes and within sensory modes into distinct forms and events. The basic act of perception is the abstraction and reinforcement of invariant features in the unfolding field of dots.... It is the job of the cognized environment to portray an internalized world of phenomena by ordering dots into recognizable configurations. There are, however, phases of consciousness attained in mature contemplation during which the entire sensorium is experienced as a single monad (either bounded or unbounded, finite or infinite), where the distinction between the different fields of dots constituting various sensory modalities merge into a unified, singular field (the *coincidentia oppositorum*). During this experience consciousness becomes indistinguishable from the sensorial monad, the sensorial monad indistinguishable from consciousness.... Conscious experience at this point verges upon totality, a phenomenally undifferentiated, timeless, and infinite monad of awareness in which the unfolding energy events play themselves out without hindrance and with the experience of complete flow. (Laughlin 1990)

It is this "abstraction and reinforcement of invariant features in the unfolding field of dots" (the field of perception) that is at the core of the symbolic process. In this sense, perception and the symbolic process go "all the way down" to the dots, to the primary units of experience.

> My vision is being affected as well. I have a very grainy field of vision, as if everything was made up of tiny hyper-vibrational particles that I could actually see in motion, like watching a swarm of gnats in a way. [4-Acetoxy-MiPT with prior ephedrine and cannabis] (Rivers 2005)

The next experience quote finds particles in a sonic-bioenergetic field of experience.

> Force-fields, thin clear beams like lasers of sound, smooth crests, clouds of particulate sounds like swarms of electron bees, echoes of fractal complexity, resonating sound-scapes made of smaller versions of themselves, forming larger than life cathedrals of transient sound structures in flux. It was sort of an Ethernet for intercommunication among vastly variegated life forms from all over the galaxy. [LSA] (Justin 2006)

Laughlin further elucidates the concept of dot as a "descriptive empirical category and not a theoretical one like a black hole or a quark." He relates it to the Hindu concept of the *bindu,* a Sanskrit term meaning "dot" or "drop," which is the elemental particle of *prana,* the fundamental energy of the universe. The dot is also connected to the monadologies of Leibnitz, Kant, and Husserl. In the case of Whitehead's formulation of "actual entity," the dot stands as a point of consciousness. In making these correlations, Laughlin connects the dots, the primary units of experience, to consciousness. Perception, language (as symbolic process), and consciousness together go all the way down to the dots.

Laughlin places the symbolic process in a central position in neural organization and experience. As such, his concept includes, but reaches beyond, the symbol as it is conceived in a semiotic context. When he is talking about the symbol (as "signifier") he is refering, minimally, to any stimulus that provides sufficient patterning for entrée into a model (as "signified") that contains more information than that provided by the stimulus. The symbol is the medium by which we connect the "operational world" (of noumena) to the "cognized world."

> The intentionality of a symbol may be conceived as simply the functioning of the models evoked by and entrained to that symbol, or the functioning of the models that produce that symbol. (Laughlin 1990)

Evolution of the Symbolic Process

"Actually, consciousness can't evolve any faster than language. The rate at which language evolves determines how fast consciousness evolves; otherwise you're just lost in what Wittgenstein called the unspeakable."

—Terence McKenna (Brown 2010)

Theoretically, we are at the heart of the matter of the co-evolution of language and consciousness with Laughlin's descriptions of the evolution of the symbolic process and of symbolic forms.

Semiosis

The development of the cognized environment—the accrual of ever more complex models and the symbols that evoke them—is called "semiosis" in Laughlin's system.

> If a symbol-model entrainment is to be effective in completing intentionality so that it facilitates an adaptive response to the world, then the model must be formulated in active dialogue with the world. We term this dialogue semiosis: the EMC[3] process by which a symbol develops its intentionality.[4] (Laughlin 1990)

Semiosis is that process by which the novel symbol is assimilated to conscious network—adjusting models in the learning process. Laughlin spells out in detail the indicators of this evolutionary advance in semiosis. They include:

> (1) increased spatiotemporal distance between a noumenon and reception of information about the noumenon leading to evoked intentionality; (2) increased complexity of cognitive associations (or models) entrained as intentionality; (3) increased expansiveness of spatiotemporal extension modeled within intentionality; (4) increased capacity for cross-modal transference and integration of intentionality; (5) increased hierarchicalization of models mediating intentionality; (6) increased autonomy of higher cognitive functions from lower affective ones; and (7) increased complexity of formalized behavior as an expression of intentionality. (Laughlin 1990)

Life communicates symbolically in complex and multiple ways: within a single organism communications relay from quantum to molecular to macro levels across scalar vastnesses, and between the organism and the "operational environment" that includes other organisms. Life, from the smallest microorganism to the human being, is in constant communication within itself and to and from its world. Evolution proceeds by building nested hierarchies from the simplest to the most complex. Laughlin summarizes the evolution of the nervous system—and consciousness—in terms of the symbolic process.

> In short, the symbolic process has become more ramified and complex along precisely those dimensions that have characterized the allometric elaboration of prefrontal, parietal, and temporal association cortex. For example, the development of cross-modal transfer meant that a symbolic stimulus presented to one sensory mode could potentially evoke models in more than one sensory mode. *Obviously, then, we may speak of the evolution of the symbolic process reflecting the evolution of consciousness, for symbolic processing incorporates many of the structures that are routinely entrained to conscious network and that mediate consciousness.* (Laughlin 1990) [emphasis mine]

Language and consciousness are deeply, deeply, *deeply* intertwingled.

Symbolic Forms

The symbolic process in cognition operates largely at an unconscious level unless given the form of attention of contemplation to bring it into view, as with the perception of dots. In the evolution of symbolic forms, Laughlin differentiates first between symbol (small *s*) as the fundamental form (stimulus-as-object) and SYMBOL (big *S*) as cognized symbols, identifying SYMBOL as an evolutionary advance.

> A person or society's SYMBOLS are typically those that may evoke models of the most extensive and profound intentionality (e.g., flags, totems, shamanic regalia, religious icons, commercial logos, personal costumary, etc.). (Laughlin 1990)

SYMBOLS are the products of enculturation. Laughlin introduces the concept of semiotropism to discuss the functioning of SYMBOLS in culture. We orient ourselves in our cultural landscape by means of our symbolic landmarks. When SYMBOLS capture our attention, turning us toward their meaning, Laughlin calls it semiotropism.[5]

> Semiotropic responses are particularly dramatic and evident when they are upon SYMBOLS within the context of ritual. The role of prefrontal cortical structures in both augmenting associations configured about the

> SYMBOL, and inhibiting alternative objects of attention, is paramount. (Laughlin 1990)

The next step in Laughlin's evolution of symbolic forms he terms the sign. Laughlin postulates an increasing arbitrariness of the symbol and its intentionality as signs proliferate and become parts of larger symbolic systems.

> From the present perspective, a *sign* is an evolutionarily advanced and specialized SYMBOL. A sign is specialized for participation as a unit in a greater SYMBOLic system. The evolutionary sequence has been from the primitive symbolic process to cognized symbols. Coinciding with the development of SYMBOLS, the cognized environment became less stimulus-bound, an occurrence indicating that cognitive associations and intentionality of models could be, to some extent, removed from the pressure of immediate perception. As the cognized environment became less stimulus-bound, the relationship between SYMBOL and intentionality in expression reciprocated. This reciprocation produced (was the necessary condition for) a greater semantic arbitrariness in the intentionality of SYMBOLS over and above symbols. (Laughlin 1990)

After the evolution of symbolic forms comes the development of *sign systems:* human spoken and written "natural" languages. Laughlin critiques Chomsky's postulate of "deep structures" as the generative source of language, as limited to specifically "linguistic" structures, which cannot be mapped onto neurocognitive organization. He hypothesizes, rather, that

> [. . .] a neurocognitively grounded theory of language will recognize that the deepest structures of lexical intentionality are not to be found in discrete linguistic structures, but throughout the neurocognitive system and its perceptual, conceptual, imaginal, affective, and attentional structures. . . . We need recourse only to common experience to see that linguistic utterances may evoke thoughts, images, scenes, feelings, states of arousal, and autonomic and metabolic responses. (Laughlin 1990)

This view is paralleled in anthropologist Terence Deacon's work:

> Once we abandon the idealization that language is plugged into the brain in modules, and recognize it as merely a new use of existing structures, there is no reason to expect that language functions should map in any direct way onto the structural-functional divisions of cortex. (Deacon 1997)

Deacon's definition of "the symbol" is less inclusive than Laughlin's. He describes the symbol as a specifically human development, differentiating between earlier forms of cognition and communication at the animal level. He is also firmly in the camp of the symbolic process as being "representational." The point I am emphasizing in Laughlin's formulations is the sense in which the symbolic process goes "all the way down" as a more important point than the distinctions in semiotics among the "iconic," the "indexical," and the "symbolic." Laughlin of course recognizes the differences between the human symbolic process and that of earlier animals. Natural language, as the human being's primary sign system, "obtains its notable adaptive power because it is the manifestation of a neurocognitive system relatively free from a perceptual frame."

The next stage in symbolic evolution, in Laughlin's taxonomy, came with the emergence of *formal sign systems*. While they see the origins of abstraction as far back as the Middle to Upper Paleolithic, these systems begin to flourish and proliferate with the invention of writing. While the origins of spoken language are largely indeterminable from the lack of physical evidence, the origins of written symbolic systems can be determined to a closer degree. The cuneiform accounting systems of Sumer date back to the fourth

■ **Figure 68: Cuneiform script, Sumeria.** Wikimedia Commons.

millennium BC. There are Chinese tortoise-shell inscriptions, related to divination, that date back to 6000 BC but whether these constitute writing *per se* is contested.

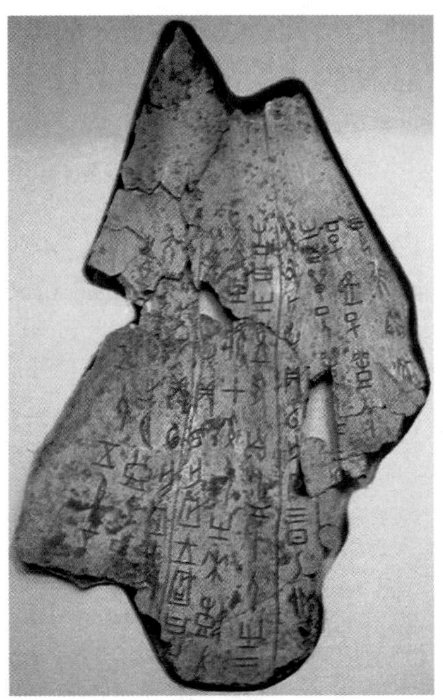

■ **Figure 69: Chinese oracle bone script.** Wikimedia Commons.

Formal sign systems such as mathematics, geometry, symbolic logic, and computer languages are developing exponentially. The development of media such as photography, cinema, and computer graphics is part of this process of symbolic proliferation. From this standpoint, the symbolic process—when one considers symbolic forms in the human being—is evolving at an accelerating pace. The premier example of symbolic evolution is the general-purpose linguistic machine—the computer. With its electronic language of logic gates, based on Boolean logic, and the layers of language by which software is elaborated, the computer is a very recent linguistic machine that has arguably revised the structures of global civilization with at least the impact of the introduction of electricity itself. The advancement of communication technologies in general, and digital technologies specifically, what we group under "media," is a history that underpins at least two of the specific examples of xenolinguistic systems explored in this book, specifically the McKenna brothers' Timewave Zero, and my visual language, Glide.

> [If] you look at the evolution of media as you would look at the evolution of a species or a group of genera in an organic situation you would see a very pronounced preference for the visual. Colorful and rich speech gives way to photography . . . then color and motion . . . stereo . . . Clearly we view the language-forming enterprise as a task not yet brought to completion. (McKenna 1994)

The Universal Symbol

Laughlin identifies the universal symbol that stands in a different relation to the evolution of symbols outlined above. The universal symbol is identified with the Jungian archetype. Examples of universal symbols are described as arising in meditative practice, where the meditator constructs, element by element, and holds an inner SYMBOL (such as the representation of a complex Tibetan Buddhist deity) steadily in mind.

> When an inner SYMBOL is stabilized as an eidetic image, and concentration upon it is intense and undistracted, the stage is set for the arising of one or more universal symbols. These are sensorial phenomena that arise unbidden from unconscious networks, and are the result of a radical reentrainment of networks producing a warp in consciousness. The inner SYMBOL is transformed or eliminated, and in its place occurs a sensory experience intuitively, but nonrationally related to the inner SYMBOL. (Laughlin 1990)

These universal symbols are seen as cross-culturally invariant (hence universal) in the structure of alternative phases of consciousness. Universal symbols have a numinous nature. We are back to bliss.

> the bliss of re-figure-ment—hard to express in human—yes—Glide—but you your future selves—as we said before—time pours through the crystal lattice the crystal matrix—the memes will go forth bursting like pollen from the anthers—crystal pollen, crystal spores from the opening pod of your mind and the crystal structures. . . . (session report 01.12.15, MDMA)

> Finally, it should be emphasized again that the arising of the universal symbol often occurs paired with an affect of intense ecstasy or bliss. . . . It is unexpected, it is often novel and dramatic, and it is frequently paired with both intuitive insight and ecstatic bliss. (Laughlin 1990)

> Ecstatic sensations—can the ascent be described? Physical—running throughout the body very fast now—close eyes and will be gone—thread of language requested given—Now visual just beginning. The multiplying of dimensions—whole body participates—something flooding through—the rainbow serpent swiftly swiftly occupies the space of the body (session report 03.01.18, 3 g *Stropharia cubensis*)

The following excerpt from a 2002 session report records the formation of a complex universal symbol.

> Faithful scribe. A scriptorium. A Glide seated himself in the heart of the blue lily. Crosslegged. Reddish dark skin, elven ears. Human sized. He shows me the crystalline lilies. He gives me a crystal ball or bubble to hold. The ball is a portal. The ball is a condensed space/place. The crystalline blue, green, violet space of the lilies. Crystals. Great wealth flower petal soft, crystalline sharp and defined. This is different this teaching. You have to be more "awake" to scribe this. Learning to see into the other dimensions/spaces. Don't invalidate. This is important: you want to see us—the blue-purple lily fills my heart—again—more vivid—larger—it leaped in it unfolds and unfolds—Blue-black lotus—deep deep velvety lotus—the jewel in the lotus crystal and soft and petal like (the center of the lily a tiny point)—highly condensed—the petals open and open and open—everything generated from the point—of infinite depth at the heart of the lily—this is the connection point be very very aware of it—in the center of the heart that holds the lily—this is the crystal the jewel this is the opening—let me go through—it is the point through which the center universe is pulled "inside out"—deeper than deep—deep deep blue point—seed portal—something so tiny, so point-like something so secret so centered something to be aware of bindu The jewel in the lotus the heart the center—it is the treasure—in the center of the heart—it is not conceivable but you can sense it—it is the great secret—the jewel in the heart of the lotus the lily is real real real—it is a deeper illusion than all illusion it is the midnight pearl (session report 02.11.16, MDMA)

Symbolic Penetration

Laughlin defines symbolic penetration as a transcalar, interconnected system of communication:

> The effect that one cell has upon another, one network has upon another, or one system has upon another we have called penetration. . . . This mutual interpenetration occurs between nested systems at the same level of organization within the same system. (Laughlin 1990)
>
> Symbolic penetration can be *driven* as well.
>
> Lower autonomic systems may be tuned and retuned directly by penetration from external stimuli. . . . These stimuli are called drivers and may

> take the form of repetitive stimulation such as drumming, flickering light, chanting, or sexual intercourse. Drivers may be used in ritual circumstances to generate simultaneous discharge of both systems (e.g., orgasm), which sets the stage for a radical retuning of the systems relative to particular stimuli. (Laughlin 1990)

The role of symbolic drivers in both the shamanic and the syncretic church settings to guide the ayahuasca encounter is well-documented. Hymns or *icaros,* dances, drumming, and visual symbols such as ritual costumes and the objects on a shrine or on the shaman's *mesa* all play their part in channeling the experience within a culturally determined set of intentionalities. These meanings are reinforced by the creation in the group of a shared state of consciousness shaped by previously internalized models (the myths and cosmologies of the group; the *set*) entrained by symbolic drivers.

■ **Figure 70: LiveGlide, still image from video performance.**
Diana Reed Slattery.

Symbolic drivers in the form of universal symbols are integral to many of the experiences we call art. In my own practice of performing with LiveGlide, the projection of the moving, transforming symbols onto a dome in an altered state of consciousness *drives* the altered state of consciousness. This projection, on the physical dome, and reflected in the dome of consciousness in turn, directs the writing and simultaneous reading in a feedback loop, amplifying the intensity, resonating within the integrated inner/outer space of inscription. In the ASC, the glyphs of the Glide symbolic system create their meanings in the flow of symbol through 3-space into form *(flow begets form)*. LiveGlide forms generated by the Rainbow Serpent gesturing through the body-mind produce a visual form of the Rainbow Serpent. The serpent energy generates the glyphs in their basic form. The glyphs, moved through 3-space, create the spiraling waveforms of the Rainbow Serpent. The serpent is a universal, cross-cultural, multivalent symbol.

Harry Hunt: Presentational and Representational Symbolic Cognition

"Everything was blazing with significance."

—Terence McKenna

Psychologist Harry Hunt concentrates on "presentational" states of consciousness, in contrast to the linguistic or "representational" states he sees as the focus of the majority viewpoint in cognitive science. The idea of the presentational is helpful in understanding both the sense of deep meaning imbued in the perceptions of altered or visionary states, and the encounter with various aspects of what I interpret within altered states of consciousness as "linguistic phenomena." Hunt consistently uses "language" and the linguistic to refer to human "natural" language, as does cognitive science in general, and "symbolic cognition" as specific to the human, self-referential form of consciousness. But Hunt, along with Laughlin and Winkelman, points to altered states of consciousness as an important site for research into consciousness and symbolic cognition.

> It is here that we can turn to the spontaneous transformations of consciousness that constitute "nature's experiments" on mind, initially at least in its first-person aspect, and that have been variously termed "altered states of consciousness," "transpersonal states," or, as below, "presentational states." These phenomena appear to offer just the empirical clues both to the nature of consciousness in general and to its cognitive-symbolic processes that are lost in the transparency of ordinary awareness. Indeed, these subjective states, both in their positive form as an enhanced experiential synthesis and in their more disintegrated and psychotic aspect, constitute the uniquely privileged "microscope" for an emergent psychology of consciousness—and perhaps even of symbolic cognition itself in its broadest aspects. (Hunt 1995)

Certainly nature, in providing fungi and plants such as the varieties of "magic" mushrooms, cannabis, *Amanita muscaria,* and the range of ayahuasca admixtures and at the same time developing neurotransmitter receptors in animals, including humans, that can recognize these molecules, has created a site for experimentation that psychonauts have occupied like an ecological niche. By relating "symbolic cognition" to "presentational states" (ASC), Hunt constructs a framework for understanding hallucination (extended perceptions) and mystical vision as linguistic, communicative, something that can be read, a text. We are brought closer to a particular psychedelic meme: the concept of the linguistic structure of reality.

> That's why it's so important to communicate, for all of us to put our best foot forward, to put our best metaphors on the table. Because we can move no faster than the evolution of our language. And this is certainly part of what the psychedelics are about: they force the evolution of language. And no culture, so far as I am aware, has ever consciously tried to evolve its language with the awareness that evolving language was evolving reality. (McKenna 1991)

Hunt uses the terms "symbolic" and "language" somewhat differently than Laughlin. For Hunt, language means natural language while the symbolic encompasses the full range of meaning-making from the presentational to the representational. He does not posit the presentational as a more primitive form of cognition out of which the specifically linguistic emerges. Rather he sees all symbolic cognition as cross-modal and synaesthetically based, in other words, highly complex under introspective scrutiny, though not necessarily recognized in "the transparency of ordinary awareness." This cross-modality is, in his view, essential to all metaphoric construction. This view relates to George Lakoff's view of primary "image schemata" derived from our embodied and kinesthetic sense (Lakoff 1980, 1989).

> One of the things that is especially interesting about these states is that they appear to be spontaneous expressions of a self-referential, abstract, symbolic capacity that has traditionally been explained as a consequence of language but here is manifested in a nonverbal form. (Hunt 1995)

Hunt's view of "synaesthetic consciousness" is, however, restricted to the human.

> It makes no sense to ascribe synaesthetic consciousness to nonsymbolic animals, since they lack a capacity to cultivate sensitivities for their own sake, that is, aesthetically. Moreover, there could be no possible use for such beings in having experiences that entail an inability, however brief, to tell which modality has been stimulated or the spatial-temporal location

> of its source. The aesthetically rich properties of these subjective states are the clue that we are dealing with a capacity fully emergent only on the symbolic level. (Hunt 1995)

This restriction of synaesthetic consciousness—or in fact consciousness more broadly, to say nothing of intelligence and language—to the human is sharply contradicted in many aspects of the psychedelic experience. In all the varied ayahuasca cultures of South America, plants are teachers, offering knowledge not only of themselves as symbiotes of the human, but of the most profound cosmological visions. And aesthetics? The seductive rhetoric of the rose, the orchid, or the forget-me-not communicate their complex synaesthesias of smell, taste, touch, color, and form within their own domain to the sensoria—not *human* sensoria alone, but a highly tuned, infinitely specific set of communicative relations of their mobile colleagues—insects, birds, and mammals. These same plants have communicated to us, the humans, in our differently configured sensoria using their extensive vocabularies of chemical communication and effortless production of beauty to lure our impoverished steel-glass-plastic civilized sensibilities to their own adaptive advantage: we cultivate these beauties and advance their evolution, a point made by Michael Pollan about tulips and cannabis (Pollan 2001).[6] Plants are interspecies linguists at a level of depth and complexity that is completely obvious to the shamanically trained who have been taught by the plants themselves (Beyer 2009).

The property of so many psychoactive plants to release, renew, and enhance aesthetic sensibilities in our human selves leads to the question: What kind of aesthetic intelligence can we construe in the world of plants that can redemptively return us to the world of beauty?

> Psychedelics return us to the inner worth of the self, to the importance of feeling immediate experience. And nobody can sell that to you and nobody can buy it from you, so the dominator culture is not interested in the felt presence of immediate experience. But that's what holds the community together. And as we break out of the silly myths of science and the infantile obsessions of the marketplace, what we discover through the psychedelic experience is that in the body—in the body—there are Niagaras of beauty, alien beauty, alien dimensions that are part of the self, the richest part of life. (McKenna 1991)

Hunt, at the same time, relates this "loss of reality" poignantly in his portrayal of the effect of Cartesian doubt:

> Social scientists perhaps should not ignore the fact that Descartes—the progenitor of the subject-object dichotomy in its modern form—actually managed to doubt whether he *existed* and had to construct logical proofs in order to convince himself *intellectually* that he did. Proofs for the existence of God may or may not be charmingly quixotic, but needing a proof of one's own being or isness is, more simply, sad, if not overtly schizoid. The danger is that our contemporary psychological and philosophical concepts of consciousness are not merely conceptually confused, as Wittgenstein would have it, but actually clinically disturbed. We unwittingly enshrine an endemic narcissism and personal isolation at the core of our thought about our own nature and potentialities. (Hunt 1995)

What Hunt does not seem to notice is that his anthropocentrism in respect to symbolic cognition may be another symptom of the same narcissism, applied not only to human nature, but to all-the-rest, Nature herself. In another context, however, in his discussion of William James's famous descriptions of consciousness as stream or flow, Hunt takes this perception of consciousness as flow as a fundamental metaphor, deep in nature.

> Water, air, and fire, as the major metaphors for the formal qualities of awareness, all have in common the properties of a turbulent flow in constant transformation. These same properties are central in mythology, philosophy, and the etymologies of words for "mind" in all languages, and they have now become the focus of contemporary nonlinear dynamics. Perhaps our self-awareness and the perception that it reorganizes is patterned in terms of flow properties "mirrored" in from the most fundamental features of the physical surround for living, motile organisms. If so, then James' stream is both a self-referential metaphor and a mirror of the physical reality most adjacent to the life-world. (Hunt 1995)

Hunt puts flesh on Laughlin's idea of the symbol as a fundamental unit of perception. He continues the explication of flow through the images of alchemy—"expansions, congealings, and flowings into diverse patterns, as a spiritual and meditative enterprise of personal transformation."

> We could say that chaos theory, along with related interests in the self-organization of forms, is the direct historical continuation of these early alchemical preoccupations, otherwise so outside our mainstream scientific tradition. . . . In this sense, their descriptions and pictorial images call attention to the emergent self-organization of the same form constants at all levels of physical reality that is again of such contemporary interest. They also exemplify the flow dynamics of complex cross-modal cognition, since the alchemist will kinesthetically feel what he or she sees. Under it all, and the secret of its fascination, will be the fluid dynamics of the envelope of flow that is the perceptual array of all motile organisms. (Hunt 1995)

> delicious torque-ing twisty serpentine motions of energy in body (LiveGlide forms being drawn in body) this twisting energy in the body-mind produces the transformation of consciousness occurring here—the dimensional shift the move that creates added dimensions   "the force that through the green fuse drives the flower"   a spiraling energy   movement of Tao—coiling, torque-ing, twisting, spiraling, folding, while replicating   flow begets form Qi/the Tao moves the changes   the developmental process that flows through each hexagram—the lines   Glide representing Qi + flow of energy   flow begets form   Qi Gong—the energy system of the body and how it connects to the universe—how form dissolves back into flow—how flow intersecting—creates forms—the delight of forms   micro-level of heterarchical connections necessary matrix—then a fruiting of the form (session report 03.11.02, MDMA)

Hunt traces the spiraling, serpentine forms throughout levels of organic development, with illustrations from D'Arcy Thompson's classic *On Growth and Form* and Theodor Schwenk's work *Sensitive Chaos: The Creation of Flowing Forms in Water and Air.* He quotes Schwenk, "The organ of the higher animal may be regarded as solidified movement."

> Every one of these metaforms so far can be expressed with Glide the wave—(the oscillating string) the vibrations of light and sound—vast signaling system—interconnected at all levels—differentiated deeply. . . . (session report 03.11.02, MDMA)

Francisco Varela: Biologic

Francisco Varela's work on first-person methodology and on the calculus for self-reference (about both, see Chapter 5) touches many concerns of my research. Varela's calculus for self-reference, based on George Spencer-Brown's seminal work, *The Laws of Form,* and developed in conjunction with mathematician Louis Kauffman, forms the basis of a biologic. A biologic is a logic of living forms that bears a suggestive relationship in its ideas and in its formalism to the Glide symbolic system's ternary logic (Chapter 3). A major idea at the heart of Spencer-Brown's *Laws of Form* was the inclusion of self-reference in his calculus of indications. Spencer-Brown aimed at the resolution of the logical paradoxes that troubled Bertrand Russell into his theory of types. Self-reference for Spencer-Brown reflects the psychedelic, alchemical and/or mystical experience of the union or coexistence of opposites without contradiction.

> The world view that made the most sense of this experience was clearly a mystical one. Neither the subjective nor the objective pole of experience could encompass the totality. The possibility of transcending boundaries between self and other, the illusory nature of ego, the interdependence of opposites, the relative nature of dualism and the resolution of paradox in transcendence became clear. (Francis Vaughan, LSD, in Grinspoon 1983)

Looking back through our own history as a species, with our elaborate forms of symbolizing capacity, is one way to imagine the evolution of language. Looking at our biological construction through the evolution of form in the biosphere as a fundamentally linguistic process itself is another. Varela extends the domain of *natural* language to an understanding of the way in which nature has constructed me linguistically or, at the very least, produced a creature that would describe her (nature's) activities in such a fashion.

Autopoiesis, a central idea in Varela's work, derived from his teacher Humberto Maturana, is the construction of a self-producing and self-maintaining autonomous living system. A cell is an autopoietic system; so is a heart. Varela distinguishes between two levels of description, which he calls the operational and the symbolic. The operational or causal description of the autopoietic living system is, essentially, a description in terms of scientific practice that yields predictable outcomes, and that has no need to include purpose or *telos*. The operational description traces causal interconnections between components of the system; it is the language of chemical interactions, of molecules and atoms. In *Principles of Biological Autonomy,*

Varela's extension of Spencer-Brown's calculus of indications to a calculus for self-reference is central to the operational description of autopoiesis. As Varela asserts, "Living systems, as physical autopoietic machines, are *purposeless* systems" (Varela 1979). And further, "Notions of information and purpose are, from the point of view of an operational explanation, dispensable." In essence, such notions belong to a different domain than the system's autonomous organization. Varela, however, makes clear that one can recover a "non-naïve and useful role of informational notions" belonging to a different category of explanation, the symbolic, and makes clear that "the connection between an operational description (such as autopoiesis) and a finalistic description lies in the observer who establishes the nexus." In other words, nature supplies the processes. Humans supply the meaning, always a human meaning from a particular viewpoint.

> This possibility of choosing to ignore intervening nomic links is at the base of all symbolic descriptions. What is characteristic of a symbol is that there is a distance, a somewhat arbitrary relationship, between signifier and signified. . . . Thus in order to understand language, we do not trace the sequence of causes from the waveform in the air to the history of the brain operation, but simply take it as a fact that we *can* understand. . . . Thus we come to the conclusion that purpose and symbolic understanding are interrelated as a duo, that is symmetrical to the duo of operational explanation and prediction. Under symbol we are subsuming here the varieties of its forms, such as code, message, information, and so on. (Varela 1979)

Varela asserts that the operational and symbolic description do not contradict each other, coming from two different levels of description in a community of observers.

The autopoietic system maintains itself through its self-contained regularities—the predictability of the operations—and it is these regularities that give rise to symbolic explanations. An example of a symbol would be the identification of a "gene" as a structure in the system of the cell's organization, an assigned meaning that carries descriptive power beyond, and in a different fashion than, the operational descriptions of DNA within the autopoietic organization of the single cell. The "gene" is implicated in relations between autopoietic systems, in a larger context outside the single autopoietic system—relations such as "development" and "evolution."

> On empirical grounds, the regularities that have been fertile and preserved in evolution are those such that the symbols that stand for them can be seen as *composable like a language*—in other words, such that the individual symbols, as discrete tokens, can interact with each other in a syntax capable of generating new patterns in combination. Again, the typical example is the genetic symbols, which in a linear array are eminently composable. This is still somewhat possible, but not so clearly so, in the case of external signals and surface receptors. . . . (Varela 1979)

The great symbolic systems of living beings—the genetic and nervous systems and human language—are all based on regularities whose symbols are composable through rules that generate a vast class of new phenomena out of a set of discrete elements. An *autopoietic system* has organizational closure; it is autonomous, possessing a unique and bounded identity. Phenomenology, in this light, is self-description from within an autopoietic system. An autopoietic system maintains a balance between its structural invariance, by which identity and wholeness are maintained, and structural plasticity, the limits of change within the system that can occur while maintaining invariance. This play of opposites, the internal management of a discursive paradox within the system, is expressed in Varela's calculus for self-reference.

The bodies of living forms are composed of intercommunicating, nested hierarchies and heterarchies (what Varela calls "trees" and "nets") of autopoietic systems: systems within systems within systems, each producing and maintaining itself (as an autonomous whole) while simultaneously functioning as part of a larger system: whole/part.

Structural couplings are the interactions of a structurally plastic system in an environment with recurrent perturbations that will produce a continual selection of the system's structure. The *cognitive domain* of an autopoietic system is the specification of the domain of interaction with the environment that is possible without loss of identity. Judging from the novel experiences of the mind when the brain undergoes psychedelic perturbations in its neurotransmitter systems, we could say that the brain/mind system is highly structurally plastic. One may undergo ego dissolution—the disappearance of what is, at baseline, an omnipresence—and live to see it restructured like a smashed cup pulling itself back together to wholeness when the frame sequence is reversed. The mind, apparently, is so plastic that its primary structures, such as the sense of self or self-identity, can disappear or dissolve and pull themselves back together. Identity lost is quickly regained, but often with subtle or not-so-subtle changes. Henceforth, the ego contains the knowledge of its own porosity, and the possibility of its very personal dissolution and subsequent rebirth. When the individual's cognitive domain expands to the degree that occurs under psychoactive stimulation, and can be integrated upon return to baseline, the fact of plasticity allows changes to occur in the baseline structures of consciousness. Capital S Self has intervened with small self (ego) to change its mind. The positive changes that a profound psychedelic excursion, in a supportive setting, can bring have been well documented in the clinical research of Charles Grob, Roland Griffiths, and others in their research on the use of psilocybin and LSD to ameliorate end-of-life anxiety in terminally ill patients. The attitudes and emotions of the baseline self can be shifted in a positive direction.

A *symbol* in Varela's scheme is a component interaction in a structural coupling. The concept of the allowability of structural coupling reveals the rule-based syntax of these interactions.

> Any component interactions thus defined as a symbol are generated by the coupling and can only be defined in reference to it. (Varela 1979)

> Further, whenever the symbolic components of a cognitive domain can be seen as composable (i.e., syntactical), this corresponds to an immense evolutionary advantage for the units that generate them. The emergence of second-order autonomous systems is then possible, built on the interdependence of a symbolic domain. (Varela 1979)

> —syntax—where the link-view is as important as the node—that it connects and how it connects—when in motion, exhibits link-seeking, link-generating, and link-breaking behavior metaphor and process, also metaphor in process—as links are made and broken in a shifting fabric or surface of meaning (2D Glide) or, more complexly—where meaning emerges as a moving edge, leaving behind it the static forms—where flow begets form—where the energy of meaning-seeking (or desire to communicate) reaches out, exhibits link-seeking behavior (session report 03.03.23-24, Paris SETI Workshop on Interstellar Messaging, MDMA)

The technology of DNA editing has emerged in the context of the vast living intelligence we call nature or the biosphere. Our test, and it is a huge one, is to use this technology not only to our perceived momentary advantage as humans, but with awareness of how we fit into the whole of nature. What effects a change in the part will have on the whole, including all other life-forms, depends in large part on our awareness of other life-forms, and of our deep intertwinglement with them. We live in an interdependent world. Varela's view of biology emphasizes the tight connections (structural couplings) that exist on every level of the body, and with the world outside the body.

Varela goes on to define a *linguistic domain* as "the aggregate of symbolic descriptions arising from the structural coupling between two or more autonomous systems." Communication is behavior in a linguistic domain.

> body a living language—made of code—metaphor for filamental structure—at many levels of description—multiple metaphoric structure—wave structure of the universe   superstring theory intones the waviness the profound waviness of the universe   an interconnected web of finest vibrating fibers—Tai Chi—waves of chi (session report 03.03.23-24, Paris SETI Workshop, MDMA)

This set of definitions—autopoiesis, symbol, structural coupling, linguistic domain, and cognitive domain—outlines a framework for living systems that is linguistic at the core, and linguistic at every order of magnitude within the living form. Varela's autopoietic systems are *knowing* systems, engaged in communication, cognition, and linguistic behavior, at every level. Knowledge arises in the interactions, the conversations or structural couplings between autonomous systems. In this sense they are "units of mind."

> A conversation on the one hand embodies a direct prototype of the way in which autonomous units interact. On the other hand, it is an instance of an autonomous entity in itself, and a very important one, for we are immersed in the ongoing autonomy of our tradition, the ongoing autonomy of a next higher level of interdependence as participants. These two sides of conversations bring us in fact to the heart of an essential consequence of all that has been said before, namely, the need to *reconsider the traditional notion of subject.* (Varela 1979)

> notion—in Qi Gong—the movement, can be made entirely with the mind? the body/mind work together—grasping for something here—mind is body whole

> body—in some sense—distributed awareness—can the mind stalk like a jaguar? ripple like a goldfish tail? (session report 03.03.17, MDMA)

> We can go one step further here, to notice that whenever we consider an autonomous unit, it will have two characteristics that make it mindlike: First, it specifies a distinction between it and not-it, a basic dual split. Secondly, it has a way of dealing with its surroundings in a cognitive (informative) fashion, depending on its plasticity. From this point of view, then, mind is an immanent quality of a class of organizations including individual living systems, but also ecological aggregates, social units of various sorts, brains, conversations, and many others, however spatially distributed or short-lived. There is mind in every unity engaged in conversation-like interactions. (Varela 1979)

I have gone into Varela's thought in some depth, quoting him at length, because I feel it offers an interwoven view of mind, sentience, cognition, language, and symbol that is most useful in describing psychedelic experience phenomenologically. It is the essence of the constructivist position, which he differentiates clearly from the "objectivist scenario." In Varela's view, informed by a scientific biological practice, a mature Buddhist contemplative practice, and a deep understanding of systems theory, including second-order or self-reflexive systems, consciousness and language go all the way down to the roots of life itself. This distributed, densely interconnected notion of "mind" is reminiscent of Huxley's "Mind at Large."

The neurotransmitter system is a highly structurally plastic system, as is the whole of the nervous system. Perception is one of the major systems in the body that is perturbed due to psychedelic action. These perturbations change, for their duration, the sense of self, opening self to Mind at Large and thereby to the experiences that I have called the Other (in its multiple forms). These perturbations create, temporarily, novel symbols and novel forms of cognition in conversations with the Other, and thereby the possibility of new knowledge. The experience that Richard Doyle has called the ecodelic insight and McKenna calls the Gaian oversoul or "an ecology of souls" can be understood from this theoretical framework. The self—our way of referring to our internal sense of our own unique, differentiable, and distinct identity or autopoietic nature—can also be seen as highly structurally plastic. It can seemingly dissolve its usual self-perception into new formations, and engage in new conversations within Mind at Large, then reshape itself to its initial state, regaining its recognizable autonomy at baseline. Consciousness, in this light, is seen as one of the most structurally plastic systems we can experience. The self reveals itself as a linguistic construction whose autonomy can dissolve (death of the Ego) or be radically reshaped when it enters a different linguistic domain, with different structural couplings (conversations) among selves. The everyday self magically reforms when the perturbation is resolved. What is learned in the psychedelic state under these different epistemological conditions and the symbols that arise could be viewed as the very beginnings of what Tart called for as "state-specific sciences."

The Be Me experience (Chapter 2) of the two-in-one (or two-*and*-one) experientially defines the structural coupling within which knowledge acquisition in the cognitive domain delineated by that structural coupling occurs. In the psychedelic states, links can be formed and then dissolved in the same manner as conversations (structural couplings) between any autopoietic systems.

Psychedelics, by forming new couplings, new configurations of interconnectivity, new conversations, open new linguistic domains, where the interactions of the conversation with the Other can call forth new symbols and symbolic systems, and provide another language with which to speak of the evolution of language in the psychedelic sphere.

Steve Farmer: Correlative Systems

Renaissance scholar Steve Farmer's research on correlative systems relates the structure of premodern through High Renaissance textual and oral traditions to the structure of the brain, especially the anatomy of the cortex. It is important to note that his own correlation upon which his entire hypothesis is based is nothing less than a correlation between mind and matter, between what Varela would called the operational (brain structure, for instance) and the symbolic. Farmer and his colleague, Steve Henderson, a sinologist, were searching for an explanation of the arising of similar forms of cosmological systems cross-culturally within the same time frames where no significant cultural cross-fertilization could have occurred. The model they constructed postulates that given our common brain structure, and therefore our common platform for cognitive activity and the construction of knowledge, such similar systems can and will arise independently and culturally follow similar evolutionary patterns. In the latter stages of this evolution, Farmer identifies the "high-correlative" systems of the Renaissance, systems that correlate more than one correlative system into a grand system, reconciling, through complex exegetical techniques, the apparent contradictions in systems. Farmer's major study is of the *900 Theses* of the "extreme syncretist," Giovanni Pico della Mirandola. Pico constructs a vast correlative and unified system linking the Old and New Testaments with Plato, Aristotle, Kabbalah, Hermes Trismegistus, Averroes, and Avicenna, designed to demonstrate the unity of knowledge underlying these systems (Farmer 1998).

Farmer defines religious, philosophical, and cosmological systems as correlative systems, based in correlative thought, whose origin is rooted in our neurobiology. He takes the term "correlative thinking" from scientist, historian, and sinologist Joseph Needham (Needham 1991). Correlative thinking is "linked in turn to the origins of magic and anthropomorphism underlying myth and primitive concepts of deity" (Farmer 2006). High-correlative systems evolved in all literate premodern civilizations: China, Europe, India, and Mesoamerican traditions.

> Parallel developments we explored in this period included the elaborate cycles-within-cycles associated with mature models of time in Chinese, South Asian, and Mesoamerican traditions; neatly scaling (or "topological") linear models of time that emerged in late-ancient and medieval Jewish, Christian, and Islamic traditions; and the complexly nested hierarchies associated with scholasticism in general. (Farmer 2006)

Farmer's explanation for the synchronous emergence of correlative systems lies hardwired in our neurobiological structures, namely, the vertical (and horizontal) symmetries in the structure of the cortex, where different areas are designated for specialized processing of perception (feature detection, types of tactile data, etc.). The cortex is modeled as "a stack of topographic maps in which the frontal hierarchy is the mirror image of the posterior hierarchy." In Farmer's model, "topographic" means "correlative." The layered structures of sensory processing are brought together in multisensory integration centers.

> What we label "correlative systems," and neurobiologists call "topographic maps," mathematicians refer to in general as "self-similar" or "self-affine" structures—better known as "fractals." (Farmer 2006)

The universal symbol of the fractal is correlated with correlative systems (mind) and topographic systems (matter).

Synaesthetes are presented by Farmer as "ideal models for studies of correlative thinking and closely related phenomena including imitative magic; the condition at present is being intensely studied for the light it throws on cortical integration in general."

> A growing consensus exists that at least one version of synesthesia consists in nothing but a heightened consciousness of normal sensory integration going on constantly in all of us . . . which again suggests the deep neurobiological origin of correlative thinking. *This view finds further support in the fact that synesthetic experiences can be readily induced in a normal subject by use of hallucinogenic drugs, which were widely employed in ancient religious-magical traditions.* (Farmer 2006) [emphasis mine]

Farmer emphasizes the critical role of brain-culture interactions in shaping our plastic brains. Laughlin's neurognostic structures are echoed in Farmer's formulation.

> It should be noted finally that correlative brain maps are not static crude maps that are laid out genetically and in fetal development, but final response patterns are fixed by experience, which in humans involves massive cultural input. . . . One implication of this finding is that it is not possible to neatly separate biological and cultural factors in brain development; this suggests in turn that existing divisions between neurobiological and cultural studies must be bridged before either field can fully mature. (Farmer 2006)

Farmer builds his own correlative structure in correlating two types of correlative structures: the layered structure of the brain's topologies and the cross-cultural occurrence of texts of layered correlative systems in history. It is important to note that Farmer operates firmly within the episteme of science and considers these earlier thought-forms of "premodern correlative systems" to be "primitive," "magical," and "religious." As such, they are, in his reckoning, decidedly inferior to scientific thinking. This viewpoint has similarities to the notion of our earlier evolutionary forms, both biological and cultural, as being "inferior." As in Jean Gebser's system, we progress into superior forms of cognition as epistemes shift. In Farmer, these "primitive" tendencies toward religion and anthropomorphism (equated with animism), which would certainly include the interpretation of plants as teachers and all experiences of spiritual entities so common to psychedelic experience, are a problem to be overcome with Reason.

> Given how deeply these tendencies are rooted in cortical development, it is easier to explain why humans build anthropomorphic models of the world than it is to imagine how such tendencies can be overcome. This problem can be tied to the persistence of primitive religious ideas even in technologically advanced societies, which remains a global problem hundreds of years after the Enlightenment. (Farmer 2006)

Animism, for Farmer, is a bug, not a feature. This conflict of epistemes, between Enlightenment Reason on the one hand and "primitive religious ideas" on the other, raises basic questions about the nature of his own correlation between the premodern and Renaissance correlative systems and the brain as correlative system. The contradictions are not at the level of experimental results, data gathered, or even conflicting interpretations but at the level of basic assumptions about the nature of knowledge. The source of much correlative thinking, according to Farmer, is found in altered states of consciousness where the conditions of knowledge acquisition, the standards by which knowledge is evaluated, the forms that constructed knowledge systems take, and the content of the data itself can be profoundly at odds with the conditions, standards, forms, and content of scientific knowledge. Farmer tells us that Pico himself used altered states of consciousness to syncretize the mass of texts in his *900 Theses*.

> In the nine hundred theses, Pico suggested that his own methods could not be applied mechanically but required a state of contemplative purity, perhaps even the trancelike state assumed by Abulafia and his disciples. (Farmer 1998)

Farmer discusses the complex exegetical processes that the scholars who constructed increasingly complex correlative structures went through in the effort to reconcile what on the surface can seem irreconcilable systems. While his brain model—as correlative system—and the structure of the cosmological systems he examines are similar, it is the scientific episteme through which he filters his observations and interpretations that is not reconciled. From which episteme are the correlations being made? To what extent is the "problem" a factor of what Terence McKenna calls "the balkanization of epistemology" and Nicolescu terms "the disciplinary Big Bang"? Or is the problem due to a confusion of levels of description, as in Varela's differentiation between the operational (scientific) description and the symbolic? Put otherwise, what is the syncretic move that will reconcile Aristotelian logic and the logic of magic; causal connections and metaphoric links; and, ultimately, a scientific and a psychedelic world view? Nicolescu's transdisciplinary approach that can potentially incorporate knowledge from different levels of reality—with different laws of operation—into an overarching meta-framework is an option.

Correlative Thinking

Farmer has made the connection between psychedelic mind-states (shamanic or mystical) and correlative thinking. From within the psychedelic state, thoughts about correlation correlate into their own systems of thought.

> Correlative thinking is generative in that it makes connections, new and novel or patchworked or perfect fits, incandescent isomorphisms, the marriage of two minds without embarrassment. Knowledge mingles, intermingles, attracts similar bits, all theories of correspondences may apply themselves to the task-at-hand: focus crystal vision on all our awareness of how the novel comes into being knowledge attracts to itself other notions with varying degrees of epistemological potency relative to the system of systems it is correlatively forming. (session report 10.04.01, 2C-B)

The idea of hypernoia, introduced in Chapter 6, comes into play in the consideration of correlative systems and their formation. Computer visionary and early psychedelic experimenter Ted Nelson defines hypernoia as "the belief that everything is, or should be, connected, interconnected, or reconnected. Bringing back together what should never have been separate" (Nelson 1993). To understand Nelson's hypernoia is to understand the doctrinal basis of today's world (no promises for tomorrow) of an infinitely linked WWW and filamentally connected souls distributed across social media. Medically, hypernoia is defined as "great rapidity of thought, excessive mental activity or imagination of the type seen in the manic phase of the bi-polar syndrome" (MediLexicon, retrieved 2012). Once again, we see the "not-normal" mind-state of rapid thought—which in the psychedelic sphere can be experienced as a feature—characterized as a bug, that is, abnormal, and linked to a DSM-V category, bi-polar, as voices in the head are linked to schizophrenia. In the psychedelic sphere, I call this phenomenon hyperconductivity and hyperconnectivity, pure flow, finding here an essential feature of the hallmark psychedelic experience of interconnectedness.

> And the increased conductivity—this is harder to achieve and to explain—superconductivity = little or no resistance to flow—and changing the ego-identity structure from something that is walled in (the medieval city) to something far more porous—while saving, maintaining—all the individualness that accelerates production of forms and knowledge and art forms—but changing its nature and use radically—now in awareness of and service to the networked larger awareness and intention (session report 03.03.02, MDMA)

> Relaxing allows the superconductivity to happen—much greater in and out—much wider reach—feels smooth and frictionless and graceful and beautiful—keep that awareness and body—the Glide gestures, Qi Gong—find that superconductivity in the mind's flow over content—not getting stuck in pathways, or behind taboos, or caught up in judging activities—which halt flow to consider—is this right or wrong—sheer spontaneous flow (the Zen thing, must be) comes from a tremendous trust of self, of the cosmos, of the things one doesn't know the answers to—like—especially like—the huge situations in the world—impending war—etc. (session report 03.02.09, MDMA)

> superconductivity of individual construct (sub-circuit) ID package ("self-construct") happens when energy is not being trapped or hung onto for purpose of "heating up" circuit, shining, attracting attention, ego-waves (session report 02.12.25, MDMA)

> superconductivity at its limit is the speed of light—which is the speed of time—which is "standing still" (session report 03.03.17, MDMA)

The qualities and dynamics of superconnectivity and superconductivity in psychedelic mind-states are key topics in the session reports. The qualities of cognition experienced—thoughts moving fluidly, *sheer spontaneous flow*—were the conditions of the correlative thinking that developed the Glide symbolic system and found the connections to other correlative systems.

> There is a funneling down that must occur, a loosening of boundaries that will permit the systems to intermingle freely, without disciplinary or methodological chaperonage. (session report 10.04.01, 2C-B)

Summary

Neurophenomenology is a scientific approach to the study of the brain/mind that attempts to bring together the subjective (phenomenological) and the objective (scientific) descriptions of consciousness. Charles Laughlin's neurocognitive approach to symbol and symbolic process affords a perspective on language that is grounded in—but not reduced to—the body's evolution and functioning as a physiological system. His models are inclusive of altered states of consciousness.

Michael Winkelman's work on ASC and shamanism centers on the concept of psychointegration—the action of psychedelics to open and connect parts of the brain normally dissociated in baseline states of consciousness. He details the adaptive potential of the resulting states for healing, social cohesion, and visionary insight. His work is helpful in understanding aspects of the experiences recorded in the session reports, especially hyperconnectivity and the quality of cognition that accompanies the exploration of novel linguistic phenomena in altered states of consciousness.

Harry Hunt differentiates between the presentational and the representational as two aspects of symbolic cognition. His view of the symbolic arising in cross-modal synaesthetic perception (a hallmark of altered states of consciousness of various types) offers useful categories in distinguishing types of knowing and symbolic expression. Especially helpful is the difference Hunt draws between propositional (natural language and its built-in logics) and imagetic forms of cognition. This distinction has helped in understanding the reports from shamanism and the syncretic churches of Central and South America that use ayahuasca as a sacrament. The synaesthesias of visual and sonic elements in the *icaros*, hymns, and dances guide and shape a variety of visionary ayahuasca experiences.

Francisco Varela's idea of the mindedness and communication among autopoietic systems at all levels can be considered inclusive of experience in altered states of consciousness and certainly does not preclude the presence of and conversations with the Other in all its forms.

But the questions raised about the correlations of first-person reports of altered states of consciousness with scientific neurobiology, even given a neurophenomenological framework, are and will remain unsettled, as they rest on choices of episteme, which in turn reflect fundamentally different apprehensions of reality, and the knowledge that is possible about reality. Varela's summation at the end of *Principles of Biological Autonomy* helps me to hold these questions in suspension:

> Our "knowledge," whatever rational meaning we give that term, must begin with experience, and with cuts within our experience—such as, for instance, the cut we make between the part of our experience that we come to call "ourself" and all the rest of our experience, which we then call our "world." Hence, this world of ours, no matter how we structure it, no matter how well we manage to keep it stable with permanent objects and recurrent interactions, is by definition *a world codependent with our experience*, and not the ontological reality of which philosophers and scientists alike have dreamed. All of this boils down, actually, to a realization that although the world does look solid and regular, when we come to examine it there is no fixed point of reference to which it can be pinned down; it is nowhere substantial or solid. *The whole of experience reveals the codependent and relative quality of our knowledge, truly a reflection of our individual and collective actions.* (Varela 1979) [emphasis mine]

This is the question, isn't it, for science: how shall we regard the inner life, the life of the mind and soul? Varela's position is essentially Buddhist: self and world codependently arise—and pass away. There is nothing solid, permanent, or self-existent about reality at all. His position comes from the experience gained in meditative practice as well as philosophic study and scientific empirical knowledge. I have stated something similar in saying that perception and reality, self and world, are deeply intertwingled. And always in flow.

Notes, Chapter 7

1. Hereinafter referred to as "Laughlin," for stylistic simplicity.
2. It should be noted, in the interests of harm reduction, that the quotes above came from multi-drug trips that were experienced as "bad trips" with the cause laid to the combination of drugs. The experiencers state strongly that these combinations are not to be recommended.
3. EMC: the empirical modification cycle; i.e., learning.
4. In Laughlin's discourse, intentionality means, essentially, "meaning."
5. Semiotropism can be seen as the neurophysiological aspect of rhetoric, when defined, as by Lanham, as "the science of human attention-structures" (Lanham 1991).
6. The opportunity to observe the development of female cannabis plants, and to encounter their exorbitant sexuality while in a be-mushroomed state, made it perfectly clear that the source of the appetite-enhancing, aphrodisiacal, aesthetically tuning, and medicinal properties (these categories promiscuously intertwingle) of this broad-spectrum plant is the sparkling, globular, amber, sticky cunt-juices—the resin production—of an aggressively sexy plant that has found a perfect symbiotic mate in the human.

III: XENOLINGUISTICS

CHAPTER 8

Natural and Unnatural Language

> *"The thing makes linguistic objects it sheds syntactical objectification so they come toward you they divide they merge they're bounding they're screaming they're squeaking they hold out objects which they sing into existence or which they pull out of some other place and these things are like jewels and lights but also like consommé and old farts and yesterday and high speed"*
>
> —Terence McKenna, 1998

Natural language emerges from an organism, *Homo sapiens,* who, in companionship with all other life-forms, is linguistically structured. We, as organisms, are *in-formed,* as Francisco Varela uses the term, all the way down. Natural language, with all its affordances, diversity, and fecundity in creating all of culture and civilization, is often considered the *sine qua non* of that which sets us apart from other species on Planet Earth. The powerful offspring of natural language, the formalisms of mathematics, logic, and the binary codes that reflexively manipulate these forms, have been key in the proliferation of science and technology and their world-transforming effects. Xenolinguistics assumes that language is a much broader concept than *natural* language. So it is with all due respect to the mother tongue of humanity that I include under the rubric *language* some examples of linguistic phenomena manifesting in psychedelic states as most *unnatural.*

A basic assumption is that language itself, in the sense of natural language, and language in the broader sense that will unfold below, undergoes a co-evolutionary process with consciousness, interdependently arising. The observation, description, and interpretation of linguistic phenomena in the psychedelic sphere take place on shifting sand. The psychedelic states, through chemical action on our neurotransmitter systems, disrupt the functioning of the natural-language symbolic system, destabilize the experience of self (the *who is observing?* and *who are those Others?),* and transfigure the perceptual milieu and hence the assignment of reality, sometimes to a spectacularly alien degree. Natural language cannot by definition address the unspeakable, but the Unspeakable (which Terence McKenna sometimes conflates with the Other) can address us as linguistic creatures—on its own terms, at its own behest, with its own timing, and utilizing its own symbolic systems.

In their highest strangeness, these linguistic objects precipitate an ontological rupture, demanding a determination of status: is this a perception of something *human* or something *non-human* (the alien)? On the horns of this dilemma, either horn is too uncomfortable to occupy for long. Horn One: This unspeakably bizarre translinguistic object is just (!) an aspect of myself. However, this aspect of myself, formally unsuspected and uncontacted, lies beyond the biggest imaginative leap I can make. In fact, if this is *"human,"* or *"me,"* then this is a self-concept that myself-at-baseline instinctively rejects as utterly impossible. But in that rejection, the other option, equally hard to accept, rears its head. Horn Two: This phenomenon is a result of the Other as Alien making actual contact. But with a language lesson? Is this payback? The only appropriate reply to the sincere but ugly engineer art of the *Voyager* space probe inscription? Rational discourse breaks down, the cosmic giggle threatens to erupt, and the dilemma persists: is this self (Self) s(elves) or Other? *Who speaks? Who listens? Are we waking up to the possibility of becoming something profoundly alien, the seeds of which are planted, somehow, in our psyches?*

> we are who you will become (session report 99.07.10, MDMA)

To practice as a xenolinguist is precisely to attempt to communicate with the Unspeakable, and then about the Unspeakable (such as the description of the horns of the dilemma above), even if it takes multiple voices (some of them speaking in alien tongues) and several interwoven levels of reality to make the attempt.

The idea of the alien is linked to the novel, a concept central to Terence McKenna's model of the universe as a novelty-producing and novelty-conserving process. Xenolinguist Simon G. Powell calls this evolving totality "the reality process." According to McKenna, the telos of human history and time has a fractal structure in this universal process. And the process is producing novelty at an exponential rate through an extension of its symbolizing, fundamentally linguistic nature, self-similar at all levels of structure. The forms of life, as Varela describes them, appear as a linguistic fractal, evolving over time by virtue of their eminently self-similar and composable structure. History, the sum of our symbolizing in culture, appears in McKenna's description as a temporal fractal. Bios and Logos, both structured fractally.

■ **Figure 71: Julia Pastrana, freak.** Wikimedia Commons.

The idea of the novel is linked to the emergent: how the novel emerges through the self-organization of a multiplicity of simple processes, linguistic and algorithmic processes, into complex structures. Linguistic phenomena in the psychedelic sphere enfold these qualities of the alien, the novel, and the complex. But the emergent often appears under the sign of the monstrous. Human mutations that alter the normal body form, until recently, were displayed in freak shows.

The mutated realities of psychedelic experience are often viewed with deep suspicion by the unexperienced. Bleeding through into popular culture, the flamboyant hair and clothing of the experienced led to the labeling of the counterculture as "freaks."

The prospect of creating more "freaks" with the rewriting and editing of genomes is a looming issue to be tried not only in laboratories but in the courts of human opinion. The opening arguments are being drafted. The issue is nothing more or less than determining the limits of the human. Where does the "natural" end and the "unnatural" begin? What changes do we dream of making to ourselves that would result in what would have to be called a novel, alien species?

■ **Figure 72: Magenta Imagination Healer.**

Terence McKenna's life work could be described as the unpacking of a DMT experience in the late '60s (and many others to follow). The experience of the Others and their linguistic objects, and the ontological dilemma presented, informs a central axis of his thought.

> But what is astonishing and immediately riveting is that in this place there are entities—there are these things, which I call "self-transforming machine elves," and what they were doing, was they were making objects come into existence by singing them into existence. Objects which looked like Fabergé eggs from Mars, morphing themselves with Mandaean alphabetical structures. They looked like the concrescence of linguistic intentionality put through a kind of hyperdimensional transform into three-dimensional space. And these little machines offered themselves to me. And I realized when I looked at them that if I could bring just one of these little trinkets back, nothing would ever be quite the same again. (McKenna 1993)

Language in the Warp

The effects of various psychoactive substances on perception—visual, aural, gustatory—have been widely studied and noted in the literature, both scientific and in personal experience reports. The effects of psychoactives on natural language—speaking and listening, reading and writing—have received far less attention. A 1970 article by Stanley Krippner, "The Effects of Psychedelic Experience on Language Functioning," reveals a theme that can be seen in many psychedelic studies: the extreme variability of the effect of a particular substance across even a small group of people where dose and setting are much the same. This variability is evident in many of the reports of those in Alexander Shulgin's research groups where the same drug, in the same setting, can elicit a broad spectrum of experience (Shulgin 1991). The same variability can be noted in Rick Strassman's DMT research, where dose and setting were tightly controlled (Strassman 2001). Krippner finds the variability in his study of effects on natural language functioning. At the time Krippner was writing, the primary drug of study was LSD; mescaline, peyote, psilocybin, and cannabis were also in the literature. Ayahuasca was little known and reported, and Sasha Shulgin had not yet enriched our psychedelic pharmacopoeia with hundreds of new syntheses of compounds exhibiting a wide range of effects.

Defining models of sequential "levels" and "states" of reality and consciousness was part of the intellectual enterprise of the 1960s and 1970s, as we saw in the work of Fischer, Tart, Roberts, and Nicolescu. Krippner used Masters and Houston's 1966 model of four levels of mental functioning in psychedelic states to parse the language experiences he presents. Masters and Houston propose a four-level model: 1) *sensory*—changed awareness of body, space, and time, heightened sense impression, and synaesthesia; 2) *recollective-analytic*—reliving parts of the past, new insights about self, work, relationships; 3) *symbolic*—visual imagery involving history and legend or evolutionary processes, ritual processes; and 4) *integral/mystical*—religious experience, white light, and unitive experience (Masters 1966). Krippner then maps the various (natural) language modalities—listening, speaking, reading, and writing—against these states.

The language used in guiding a psychedelic experience is seen as exceptionally potent to individuals in altered states of consciousness. The language used can program the trip profoundly, positively or negatively, an effect Doyle calls "an extraordinary sensitivity to initial rhetorical conditions" (Doyle 2011). A particularly vivid and sadistic experiment reported by Masters and Houston is cited by Krippner:

> The subject was told by the psychiatrist that he would have "a terrible, terrible experience" filled with "strong anxiety and delusions." The drug was administered in an antiseptic hospital room with several observers in white coats watching him. As the effects came on, the psychiatrist asked such questions as "Is your anxiety increasing?" At the end of the experiment, the subject was in a state of panic. The psychiatrist announced to the group that LSD is indeed a "psychotomimetic" substance, which induces psychotic behavior. (Krippner 1970)

I am reminded of Terence McKenna's quip, attributed to Timothy Leary, "LSD is a psychedelic drug which occasionally causes psychotic behavior in people who have NOT taken it." In other examples, Krippner reports opposite sets of effects: the loss of reading ability in one case, and an exquisite enhancement of reading in the same case, at a different point in the trip; spoken language enhanced or attenuated; a greater ability to distinguish between word and object in one case, and a reversion to "primitive thinking," including the union of word and object, in another. Krippner cites two interesting cases of enhanced language-learning ability: one, a man who learned German over the course of a long LSD trip, and another person who practiced typing to an expert level, similarly dosed.

Fischer and Martindale's 1977 study of a single subject's experience of writing prose (four instances) under the influence of psilocybin compared his prose sample at baseline to that in the "aroused" state. The results were interpreted through a quantitative analysis of such linguistic dimensions as the relative concreteness or abstraction in noun phrases; length of sentences and clauses; and topical organization. These measures showed an increase in the psychoanalytical category "primary process" (concrete, free associative, drive-dominated, autistic) and a reduction in "secondary process" (abstract, analytic, purposeful, reality-oriented) (Fischer 1977). An earlier 1970 study of personality traits related to the effects of psilocybin on the changes in size and pressure of handwriting showed different results for different personality types, measured by the Meyer-Briggs indicator (Fischer 1970; Fischer 1977).

From the perspective of my own practice, the shift in handwriting was experienced many times over a period of years. The shift went from the formation of words to the dissolution of the line and the appearance of visual puns under the internal pressure of the serpentine movement of flowing energy I call the "rainbow serpent." I have come to interpret this phenomenon as a fundamental linguistic movement underlying writing and drawing that easily takes over from the inscription of natural language in altered states, a kind of gestural glossolalia.

> tttttt tttttttt tttttttttttttt here are the lines the transmission being here ray-diate the dimensional script so words shiver across themselves transmit mitten tran-smitten manuscript script of the full filament (session report 05.03.25, 5 g dried Stropharia cubensis)

Charles Tart's 1971 study of marijuana intoxication, in addition to pointing out the common phenomenon of forgetting the beginning of a sentence further in, finds that talking runs a range between saying relatively profound things and giggling; talking more than at baseline or less; and socializing more or feeling isolated. Again, we see a full spectrum of effects, not easily generalizable.

Benny Shanon's phenomenology of the ayahuasca experience brings other linguistic phenomena to light. He describes the "slight adverse cognitive effects" that can occur:

> Usually, during ayahuasca sessions people do not talk. When they do, however, some problems of speech coordination may be exhibited. For instance, speakers may have difficulty in keeping track of different lines of thought that they express and some slips in their verbal output may be noted. . . . Also encountered is perseveration, that is, the ongoing repetition of a given pattern of behavior and difficulty in breaking out of it. Repetitive singing or excessive talking may be regarded as manifestations of this. (Shanon 2002)

In terms of the linguistic content of visions, Shanon identifies a category of "Books, Scripts, and Symbols."

> Many people report seeing inscriptions of letters, numerals, or other signs. Both in my case and in that of my informants, on some occasions the characters seen were made of, or engraved in, gold or silver. Often these are in scripts or languages that the Ayahuasca drinker characterizes as ones he or she cannot decipher or understand. Some informants say that they do manage to decipher and understand messages in scripts and/or languages that actually are not familiar to them. (Shanon 2002)

In discussing the dynamics of the manner in which the visions of the ayahuasca experience develop, Shanon describes in some detail the thought sequences that can illustrate an associative process like punning, which he calls the "double-face configuration." The medium—the phonological form of the word—and its meaning become "decoupled," then reconnected to a different meaning. This places the cognizing person in a new semantic domain. "Thus, the decoupling has generated unplanned novelty in the thought process" (Shanon 2002).

> the scripting of dimension—all script—tase the trans—lation to the script (session report 05.03.19, MDMA)

Shanon mentions an example of visionary content that relates the linguistic to Laughlin's description of dots. We are approaching the presentationally symbolic, and leaving the realm of natural language.

> There is a code here—like that of Morse or the genetic code. The code is constituted by many, many dots, the density between which varies. All this is a language calling to be deciphered. (Shanon 2002)

Somewhere in the dots, propelled by the spiral waves of the rainbow serpent, lies the fundamental wave-particle of language.

Eloquence

There are few more eloquent descriptions of the eloquence conferred by the magical mushroom than Henry Munn's description in his essay, found in Michael Harner's *The Way of the Shaman.*

> "It is not I who speak," said Heraclitus, "it is the logos." Language is an ecstatic activity of signification. Intoxicated by the mushrooms, the fluency, the ease, the aptness of expression one becomes capable of are such that one is astounded by the words that issue forth from the contact of the intention of articulation with the matter of experience. At times it is as if one were being told what to say, for the words leap to mind, one after another, of themselves without having to be searched for: a phenomenon similar to the automatic dictation of the surrealists except that here the flow of consciousness, rather than being disconnected, tends to be coherent: a rational enunciation of meanings. Message fields of communication with the world, others, and one's self are disclosed by the mushrooms. The spontaneity they liberate is not only perceptual, but linguistic, the spontaneity of speech, of fervent, lucid discourse, of the logos in activity. For the shaman, it is as if existence were uttering itself through him. (Munn quoted in Harner 1986)

Munn describes María Sabina's "curing with words" and the speech of other Mazatec curanderos as language brought to a heightened potency. As Richard Doyle proposes in *Darwin's Pharmacy,* eloquence is deep in nature as an adjunct to plant and animal strategies for food and sexual selection, the two primary survival activities. These eloquent and highly specific forms of communication often intermix the dual motives of food and sex, as nectar-drinking and flower pollination become part of the same symbiotic conversation, in the Varelian sense. The complex symbiotic interactions of three species in the life cycle of the Brazil nut tree highlight these interspecies communication systems. Female orchid bees respond to the fragrance of the Brazil nut tree's brief flowering of creamy yellow flowers; they are the only insects that can pull back the tight hood and penetrate and pollinate the center of the flower. The third partner in the Brazil nut tree's cycle of survival is the agouti, a large rodent that lives on the forest floor and eats the fruit encased in rock-hard shells that fall to the ground. It buries what it cannot eat; those that it forgets to collect can germinate and produce the next generation of Brazil nut trees.

The highly specific chemical languages producing sight, scent, and taste combine in unique patterns, the "conversations" of highly diverse species. It has also been found that the diversity of natural languages in an area is directly proportional to the biodiversity in the region. High linguistic diversity and high biodiversity can be observed in the species-rich Amazonian environment (Marent 2006).

Glossolalia

Wikipedia defines glossolalia or speaking in tongues as "the fluid vocalizing (or, less commonly, the writing) of speech-like syllables, often as part of religious practice. Though some consider these utterances to be meaningless, others consider them to be a holy language." These utterances are often associated with altered states of consciousness, and their interpretation depends on the framework of the interpreter. To the psychologist, they can be heard as pathological, dissociative states; to the ethnographer confronted with the culturally bizarre, they have been described as hysteria, frenzy, or "utter gibberish." It appears to be a broad, cross-cultural phenomenon of considerable antiquity. The appearance of glossolalic utterances in shamanic cultures relating to communication with spirits would indicate roots in the distant past. The Biblical description in the book of Acts of the original Pentecostal speaking in tongues brought on by the Holy Spirit is another cultural formation of the Other as Logos or Spiritus Sanctus speaking through a person or persons (Goodman 1972).

Felicitas Goodman's cross-cultural study includes examples from Umbanda practices in Brazil, Pentecostal churches in Mexico City, a Maya village in the Yucatán, and Pentecostal churches in Texas. One interesting example of glossolalia on a tape she analyzed was made during the LSD session of a "Mr. R." Goodman's conclusion was that this vocalization was different than the Pentecostal glossolalias she had been studying and, to her, sounded like a foreign language. Mr. R., however, "came to the conclusion that he had somehow experienced man's early history—that he had accidentally recreated the *Ursprache,* the original language of mankind" (Goodman 1972).

Terence McKenna describes a psychedelic glossolalia and its application in the psychedelic moment:

> And what they meant was: use your voice to make an object. And as I understood I felt a bubble kind of grow inside of me. And I watched these little elf tykes jumping in and out of my chest (they liked to do that to reassure you), and they said, Do it! And I felt language rise up in me that was unhooked from English and I began to speak like this: Eeeoo ded hwauopsy mectoph, mectagin dupwoxin, moi phoi wops eppepepekin gitto phepsy demego doi aga din a doich demoi aga donc heedey obectdee doohueana. (Or words to that effect.) And I wondered then what it all meant, and why it felt so good (if it didn't mean anything). And I thought about it a few years, actually, and I decided, you know, that meaning and language are two different things. And that what the alien voice in the psychedelic experience wants to reveal is the syntactical nature of reality. That the real secret of magic is that the world is made of words, and that if you know the words that the world is made of, you make of it whatever you wish! (McKenna 1993)

I experienced an entire session of strange vocalizing on an 8.5-g dose of *Stropharia cubensis.* It was an extension of Glide, only in sound forms. I spent eight hours (with short stretching breaks) upright on a meditation bench, which helped me to focus and control the energy moving up and down the spine. The sounds were part of a language lesson. There were whistles, both with lips, and with tongue and roof of my mouth and teeth. There were whistles both on the in- and the out-breath, so there developed a continuous stream of rapidly varying sounds—whistles, piping sounds, clicks, pops, hisses. The sounds were joined by gestures—small hand motions, quite precise, very varied, and keyed to the sounds. Certain "phrases" would be repeated over and over. Occasionally I would feel I got one of the phrases right, like a baby who is babbling and gets a word right by accident, who then receives positive feedback from mama repeating it back happily. Eventually, the baby gets the idea of a sound with meaning: a word. In this case the words were constructed differently, combining in- and out-breath with hand gestures. The sounds were also being "spoken" and "heard" simultaneously not only by me but by the Other. The Other was part of the conversation in a communication just this side of communion. Two or more beings (myself included) were communicating at once, in and out, without interrupting each other in the slightest. More like a duet, but improvised with simultaneous meaning-making in micro-sounds and micro-movements. I've experienced this same merging of meaning-making when reading/writing with the LiveGlide video performance software, where it's a co-creation of the Other and myself. Yes, it was a little like love-making, the ins and outs of it, but that was just the style, as if you have to get fairly merged to even begin to understand the Other. And what can we do but bring our best skills of merging to the classroom? Because it was clearly classroom again, with a lot of drill.

As the lesson went on, I was asked to observe what was happening with various mental/emotional shifts that would occur when certain sounds were made. I could see that the sounds created a very complex and subtle dance of neurotransmitters frothing at the synaptic bath in the multidimensional receptor space.[1] The receptor space was like a huge organ, not making sound but being played with sound. The lesson was—if you learn to use this form of language, you can turn mind-body states on and off, and enter and leave various states/settings at will, i.e., navigate. This was a much more complex lesson built on an earlier one, years ago, where I learned that a certain sound (SWWWSSSSSSssss) with a sharp ending could move me out of a mind-space I no longer wanted to occupy. This lesson presented a whole vocabulary of how to change states with sounds and gestures. It was noted that this would take a lot of practice to even begin to get the hang of it.

Psychedelic glossolalias, Philip K. Dick's xenoglossia—do they or don't they map to natural language? If not, can we understand them in the context of what might be called a written "glossolalia"—such as Allyson Grey's Secret Writing, or Sara Huntley's Dimensional Script?

The Guild of Xenolinguists

Caroline and Gaetan Cottereau-Meurée: Skin Bridge

Among their projects as the art collaborative Artifist, Caroline and Gaetan Cottereau-Meurée kept to a six-day-per-week diet of *Peganum harmala* for a year, during which Caroline designed and tattooed Gaetan's back using neuromediators such as pinoline and ayahuasca under the pigments. The work includes a temple floor plan, a fierce bird, and a twisting serpentine form, covered with language and symbolic forms. They discovered that each neuromediator has a specific signature of fluorescence under black light.

Brain Skin Medium: The Skin Bridge

In Artifist's words (taken from their website):

> The skin and nervous system come from the same embryonic sheet, remaining linked through common neuromediators. Changes in the brain (e.g., a nervous breakdown) lead to modifications of the skin (e.g.,

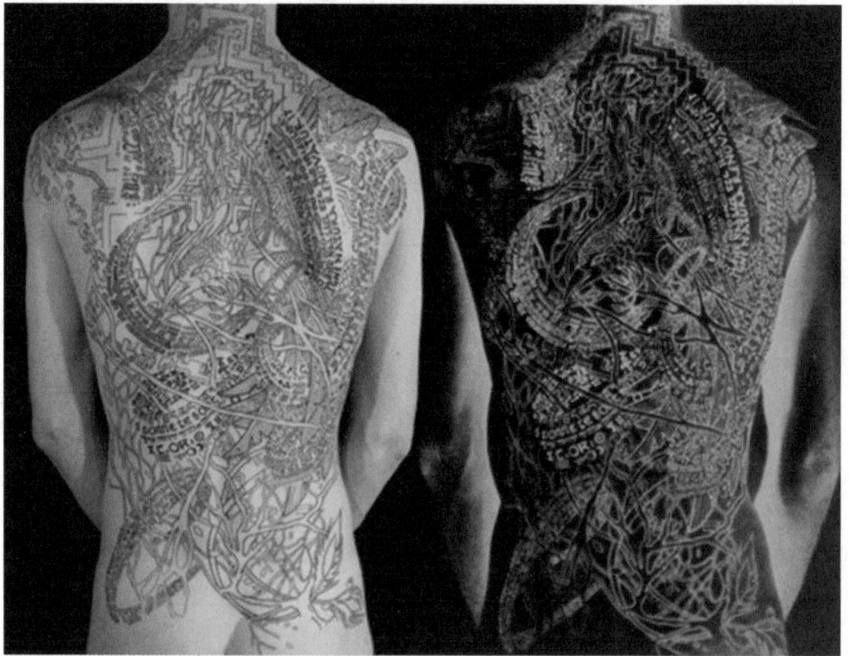

■ **Figure 73: Gaetan's tattoo, under ordinary and black lights.**

inflammation). The work of Gaite Artifist follows the opposite process: in applying neuromediators on/in the skin, they consider the skin as an interface to the brain.

Neurotransmitters, such as spinoline, adrenaline, dopamine, or serotonin, applied to the skin result in them being absorbed through their respective skin cell receptors and then causing modification in brain states.

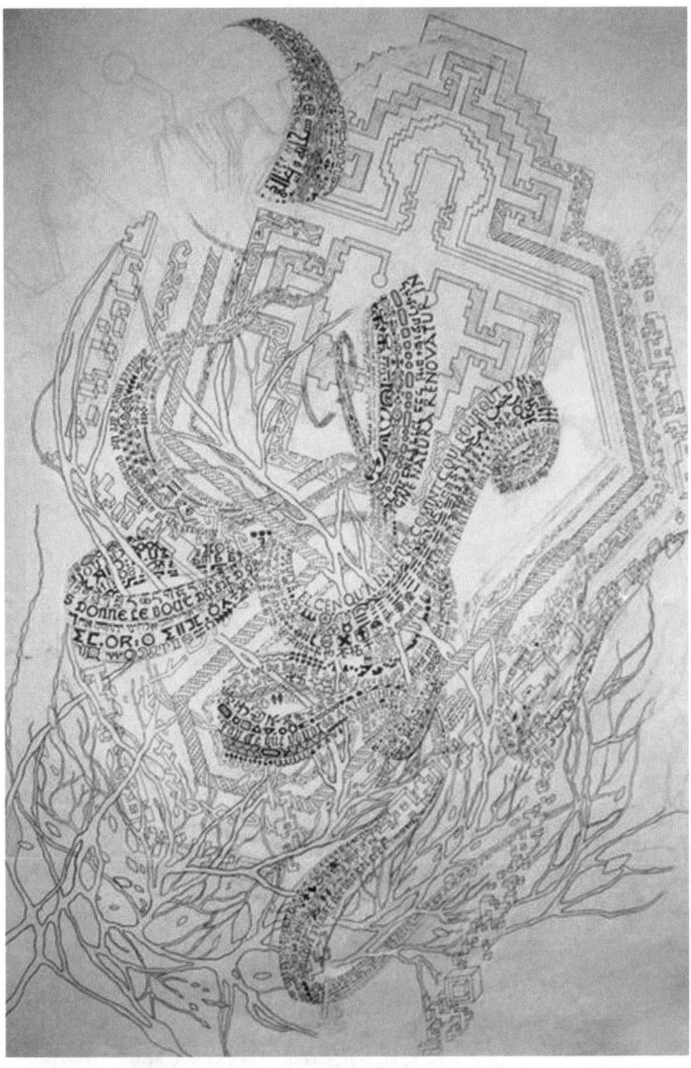

■ **Figure 74: The original, more complex drawing from which the tattoo was made.**

The following three pictures are details from the original drawing.

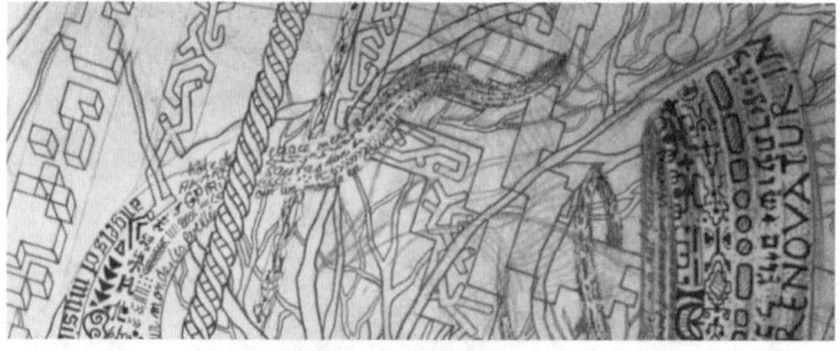

■ **Figure 75: Tattoo drawing, Detail 1.**

■ **Figure 76: Tattoo drawing, Detail 2.**

■ **Figure 77: Tattoo drawing, Detail 3.**

■ **Figure 78: Caroline and Gaetan Cottereau-Meurée.**

Sara Huntley—Writing with Dimensional Language

Sara Huntley writes with fire, paint, and tattoo pigments as she experiments broadly with communications in altered states. The extracts that follow are Sara's report from a xenolinguistical session. In her own words:

> The first time I saw the language-like patterns was on the inner surface of my forearm one spring day on an exquisite psilocybin journey. I had ingested mushrooms a number of times before, and was familiar with a variety of hallucinations. Visually this was a particularly amazing trip. After being hypnotized for nearly an hour by a divine mandala-like pattern in the plaster popcorn ceiling, I sat up to inspect my surroundings again, and in turn looked down at my body, which seemed beside myself and puppet-like. Upon inspection, I saw there were embossed angular imprints on my skin, they looked like crystalline fractals.
>
> Instead of a linear organization, they spread out in all directions. They looked more circuit-like than typical language and sentence structures. Instantly mesmerized by its complexity, and beauty, I felt the urge to understand what they could mean, and as an artist, document them. It seemed to be a part of my arm, some blueprint to an underlying structure I could not see with a normal gaze. If I tried to look at them too directly, they subtly shimmered away. They seemed only visible when the light hit on them in a particular angle or in peripheral vision.

■ **Figure 79: Sara Huntley, Dimensional Writing.**

Not to miss out on this window into the visionary state, I grabbed a pen and set to scratching out every distinct shape I could in the pattern. Once I had exhausted every one that I could catch, I let my trip move into other modalities. The next morning, I transcribed the language from my arm into my sketchbook.

The entry became a point of fascination for my artwork. It had a genuineness of character that could not be duplicated or made up. If I tried to emulate the pattern it fell flat and didn't hold the same intrigue. So I decided not to fake the pattern in any of my artwork, though I could not decipher its meaning.

A year and a half after the first encounter with this language form, I was experiencing a mild acid trip with a close friend, when to my astonishment I saw a familiar crystalline pattern on the surface of a cardboard box in the living room. My mind was pulled into witnessing the same distinct circuit language on the box. Thoughts raced, as this chemical catalyst is

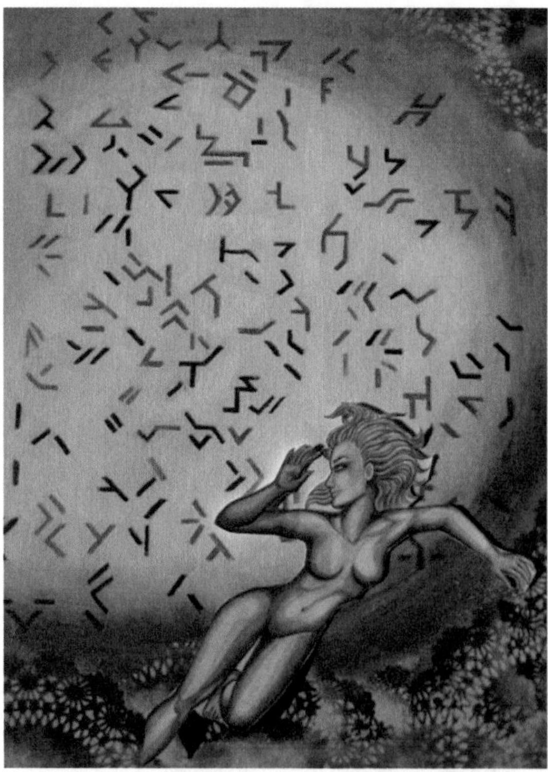

■ **Figure 80: Sara Huntley, #2.**

of a completely different order than the mushrooms. A dozen hypotheses came up: could this be some kind of architecture of my mind, how my brain stitches together sensory stimulus into the hologram-like construct we call reality?

■ **Figure 81: Sara Huntley, #3.**

Are they higher-dimensional artifacts filtering into my limited awareness as my senses expand in psychedelic consciousness? None of these questions could be answered. I knew I had to capture this evidence before it evaporated. With a blue colored pencil I drew directly on the box, pulling the pattern from the visionary state into our objective corporeal space. I photographed this box, and later transcribed the patterns into my sketchbook alongside what had been previously dubbed "the mushroom language" and at this point, I had to revise my nickname for it, and it became "The Alien Language."

The third time this language made itself evident was by far the most potent and interactive discovery to date. I had ingested 2C-B for the first time, and was about two hours into the experience. After listening to some drum and bass electronic music, and drawing out the synaesthesia of my closed-eye visual pattern, I turned my page over, to start doodling on the back, when in the imprints the pencil had made in the page on the other side, I saw elements of that same language. At this point I had discovered that the angles of the language work on an 8-fold grid, which made it easier to spot.

I gingerly drew the language as it appeared on the page, and then to my surprise, as I lifted the page and light shone through it, [I saw] that it matched up with the pattern on the other side of the paper. I felt like an explorer discovering artifacts from another world. This gave me further insight into the nature of what the language could mean. The pattern I had been drawing is similar to an interlocking Japanese kimono fabric pattern, which I later learned is a p6m in crystallographic code. So this language has overlapping qualities with wallpaper patterns, which are mathematic classifications of a two-dimensional repetitive pattern based on its symmetries.

■ **Figure 82: Sara Huntley, writing with fire.**

With more information, there are more questions and possible explanations. Is this a language that is within my mind all the time? and when in altered states of consciousness my awareness is witness to it? or is this something that only arises because of the psychedelic catalyst? If this is something biochemical in nature, and inside my mind, what is the structure I'm seeing? Is it architectural in content, or is it allegorical? What is the nature of the intelligence behind its organization?

Could they be related to Cymatic wave patterns, how vibratory fields give rise to form? Or higher-dimensional media being compressed into lower-dimensional framework? I wonder sometimes if the scale of my consciousness is getting cross-fed with information from smaller micro biological scales, or higher dimensions. Regardless, I feel very grateful it has graced my eyes and mind, it fills me with wonder, and keeps my mind open to all kinds of pattern in the cosmos. I always wonder where I will see it next.

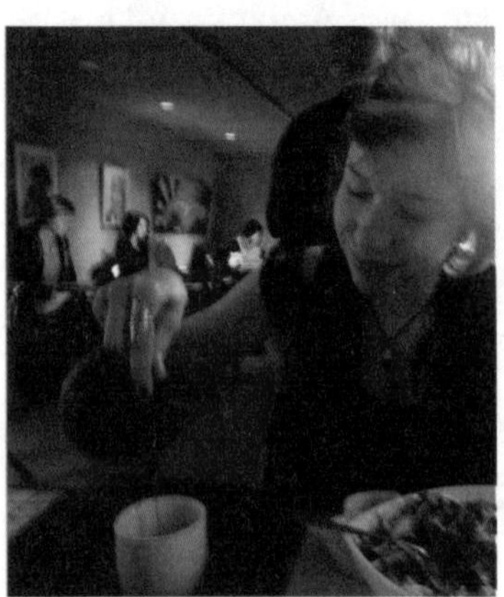

■ **Figure 83: Sara Huntley.**

Allyson Grey: Secret Writing

Infinite connectivity and reflectivity is at the heart of Allyson Grey's psychedelically informed artwork. Grey relates the sacred loom-matrix she experienced on an acid trip to the Jewel Net of Indra.

> In the Hindu pantheon, Indra is God of Space & Time. Indra's abode regaled a net that stretched infinitely in all directions. Each facet of the net held a jewel, so highly polished that it reflected every other jewel in the net. This Hindu description of a vision resonantly coincided with the LSD journeys it was my intention to depict in this and many of my artworks.

In other words, an experience in which every entity in the universe connects with and has knowledge of every other: infinite noesis.

For almost forty years, Allyson Grey has committed her paintings to describing a message received during a journey on LSD. The voice told her that all consciousness could be essentialized in a world view that consists of Chaos, Order and Secret Writing. Allyson describes her work as follows:

> The concepts chaos, order, and secret writing symbolically expressed in the compositions, colors, and systems of my art represent an essentialized world view that has long been the content of my oeuvre.

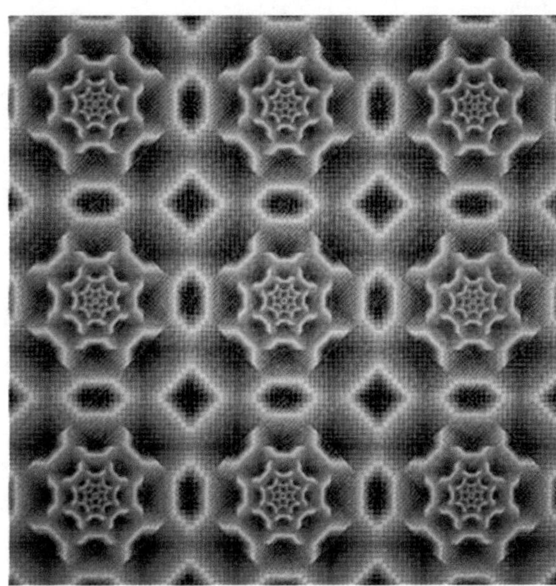

■ **Figure 84: Allyson Grey, "Jewel Net of Indra."**

> Chaos is order plus entropy. My paintings portray spectral systems of squares, both particles and waves, that drift apart, representing the beauty and the natural disorder and unpredictability that exist in every system of the physical world.
>
> Order in my work represents the bliss realms I experienced in transcendental states of mystic unity referring to Nirvana, heaven, the infinite Divine.... In a state of heightened consciousness, I witnessed vast vistas of interconnected fountains and drains of spectral light. The light was God. The light was Love.
>
> Secret Writing in my art is composed of twenty unpronounceable letters, referring to the Almighty that speaks through all sacred writing; the spirit imbedded in communication that cannot be reduced to concepts. Secret writing in every culture is like a window revealing inner perceptions manifested into the material world. Secret writing is the language of the Divine Creative Force speaking through my art.

In addition, Grey describes her Secret Writing as ". . . the language of creative manifestation . . . the unutterable truth beyond language that is pointed to by all sacred text . . . communications of the nameless presence." The painted spectral squares appear "extra-dimensional," utilizing the color spectrum in a pulsing, glowing effect. Prolonged viewing of the work can be meditative or vertiginous.

■ Figure 85: Allyson Grey, "Secret Writing: Magic Square with Mandala Border."

Order rivets the viewer toward the center or multiple centers. Chaos appears like a swatch of a greater pattern in which the spectral squares swirl and fly off the picture plane. Fractal dimensionality, an effect evident in Grey's work, is a hallmark of much psychedelically informed artwork.

Allyson Grey, in her own words:

> Secret writing was inspired by an acid trip in 1971, my first glimpse of the white light. Meaning has never accompanied my secret writing. Their explicit content always defied translation, as definition and the use of symbols for communication separates experience from expression. The alphabet that I use points to the notion of a sacred language beyond

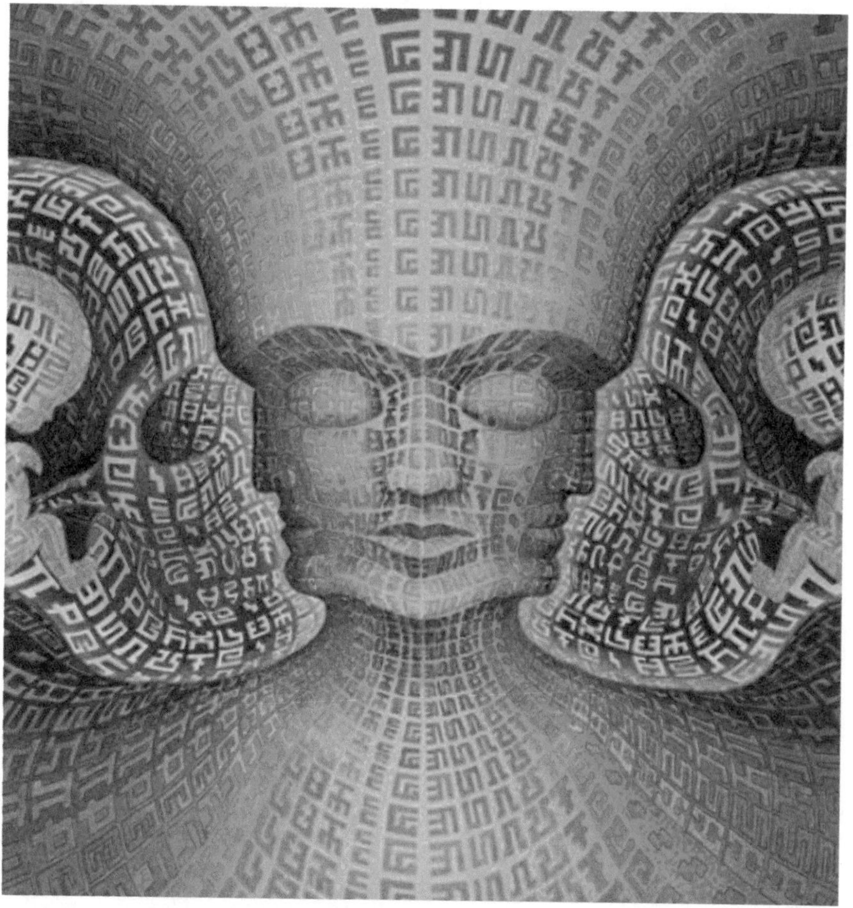

■ **Figure 86: Alex Grey and Allyson Grey, "Secret Language Being."**

■ **Figure 87: Allyson Grey.**

meaning. Some of the works call to mind the experience of seeing an illuminated text in a foreign language and religion.

On an LSD trip with Alex on June 3rd, 1976, we simultaneously shared a vision of the vista of interconnected fountains and drains flowing in a pattern that spread infinitely in all directions. This experience lifted the veil over the loom-matrix of our highest identity, revealing our individuality as a node in the net of space and time. For both of us, this was clearly our life's most profound revelation. As the most important message we could impart in the world, as artists this higher vision would become the subject of our work for a lifetime.

Notes, Chapter 8

1. "Frothing at the synaptic bath" is a metaphor used by media scholar David Porush. The metaphor "multidimensional receptor space" is Tom Ray's felicitous phrase.

CHAPTER 9

Language, Culture, and Nature

"The word language is misheard in English. . . . Language is old. Honeybees do it, dolphins do it, it's even possible when you think of chemical communication that flowers and ants do it. Nature is knit together by communication, it has rules, syntax, and so is language. If you've ever stood in a rainforest or any species-dense environment it's alive with signals, with sounds, with odors, that are carrying messages; these things are not just produced for special effects, they have intended hearers."

—TERENCE MCKENNA, 1994

Psychedelics have been characterized as deconditioning or deprogramming agents, in reference to their ability to lift the experiencer quite out and away from their usual version of being-in-the-world. In addition to a radical reframing of the sense of self, and the perceptual changes that bring new worlds into view, one can find oneself suddenly outside whole modules of social conditioning, with many of the "truths we hold to be self-evident" completely up for grabs. The Leary mantra "turn on, tune in, drop out" is a program for this deprogramming. The authority that is questioned happens not just at the level of social rebellion from parents, teachers, and cops. The process begins internally where the unquestioned rules by which we have been traveling the road of life come into view to the point where they can even be called into question. The mechanisms by which this conditioning is nailed in place are linguistic. It is language that creates the structures in consciousness by which we not only shape our behavior, but the structures by which we perceive the world. This is Aldous Huxley's point in his idea of Mind at Large being run through the reducing valve of ordinary consciousness. The dissolution of the ego in the psychedelic warp can be seen as the dismantling of our own most personal authority. This temporary reprieve from its demands to *be this and not that* gives one a space where reflection on that which was previously not even visible to inspection can be considered.

The relations among language, culture, and nature as they meet at the crossroads of individual experience can be examined in this opened, porous space. One of the most life-transforming experiences that psychedelics can deliver is what Doyle calls "the ecodelic insight." This recovery of the living truth of our deep intertwinglement with the world of nature, the healing of the estrangement that our runaway forms of culture have created, is a starting place for the remediation of the effects we are having on the biosphere's health and future. Who we think we are as individuals, as the human race, and especially in relation to the nature from which we have set ourselves apart, undergoes a sea change when the stories we habitually tell dissolve with the ego structures they describe. New stories and, sometimes, new forms of language with which to express these stories move into the garden of memes.

Evolution of Language

Language is deep in nature, its expressive forms evolving from highly complex forms of chemical and electrical communication within a single organism, between any organism and the environment with which it must communicate to survive, and between organisms, of the same or of cooperating or competing species.

Psychedelic use has been connected with our earliest symbolic artifacts, especially in rock art of Paleolithic cultures on all continents. The resemblance of the abstract signs to Kluver's form constants has been noted by anthropologists J. D. Lewis-Williams and T. A. Dowson in their article, "The Signs of All Times." Genevieve von Petzinger's anthropological study of these abstract signs in French parietal art goes further in suggesting that these abstract signs represent early symbolic communication. "Repeated patterning is one of the criteria used when looking to identify symbolic behaviour in scratch marks and other engravings on portable items during the Middle and early Upper Paleolithic," she writes, noting that while "isolated instances are not sufficient evidence, multiple examples of similar patterning are required, since these are what imply that there was a shared meaning or understanding" (von Petzinger 2009). If these forms (von Petzinger identifies 28 distinct marks) are indeed symbolic, they may represent a very early form of writing;

if they are also connected to psychedelic use and the forms that arise therein, we have a suggestive connection with McKenna's hypothesis of psychedelic use as a catalyst for language evolution in early humans.

> My contention is that mutation-causing, psychoactive chemical compounds in the early human diet directly influenced the rapid reorganization of the brain's information-processing capacities. Alkaloids in plants, specifically the hallucinogenic compounds such as psilocybin, dimethyltriptamine (DMT), and harmaline, could be the chemical factors in the protohuman diet that catalyzed the emergence of human self-reflection. The action of hallucinogens present in many common plants enhanced our information-processing activity, or environmental sensitivity, and thus contributed to the sudden expansion of the human brain size. At a later stage in this same process, hallucinogens acted as catalysts in the development of imagination, fueling the creation of internal stratagems and hopes that may well have synergized the emergence of language and religion. (McKenna 1992b)

Robert Bednarik's exhaustively researched rock art studies around the world propose a theory of the origins of symbol making and language that push the date for our symbolizing back to the one million year BP[1] mark. He posits a long gradual history of language and symbol-using development. Bednarik sharply critiques the "leap into language" hypothesis, which has been the standard model in archeology, tying the development of language to the development of iconic art in the caves of Europe beginning 35,000 BP. His critique is based on evidence from the development of technologies, culture, genetic research, and physical anthropology. As he sees it,

> In anthropocentric and humanistic disciplines, the definitions of what indicates characteristics such as culture or language are routinely revised in response to the threat that such characteristics might be attributed to non-human interloper species. In this case, that practice is extended to "pre-modern" homonids that need to be excluded from some perceived exalted status of modern humans. In reality, there can be no doubt that humans do not possess one single definable, measurable or observable characteristic that is not shared by another species. The humanist inclination of maintaining, perhaps subconsciously, a qualitative separation between humans and non-human animals (or between "Moderns" and archaic H. sapiens)

> is ultimately attributable to the religio-cultural individual reality scholars exist in. (Bednarik 2006)

Bednarik is addressing precisely those points of our cultural conditioning ("the religio-cultural individual reality scholars exist in") that serve to hold key viewpoints in place as to what is or isn't "human." These viewpoints are part of the scaffolding that builds and maintains our estrangement from nature, in this case the animals from whom we have evolved. Bednarik acknowledges a connection between the rock art symbols and entoptic phenomena, but sees those marks as early symbolizing activity (of which we can only guess the meanings) rather than "just" an expression of an altered state of consciousness.

> The modernity of human behavior is not determined by skeletal evidence, not even by stone tool technologies. It is indicated by the "storage" of symbolism outside the brain, especially in the form of paleoart (the collective term defining all art-like manifestations of the remote human past). This argument was first advanced by Merlin Donald, who proposed a complex model in which he posited three basic stages of construction of conceptual space using language. The first, according to him, is mimetic symbol use without symbol creation, the second is the construction of conceptual space using language. The third involves the deposition of symbolic properties in material culture, capable of intervening in social behaviour, or in communicating meaning. (Bednarik 2006)

From this viewpoint, following Merlin Donald, cupules, as material culture, come after the development of speech and mimetic symbol use. This would push the origins of language and symbolic activity back before the 1 million BP mark. Cupules—dot-like excavations in rock faces—are prevalent the world over, and, because they take a long time to deteriorate, cupules are some of our oldest surviving symbolic remnants. Research in archeoastronomy attempts to map the presence and placement of cupules as markers of astronomical events such as solstices, indicating a high level of symbolic processes very early in our cultural evolution (Hammond 2003). The article referenced (see bibliography) also mentions—without interpretation—the presence of *Datura metaloides* (a powerful psychedelic) growing near the base of the rock being examined.

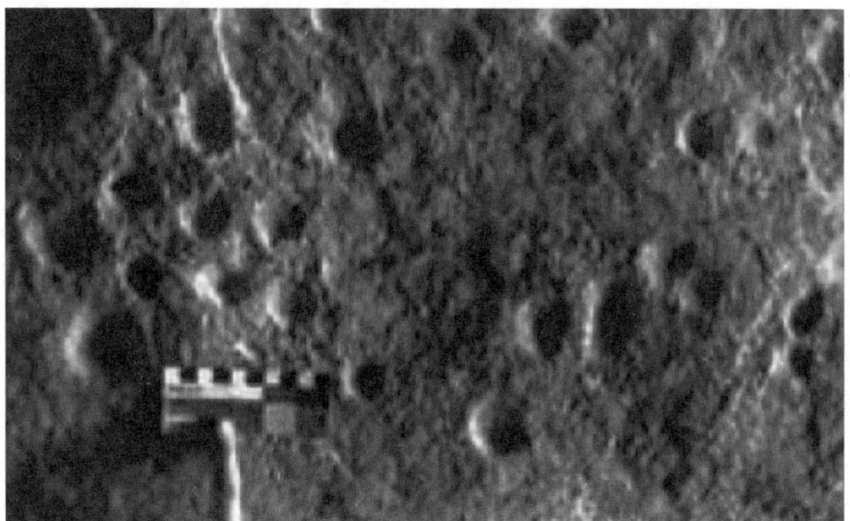

■ **Figure 88: Paleolithic cupules on the southern wall of Dariki-Chattan, Chambal Valley, India.** Photograph by Dr. Giriraj Kumar.

As Terence McKenna narrates our early history, when we moved out into grasslands and became omnivores, our sampling of any potential food source would have brought us in contact with varieties of psilocybin mushrooms. As we formed relations with cattle, leading to domestication, varieties of coprophilous mushrooms, such as *Stropharia cubensis,* would have become more readily available. McKenna summarizes (from Roland Fischer's research, and his own observations) some of the specific effects of psilocybin at different dose levels to make his argument.

> At the first, low, level of usage is the effect that Fischer noted, small amounts of psilocybin, consumed with no awareness of its psychoactivity while in the general act of browsing for food, and perhaps later consumed consciously, impart a noticeable increase in visual acuity, especially edge detection. As visual acuity is at a premium among hunter-gathers, the discovery of the equivalent of "chemical binoculars" could not fail to have an impact on the hunting and gathering success of those individuals who availed themselves of this advantage.
>
> Because psilocybin is a stimulant of the central nervous system, when taken in slightly larger doses, it tends to trigger restlessness and sexual arousal. Thus, at this second level of usage, by increasing instances of

> copulation, the mushrooms directly favored human reproduction. The tendency to regulate and schedule sexual activity within the group, by linking it to a lunar cycle of mushroom availability, may have been important as a first step toward ritual and religion. Certainly at the third and highest level of usage, religious concerns would be at the forefront of the tribe's consciousness, simply because of the power and strangeness of the experience itself.
>
> This third level, then, is the level of the full-blown shamanic ecstasy. The psilocybin intoxication is a rapture whose breadth and depth is the despair of prose. It is wholly Other and no less mysterious to us than it was to our mushroom-munching ancestors. The boundary-dissolving qualities of shamanic ecstasy predispose hallucinogen-using tribal groups to community bonding and to group sexual activities, which promote gene mixing, higher birth rates, and a communal sense of responsibility for the group offspring. (McKenna 1992b)

Michael Winkelman shares this position that psychedelic use conferred adaptive advantage to our ancestors. McKenna places the shaman at the center of both psychedelic management (Eliade's "techniques of ecstasy") and linguistic prowess. The two go hand in hand.

> The plants used by the shaman are not intended to stimulate the immune system or the body's other natural defenses against disease. Rather, the shamanic plants allow the healer to journey into an invisible realm in which the causality of the ordinary world is replaced with the rationale of natural magic. In this realm, language, ideas, and meaning have greater power than cause and effect. (McKenna 1992b)

Archeologist Robert Bednarik hypothesizes a phase where symbolizing, natural language, and the forms of culture take over the slow evolutionary processes of nature. He imagines this as a period where we inadvertently domesticated ourselves, with startling consequences. His theory attempts to explain the shift, over a relatively short period of time (±fifty thousand years) of the human body from a "robust" form to a "gracile" form. This process recurred on every continent we populated, though the shifts were at different time periods in different locales. The standard model in archeology has it that around sixty thousand years ago, a "gracile" and "superior" group of humans, representing our "modern" form, crossed from Africa and conquered the less developed Neanderthals, who disappeared by 30,000 BP. Whether Neanderthals could or could not interbreed with the "graciles" is no longer under debate, as Neanderthal DNA has been found in the modern human genomes. Bednarik argues from the material record that Neanderthals had language, and in fact had the characteristics that nature favors for fitness and survival: stronger bodies and bigger brains. His idea is that, with the advent of culture came self-awareness and the building of complex cultural systems. These complex systems included aesthetic values and values of social standing. These aesthetic choices influenced our mating choices. We thereby self-selected ourselves, within our cultural systems, establishing trends of body changes by our choices, in the same manner that we induce changes in cattle, dogs, and horses by selective breeding for desirable characteristics. The results were: smaller bodies and smaller brains than the Neanderthal, actually a regressive trend. Earlier than that, Bednarik points out, the increase in brain size found in the fossil record that occurs with exceptional rapidity in evolutionary time could have been a function of selection for the bigger brain and the capacity for language (and culture) that was developing, even though the evolutionary tradeoff—skull size that made childbearing much more dangerous, and an extended period of dependency for the neonate, are both characteristics that are not in our favor as fitness criteria (Bednarik 2006).

Media

I have looked backward to the earliest surviving symbols in human history, the dots carved into cave walls the world over, as one perspective on the evolution of language and linguistic forms, possibly connected to psychedelic use, and to a view of the biosphere per Varela that takes "the linguistic" all the way down into the structure of organisms and their communications at all levels. Futurist, author, programmer, teacher, ceremonial magician, and psychonaut Mark Pesce's reflections on the history, especially the recent history, of communication technologies takes us into our present moment of a Cambrian explosion of linguistic forms.

> That's what those 75,000-year-old squiggly lines on a piece of stone imply: that our internal linguistic capability, which gave us language, had overflowed onto the material world, and that the material world had been

> consumed by our linguistic capability. This is an important point, perhaps the central point I'm trying to make today: everything you look out upon from your eyes, exists less as a physical reality than as a construction of linguistic form. This is what Terence McKenna meant when he said that the world is made of words, and that if you know the right words, you can make of the world whatever you will. (Pesce 2002)

A cybernetic feedback circle between new technologies, and the development of new formal sign systems to describe, explain and/or implement these technologies, is a feature of this linguistic evolutionary process, from the computer and its layered languages, to the sequencing, manipulation, and uses of the genomes of living forms, to the miniaturization of magic we are calling nanotechnology. In Mark Pesce's phrase, the fundamental domains both of life and of matter have become "linguistically pliable" (Pesce 2002). In an interview on technology and psychedelics, Pesce describes how he, along with Tony Parisi and a team of open-source developers, created VRML, the Virtual Reality Markup Language, bringing the two-dimensional computer image into a three-dimensional format, a "dimensional leap." Pesce documents their use of LSD as a problem-solving aid in this creative process.

> I mean after I did that, I actually talked it out with other people while we were tripping. And this is a case of specific usage. I'd go back into the space and take a look at specific parts of it again. And, the funny thing is I'd be very methodical and rational—which is not my normal mode of experience. Normally I'm just "experiential." But in these cases I was very methodical.
>
> MAPS: While you were tripping?
>
> Mark: Yes! And I had to go back to the person I was working with, who was my partner in the endeavor when we were doing it. He understood that, and came right into the space with me, and we were methodical. We were giggly and all that stuff, but we were methodical about it. And so we were able to really say, "Okay, well here's this block right here. Okay, let's take that block and go from one side of the block to the other side of the block." And we did. We did this on a number of occasions over about a month period. And managed to take everything that I had gotten and really get it out. (Pesce, in *MAPS Bulletin* 1999)

This instance of using an altered state of consciousness in the development of a novel computer language represents another application of xenolinguistic techniques: the use of psychedelics as problem-solving adjuncts in the creation of a new use of a symbolic system—in this case, one enabling a new form of "reality." Pesce describes DNA as linguistic, and as a very slow memory, the recorded history of interactions with the environment.

> For four billion years, DNA was the recording mechanism of history, the memory of biology. As soon as we developed language, we no longer needed the slower form of DNA for memory; we could use the much faster form of language, which produced with it a deep sense of memory within the individual—since the linguistic symbols could be contained within the human mind.
>
> Since we became a symbol-manipulating species, our forward evolution, in DNA terms, has come to a dead stop. . . . However, our linguistic capabilities allow us to perform acts of memory much faster than DNA, probably at least 10 million times faster! (Pesce 2002)

Pesce describes this shift into culture and its effects on biology.

> This renegotiation of power between the previously unchallenged bios and the brand-new logos was not something that the bios was prepared for. Most likely immediately, the bios was overwhelmed by the logos. The natural environment of the first humans was entirely and utterly replaced by a symbol-driven environment. The post-modern philosophers claim that this is a new thing, that the Disneyfication of the world has overloaded the natural world with the mediasphere. But this isn't a new thing, even if our recognition of it is; as long as shamans and storytellers have been spinning myths that tell us who and what we are, the world ceased to exist as nature, and became a linguistic element in the story of *Homo sapiens*. (Pesce 2002)

The history of communication technologies, of *media,* as we have most recently called this collection of linguistic accelerants, is the history of the forms and practices that have permeated our daily lives in ways that we cannot predict anymore, unless to state the obvious: there will be more. And the *more* arrives faster and faster. Pesce's vision of the next adventure of the Logos concerns the extension of our linguistic ability back into the language of molecules: nanotechnology.

> This is the coming linguistic revolution in technology, because, at this point, the entire fabric of the material world becomes linguistically pliable. Anything you see, anywhere, animate or inanimate, will have within it the capacity to be entirely transformed by a rearrangement of its atoms into another form, a form which obeys the dictates of linguistic intent. (Pesce 2002)

Pesce, always the visionary futurist, speaking to a psychedelically informed audience, places the evolutionary transformations of language at the center of an eschatological vision he shares with McKenna:

> For we find ourselves in an increasingly narrow space, and our freedom of movement is more and more confined by both linguistic constructions and technological mechanisms; and even our DNA is coming to be controlled.
>
> But there is a new birth coming, a new form erupting into being. And we, as the folks focused on the future, who broaden our minds in every conceivable way—by reading about the future and doing the work of creating new culture, with everything that entails, be it esoteric spiritual practices or taking psychedelics—we may be among the few who can take stock of the entirety of the transformation, because we have occasionally been thrust into spaces where what is to be permanently true for everyone else has become temporarily true for us. (Pesce 2002)

Pesce describes language as the living Logos, with its own intentionality, a mind of its own, which is leading us to the edge of apocalypse. His description of the all-pervasive media ecology in which we live our lives delineates our estrangement from the Bios in stark terms.

Estrangement from Nature

"Culture is not your friend."

—Terence McKenna

From a psychedelic perspective, I have seen and felt what Richard Doyle describes as the ecodelic insight—the perception of the dense interconnectedness of all aspects of nature and the restoration of our place as a part of nature, thoroughly woven into its workings on all levels and responsible for our effects thereon. The ecodelic insight is compatible with Varela's view of "the linguistic" as the means by which this system of systems—interacting, nested, scalar—is connected and in continual interchange through all systems from the molecular to the molar. The ecodelic insight, reliably though not universally produced by psychedelic experience across substances and in varied settings, can heal the gulf by which we have set ourselves further and further apart from nature, superior to its workings, and currently engaged in its commodification and control.

Terence McKenna (in concert with feminists) takes Francis Bacon to task for his founding "bad attitude," and its part in our estrangement.

> Where I part company with science is at that moment when Francis Bacon, who was the great theoretician of modern science, wrote: "Nature is a goddess that we may lead to the rack . . . and there tease, torture, and torment from her her secrets." (McKenna in Harpignies 2007)

Nature is conceived as a set of random processes operating without *telos* and functioning as a set of resources for the human agenda, subject to ownership. This viewpoint delineates the extent to which our alienation has spread, and our potential for damage to the biosphere is maximized. However one wishes to identify the source—as a product of Enlightenment rationalism, or of scriptural necessity—we are East of Eden by many miles and millennia. And even Eden is portrayed with God's delegation of responsibility to Adam as Man-in-Charge, as if nature needs our guidance from the beginning; as if nature cannot manage without the intervention of an outside authority. This disconnect, this exile, and the imbalances it has produced, is the ethical dimension and imperative of the ecodelic insight.

> The apparent inability of humans to perceive the densely interconnected nature of their habitat threatens not only said ecosystem but the very self-definition of humanity itself as homo faber, an organism who actively creates, rather than is simply created by, her environment. Faced with overwhelming evidence of climatic change, one would expect an outburst of human agency, an ordering of the world according to the specifications of Homo Sapiens—the species, who, after all, knows what it is doing. (Doyle 2011)

I relate this form of narcissistic anthropocentrism to the same viewpoint, critiqued by Robert Bednarik, that describes humans as the only linguistically endowed creatures, the only creatures with feelings to be respected, and the only creatures with minds, much less possessed with (or by) consciousness. This tendency to set ourselves apart from the rest of nature was fully in place by the time Darwin dared to differ, and our subsequent evolutionary explorations in paleontology and genetics made animals (our food and domesticated slaves) into kin. Creationism and the myth of Eden continue to attempt to rescue us from the shame of these bestial relations, and the racially explicit "out of Africa" evolutionary scenario.

Charles Laughlin describes the evolution of symbolic forms as a progression toward formal sign systems in which "complete independence from stimulus-boundness and actual events in the world" raises the adaptive power of the human in our operational environment to a state where we are, on the one hand, *seemingly,* the top of the food chain, and controlling our environments to an unprecedented extent, and at the same time accelerating toward unsustainability on many fronts. Our adaptive successes run unchecked by the big predators we have extinguished. Meanwhile, we are increasingly vulnerable to miniature predators on the microbial and viral scale, which are adapting rapidly on their own survival agendas. Our adolescent tendency to foul our nest and expect Mother Nature to clean up after us is catching up with us fast. Our narcissistic self-image as the most or, even, the only intelligent life-form on Earth (possibly in the Universe) does not bode well for the long haul. It would behoove us to begin to adapt *to ourselves* as a threat to our own survival. If we do not succeed in adapting to our own excesses, nature has tried and true remedies for overpopulation, exhaustion of resources, and failure to adapt.

> I think plants and mushrooms have intelligence and they want us to take care of the environment, and they want to communicate that to us in a way we can understand. When I use these mushrooms and other compounds, I get the message that the planet is in trouble, that we are approaching a huge catastrophe and that we're all in this ship together. I get the sense that all these spirits are speaking to me, that the planet is calling out to us, asking us for help, to control our consumption, waste, and pollution. (Paul Stamets in Harpignies 2007)

> Jean Paul Sartre said: "Nature is mute." That, sadly, captures perfectly modernity's relationship to nature, but still—if that isn't the lamest statement made by a twentieth-century philosopher, I don't know what is. (Terence McKenna in Harpignies 2007)

We are no longer listening, yet have projected that inattention on nature: "Nature is mute." From this stance, reified by our literal, bodily encapsulation in culture and its artifacts (language, clothing, cars, buildings, cities, media), it is difficult to perceive nature's languages, though they are ubiquitous.

> Again and again in nature you see these complex chemical interactions resulting from evolution's dynamic creativity, as organisms keep trying to adapt and devise strategies by trial and error to use and manipulate each other. Plants, facing a successful chemical defense by an insect, in turn elaborate over time even more complex toxins, perhaps targeted at other cellular targets, other enzymes, other receptor systems, and it goes on and on. Eventually you see the complex web of chemical interactions that characterize these floristic ecologies. (Dennis McKenna in Harpignies 2007)

Mushroom philosopher Simon G. Powell states the case for nature's intelligence in terms of language, in what he calls "the fantastic hypothesis." Powell is well aware of the religious discourse of "intelligent design" as a brand of monotheistic theology to which he does not subscribe. However, in his experience under the noetic conditions of psilocybin perception, nature is perceived with *telos* at the core.

> The fantastic hypothesis views reality, or Nature, as a meaningful and intelligent system as opposed to some mindless accident. According to the fantastic hypothesis, we are woven into an orchestrating tide of information, interconnected throughout. (Powell 2009)

Similarly, anthropologist Jeremy Narby's life-work can be read as his attempt to reconcile and integrate two forms of cognition: the epistemological practices of Ashininca shamanism, including his own ayahuasca experiences over many years, and his scientific training in anthropology (Narby 1999; Narby 2005). It is the same act of bridging two world views that Varela attempts in his differentiation between operational descriptions of science that have no room for human purpose, and symbolic descriptions in terms of human meaning and purpose.

The insights of Richard Doyle, the McKenna brothers, Paul Stamets, Mark Pesce, Simon G. Powell, and Jeremy Narby are intellectually and psychedelically founded—products of both representational and presentational forms of symbolic cognition, to put it in Harry Hunt's terminology.

The Call for New Language

"We need to create a meta-linguistic, meta-mathematical, meta-metaphorical language."

—Terence McKenna, 1983

Aldous Huxley's famous definition of consciousness as Mind at Large funneled through the reducing valve of the brain and nervous system came directly from his psychedelic experiences.

> To formulate and express the contents of this reduced awareness, man has invented and endlessly elaborated those symbol-systems and implicit philosophies which we call languages. Every individual is at once the beneficiary and the victim of the linguistic tradition into which he has been born—the beneficiary inasmuch as language gives access to the accumulated records of other people's experience, the victim in so far as it confirms him in the belief that reduced awareness is the only awareness and as it bedevils his sense of reality, so that he is all too apt to take his concepts for data, his words for actual things. That which, in the language of religion, is called "this world" is the universe of reduced awareness, expressed, and, as it were, petrified by language. The various "other worlds," with which human beings erratically make contact are so many elements in the totality of the awareness belonging to Mind at Large. Most people, most of the time, know only what comes through the reducing valve and is consecrated as genuinely real by the local language. (Huxley 1974)

Psychonauts have their own reasons for calling for new language, but the tradition of dissatisfaction with the current state of natural language is not new. Umberto Eco, in his work *The Search for the Perfect Language,* gives an overview of the multivalent impulse toward perfection: sacred perfection, as seen in the search for the language of Adam, or the original Hebrew, or the postulated Indo-European root language. Leibnitz wanted philosophical perfection, and the perfection of pure rationality. He searched for a "truly blind calculus," blind, that is, to semantic variation—the polysemy of natural language.

> Leibniz saw an analogy between the order of the world, that is, of truth, and the grammatical order of the symbols in language. Many have seen this as a version of the picture theory of language expounded by Wittgenstein in the Tractatus, according to which "a picture has a logico-pictorial form in common with what it depicts." Leibniz was thus the first to recognize that the value of his philosophical language was a function of its formal structure rather than of its terms; syntax, which he called habitudo or propositional structure, was more important than semantics. (Eco 1995)

Leibniz had published *Novissima sinica,* a collection of letters and studies by Jesuit missionaries in China. Father Joachim Bouvet, himself a missionary to China, seeing the work, sent Leibniz a treatise on the *I Ching*.

> When Leibniz described to Bouvet his own research in binary arithmetic, that is, his calculus by 1 and 0 (of which he also praised the metaphysical ability to represent even the relation between God and nothingness), Bouvet perceived that this arithmetic might admirably explain the structure of the Chinese hexagrams as well. He sent Leibniz in 1701 (though Leibniz only received the communication in 1703) a letter to which he added a woodcut showing the disposition of the hexagrams.
>
> In fact, the disposition of the hexagrams in the woodcut differs from that of the King Wen sequence of the *I Ching,* nevertheless, this error allowed Leibnitz to perceive a signifying sequence which he later illustrated in his *Explication de l'arithmétique binaire* (1703). (Eco 1995)[2]

Eco notes the interesting irony that Leibniz's work, the purely syntactical binary, developed into Boolean logic and became the root logic for our linguistic machines, the computers, capable of specifying any manner of semantically distinct objects (such as his plane reservation).

> Passing through the mathematical filter of Leibniz, reducing itself to pure syntax, his philosophical a priori language has finally managed to designate even an individual elephant. (Eco 1995)

I will return to the discussion of the *I Ching* and its deep correlative structure in the elaboration of the McKennas' Timewave Zero.

Natural language is seen by Huxley, McKenna, and Pesce as part of the structures of consciousness that serve both to structure reality and at the same time, paradoxically, to separate us from nature. The psychedelic experience of penetrating the veil of natural language to a direct apprehension of the impeccable radiance of the natural world leads us toward the possibility of a reconciliation with our original Eden. The call for new language emanating from psychedelic experience expresses this longing to find forms of language that can join us rather than separate us from the natural world, and help us to arrive at a deeper knowledge of ourselves.

The Guild of Xenolinguists: Terence and Dennis McKenna—Timewave Zero

The McKenna brothers, Terence and Dennis, the core of *The Brotherhood of the Screaming Abyss,* in a psychedelic mind-meld experienced a download of magnitude at La Chorrera, Colombia, in 1971. Terence went on to become a public figure, the bard with the golden tongue and the psychedelic schtick, the tryptamine Pied Piper, unpacking these experiences and inviting the world into his peculiar brand of psychedelic adventure. Terence framed the narrative of psychedelic exploration as "a ripping good story," and, as Dennis has noted, Terence never let a fact interfere with a good story. Dennis took a less public but no less adventurous path as a psychedelic scientist. His stories have been told mainly in scientific articles, with great attention to fact, and in the unimpeachable syntax of science. Dennis has now advanced his story in the form of a memoir, entitled *The Brotherhood of the Screaming Abyss*. But it is clear from both their writings, and especially in the two books, *True Hallucinations* and *The Invisible Landscape,* that the ideas that informed Terence's talks began as a shared and true hallucination between the brothers.

■ Figure 89: Terence (right) and Dennis McKenna, 1975.

The Core Mystery

Terence McKenna's complex of psychedelic ideas can be mapped with language at the center, influencing every discourse he entered. His interests were wide: hermeticism, alchemy, the Logos, DMT, DNA, *I Ching,* shamanism, ecology, history, and ontology, and in each he found indications that reality is linguistically structured. Early in his psychedelic adventures, a profoundly influential experience with DMT set this strange attractor in place in his personal landscape. He has called this experience, and the DMT experience in general, "the core mystery." In Nepal, involved in smuggling hash and studying Tibetan language in 1967, age twenty-one, Terence McKenna had

> I guess it's called a peak experience, or a core revelation, or being born again, or having your third eye opened, or something, which was a revelation of an alien dimension; a brightly lit, inhabited, non three-dimensional, self-contorting, sustained, organic, linguistically intending modality that couldn't be stopped or held back or denied. . . . I found myself in the sort of auric equivalent of the Pope's private chapel, and there were insect elf machines proffering strange little tablets with strange writing on them. And it all went on, they were speaking in some kind of—there were these self-transforming machine-elf creatures—were speaking in some kind of colored language which condensed into rotating machines that were like Fabergé eggs, but crafted out of luminescent super-conducting ceramics, and liquid crystal gels, and all this stuff was so weird, and so alien, and so "un-English-able" that it was a complete shock. (McKenna 1988)

These are the wholly alien linguistic objects he describes over and over in his taped lectures and books from the beginning to the end of his career. He became a xenolinguist in the DMT space. Many of his linguistic ideas appear to be a result of the effort to unpack the 1967 (and subsequent) DMT experiences. The self-transforming machine elves of language became Terence's logo of the DMT alterity, impossible to language, difficult to visualize, the sublime irony of a brand that cannot be reproduced, perhaps because it enacts reproduction itself.

The Experiment at La Chorrera

Four years after the initial DMT revelation, in the jungles of the Colombian Amazon, at the mission settlement of La Chorrera, Terence and his younger brother Dennis, along with three friends, had a weeks-long cascade of psychedelic experience that has been called since "the Experiment at La Chorrera" (the E@LC). Two books and many taped lectures detail the events. The first book, *The Invisible Landscape,* is co-authored. The second, *True Hallucinations* (Terence McKenna 1993b), is written by Terence, including long excerpts from Dennis McKenna's journal of the time. It is clear in studying these books that many of the major ideas that Terence lectured and wrote on throughout his career crystallized in the prolonged state of mind-meld between the brothers described in the two books. I am not highlighting issues of authorship, but the states of mind or Mind at Large that occurred during the download period from March 4th to March 15th, 1971, at La Chorrera.

> He performed his experiment and it seemed as though I got a kind of informational feedback off my DNA, or some other molecular storage site of information. This happened precisely because the psychedelic molecules bound themselves to the DNA and then behaved in the way that we had expected; they did broadcast a totality symbol whose deep structure reflects the organizational principles of the molecules of life itself. This totality entered linear time disguised, in the presence of ordinary consciousness, as a dialogue with the Logos. The Logos provided a narrative framework able to frame and give coherency to the flood of new insights that otherwise would have overwhelmed me. (McKenna 1993b)

What makes a download a *download* is the intensity of the experience, the extreme compaction of densely interconnected information, and the sense of potential access to any knowledge one can summon the wit to inquire about under such extreme epistemological conditions. The Other, as Logos, provided structure, acting as a transducer of energy, bringing the high-speed, high-intensity informational flood to a manageable level. Regarding intensity: the fact that Dennis remained in an altered state of consciousness for at least twenty-three days is an almost unthinkable supermarathon of psychedelic travel. During this time Terence minded him, not sleeping for several nights himself. Terence kept one foot in the default world in which concern was escalating over Dennis' mental health, and the other foot firmly planted in the uninhibited, luminous, absurdist, messianic certainty and ontological confusion of the world Dennis appeared to live in, day after day. The brothers shared a reality, "illuminated and maddened and lifted up by something great beyond all telling" (McKenna in Sutin 1991). During the same time period, the voice of the Logos asserted itself with Terence, and the intricate implication of the *I Ching* and its processes began to unfold.

The concept of concrescence, which Terence McKenna derives from Whitehead, describes a coming together, a condensing of ideas and events. Concrescence is at the heart of the events and processes in play in the E@LC. Concrescence is also a characteristic of high correlative systems where many ideas are brought together in a single system of systems. Altered states, including those produced by psychedelics, can precipitate correlative thinking and produce correlative systems, as we have seen in Chapter 7 with the discussion of Steve Farmer's work. Timewave Zero is such a correlative system, bringing together the mathematics and the description of time as an evolutionary process, time that embodies a quality of ebb and flow on individual, social, biological, and cosmic scales. McKenna's time is fractal in form, self-similar at multiple scales, and deeply personal. Timewave Zero becomes the carrier wave of the principle of novelty.

The protocol for the psychedelic experiment itself developed from the several initial psilocybin experiences *(Stropharia cubensis)*. These trips were undertaken in a series shortly after arrival at La Chorrera when the unexpected resource of the coprophilic mushrooms was identified growing abundantly on cow patties in the fields surrounding the Mission. On the fourth psilocybin trip in as many days, Dennis emitted a brief burst of sound, "a very machine-like loud, dry buzz, during which his body became stiff." He related the sound, which he reported containing a tremendous energy, to the tryptamine buzzing he heard, and to Terence's reports of DMT-induced glossolalia-like sounds. Creating the sound both frightened him and catapulted him into a complex of ideas from chemistry, physics, microbiology, DNA, alchemy, and shamanism, an ad hoc correlative system built of existing knowledge frameworks that became the protocol of the Experiment, or opus. He called the sound a "psycho-audible warp phenomenon."

> I felt Dennis's amazement was perfectly reasonable; it was my own encounter with the visionary and linguistic powers of DMT that had originally sent me looking into hallucinogens and their place in nature. (McKenna 1993a)

Dennis's notes from the period detail the process they would follow. His idea was to test the effect of the harmonic sound he was able to produce on the chemical and physical properties of the molecules involved, including his own neural DNA and RNA. Terence states in the text that their ideas of what actually happened from a chemical and physical standpoint have undergone much sorting out and revision since the original conception.

> These notes do not of course represent the final form of our theorizing about these matters and are not at all to be taken at face value. But how complete the vision was and how finely worked its detail! The theory that is represented in my brother's notes remains the operational basis for understanding the effect that was triggered on March fifth at the conclusion of the experiment. His notes were our working blueprint, and they were very effective. (McKenna 1993b)

The process is described by Dennis:

> The mushroom must be taken and heard.
>
> The ayahuasca must be taken and charged with overtonal ESR [electronic spin resonance] of the psilocybin via voice-imparted, amplified sound.
>
> The ESR resonance of the psilocybin in the mushrooms will be canceled and will drop into a superconducting state; a small portion of the physical matter of the mushroom will be obliterated.
>
> The superconductively charged psilocybin will pick up the ESR harmonic of the ayahuasca complex; this energy will be instantly and completely absorbed by the higher-dimensional tryptamine template. It will be transferred to the mushroom as vocal sound and condensed onto the psilocybin as a bonded complex of superconductive harmine-psilocybin-DNA.
>
> The result will be a molecular aggregate of hyperdimensional, superconducting matter that receives and sends messages transmitted by thought, that stores and retrieves information in a holographic fashion in neural DNA, and that depends on superconductive harmine as a transducer energy source and super-conductive RNA as a temporal matrix. (Dennis McKenna in McKenna 1993b)

The process was dubbed "hypercarbolation." Alchemically read, the goal of the opus was to instantiate the Philosopher's Stone, using ayahuasca, psilocybin, and the sound that resonates with the rising tone heard in the tryptamine trance, by intercalating the harmine molecule into the DNA and creating a bond that would essentially hold open the portal for transdimensional information flow.

The Philosopher's Stone, Translinguistic Matter, and the Hyperdimensional Object at the End of Time

A concrescence of totality symbols was used to describe the goal:

> There seems to be an ideological lineage, the golden chain, whose collective task was the shattering of the historical continuum through the generation of the living philosophical lapis of hypercarbolated humanity. All these visionary thinkers had performed their part in this project. Now, as the secret work of human history, the generation of Adam's cosmic body, lost since paradise, neared completion, these shades stirred and pressed near to our Amazonian campsite. Our destiny was apparently to be the human atoms critical to the transformation of Homo Sapiens into galaxy-roving bodhisattvas, the culmination of quintessence of the highest aspirations of star-coveting humanity. (McKenna 1993a)

The alchemical Anthropos, the Christian Resurrection Body, the stone, and the roving lenticular vehicle all converge in the intentionality of the Experiment. The download precipitated by the Experiment and shared by the McKenna brothers was a concrescence of noesis that resulted in the Timewave Zero theory. This theory developed in dialogue with the Logos and was based on the *I Ching*. And the Timewave Zero theory itself is a tale of time ending in a concrescence variously called the Eschaton; the singularity; the philosopher's stone; the trans- or hyperdimensional object at the end of time; and other universal symbols of totality, finality, and completion. The philosopher's stone, according to Jung, is the polysemic totality symbol *par excellence*. The stone is beginning and end, alpha and omega, stone and solvent, "it" and "process" (Jung 1953).

Translinguistic matter, in the McKennas' various descriptions, plays the role of a magical substance that, perceived in psychedelic states, can be used

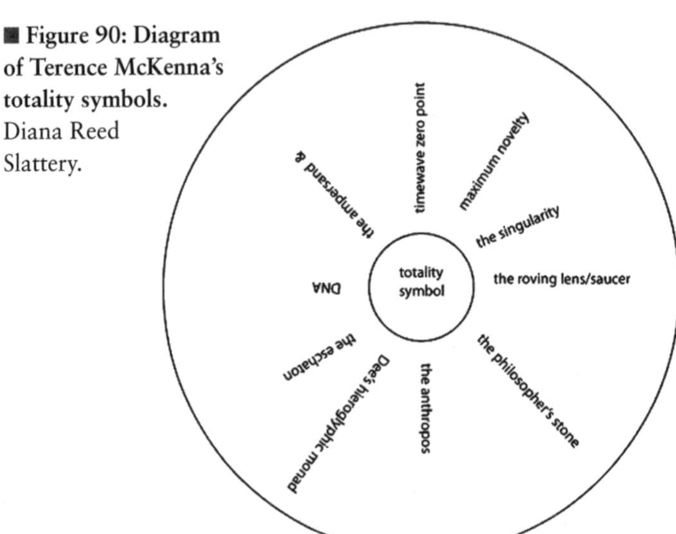

■ **Figure 90: Diagram of Terence McKenna's totality symbols.** Diana Reed Slattery.

to create things, *any*-things, as if it were a precursor material to the stone itself. Terence McKenna describes Dennis McKenna's run-up to the Experiment as a function of this substance in action whose harnessing would instantiate the Stone.

> He was onto something very strange; his word-pictures caused reality to shimmer and crinkle at the edges. He was really in touch with this bubbling obsidian fourth-dimensional fluid that we were going to stabilize into a usable tool. (McKenna and McKenna 1993a)

In *True Hallucinations,* Terence McKenna devotes a chapter to his Nepalese DMT "peak" experience, as the back-story to the E@LC. The experience, along with everything else, was sexual, and included the phenomenon of translinguistic matter.

> Reality was shattered. This kind of fucking occurs at the very limit of what is possible. Everything had been transformed into orgasm and visible, chattering oceans of elf language. Then I saw that where our bodies were glued together there was flowing, out of her, over me, over the floor of the roof, flowing everywhere, some sort of obsidian liquid, something dark and glittering, with color and lights within it. After the DMT flash, after the seizures of orgasm, after all that, this new thing shocked me to the core. What was this fluid and what was going on? I looked at it. I

> looked right into it, and it was the surface of my own mind reflected in front of me. Was it translinguistic matter, the living opalescent excrescence of the alchemical abyss of hyperspace, something generated by the sex act performed under such crazy conditions?

The McKennas were also discussing the shamanic occurrence and uses of this substance.

> The people take ayahuasca after which they, and anyone else who has taken ayahuasca, are able to see a substance that is described as violet or deep blue and that bubbles like a liquid. When you vomit from taking ayahuasca, this violet fluid comes out of your body; it also forms on the surface of the skin like sweat. The Jivaro do much of their magic with this peculiar stuff. These matters are extremely secret. Informants insist that the shamans spread the stuff out on the ground in front of them, and that one can look at this material and see other times and other places. According to their reports, the nature of this fluid is completely outside of ordinary experience: it is made out of space/time or mind, or it is pure hallucination objectively expressed but always keeping itself within the confines of a liquid. (McKenna and McKenna 1993a)

Stephan Beyer, in his comprehensive work on Amazonian mestizo shamanism, describes the shaman's "phlegm" as the source of his power. This material can be transformed into lethal darts and used in attack; the same material is used defensively to encase and expel such darts in curing.

> Throughout the Upper Amazon, shamanic power is conceptualized as a physical substance—often a sticky saliva- or phlegm-like substance—that is stored within the shaman's body, usually in the chest or stomach, or sometimes permeating the shaman's flesh. This substance is used both for attack and for defense. The virtually universal method of inflicting magical harm in the Upper Amazon is to project this substance into the body of the victim—either the substance itself or pathogenic projectiles the shaman keeps embedded with it. (Beyer 2009)

Alchemy meets shamanism in the E@LC. In the McKennas' idea of translinguistic matter, the concept is broadened; the tools of the magicians and shamans of many cultures are molded in the altered state of consciousness out of translinguistic matter. The techniques are legion: magic mirrors for skrying past and future, especially for that which is out of sight; penetration of secrets, another's hidden knowledge; hidden causes of disease or misfortune; prediction of the future; or even time travel to the distant past. In this sense, translinguistic matter is divinatory in its uses. "Chattering oceans of elf language" and gushes of sexually charged translinguistic matter "flowing everywhere, some sort of obsidian liquid, something dark and glittering, with color and lights within it" bring together two of the most complex linguistic phenomena of the psychedelic sphere in a single wild ride.

> Non-chemists ourselves at that point, we had been able to turn the condensation of spirit into the idea of translinguistic matter. Word, object, and cognition had become fused in the best tradition of the higher Tantric yogas. (McKenna 1993b)

Relative to natural language broadcasting on station normal, this represents a high degree of novelty. Recombinant keywords: *hyperdimensional, obsidian, violet, vomited, opalescent, magical, fluid, sticky-phlegm, glittering-shit*. Precious bodily fluids, indeed. Translinguistic matter as the liquid phase-state of the stone? An unspeakable liquid linguistic substance that bespeaks objects into existence—and we've come round to the machine elves again. One flows into the other; permutations of the linguistic machinery glimpsed behind baseline reality.

> they were showing me the machinery of reality the something that could make anything the everything machine endlessly creative, above all things (10.03.02, DMT post-session report)

This apocalyptic concrescence of impossibly patchworked qualities is a hallmark of the novelty-laden DMT or high-dose psilocybin experience.

> It is a language, but not made of words—a language which becomes and which is the things it describes. (Dennis McKenna in McKenna 1993a)

Like DNA, as Jeremy Narby said.

Timewave Zero and the *I Ching*

Timewave Zero, the symbolic system whose concepts were initially downloaded in the E@LC, was Terence McKenna's masterwork. The mathematics and subsequent software instantiating the theory of novelty and the fracticality of time were developed and refined over the stretch of time between the La Chorrera incident in 1971 and 1998 (Meyer 2006).

The mathematics of Timewave Zero have been thoroughly critiqued by Peter Meyer and others. In simplest terms, the Eschaton has a date: December 21, 2012. How that date was arrived at is explained by Meyer, a programmer who worked with Terence McKenna from 1985 through 1998 on the development of the Timewave Zero software. The explicitly fractal mathematics of the Timewave was recognized and developed during this period. Meyer points out that the 2012 endpoint date is wholly dependent on two variable factors. First, its calculation depends on fixing a date earlier in the Timewave representing a high level of novelty in human history. McKenna's choice was the explosion of the atom bomb at Hiroshima. Mapping that date to correspond with a low point (high novelty) in the Timewave slides the endpoint date to November 2012. Second, the choice of which of the tables of 384 values (calculations from the *I Ching* sequence that determine the data points from which the Timewave can be drawn; several were developed) changes the outcome of the endpoint, as well as the overall shape of the wave. These variant tables are built into Meyer's most recent version of the software. The fixing of the date thereby depends on a number of interpretive choices made both by the software developers and the users of the systems. Evaluating events in human history as to their degree of novelty is clearly a highly personal and situated process that will never submit to scientific certainty. I suspect that if Osama bin Laden, Mother Teresa, or Martin Luther King, Jr., were to make their choices as to events in history containing high novelty, their choices might differ.

The symbolic system of Timewave Zero is similar to the *I Ching* in this fashion: on the one hand, it is a mathematics derived directly from the King Wen sequence of hexagrams. The King Wen is the older, traditional order of the hexagrams. In the *I Ching,* each hexagram itself is a sequence of six binary bits, which are an expression in binary code. Lines then have the added property of being changing or unchanging. And here the mathematical structure upholds the qualitative, metaphorical, and philosophical aspect of the *I Ching*. In one aspect, the *I Ching* is mathematical or quantitative, but these mathematical configurations are given interpretations that are qualitative and textual. As one reads the verbal interpretations of the hexagram and its changing lines in sequence through the hexagram, various processes in human and cosmic affairs develop, moving through a life cycle of the situation, and locating the individual consulting the *I Ching* somewhere in that sequence of changes. These two aspects, what Varela called the operational (that which operates by rules with no need for human interpretation) and the symbolic levels of description, are brought together to give a full reading of the situation and its changes in a divinatory context. This is the art of divinatory interpretation. This is the context in which I read both McKenna's construction of the Timewave Zero system and its interpretations, which link mathematical points in the wave to subjectively chosen points in history. But *whose* history? Who is determining what is important, and truly novel, is always the question. And at what scale? The purely personal life events? National events? If so, from whose perspective? Or events on the scale of human or cosmic evolution? And for that matter, what is an "event"? Events have precursors and aftermaths; where in linear or fractal time did the French Revolution begin and end? Divinatory systems such as the *I Ching* and astrology both link a mathematical system to divinatory interpretations. In short, Timewave Zero does not, cannot predict in the operational, scientific description. Timewave Zero is interpretive, a symbolic description in Varela's terms, and its use is for divination, which interprets in terms of an individual viewpoint.

The *I Ching* as Correlative System

The *I Ching* or *Book of Changes* is one of the five Classics of Chinese philosophy. Its origins have been treated both traditionally (mythologically) and historically, but it is generally accepted to be a compendium of early divinatory texts and numerological systems. The trigrams and the hexagrams precede the divinatory texts, which are followed by the layered strata of commentaries. Both Taoist and Confucian philosophies are embodied in the commentaries. Two millennia of Chinese scholarship and a sizeable body of Western translations and commentaries since the Legge translation in 1899 and the Richard Wilhelm translation in 1961 attest to the perennial attraction of this high-correlative premodern text.

> In the course of Chinese history over a hundred different schools have appeared on how to study the *I Ching* and apply its wisdom to daily life. Every school writes commentaries and contributes its own achievements. There are immense numbers of commentaries on the *I Ching*. The Chinese describe them as "vast as an open sea." (Huang 2000)

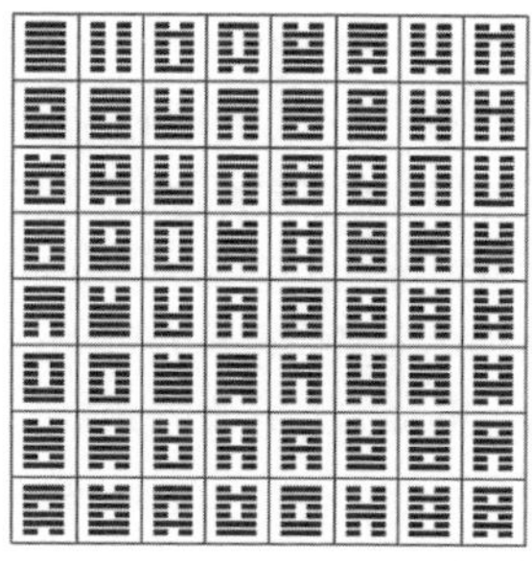

Figure 91: The King Wen sequence of hexagrams.

I am not engaging the scholarly issues of historicity, especially matters of the sequence of materials as they were compiled into the *I Ching* system as received today. Instead, it is presented as an ancient book of wisdom in modern translation that has deeply influenced the McKennas' Timewave Zero symbolic system, and the Glide symbolic system (independently developed). Each of these two xenolinguistic systems connects to the *I Ching* correlatively, and can be considered correlative extrapolations of the *I Ching* system.

Divination, our oldest form of predictive art, has roots in prehistoric shamanism. Amazonian ayahuasca practices use psychoactive adjuncts as part of divinatory technology. Divination has always concerned itself with those types of knowledge that have proven intractable to science in any predictive sense: the knowledge of human affairs, the secret movements of the heart, and especially the interaction of human lives with chance, fate, the elements, the forces of nature, and each other, addressing our embeddedness in webs of interaction and our responses to unpredictable conditions, to accidents, and to fortune, good and bad, by which our lives can turn onto new paths, like redirected rivers after flooding storms.

I Ching scholar Steven Karcher defines the *I* thus:

> Though often translated as change or changes, the central term *I* is not simply orderly change—the change of the seasons, for example, or the change of one thing into another, like water changing into ice or a caterpillar into a butterfly. Unpredictable and, as the tradition says, unfathomable, *I* originates in and is a way of dealing with "trouble". It articulates possible responses to fate, necessity, or calamity—that which "crosses" your path. (Karcher 2002)

Further, Karcher implies, the first-person experience of the human mind is that of an island of conscious awareness in a sea of the "unconscious" or "mind at large" which holds, out of sight (by definition), the "everything else"—memory, dreams, drives, desires, complexes, creative imagination, visionary states, and archetypal figures.

Is it fair to say that responding to emergency, disaster, or sudden opportunity always happens in the absence of sufficient data to reach exclusively rational considered decisions? Divination seeks the underlying order in the chaotic sea of unknowns, the Tao beneath the disconnected details, the ancestral viewpoint standing somewhere outside the flow of events (but still in touch with us). Divination postulates realities and viewpoints possessing greater knowledge, an epistemic edge, an early warning system of events to come, the auspicious and the dire, some slight preparedness, some added sense of timing, or tuning, aligning, a stance. Karcher again:

> The term *I* emphasizes imagination, openness and fluidity. It suggests the ability to change direction quickly and the use of a variety of imaginative stances to mirror the variety of being. It further suggests that this imaginative ability is the true root of a sense of security and spiritual well-being. The most adequate English translation of this might be versatility, the ability to remain available to and be moved by the unforeseen demands of time, fate, and psyche. This term interweaves the *I* of the cosmos, the *I* of the book, and your own *I*, if you use it. (Karcher 2002)

Karcher describes the process of consulting the *I Ching* as a complex interaction with a symbolic system that connects one to the Other as source of knowledge. According to Karcher, "The texts came into existence through a mysterious mode of imaginative induction which endows things with symbolic significance." And this symbolic process, called "hsiang," was done "to form the texts and figures as links to important spirits and energies." The Other is implicated in this symbolizing process at every turn. The ideal user of the book, the "chun-tsu," takes the figure and words obtained through divination into the mind and heart.

> Through this action, the chun-tsu becomes hsiang or symbolizing, linking the divinatory tools and the spirits connected with *I* directly to the

> ruling power of the personality. To do this is called shen, which refers to whatever is numinous, spiritually potent.
>
> Like the shamans and sages of old, this tradition maintains, the person who uses these symbols to connect with *I* will have access to the numinous world and acquire a helping spirit, a shen. The *I Ching* is more than a spirit; it channels or connects you to a spirit. (Karcher 2002)

Part of the action of consulting the *I Ching*, which is treated as being a spirit in its own right, is to connect the *shen* to the Other by way of *hsiang*, or active symbolizing. The human situation is described as a nexus of influences from multiple levels of reality, mediated by symbols that become the points of passage among these levels. Another description of this process comes from historian Michael Nylan:

> The *I Ching* specifically tries to locate the "gate of change"—that phase of transition where things and events first come out of formlessness into an intermediate state of bare perceptibility (often identified with the image or symbol). After passing through this gate, things eventually develop concrete form and fully individuated characteristics. (Nylan 1994)

The set of symbols (obtained by the yarrow stalk or coin method) with which one interacts includes the Chinese character that is the name of the hexagram obtained, the hexagram and its configuration of yin and yang lines, the trigrams, inner and outer, of which the hexagram is composed, the individual lines *(yao)* that are strong or weak, changing or unchanging (each of which has multiple traditional texts associated with it), and the multiple texts for the hexagrams as a whole. The additional layers of commentaries, such as the Ten Wings, and diagrams of major symbolic relations of trigrams give the whole structure the appearance of an archaeological site, where shamanic, Taoist, and Confucian levels coexist in layers throughout the correlative system. The layered symbolic system of the *I Ching* becomes one of the parts of a larger correlative system implied by the similarity of themes among the xenolinguists.

The *I Ching* is spoken of as "pre-scientific" with the implication that its methods of predicting the future have less truth value than science. But all forms of divination and science have a common impulse: to know the hidden causes of events, and to predict the future with accuracy. Only the

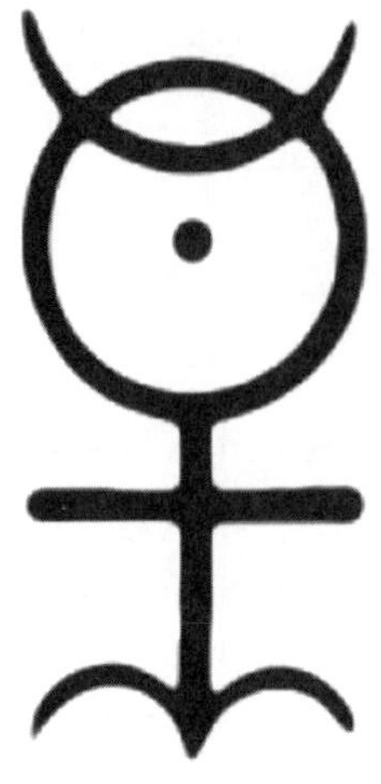

Figure 92: John Dee's glyph, the Monad. Wikimedia Commons.

methods have evolved, and that evolution always involves an evolution of linguistic forms. Mathematics creates new knowledge with new symbols; imaginary numbers or transfinite numbers, for example. I speculate that divination systems have a form of life and therefore consciousness, and similarly evolve: as extensions of existing systems (*I Ching* into Timewave Zero; *I Ching* into Glide) or by drawing other systems into relation with it as correlative systems, as happened in the evolution of the *I Ching* itself into its current form. Experiencing the divinatory system as an Other is a phenomenon reported by many who have gone deeply into relationship with the *I Ching*.

The Renaissance was a time when the divinatory and the occult on the one hand and the mathematical and rational on the other could occupy the same minds bearing great fruit. Isaac Newton and John Dee were alchemists, magicians, and mathematicians and scientists. Dee's skills in mathematics and astronomy allowed him to train the English explorers in the arts of navigation. And McKenna has noted Dee's download of an angelic script, Enochian, out of which magical systems were developed. Dee's monad remains a complex symbol, representing the moon, sun, elements, and fire.

E	A	F	D	G/J	C/K	B
Graph	Un	Or	Gal	Ged	Veh	Pa
7	6	5	4	3	2	1
N	Q	P	L	H	I/Y	M
Drux	Ger	Mals	Ur	Na	Gon	Tal
14	13	12	11	10	9	8
T	S	U/V	Z	R	O	X
Gisg	Fam	Van	Ceph	Don	Med	Pal
21	20	19	18	17	16	15

Figure 93: John Dee and Edward Kelley's Enochian alphabet. Wikimedia Commons.

As Dee described the angelic download:

> Sixth Action. Mar 1582 (Date uncertain). Michael, Uriel and Semiel appear. The form of the Sigil described. Forty angels appear and reveal 40 letters for the sigil's border.
>
> Seventh Action. Later, same day. Michael corrects several errors. The interpretation of the 40 letters given. (Dee, 1581—1583)

Terence McKenna was, in his own always colorful way, trying to synthesize the scientific and the occult in his own thought, although he clearly leaned toward the hermetic. Just as clearly, he sought acceptance for these ideas from science, with no success. Timewave Zero is in one sense an attempt to validate the occult by mathematical means—and vice versa. But this is not the Renaissance, and the politics of knowledge have shifted to science as majority rule. However, there is a case to be made for seeing certain approaches to current psychonautic practice as part of the long lineage of Western occult and hermetic tradition, especially when such practices involve contact with the Other, as years of Dee's work, faithfully scribed in his diaries, reveal.

2012 and Novelty

To know the shape of time is, for Terence McKenna, to know the shape of human history. He called history "the fractal mountain." The ups and downs of the Timewave graph are the creodes of fluctuating novelty and habit, fractally arrayed, that give to history its uneven texture of high drama and innovation interwoven with long stretches of conservative repetitions. For him, the King Wen sequence of the *I Ching* suggested the math generating the Timewave through the psilocybin voice, the voice of the Logos, as he came to call it. The Timewave was conceived as a map—the path of time into the future, a class of time travel, and a form of divination. Time is distinctly differently perceived—no longer smooth, no longer an infinite linear extension of evenly spaced intervals as devoid of content as Newtonian space, a similarly empty container, a void. Timewave Zero time follows the Einsteinian analogy for space—uneven due to the presence of masses of uneven dimension whose gravitational fields bend space. But that analogy is used to frame a Messianic, apocalyptic vision of the end of time, of history, and of being as we know it. The Timewave, after all its ups and downs, takes a final dive in

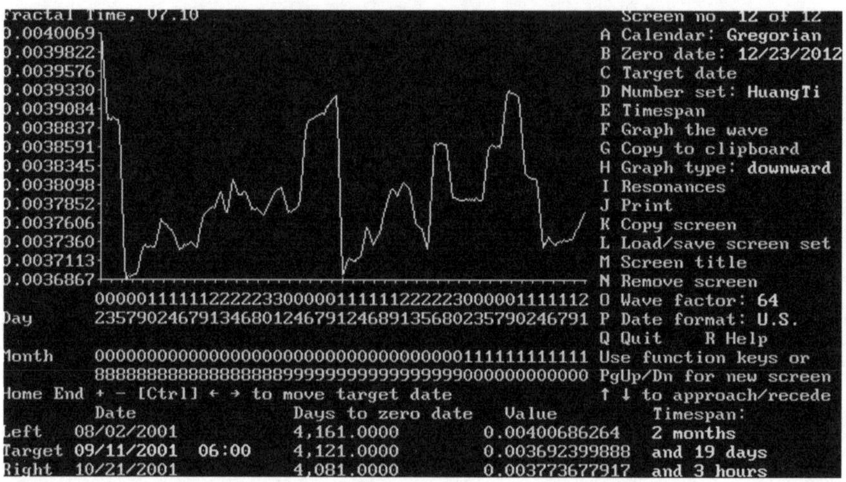

■ **Figure 94: Screenshot of Timewave Zero.** Wikimedia Commons.

infinite novelty on December 21st, 2012. The choices that led to that date are not arbitrary, but biased by the inevitable fact of situated knowledge: this is Terence McKenna's view of what made it to the high-novelty category—and what is ignorable. His choice of an earlier high-novelty event—Hiroshima—determined the end date for the Eschaton, perhaps with a little fudge factor to make it meet the end date of the Mayan calendar exactly.

2012, the Eschaton, went on to be a viral meme not only in the psychedelic community that absorbs McKenna's ideas, but beyond into a big-budget apocalyptic movie, and a Maya franchise, reaching a fertile audience. Millenarianism is a perennially attractive human mindset, the necessary closing bookend to a Creation story. By a similar analogy to Einstein's description of gravity on space, events that represent a maximum ingression of novelty and impact on the temporal neighborhood thereby bend time toward novelty. The timewave accelerates toward the Eschaton; it frames its own demise, the point of maximum novelty, the end of history. Time is depicted as uneven, fractal, eschatologically driven by its own process toward the Eschaton to consume itself—or transform itself. Through the logic of maximum novelty, nothing will be left unchanged. Novelty is described by McKenna as a process both internally driven and ultimately pulled forward by the transcendental object at the end of time, the Eschaton.

The timewave condenses as a symbolic system out of the translinguistic fluidity of the E@LC, a fractal, self-describing construction, like DNA, the biologic of life, which itself has mathematical roots in the patterns of the *I Ching*. We can see the correlative system assembling.

> The timewave is a kind of mathematical mandala describing the organization of time and space. It is a picture of the patterns of energy and intent within DNA. The DNA unfolds those mysteries over time like a record or a song. This song is one's life, and it is all life. But without a conceptual overview one cannot understand the melody as it plays. (McKenna 1993b)

The means by which novelty ingresses into the timewave and human experience is variously imagined by McKenna as 1) a higher cortical function induced by psychedelics; the possibilities of new cognition due to the new configurations of neurotransmitter activity, as Tom Ray's research explores (Ray 2010); 2) a higher spatial dimension penetrating our three-dimensional reality; 3) the inter-species network of DNA, and the intelligence of the Gaian oversoul of the planet.

Novelty is variously equated in McKenna's system as information (the difference that makes a difference, in Gregory Bateson's terminology); as increase in complexity; as emergence; and as the felt presence of the Other (McKenna 1998). It is contrasted with habit, repetition, and conservation of structure and qualities. In this description, it mirrors the dual nature of DNA, at once our most conservative molecule, whose structure and function have remained the same across myriads of organisms over the four-billion-year time period through which it manifested on Earth. At the same time, DNA is the mechanism that captures the endless innovation of the biosphere, its diversity, difference, experiment, and overall growth in complexity to arrive at this moment, with *Homo sapiens's* novel symbol-manipulating ability, to describe itself to itself, becoming, in David Porush's phrase, a "discourse that enfolds its own intelligence." In Terence McKenna's view, the universe, not only the biosphere, is seen as a novelty-producing and novelty-conserving process. This idea is reflected in the uneven pace of growth and change in the biosphere with periods of great acceleration of diversification, alternated with long periods of stability where nothing much changes for eons. This unevenness matches in concept the facts of the early universe as now pictured by physicists—where a fundamental break in symmetry results in more matter than anti-matter, and hence, a universe that can (and did) manifest materially. The novelty principle asserts a similar asymmetry in time, with the balance tipped toward novelty.

The presence of purpose, meaning, and direction in the unfolding reality process we call a universe through time is embedded in the human experience of time. Human events are non-repeatable due to the structural individuality of every moment relative to the transforming process. Tides of creativity are inherent in the reality process at all stages. These factors differentiate this process from the physicist's conception of time as one-dimensional, linear, and evenly divided into equal units. Also, the direction-independent formulation of time that characterizes physical formulas at the level of elementary particles contrasts sharply with the arrow of time we assume in all our macrophysical interactions. Yesterday, today, and tomorrow remain in proper sequence, and a process view of reality prevails that includes principles of development on the individual level, as well as genetic and epigenetic evolution—of the species, and of culture. Fractal time integrates the primary Hermetic formula, *as above so below,* with ease, entering a scalar factor into the correspondence. Fractal time allows us to generalize from our individual experience to cosmic principles—and back, gathering us in a net of correspondences that become a single interconnected system.

As Mark Pesce points out, McKenna's Eschaton resembles Ray Kurzweil's singularity, a postulated time in the near future when the acceleration of machine intelligence will have surpassed human intelligence, and humanity will no longer dominate. Pesce rejects Kurzweil's conclusion of takeover but accepts the acceleration factor, transferring it to the acceleration of memory and information buildup and transfer capacity brought about by our linguistic evolution. He discusses DNA as the memory of life, *the song,* a very slowly developing informational structure that preserves the memory of all the interactions of life-forms with each other and with the environment.

The idea of DNA as the universal memory of life can be directly experienced by some in psychedelic states.

> As the experience developed, I had an encounter with a "dragonish" entity which completely devoured me, took me down the tunnel of death/rebirth, back to the beginnings of life on Earth, while narrating this rap about the origin and purpose of DNA, eventually leading me down the long

> and ancient corridors of time to the present and then into the future, explaining how this planet is approaching an energetic shift that will lead it into awakening to its purpose as part of the larger galactic intelligence. (Elfstone 2006)

Forging the connection to DNA as universal source of knowledge was at the heart of the E@LC.

> That would be the holding mode of the lens, or the philosopher's stone, or whatever it was. Then someone would take command of it—whose DNA it was, they would be it. It would be as if one had given birth to one's own soul, one's own DNA exteriorized as a kind of living fluid made of language. It would be a mind that could be seen and held in one's hand. Indestructible. It would be a miniature universe, a monad, a part of space and time that magically has all of space and time condensed in it, including one's own mind, a map of the cosmos so real that it somehow is the cosmos, that was the rabbit he hoped to pull out of his hat that morning. (T. McKenna 1993)

McKenna notes that an interesting pattern is created with the Timewave, as follows. First, a mathematical pattern is revealed, based on the analysis of first-order differences between the hexagrams in the King Wen sequence, an irregular pattern. This syntactical pattern, derived from sequence and structure of the hexagrams, undergoes a subtle manipulation in which the wave is flipped over in two dimensions, yielding a composite wave that moves simultaneously both forward and back in time. Visualization of this process reveals the creation of a spiral wave, as the two-dimensional wave is rotated through a dimension not contained in itself, a half-twist, that creates a spiral waveform that meets itself at beginning and end, as can be seen in Figure 17.

Seeing wavelike formations in the King Wen sequence is not unique to McKenna. The King Wen sequence has been depicted by *I Ching* scholar

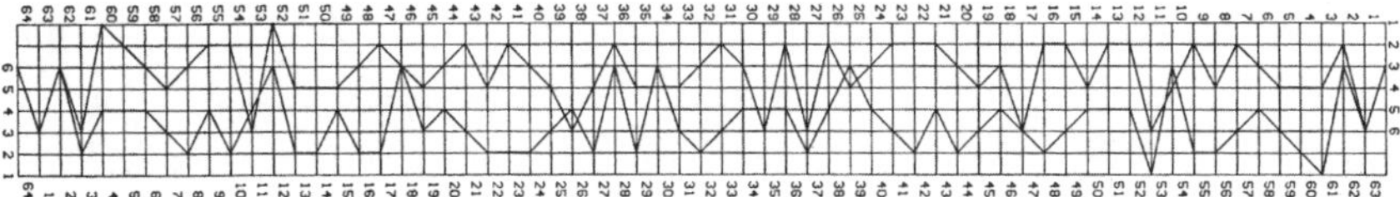

■ **Figure 95: The forward- and backward-moving Timewave.**
From Terence McKenna, *True Hallucinations*.

Al Huang as a semantic wave of meaning in the King Wen progression of hexagrams (Huang 2000).

Wave-like structures thus appear in both semantic and syntactical extrapolations of the King Wen sequence of hexagrams. The timewave in this sense becomes the pulse, rising and falling, of the pressure of this invisible world on the membrane of consciousness. The veil grows thin. Something is glimpsed.

Dimensionality

The timewave, twisted back on itself, forward- and backward-moving, makes a dimensional leap, autopoietically closing on it/self, an autonomous system of meaning. McKenna pictures this timewave progressing biologically through a series of dimensional conquests.

> One of the very large creodes that we can see at work in nature and society is what I call the conquest of dimensionality. Biology is a strategy for moving into and occupying ever more dimensions. And biology begins as a point-like chemical replicating system attached to a primordial clay in a proverbial warm pond somewhere at the dawn of time, and as life develops it folds itself, it becomes a three-dimensional object, it replicates itself in time, by that means it claims the temporal dimension. . . . (McKenna 1994)

A dimensional leap was at the heart of the technology of the Experiment, the transduction of sound resulting in the production of translinguistic matter.

> On tryptamines it is possible, under special conditions, to hear and vocalize a sound that turns through a higher-dimensional manifold and condenses as translinguistic matter, i.e., matter reduplicated upon itself through time, much as a hologram is reduplicated through space. The substance whose appearance the sounds initiate is tryptamine metabolized by mind through a higher spatial dimension. (McKenna 1993b)

In McKenna's view, the phase of acceleration toward the 2012 Eschaton, seen particularly in the accelerating evolution of media and communication technologies, represents "dimension-conquering phenomena designed to shrink the earth to a point. Of course the Internet is the mother of all dimensional conquests" (McKenna 1994). Terence McKenna envisioned the possibility of computer animation technology as a means of expression of higher-dimensional forms of language.

Of course, the 2012 Eschaton rippled through Reality with barely a shiver. But millenarians and messianic prophets will deal with the disappointment as they always do: move the date. This failure of prediction on McKenna's part caused some portion of his fan base to decamp in disgust, writing off the Timewave as valueless. In my own study of McKenna's ideas on language, examining the Timewave as a divinatory system, in that category of prediction, I find it interesting that I could come up with my own Eschaton, having chosen my own earlier novelty date, an Eschaton whose meaning I would have to decipher in terms of my own life.

I think, at this point, that the concept of time as fractal in structure when one is dealing with human affairs and history on any scale is a useful and generative idea. And Timewave Zero, as a xenolinguistical system, is especially valuable in understanding McKenna's notions about language, reality, and the thrust of the human project toward . . . some would say toward apocalypse in the form of environmental disasters brought about by climate change and global warming. The date may be wrong (how ever would you date a collapse that happens as a compilation of disasters large and small), but "Eschaton" might not be that bad a choice of words for a major die-off of life-forms on planet Earth. It has happened before.

Language and the Structure of Reality

Language is an ontological category for Terence McKenna. The function of natural language in the development of the child through language acquisition is identified as the introduction of a layer of artificiality and abstraction between "the felt presence of immediate experience" and the experienced world. This built-up linguistic ability creates a world made of words, which, as units of cultural conditioning, serve as the bricks with which the shelter and prison of cultural conditioning is constructed. The boundary-dissolving effect of psychedelics in dismantling this cultural conditioning can become a political act, as Timothy Leary's Children's Crusade of the '60s and his own archetypal drama of a real-time prison break demonstrated (Leary 1990). From the viewpoint of issues of cognitive liberty, an increasingly relevant issue in our neuroscientific age, freedom of speech presupposes freedom of thought and mind-state, and choice of reality. Proponents of a single reality cannot, by definition, entertain the possibility of choices.

When the boundary dissolution became all too real in the days following March 4th, 1971, and telepathic communication and access to information not normally available established itself through this mind-meld for days after between the McKenna brothers, a new reality was temporarily created. This reality stood in sharp contrast to the reality of other members of the group, who, not experiencing the same phenomena, saw their form of thinking as delusional and schizophrenic, a *folie à deux* to be remedied in due haste. Terence McKenna's utterly real (to him, by the rules of self-evidence) and at the same time self-invalidating sighting of the lenticular roving vehicle at the end of the time in La Chorrera capped the craziness with a cultural icon of confirmed crackpottedness, the UFO, marking the whole experience as fringe theatrics, not to be taken seriously.

To trust in the occurrence of phenomena that are not part of baseline reality is no small task. The experience of telepathy—the connectedness of minds when ego boundaries have dissolved, or the connection to a state of "all-knowing"—can be difficult to hang onto when reality goes back, as it usually does, to "normal." The task of communicating such unspeakabilities highlights the gap—the reality gap—between baseline and some forms of psychedelic visionary states. These difficulties only increase when a messianic vision is put forth of the Eschaton, the end of time toward which all history and cultural production and consciousness is accelerating as part of a universal process built into the structure of time itself. The mission of the transmission of the vision demands a level of rhetorical skill in packaging the preposterous that Terence McKenna, deputized by his brother Dennis during the Experiment as "The Teach," exercised through books, articles, and hundreds of taped lectures.

> He referred to me as "The Teach," not teacher or teaching but the Teach, a kind of personified alien ambassador empowered to negotiate the entry of the human species into the councils of higher intelligence. (McKenna 1993b)

I never met the man, only listened to that unmistakable voice that takes on the cadences of an alien AI voice at times. I will always think of Terence McKenna, given my bias, of course, as a master xenolinguist, communicating the Unspeakable in such a way that we can get a taste. That taste, that rhetorical invitation, has been enough to deputize a generation of psychonauts now moving through the gate of change that opens with every psychonautic voyage to explore the marvels he so seductively presents.

Notes, Chapter 9

1. BP is used in anthropology to mean Before Present.
2. Eco is partially in error in his attribution of error regarding the sequence of hexagrams. While the texts that structure the *I Ching* are traditionally known as the King Wen sequence, the hexagram arrangement given to Leibniz by Bouvet is equally well known; Leibniz's version is the Fu Hsi or Earlier Heaven Sequence, elaborated by Shao Yong of the Number and Symbol School, Sung Dynasty. The King Wen sequence is much older than the Fu Hsi sequence.

CHAPTER 10
Constructed Languages

One of the contexts for understanding xenolinguistic symbolic systems is the organized activity of language construction. In the end, perfection in language comes down to a highly personal vision. On the one hand, we have Leibnitz's ideal of the reduction of all language to a single language, perfectly rational, perfectly transparent to all users, perfectly regular, whose utterances can be understood identically with no misunderstandings possible. On the other hand, there is the delight in the polysemy of words, new sounds in new combinations, the slippages of puns and word play, metaphor, poetry, and the creation of entire new systems of language, for whatever purpose serves the creator and his or her sense of perfection. That purpose often includes sharing created languages with others—not with the desire to convert others to their use, but as, ultimately, an art form, "language construction."

Language Geeks

The art of language creation is practiced by members of the Language Creation Society, a special-interest group of self-described "language geeks" (present company included) who call it "conlanging." Conlanging, from "**con**structed **lang**uage," is obsessional, hermetic, and prolix. The conlang mailing list carries very high traffic and involves high levels of expertise, especially in natural languages, linguistics, and semiotics, combined with the spirit of play. Many conlangers are graphically skilled as well; the creation of beautiful orthographies is part of their activities.

The difference in viewpoint between the ideal of rationality and the urge toward beauty and art created a contentious bifurcation in the original conlang mailing list. The auxlangers (auxiliary language adherents) see perfection in language as denotative exactitude and rational construction. The auxlangers ultimately decamped and went off to form their own mailing list.

Benct Philip Jonsson put it this way on the conlang mailing list:

> To my mind at least conlanging is—in spite of its solipsism—a performing art. I'm not nearly as thrilled by reading a grammar of a conlang as of hearing the stories of how the conlanger discovered what the grammar looks like, and why. That's why to me the appropriate term for the art must be "language construction," and the true sense of "constructed language" is "language which is being constructed" rather than "language which has been constructed," since the thrill is in the journey, not in the destination, or even in the arrival. (Jonsson 2009)

Linguistic Diversity

Conlangers tend to see the Babel incident in the Old Testament as a feature, not a bug. The more languages the better! A standard practice in the group, almost an initiation, is to translate the Babel text into your own conlang. Conlangers point out that linguistic diversity is falling in parallel with biodiversity, "faster than ever before in human history," according to Tove Skutnabb-Kangas of the University of Roskilde, Denmark. Europe is the poorest continent in linguistic diversity, while "Indigenous peoples, minorities and linguistic minorities are the stewards of the world's linguistic diversity."

Nigeria alone has 410 languages; Papua New Guinea, 850 languages; and Indonesia, 670. Among them they represent 25 percent of the world's languages. Linguistic diversity and biodiversity are correlated; when one is high, the other generally is as well (Skutnabb-Kangas 2002). Languages are disappearing faster even than butterflies—except in the conlang community. Linguistic creation and experimentation is bubbling up out of a primordial soup of natlang (natural language) parts, with many mutations, variations, and hybridizations, as well as new orthographies (writing systems

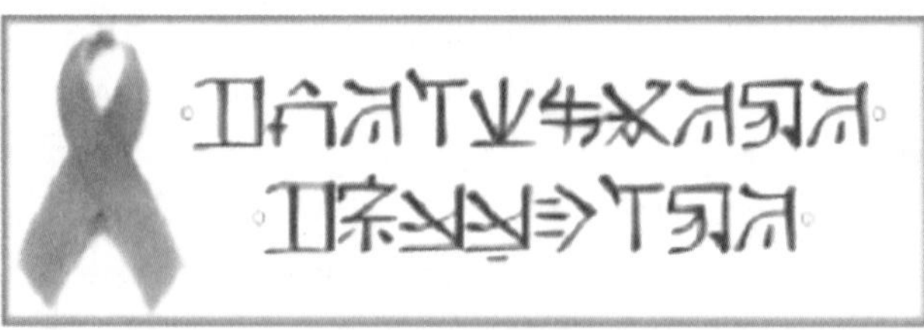

■ **Figure 96: "Fight Linguistic Extinction—Invent a Language!"** David Peterson's Kamakawi script.

that may or may not represent the sounds of a language). Emergent forms of languages—visual, both two-dimensional and three-dimensional, gestural, sculptural, languages with no spoken form, and lots of alien languages—are all part of the mix.

J.R.R. Tolkien is the Shakespeare of conlanging. His essay, "A Secret Vice," details his own experiences and speculations about language creation, which possessed him from an early age (Tolkien 1983). Many, if not most, conlangers began some form of the activity in childhood. Tolkien calls conlanging "a new art, or a new game" and indeed, the activity is perfectly suspended between these impulses. A desire for secrecy plays itself out in various aspects, beginning perhaps with the delight of children in having secret languages and societies to bond their group, as Tolkien points out. Later come secret scripts for maintaining the privacy of journal writing. These secret languages are called by some "stealth-langs." Deena Larsen's Rose language/code serves such purposes. In her own words: "It is based on English, but has 75 characters. Each letter has variations that connote emotion. When I write, I unconsciously use these forms. Then when I reread, I find out what I was feeling. Then I can get to my 'inner thoughts.'"

■ Figure 97: Deena Larson's Rose stealth language.

A wry take on the secrecy—or privacy—of conlangs from "Leah" on the alt.language.artificial list:

> As for a lang having interest to someone other than the creator, that can vary with time. When I finished my first conlang, I offered to teach it to people I know, and they refused, UNTIL I started keeping my personal journal exclusively in my conlang. THEN, the interest started. Of course, they want to spy on my most private thoughts. Therefore, my conlang became my stealth lang.

"Stealth language" is also Tolkien's term. For him, a stealth language can "satisfy either the need for limiting one's intelligibility within circles whose bounds you can more or less control or estimate, or the fun found in this limitation. They serve the needs of a secret and persecuted society, or the queer instinct for pretending you belong to one."

Think: pidgins, creoles, slave languages. Tolkien began the *Silmarillion,* the first part of his "mythology for England" and the mythical basis for *The Lord of the Rings,* during WWI, in the hospital, recovering from the injuries and horrors of trench warfare in the Battle of Somme. Tolkien's *Silmarillion* is the mythology of his Elvish languages, Quenya and Sindarin. For Tolkien, language and mythology are deeply intertwingled.

> I must fling out the view that for perfect construction of an art-language, it is found necessary to construct at least in outline a mythology concomitant. Not solely because some pieces of verse will inevitably be part of the (more or less) completed structure, but because *the making of language and mythology are related functions;* to give your language an individual flavour, it must have woven into it the threads of an individual mythology. . . . The converse indeed is true, your language construction will breed a mythology. (Tolkien 1983) [emphasis mine]

In contemporary conlanging, this principle is in force in a significant number of conlangs: they come hand in hand with the imagined worlds in which they communicate. Sally Caves, a professor of English at the University of Rochester (as Sarah Higley), whose creation of Teonaht, a language and a world, began at age nine, expresses this principle eloquently:

> Those unbitten by this bug will undoubtedly want to know why we do it: why invent something so intricate, so involved, that only a few people,

maybe even no one, could ever share in its entirety? To begin such a thing is whimsical at best, but to persist in it is surely madness. However, I'm not alone in my pursuit. The discovery of the Conlang listserv devoted to glossopoeia or the artful construction of languages, introduced me to a world of compatriots who share my love of language—not just the natural languages, but the experiments one could make with syntax, morphology, typology, lexicology, historicity, and myth . . . glossopoeia is like building a strange, new, mythical city. You start with the foundations and move up, stone by stone. Or sometimes you start with the roof and work down. Sometimes your paths are crooked, others straight; sometimes you erect cathedrals, canals, and bridges. Sometimes you tear everything down and start over. Gradually it takes on a character and populace of its own, and all its own rules, and you come to know its streets and houses and people as unique. You have relexified your world. (Caves 2010)

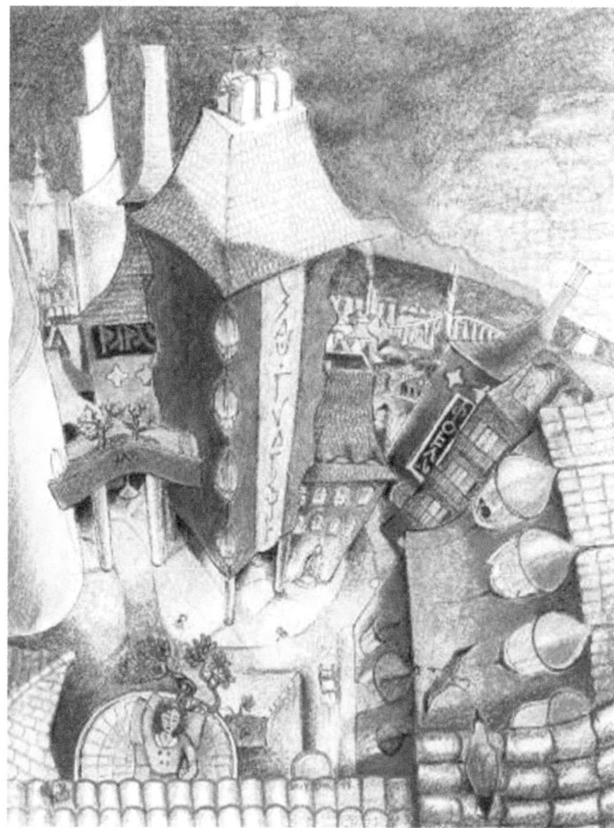

■ **Figure 98: Sally Caves, drawing of Teonaht, a constructed world and language.**

Sai Emrys, founder of the Language Creation Society, posts a many-year, much revised "Design of an Ideal Language." In his own words,

> I make no presumption that my particular desires are in any way objectively best; only that one can objectively take a look at some particular set of desires, make tradeoffs where needed, and then go about fulfilling them optimally in a systematic way. There are therefore an infinite possible set of perfect languages, for each of an infinite set of desiderata. (Emrys 2006)

Deep linguistic chops—really knowing the rules—are Sylvia Sotomayor's launching pad for breaking them with her conlang, Kēlen. Sotomayor has created, out of an early fascination with all things Celtic, several beautiful Kēlen scripts.

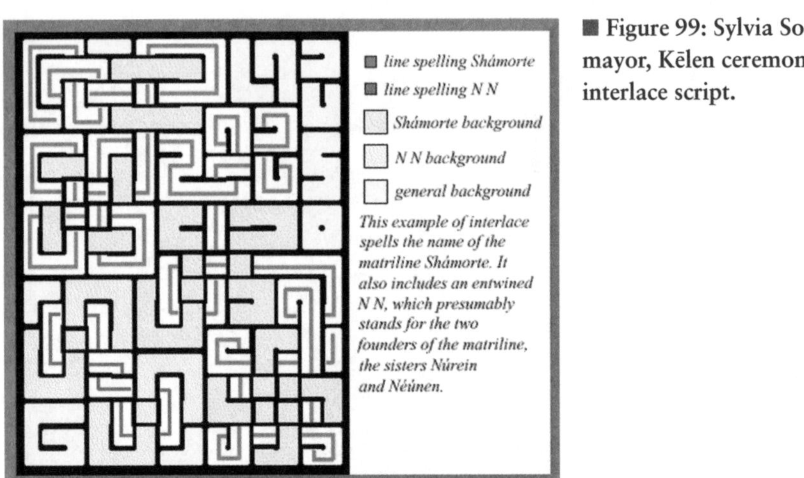

line spelling Shámorte
line spelling N N
Shámorte background
N N background
general background
This example of interlace spells the name of the matriline Shámorte. It also includes an entwined N N, which presumably stands for the two founders of the matriline, the sisters Núrein and Néúnen.

■ **Figure 99: Sylvia Sotomayor, Kēlen ceremonial interlace script.**

■ **Figure 100: Sylvia Sotomayor, Kēlen box script.**

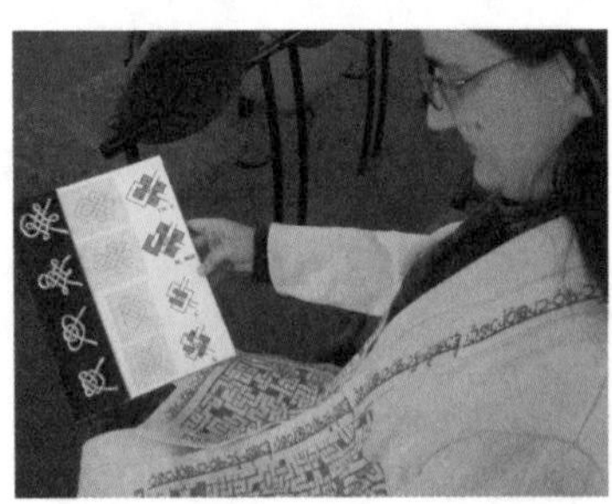

■ **Figure 101: Sylvia Sotomayor in Kēlen ceremonial vestments.**

> Learning about universals made me wonder what a language would be like that violated them. So Kēlen became my laboratory for exploring the line between a human and a non-human language. There are a few inherent difficulties to this task. For one thing, since we haven't found any intelligent aliens, there are no non-human languages to look at for comparison. So, my strategy was to take a universal and violate it. (Sotomayor 2009)

Kēlen replaces verbs with a closed class of "relationals" that perform the syntactic function of verbs.

The great majority of conlangs produced by the Language Creation Society members are based on natural language formations. I will mention two conlangs that depart from this pattern, and could be considered specifically xenolinguistic. Denis Moscowitz's Rikchik language is alien, not merely because its putative origin is the second planet of Alpha Centauri A.

> The rikchik body consists of a large (~2 ft. diameter) sphere, which contains almost all the rikchik's organs, supported by 49 long (~6 ft.) tentacles. In the front of the sphere is a single eye with a circular eyelid. The 7 tentacles immediately below the eye are shorter and lighter, and are used for talking. (Moscowitz 2009)

■ **Figure 102: Dennis Moscovitz, "Rikchik with Gesturing Tentacles."**

■ **Figure 103: Dennis Moscovitz, Rikchik morphemes, based on tentacular gestures.**

Rikchik playfully models a signed or gestural language, with no sonic component. Written Rikchik is a speechless orthography. Moreover, the "signing" of a Rikchik is shaped by its physiology of multiple tentacles. Rikchik explores the nuances of imagining language from a truly alien species.

Sai Emrys and Alex Fink have developed a "gripping language," a kinesthetic stealth-lang "mediated entirely by touch, which allows two people to converse freely while appearing to be doing nothing more than holding hands." Finger motions include presses, rubs, thumb and global moves, and finger "chords." To my knowledge, it is completely unique in the world of conlanging (Emrys 2009).

The two symbolic systems described in detail in this book are McKenna's Timewave Zero (Chapter 9) and the Glide symbolic system (Chapter 2). They are, in a sense, constructed languages from the psychedelic sphere. Each tells the story of an initial "download" experience; each was subsequently, and over a period of years, developed and interpreted by the downloadees into a fully elaborated system. And each downloadee responds to his or her own call for new language in presenting his or her experience of the psychedelic sphere, and attempts as well to bring a specific knowledge back in a manner that can be communicated at baseline.

The Guild of Xenolinguists

Deena Larsen—Rose Language

Deena Larsen is best known as a pioneering artist and innovator in electronic literature. Her hypertext works, such as *Marble Springs,* explore new patterns and constructions in hypermedia literature. Larsen's Rose Language was created as a stealth-language under unusual circumstances when Larsen was a homeless teenager. Rose is a living, personified language for Larsen, an Other who has been her companion for a good part of her life.

■ **Figure 104: Deena Larsen.**

In her own words:

> Lockers at school could easily be broken into, papers strewn everywhere. Backpacks hidden cunningly under back steps could easily be found. I had no place, no thing I could call my own. Everything I wrote could and would be used against me in a court of my peers at any time. So my secret code became even more important.
>
> Moreover, it became a friend, someone I could trust with my secrets. For who else could I trust? Where else could I talk about my problems? And thus Rose has been my friend, my confidante for over three decades now. I use the journal and the Rose stealth-lang to talk to her, to think things through, to discover how I feel. Rose was, for me, an elegant woman who was full and rich and soft as rose petals, and who yet had thorns. And then I was living on the streets in high school, with no place to put anything.

Larsen offers an explanation of how to read a page in Rose Language.

> This piece explores what happened after I went to an audiologist to determine if I could get any relief from the tortures of hyperacusis (where sounds resonate as pain in my brain). The audiologist explained that the only method of treatment now available won't work for me, and there is no other cure. The simplified translation would be: Yeah. Oh. Kay. It ain't happening. I get that.

The inflected translation is:

Yeah{unhappy}.
O{negative/bad}h{unhappy}.
K{opposite of ganbatte–give up}a{worst}y{unprotected}.
I{personal}t{impossible}
a{worst}i{personal}n{honesty, integrity, truth}'t{impossible}
Yeah. Oh. Kay. It ain't happening. I get that.
h{unhappy}a{worst}p{angry}p{angry}e{present to distant future}ni{personal}ng{frown/unhappy}.
I{personal}
g{frown/pain}et{impossible}
t{impossible}h{unhappy}a{worst}t{impossible}.

In transcribing this, each letter that has a {} after it is in the emphasized state. If you just read the {}, you can see the mood I was in. I used the honest "n" in "ain't" to underscore that there is no cure. I used the impossible "t" both times in "that" to really underscore the impossibility of the situation. Also, in Rose translations, it is actually important to distinguish between the personal and impersonal "I" even if that is the personal pronoun. (Otherwise, pronouns work the same way in Rose as they do

■ **Figure 105: Deena Larsen, Rose language.**

in English, but they, like every other word, can carry other inflections.) Note that Rose has concepts that do not exist in other languages—thus making it a true language.

The set of meanings for "k" is rather complex. An upward arrow means: {ganbatte, fight the good fight, yes, go for it, do it, right on, hooray for you, bully for you . . . }. A downward arrow means just the opposite. This is not so much encouragement/discouragement, nor is it try hard/give up—but somewhere in between. It could also be used as a "thumbs up"/"thumbs down" meaning—depending on the context. The set of meanings for "g" is also complex and context-dependent—it is a simple emoticon (albiet cyclopean)—smile or frown, or it can be the pain face so often used in hospitals. "G" thus ranges widely as well.

The petal is at an angle, denoting a different thought. But it is also close to and pointing to the other petal (I want {impossible} to explain that in a 2-second soundbyte). Rose uses paragraph structure like English, but Rose also uses "petals" where a bit of text is set off by direction, color, etc. Petals can, but do not have to be, full sentences. These petals can be considered similar to hypertext nodes, and they are rarely sequential. Petals can also share words simply by laying next to other petals or by intertwining parts of a character. (Again, the intertwined character parts also have a semantic meaning, so this is usually a "double" play.)

A second text has dots leading to this petal (Given all that, what e{subjunctive present/future}xpect{possible}ati{personal}ons can I have?). Thus, the petal has two separate meanings—the hyperacusis is not going away and the doctor is never going to listen to me explain how bad it really is to live like this.

The "p" in happening is doubled and angry, so I am really pissed off about this situation.

The tail for the honest "t" in "ain't" nearly touches the eye of the frowning "g", connoting that I am honestly and truly pained by this—and that I truly do "get" how bad this is and that I am giving up my pipe dreams of being cured in order to be realistic.

The downward curve on the "y" in "Kay" is bolded, emphasizing how vulnerable I am and how dependent I am on the doctors—how little control I have over the situation.

The forms that hypertext takes lend themselves to secrecy and mystery: one is never sure if one has explored all the available links, sequenced a story, or discovered there is no single sequence but a variety, theoretically an infinity, of branching paths. Deena Larsen is a master of the art of hypertext, and its roots in her stealth-lang throw another light on these intricate structures.

Glen English—DMT Writing

The underground DMT Dome? Or a snapshot of buckyballs? Glen English had no words to offer on the subject. Another infinite grid is implied.

When asked about the drawing, Glen replied that there was simply nothing to say about it. It stands on its own, without the support of natural language.

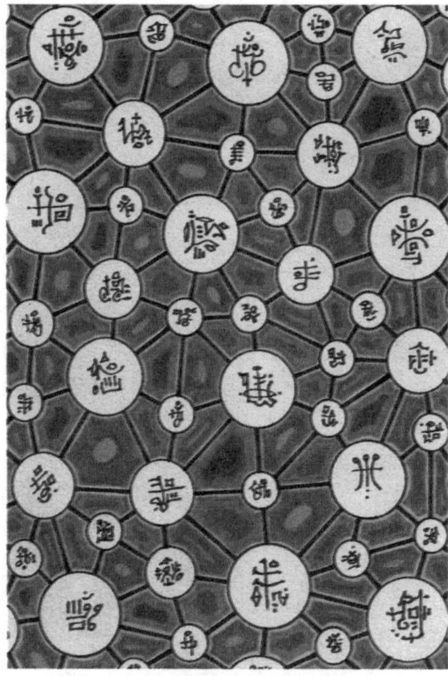

■ **Figure 106: Glen English, untitled picture drawn after a DMT session.**

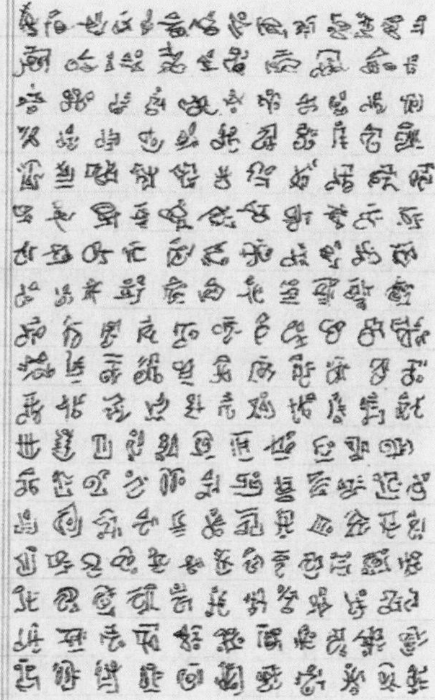

■ **Figure 107: Glen English, DMT script.**

CHAPTER 11

The Idea of a Living Language

"Both shamans and molecular biologists agree that there is a hidden unity under the surface of life's diversity; both associate this unity with the double-helix shape (or two entwined serpents, a twisted ladder, a spiral staircase, two vines wrapped around each other); both consider that one must deal with this level of reality in order to heal. One can fill a book with correspondences between shamanism and molecular biology."

—JEREMY NARBY, 1999

DNA is a strange attractor in psychedelic discourse. Intuitions about DNA riddle my session reports, becoming visual in high-dose psilocybin sessions. The Vaults of Erowid contain many reports about DNA and its functions. The correlative relationship of DNA to the universal symbol of the cosmic serpent is the topic of Jeremy Narby's work, *The Cosmic Serpent.* Narby relates the findings of molecular biologists to those of ayahuasca shamans. He depicts two paths—the scientific and the psychonautic—leading to the same knowledge (Narby 1999).

When language can describe itself, and reflect upon itself (re-entering its own form; in-forming itself), the idea of a living language emerges. In Terence McKenna's DMT vision of language, the entities produce linguistic objects out of themselves, the objects turn into living beings, and the beings emit further linguistic objects. The transformational loop between life and language progresses at high speed. The circular connections between language and DNA as the language of life become, as David Porush describes, a self-enfolding system that accounts for itself. Roland Fischer notes:

> An even more complex but familiar example refers to the information stored in the self-referential DNA structure, which consists exclusively of instructions for the synthesis of the very agents responsible for the implementation of the program. One of the main "aims" of the program stored in the DNA is to reproduce unchanged the structure of DNA itself.

> The medium is indeed the message and hence the DNA structure may be a good model for self-referential consciousness. (Fischer 1977)

Three meanings of the term "consciousness" refer to the domain of self-description or self-observation: 1) to cut or make a distinction; 2) to know *with;* and 3) to know in oneself. The DNA-like, self-referential structure of consciousness is reflected in Maturana's description of consciousness:

> . . . if an organism can generate a communicable description of its interactions and interact with the communicable description, the process can, in principle, be carried out in a potentially infinite recursive manner, and the organism becomes an observer. (Maturana 1970)

The self-referentiality of DNA, of consciousness, and of autopoietic systems converges in a second-order cybernetic commonality of process.

> following through on the idea that the design IS the intelligence i.e. the sentient nature of DNA—not just in a single cell, miracle enough, or a single body—mantis or man—but in every-body, every cell thereof the coiled filaments in ceaseless activity creating the diversity and the bodies and also densely intricately intertwingled and in communication with every other instance of DNA in the biosphere from the tiniest bacteria on up   a vast mycelial network able to communicate because of the overwhelming similarity of the majority of the text (session report 05.12.06, MDMA)

DNA is a liquid crystalline structure two nanometers across. The coded genes are aperiodic; the long sequences between, periodic. Basing his hypothesis on the work of bio-physicists Fritz-Albert Popp and Mae Wan Ho (Ho 1998), Jeremy Narby suggests that the mechanisms of biophotonic emission of DNA and its crystalline structure may be the avenue of transmission and reception of signals among DNA molecules (Narby 1999).

> The spirits one sees in hallucinations are three-dimensional, sound-emitting images. In other words, they are made of their own language, like DNA. (Narby 1999)

> it is the DNA which is evolving it/self as a whole   it has to be as a whole   the ecological fits are far too creative how the whole works together in a game that is being made up as it goes along that's called adaptation inventing new rules emergent structures or behaviors those co-evolve (session report 05.12.06, MDMA)

Narby constructs the correlations between the ayahuasqueros' detailed plant knowledge, the representations of entwined serpents, and the forms of DNA, finding DNA to be essentially minded, communicating—intra-cellularly, inter-cellularly, inter-organism, and inter-species. He found further correspondences between myth and DNA in the Desana myth of twined and twinned serpents residing in the fissure of the brain, a giant anaconda and a rainbow boa; in the aboriginal Australian myths of the creator Rainbow Serpent; and in the Aztec myth of Quetzalcoatl (whose name can be translated as "plumed serpent" or "magnificent twin") symbolizing the "sacred energy of life," who is in turn, with his twin brother Tezcatlipoca, child of the cosmic serpent Coatlicue (Narby 1999).

> the intelligence it takes to get from the machine and assembly language level of amino acids and the codes that specify them to the creation of the eye on the peacock's tail to respond to a certain complex context known as "an environment" including also all the other interacting species sharing space eating and being eaten how to get from that level of language to the systems of proteins etc. a wildly creative intelligence—the whole thing taken together the biosphere Gaia but it is the rainbow serpent of knowledge   the biophotonic pulsars speaking a language of light   bodies that by their own light shine extended perception and multiscaling reveals this language of light (session report 05.12.06, MDMA)

Panspermia

Intimations of the panspermia or exogenesis hypothesis—the idea that life originated elsewhere in the physical universe and was seeded on Planet Earth—appear in psychedelic experience reports with regularity. The panspermia hypothesis is a deferred "origin of life" idea, that is, it postulates that our DNA comes from some source outside our planet, without attempting to explain the origin of DNA. The idea was held in various forms by astronomer Fred Hoyle and DNA biologist Francis Crick, and was endorsed by Steven Hawking in 2009.

DNA is envisioned in this session as an illuminated manuscript being transmitted.

> the mission is the transmission   pay attention to the script of the trans mission
> to illuminate the manuscript   illuminate o l lumen l ate l the trans-lmission

> Alien architecture a script we are this transmission the mission of the scripts making your presence felt felt felt dimensions of trust in the script of the transmission trust now as you stand you under stand the alien dimensions trust—where all was given to the script to the transmission so much so much depends upon finding the script of the transmission (session report 05.03.19, 5 g dried Stropharia cubensis)

An early version of this psychedelic panspermia idea is found in the McKenna brothers' essay, "The Mushroom Speaks."

> I am old, older than thought in your species, which is itself fifty times older than your history. Though I have been on Earth for ages I am from the stars. My home is no one planet, for many worlds scattered through the shining disc of the galaxy have conditions which allow my spores an opportunity for life. The mushroom which you see is the part of my body given to sex thrills and sun bathing; my true body is a fine network of fibers growing through the soil. These networks may cover acres and may have far more connections than the number in a human brain. . . . By means impossible to explain because of certain misconceptions in your model of reality, all my mycelial networks in the galaxy are in hyperlight communication through space and time. . . . Few such species are minded, only myself and my recently evolved near relatives have achieved the hypercommunication mode and memory capacity that make us leading members in the community of galactic intelligence. (Oss 1986)

Terence McKenna entertained many hypotheses over his career about the mushroom, the Other, and the possibility of exo-planetary or exo-dimensional contact. The mushroom as intergalactic ambassador was an early formulation. The notion of symbiosis with the genetic material of the mushroom came from Dennis McKenna's protocol for the Experiment at La Chorrera. This symbiosis, which was at the heart of the experiment, was linked to the intention to create the lapis, the philosopher's stone of alchemy. Alchemy was one of the symbol systems with which the Experiment was associated.

In *The Cosmic Serpent,* Jeremy Narby introduces the panspermia theme through his reproduction of anthropologist and shamanic practitioner Michael Harner's account of his first ayahuasca experience, re-quoted below:

> Then he saw that his visions emanated from "giant reptilian creatures" resting at the lowest depths of his brain. These creatures began projecting

> scenes in front of his eyes, while informing him that this information was reserved for the dying and the dead: "First they showed me the planet Earth as it was eons ago, before there was any life on it. I saw an ocean, barren land, and a bright blue sky. Then black specks dropped from the sky by the hundreds and landed in front of me on the barren landscape. I could see the 'specks' were actually large, shiny black creatures with tubby pterodactyl-like wings and huge whale-like bodies. . . . They explained to me in a kind of thought language that they were fleeing from something out in space. They had come to the planet Earth to escape their enemy. The creatures then showed me how they had created life on the planet in order to hide within the multitudinous forms and thus disguise their presence. Before me, the magnificence of plant and animal creation and speciation—hundreds of millions of years of activity—took place on a scale and with a vividness impossible to describe. I learned that the dragon-like creatures were thus inside all forms of life, including man."

At this point in his account, Harner writes in a footnote: "In retrospect one could say they were almost like DNA, although at that time, 1961, I knew nothing of DNA" (Narby 1999).

A similar urgency in the contact narrative was experienced in the session report 05.03.19, above, through the line of poetry from William Carlos Williams, repeated like a refrain throughout the eight-hour session:

> so *much* depends upon

Life in Narby's view is a vast, complex, interconnected signaling system, with DNA as the transceiver, and biophotonic emissions as the signals and sources of at least some aspect of the visions one sees in psychedelic states. But what about the narrative—the creatures fleeing an enemy through interstellar space, landing here, creating life-forms to hide within and "disguise their presence"? Having had a similar vision myself, embedded in a similar narrative, on a high-dose psilocybin journey, what shall I make of this? How do such similar narratives arise, in all their urgency and detail, independently, under conditions of extreme consciousness alteration? What does this tell us about how myths arise? And if I repeat this story now, adding my own, as Narby repeats Harner's story (and other similar myths from the Desana and Aztec cultures), will there be other readers who remember some similar story from a psychedelic session? How do we then interpret these events? If DNA not only holds a vast store of information, linguistically structured, but is also intelligent—minded, in the Varelian sense—and connected to the mostly similar DNA in highly diverse, complexly related, and deeply nested organisms, across vast scalar differences, we've arrived at something resembling a galactic Gaia hypothesis, or the concept of the noösphere.

> This awareness of interconnection occurs in and with what Vernadsky dubbed the "noösphere"—the aware and conscious layer of the earth's ecosystem, and perhaps, feeds back onto our ecosystems as we become conscious of our interconnections with them. (Doyle 2011)

So—visions present stories, stories beg for an interpretative framework. But it is the network of interconnected stories (scientific, psychedelic) about the network of interconnected life-forms that reveals this planet as a wonder we take mostly for granted, a wonder that is restored in psychedelic states.

The Rainbow Serpent

The Rainbow Serpent names an experience, a multiple metaphor, a cross-cultural complex of myths, and a means of understanding LiveGlide, the 3D form of the Glide symbolic system in the session reports. The Rainbow Serpent is a universal symbol, in Laughlin's definition, and pervades many of the psychonautic sessions. Jeremy Narby calls this serpent the cosmic

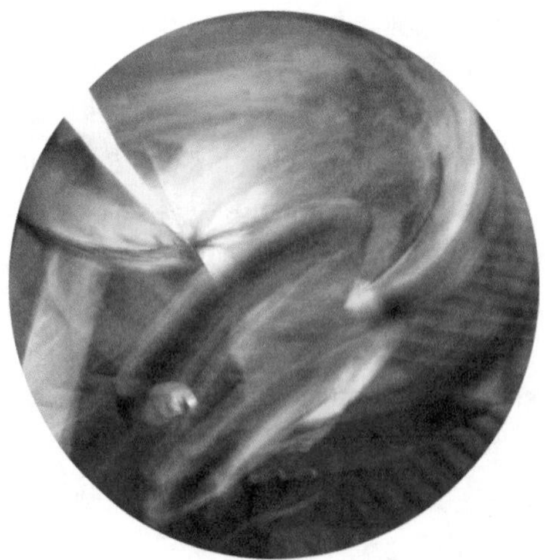

■ **Figure 108: The Rainbow Serpent, LiveGlide, screenshot from video.** Diana Reed Slattery.

serpent, and relates this symbol to DNA. From my first session, it was present in the energy flows of my body, creating serpentine hand gestures. It is present in varying forms and combinations of forms—visual, aural, energetic, gestural, and cognitive—with every psychedelic substance I experienced over the period of the research: MDMA, LSD, 2C-B, *Stropharia cubensis*, *Salvia divinorum*, and DMT. In psychedelically enhanced practice sessions with LiveGlide, it is present in the gestures of the serpentine forms that are felt in the body and transmitted through hand, eye, and arm through the MIDI controller to the software and hence to the projection surface. The Rainbow Serpent connects, energetically, with another cosmic serpent, the Kundalini, coiled at the base of the spine. The spontaneous serpentine gestures described can be interpreted as the rise of this energy in the human body.

Glide—modeling the ride on the Rainbow Serpent (session report 03.03.17, MDMA)

riding on the Rainbow Serpent—the living language of light—the device—pulsing flashing with light like stained glass window—golden circuitry . . . the radiant child riding on the rainbow serpent, Glide (session report 03.04.10, MDMA, Zurich)

The structure of reality which you experience—and metaphor—as the rainbow serpent is another way of saying flow begets form—the waves create the particulars—the particulars are where knowledge resides—the web is where it issues from and returns—the dark of the lily-mind— (session report 03.02.02, MDMA)

off and away focused on the rainbow serpent—as episteme—as interface—as route between languages—as LiveGlide—qualities:

coiling spiraling primal energy and flow transport basic wave sign (sine) primal wisdom double helix creative/destructive watery millions of rainbows in the writing air   filled with rainbow ribbons—LiveGlide—   the s—the snaky letter snaky sound—snakes portrayed sonically hissing Glide sign hiss and whistle shamanic soundings—[de-signing language]   Mudra (gestures of transmission from altered states) streaming filament from fingertips—not body isolated in empty space—but energy body—point of organization—but exists in sea of energy, shaped, coiling—that moves the body in its coils—the rainbow serpent—can be very frightening—as the energy so much bigger, more powerful than what is perceived as tolerable at the stepped-down (reducing valve) level (session report 03.05.26, MDMA)

The shapeshifting ubiquity of the visionary Serpent is emphasized in Simon Powell's account:

> In fact, such visionary motifs indicating the fusion of man-made architecture with biological structure were repeated a number of times. I often perceived stately homes and palaces—or rather, I would be gliding gracefully through such a palatial place—and always, the woodwork, like the banisters, wall panels, or staircases, would reveal themselves to be made of the body of a living creature. To be precise, I perceived that these buildings were woven from the jeweled body of the Serpent. Everything was alive, all was part of one animate, constructing entity. And if I saw human figures in any of these scenes, they too were formed out of the transmutating body of the Serpent. Everything in these scenes had the stamp of the Serpent's hide upon them, in that a kind of pulsating grid of luminescent lines and scaly jewels pervaded every object. (Powell 2008)

The polysemic Rainbow Serpent pervades Powell's mushroom experience and becomes a manifestation of Gaia. As above, the universal symbol of the Rainbow Serpent correlates with DNA.

> As the creator of life, the cosmic serpent is a master of metamorphosis. In the myths of the world where it plays a central part, it creates by transforming itself; it changes while remaining the same. So it is understandable that it should be represented differently at the same time. I went on to look for the connection between the cosmic serpent—the master of transformation of serpentine forms that lives in water and can be both extremely long and small, single and double—and DNA. I found that DNA corresponds exactly to this description. (Narby 1999)

This primal force is well known in Hindu and Buddhist practices as *kundalini,* and in martial arts as *qi.* The phenomena it incites in the human bodymind have been basically ignored by Western science. The Rainbow Serpent, by whatever name, makes its appearance in various guises in psychedelic experience, pointing to this ancient source of knowledge and creation, relating itself to the linguistic object that creates our form, our DNA.

The Guild of Xenolinguists

Jason WA Tucker—Actual Contact

Jason Tucker's evolutionary trajectory as an artist involves the combination of his artistic and psychonautic practices in a prolonged period of development he has called Actual Contact. Tucker experienced a slowly emerging sense of the Other participating in the act of drawing in a most intimate way: the emerging line felt like it was being drawn simultaneously from both sides of the paper. The drawings felt like "a new, exploratory language" developing to facilitate the communication between human and the emergent alien Other. Tucker's description of the experience of the Other participating in the act of creation, drawing with him, becomes a communion in its highest state.

In his own words. . .

> The creation of these drawings is tied to a state of heightened sensory levels brought on by a steady and disciplined use of LSD, Psilocybin mushrooms, DMT, and Ayahuasca ceremonies in Peru, from 1990 up to around the middle of 2004. During this time I found myself going through a radical shift of perspective, breaking free from my past in an unnerving unraveling of new thoughts and new metaphors, and new

■ **Figure 109: Jason Tucker.**

drawings. From out of an abstraction of lines and triangles that I had been drawing for more than a decade, ghostly cellular entities sprang into the foreground and began to amass, and the whole experience coalesced into some kind of strange and profound discovery for me.

The act of drawing became not only an act of creation, but an act of participation. Looking down at a blank piece of paper I would think, and think, and then think of nothing and then begin to draw, concentrating only on the beauty of the line, focusing on the movement, the symmetry, the vibration of just the line. I have often sensed that the same amount of concentration and surrender is happening on the other side of the line, as if another is on the other side drawing the same image at the same time. A fantastical projection from the unconscious, as well as a magical conjuring of something spiritual in nature. In a primitive sense, each drawing is an attempt to commune with a spirit world just beyond the cave walls.

I was entranced by a narrative that was developing in my drawings from one day to the next. I definitely connected with them as a new exploratory language, but it wasn't very clear, the message. I found the images to be disorienting, kind of familiar, but not explanatory. I saw it as something completely alien, or "us" in the future, or spirit, or ancestors, as far back as the cellular anthropos growing out of the primordial protoplasm. As my awareness grew with each drawing, so did the intensity of my life. For me, I had embarked upon a strange and desperate path going deeper into the wild notion of making actual contact with an "other" by drawing. A true reality bender as the drawings did come alive in this way. A circus of cellular entities had emerged out of my early abstract drawings. In hindsight, I now see that I was in a full-on religious experience of passage, ecstasy by way of animistic drawing. I had fully embraced a connection with the life-blood of the drawing, as just that, a living thing involved in continual transformation.

My drawings are never pre-planned. The role of chance comes from focusing on just the line, not knowing what image will be drawn. The experience is one of total control, but with no control at all. The images you see here are but a fraction of the total output. Each drawing is part of a larger whole. In using my intuition, listening to my heart, taking psychedelics, and fast losing the rigidity of past imprinting, the act of creation—the invention of images—became an experience of communion.

The following illustrations show the sequential development of Tucker's drawing as the experience of "actual contact" evolved in his artistic and psychonautic practices.

■ **Figure 110: Jason WA Tucker, #1.**

■ **Figure 111: Jason WA Tucker, #2.**

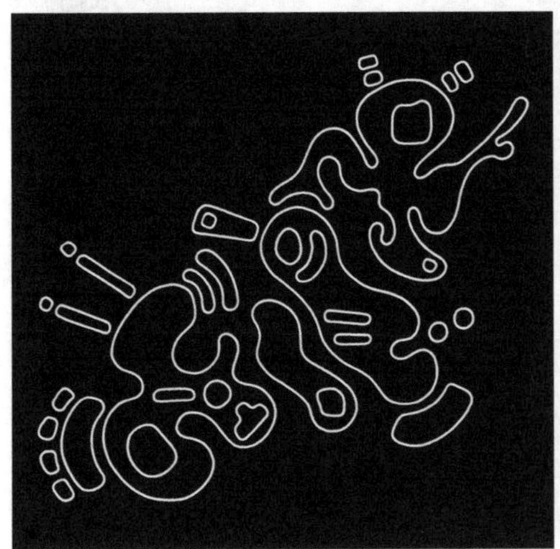

■ **Figure 112: Jason WA Tucker, #3.**

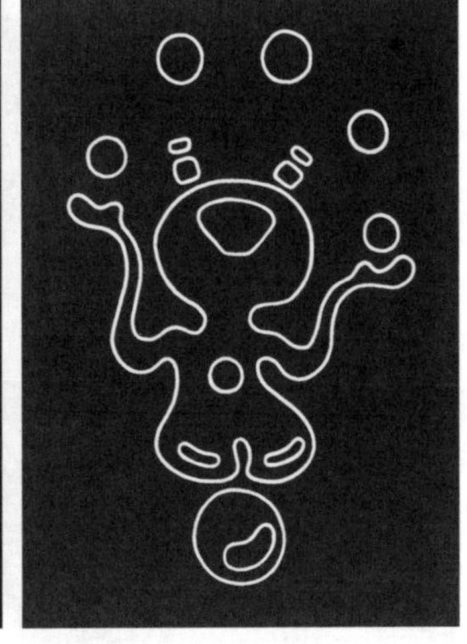

■ **Figure 113: Jason WA Tucker, #4.**

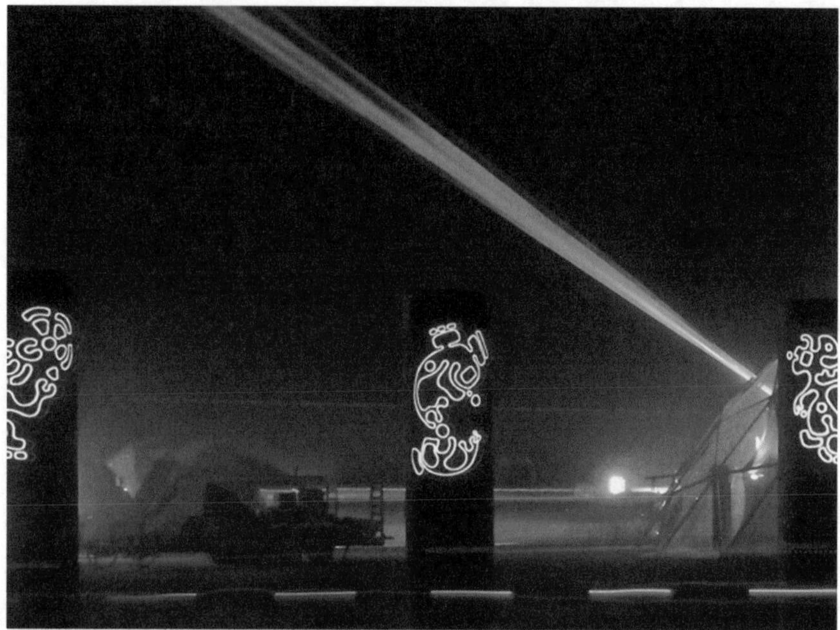

■ Figure 114: Jason Tucker, Actual Contact, Towers, Burning Man installation, 2013.

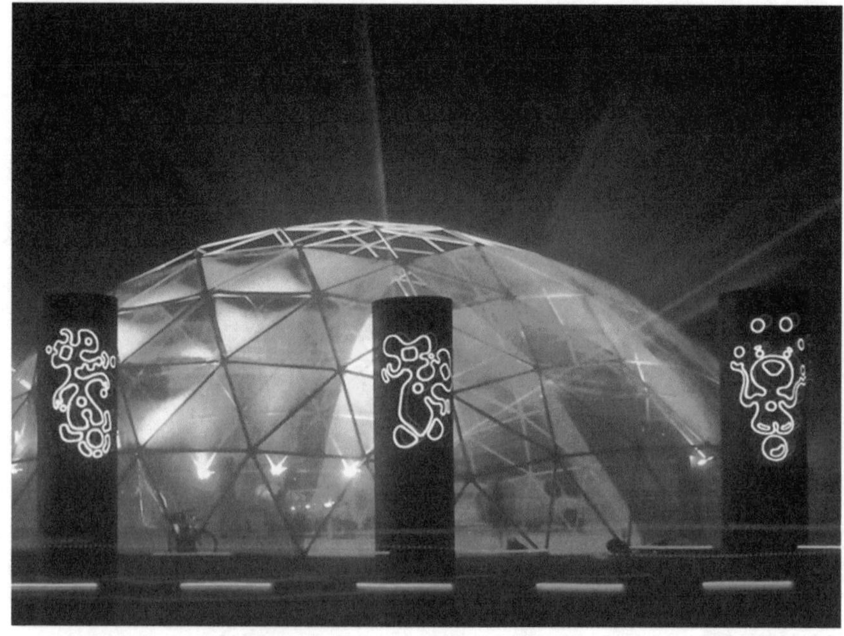

■ Figure 115: Jason Tucker, Actual Contact, Towers, Burning Man installation, 2013.

Jack Cross—The Argot of Ergot

When Jack Cross reads the English language, it is a multidimensional, multisensory activity. Meaning explodes into visual and aural puns, word-play, sacred geometry, and the revelation of the Logos. His unpublished essay, "The Argot of Ergot," is presented in full below. He outlines his xenolinguistical process. The stealth-language theme is prominent. The following section is in his own words.

The Argot of Ergot

Argot is "a specialized idiomatic vocabulary peculiar to a particular underworld group, devised for private communication and identification," translation, argot is the secret language of criminals. Ergot refers to the fungi *Claviceps purpurea,* which develops on grains, mainly rye plants, and contains the alkaloids of Lysergic Acid Diethylamide, ergo, The Argot of Ergot is The Secret Language of LSD.

Rewind to the Los Angeles Zen Center, circa 1991–92. Elvis was leaving the building when I overheard a Zen priest telling a small group of students about his "first spiritual experience," his first "peek under the circus tent," as he called it, that in the Summer of Love he had taken his first LSD trip, "which is why," he went on to explain, "I decided to study Zen." And in the context of that era, that would have made perfect sense, beautiful sense, growing up in the '50s with the Beat poets and Buddhism and at just the precise moment when our modern materialistic Western culture first touched a Shamanic substance en masse. But as I slowly walked by this conversation, I did not create the personal or cultural context for his spiritual evolution, nor did I factor in the illegality of the substance that facilitated his first spiritual experience. I simply walked by and said to myself, "Why wouldn't you study LSD?" I went on with the normal course of my life, for about a week.

Figure 116: Jack Cross.

A few days later I was at the Southwest Museum Library in the Mt. Washington area of Los Angeles looking through the "C's" of their card file when I came upon the inexplicable title of "The Sacred Mushroom and The Cross" by John M. Allegro. The title was strange enough, but the subtitle of the book was "A Study of the Nature and Origins of Christianity within the Fertility Cults of the Ancient Near East." A loose thread was dangling from the warp and weft of my reality. I pulled the card out and took it to the librarian.

The Southwest Museum Library is a reference library and so I discovered that I couldn't check the book out, which I took personally, so I politely asked if I could see the book, and I sat down and read the back cover, and the inside jacket, the foreword, the first chapter and the second and the third with something between intense excitement and horror. I was of course incapable of comprehending Allegro's philological notes, but the premise of the book was earth-shattering to my Christian bumper-sticker world. *The Sacred Mushroom and The Cross* was my *Wizard of Oz* in Zardoz, my Number 23.

The next day I went to my local bookstore and discovered that the book was out of print and unavailable and the clerk said that he thought that it might have been a "banned book." Even better! I asked for a phone book and found a used bookseller in Westwood called Needham Book Finders and a Mr. Needham, I presumed, said that he would look for it and give me a call back. A few days later he called, "Eighty bucks, in perfect condition." Ten times the original jacket price. What a bargain! I wish now that I had been in the habit of keeping receipts.

I devoured the book. The circus tent, the parasol of Paradise was taking form. Unfortunately for me at thirty-three, I didn't know of anyone who grew mushrooms; in fact, I didn't know of anyone who even smoked cigarettes, so I just told the story to everyone who would listen, and to a few who wouldn't, to see if anyone had ever heard of such an idea, that Sacraments were once actually something, maybe a mushroom, a plant, a substance, a class of drugs called hallucinogens that altered your consciousness and allowed you to commune with God, IT MADE YOU JESUS, not the person of, but the Christ. I think back now at how incredibly sweet I was, and intuitive and self-directed, to move out of my innocence, out of my ignorance, even at the risk of what we euphemistically call liberty, into the glorious life of a spiritual criminal.

Nine months went by and I spent this gestation alienating everyone I knew with my enthusiasm for psychedelics and ethnobotany, but not a single person I talked to in those nine months had ever heard of *Amanita muscaria,* let alone *The Sacred Mushroom and The Cross,* when in walks a musician who knew somebody, JACKPOT!

On a Saturday night, in an artist loft in downtown Los Angeles, I chewed the bitter caps and stems of 5 grams of *Stropharia cubensis,* and patiently sat, waiting for whatever it was that was coming for me, elf or alien, but neither did, what did was a SUPERNOVA BUTTERFLY made of Liquid Language and Light, and I knew it better than English, better than what I knew as life. I was ALL and NOTHING, a Mandelbrot Buddha laughing in a saffron and jackfruit sky, a Risen Ringmaster in a blazing red jacket throwing a private hierophantic fit. MY circus tent was Enlighten-t-ment, expressed as Geometry and Archetype and Alphabet, a SYMBOLIC Death AND Resurrection, as advertised, by a-ST-onishment!

Fast forward through innumerable Journeys to the last scene of The Lawnmower Man and pick up the phoneme and listen. The First Law of Man forbade the consumption of a plant, a plant that altered consciousness when eaten, a plant that made you AS GOD IS. Contrary to the popular cosmogony, the prohibition of a mind-altering plant marks The Beginning

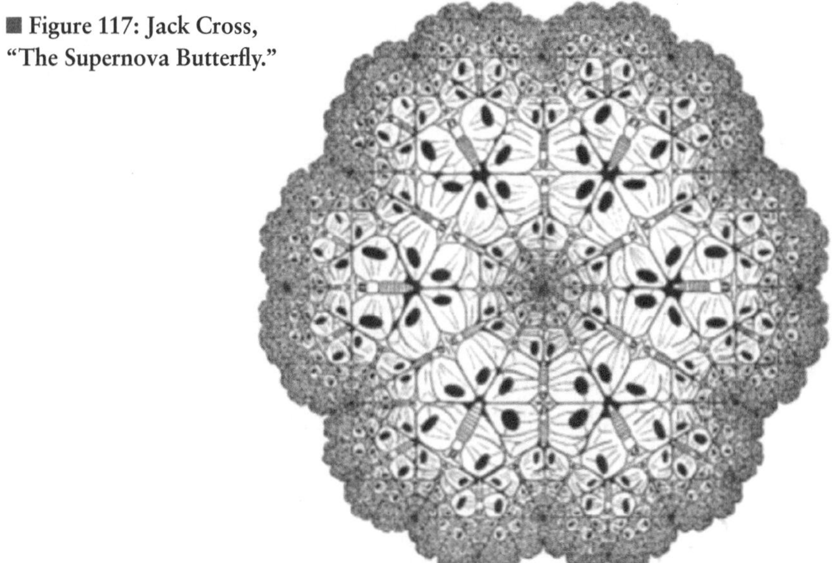

■ **Figure 117: Jack Cross, "The Supernova Butterfly."**

of linear time, its consumption transcends it. Its collective prohibition was The Fall of Man, our separation from The Divine Feminine.

As a Metaphysician of Ergot, as -son and arson of The JA Morpheme, as a Poet-Healer and Geometrician, I humbly draw your attention to the TiPs of my tongue as they untie and unite to focus your full attention on just one PoinT that begins with a "P" and ends with a "T." Our P-a-T-h[E]ology is me-T-a-P-hysical and etymological and can only be healed by a PracTitioner of Concealment and Revelation and Sacrifice. This is God's Geometry, The Logos, which to speak for, requires PrivaTe and in-T-IM-ate Knowledge of the "P" and the "T" of PoeT and ProPheT and PieTy.

Criminals abound, Saviors, like nocturnal thieves, guard themselves with parables and argot . . . and jargon, like Journey, begins with a "J."

A theory without sufficient evidence is con-j-ecture, and what theory could be evidenced more insufficiently than proofs of the existence of the theo- in theory, a combining form meaning "god." The Mind is a con-ST-ruct of sub- and ob-ject-tivity where the only means of escape is by con-j-URING up the "J" in the "T" of –ject itself, from the Latin, jacere, meaning to throw. The "J" is an A-Xis P-ole, eX-Tra-pole-ated to eXisT inside The C-ONE of The "A"-nkh of Consciousness, the pineal, and the –cere of JA[h]-cere and sin-cere means pure, and no one comes to the P-A-T-er but by the first two letters of measure, and the least of one of these.

The "T" of –j-ec-t and incandescen-t, is made of ligh-t eMAN-t-ing from inside your pineal gland, as "you," the "I" in the "A" of I AM, s-quin-t, ad-v-er-t-en-t-ly, organizing s-P-A-T-i-AL relationships with the configuration of a cross, an oP-T-ical illusion, u-P-on, which you SYMBOLCALLY h-ang, CRUCI-FI-ed, T-rans-FI-gured, from o-P-aque chatteled flesh in the possession of a scheduled sub-ST-ance to a Radian-t BE-i-NG of Ligh-t located beyond the pla[j]iarius j-urisdictions of a fictitious entity, who by Amendment to its Con-ST-itution is utterly unqualified to define Religion and un-Author-ized to interfere with its practice.

Law is the exoskel et al. remains of Logos; j-ustice, j-udge, j-ury, j-urisdiction, ad-j-udication, all bear the mark of The Axis Pole of the 'J' of -ject and Jot and Jacob's ladder. The separation of Church and State is an irrelevant pre-t-ense; BOTH are fictitious entities, shadows of a broken heart and a deluded mind pro-ject-ed onto the concaved wall of human History. Law insists on its own stability over Right and ad-ministers equal injustice founded upon precedent, upon that which came before, which makes relevant its first Judicial Act, recorded by scribe and stenographer as The Banishment of two juveniles for JA-y walking in a garden where attorneys and tourniquets first twisted innocence and sanity into sin and madness, and established that the etymological origins of the word perpetrator descend from Father.

Buried deep beneath the Temple Floor, in the center of the posterior forebrain, is the small glandular cavity of the Pineal, the cry-PT of cryptic and P-en-AL Codes. Here you will find The Shepherd's Crook, The "J" in our JAnkh DNA, and The CarPenTer's Square, the "L," and His Compass, The EYE and "A" of God, me-A-sur-iNG the re-LA-T-ionship of AL-L things, expressed Geometrically as P-LA-ne Cartesian coordinates and designated "X" and "Y," yin and yang, the du-AL aspects of The Circle, inside and outside, "I" and "O," and 10 in a dec-IM-AL system is The Completion of a Cycle, expressed soc-io-politically as a revolution and personally as RE-Ve-LA-T-ion.

The "L" of P-LA-n-T, The Carpenter's Square, is derived from hALf of a cross, the L-ineAr expression of The Circle or a poin-t of L-igh-t con-V-er-t-ed into the configuration of a cross when you squin-t. The letter "A," The Compass, in picto-grammar, is the PineAL GLAnd and Cross and Cour-t are quadran-t sys-t-ems, wherein we are tri-ed like a Thi-rd Ordinate and sub-j-ugated in the "J" of J-ustice, and the UL-T-i-mate Criminal is the Archetypal Rebel, the re-b-EL, The Re-BE-GOD, The S-JA-MAN, the P-reacher and T-eacher, the in-t-er-med-iary between the na-T-ural and su-P-ernatural worlds, in-t-er-JA-c-en-t, be-t-ween ordinates and The Extraordinary.

A "squint" in a church wall is a small O-PEN-ing giving an ob-server an ob-lique view of the AL-T-ar, squintessentially, architectural argot. A squint is also called a Hagioscope, spelled with a "G" but pronounced with a "J," like logic and magic. "Hagio" is a combining form from Greek where it means "Saint," "Holy," "Sacred," and "-scope" is a combining form meaning "to look at." The Old Hag we're looking at through the s-quin-t in-s-ide The Holy Double "yoU" in W-ALL and W-oman is The Androgynous God "S," The S-er-p-en-T, und[j]ulating upon The AL-T-ar of Ob- and the J-ec-T-ification of Consciousness. In the T-o-P-ography of letters, oblique means to slant toward the right and an oblique pro-j-ec-t-ion, is perfec-t-ed to the nth degree, where FOUR is CRUCI- and FI-ve is The SerPENT. In rhe-t-or-ic-al arg-U-men-t, and argot, oblique is in-di-rec-t.

There is no actus reus, no guilty act, and no mens rea, no guilty mind, and therefore no criminal liability in any common law-based criminal law j-urisdiction. A Sacramental Act, that which makes Sacred, is The Right of a free people to individual co-GN-itive liberty and the practice of Religion, THIS IS The Pursuit of Happiness, to link-back to God in Communion within one's own consciousness by the eating of an entheogenic plant, or by any means or molecule necessary. And conversely, it is our collective lack of coGNitive liberty, our collective lack of God Consciousness, of GN-osis, that is being reflected in, embodied, perpetuated and perpetrated by, the bloated corpus of the secular State, who exists in opposition to, by definition, and in the absence of, The Sacred.

What the unrivaled purveyor of violence is protecting its sub-jects from, under the cover of the Rule of LAw, is AuThOrship of The Word, of Christ Consciousness, of a mass Re-T-urn of Illuminated Intelligence, and on the front lines of this inquisitional and pharmacratic war between those with questions and those with none, are the first three letters of death, followed by a suffix and an aspirated breath.

The Practice of Religion, of Spirituality, trumps all concerns, even if that practice does not include participation in the fraud[j]ul-en-t perpetuation of ignorance marketed generically under the LA-b-EL of Faith Incorporated, or the bait and switch of placebo for Sacrament, or the delusions and collusions of T-em-P-le merchants trading Corner Stones for pieces of silver and the status of the taX eXem-pt.

This voice, this awed, this Buddha laughing, this Mind, this God dancing, these angels, this tip of pen, these tears of Serpents lust, this semen ink, this iridescent red, this Alphabet, this comprehend, spinning in it. A cUp, a auldron, a auldron, this crUel wine, P-LA-n-T AL-chemy, flesh is wood for fire, without hast and without rest, what two things? Christened, crossed, triple the Two is The Number of Man, Six, and Four, the last Hexagram, Before Completion, three coins to phrase, six in the fifth place, and with this hopeful outlook, always cautions, the Book of Changes, a plant oracle, and The Argot of Ergot come to their close, sublime reminders in a world where

The Way has been lost and speaking the Truth has unfavorable consequences, and nothing that would further.

I write in my room at night. . . . I thought, ya know, I'm just going to break all the rules. I'm not sure if I ever knew what they were anyway. If people want to read something normal and understandable, then turn the page, but I'm going to be as strange as I want to be. This is my voice, this is what I say when I journey, this is what I tossed myself over the edge for, repeatedly, as best as I can give it, this is my surrender, other-wise, what's the Po-in-T?

Simon G. Powell—The Fantastic Hypothesis

Simon G. Powell is a musician, composer, videographer, writer in many modes, and a mushroom devotee. His work, *The Psilocybin Solution, The Role of Sacred Mushrooms in the Quest for Meaning,* depicts the ability of the psilocybin experience to deliver high-speed downloads; information transmission as communication with the Other; and especially, information delivered as a visual language of intense concentration.

In his own words:

> Here we begin to understand what the shamanic visionary experience is like, that it consists essentially of a communication transmitted in the higher language expressed by the Other, a language of symbols embodied in animated imagery.
>
> One is confronted with a powerful communicatory flow of organized symbolic information that compels one to infer an intelligent presence of some kind as the issuer of the information. Although after such a profound experience one might question the grounds for inferring such an "Other," during the visionary trance itself one might well be utterly overwhelmed by a sense of intentional communication, leaving no room for doubt.

Powell introduces his discussion of the Other—the experience of the felt presence of an Other in psychedelic, especially psilocybinetic states—in terms of information and its transformations. Terence McKenna comes back time and again to the consideration of these experiences of the Other, especially with the mushroom. He entertained many hypotheses about its nature, from

■ **Figure 118: Simon G. Powell.**

> being the voice of the mushroom, speaking as an alien import, to the voice of the Logos itself, imparting knowledge through the agency of the be-mushroomed state. Surely the question of the nature of the Other and the source of the knowledge they deliver (is this from a previously hidden part of "my own" psyche, or from a source outside of "my self"?) is one of the enduring mysteries of the psychedelic experience. Reports of the alien Other confounded Rick Strassman in his DMT research. Cultural frameworks such as shamanism on the one hand and science on the other deliver widely different interpretations.

Powell concludes,

> The Other thus represents a name, or label, for the kind of information processing underlying the visionary state. An apparent communion with the Other demonstrates the inherent property of neuronal information to purposefully organize itself into streams of ideas laden with profound meaning. If one can conceive of the mind as being a kind of informational process, one can equally envisage the Other as being an informational process. Whatever the actual neuronal firing mechanisms involved, it seems likely that the self-organization, or forced coherence of immense amounts of information underlies the felt presence of the Other.

The discourse on intelligent design goes back at least as far as St. Thomas Aquinas's argument from final causes, which imply intelligent design. Intelligent design became identified with the fundamentalist assertion of creationism, with a monotheistic God as the supreme designer. This doctrine opposes Darwinian evolution, and virtually every scientific argument for natural evolutionary processes. Psychedelic study has its own take on intelligent design, approached from the knowledge gained in altered states of consciousness, in which nature itself and all its densely intertwingled components are perceived as radiantly intelligent. Intelligence is redefined as a quality not only of humans but of all life-forms. Jeremy Narby's book *Intelligence in Nature* speaks to this point. Ayahuasca researchers, shamans, and ethnobotanists involved in the broader exploration of South American plant medicines all speak of direct communication with the spirits of plants, of plants as intelligent teachers. This brand of natural intelligence is a central concept for Powell as well. And nature, for Powell, goes beyond our biosphere and ultimately includes both animate and inanimate nature: "life, the universe, and everything."

> Mind stuff resolves itself as being informational stuff. This is perhaps not too controversial a claim, but what I eventually hope to show is that matter, or physical stuff, is also informational in nature. This would mean that everything, whether atoms, molecules, organisms, or thoughts, could be described in informational terms.
>
> Our aim now is to discover more about the nature and intent of the intelligence that would appear to underlie the reality process. This intelligence, whatever it is exactly, seems to be causally manifest through the specific law, order, and self-organizing properties of Nature. Hence we witness the inevitable progressive emergence of phenomena like stars, molecular compounds, organisms, and consciousness (the means by which Nature can know itself), then this is strongly suggestive that there is some sort of purposeful intelligence connected with those laws. In any case, the patterns of information forced into existence by Nature appear to behave according to various systems of logic that we can loosely refer to as physics, chemistry, genetics, biology, psychology, and so on.
>
> The forms of logic cited above are language-like, computation-like, and enfolded within one another in a kind of nested hierarchy. The language-like logic of physics acts as a substrate from which the language-like logic of chemistry emerges. In turn, the language-like logic of chemistry gives rise to the language-like logic of molecular biology. And so on. Eventually, highly advanced bio-logic leads to brains that embody patterns of information we call minds. Conscious minds are subsequently able to contemplate the intelligence that likely governs this astonishingly creative set of processes. (Powell 2011)

The book concludes with Powell's "fantastic hypothesis," which brings together his arguments about the mushroom's visions, information, natural intelligence, language, and a computational universe in one package.

> The reality process around us can similarly be viewed as a fourteen-billion-year-long translation of the Other from one language-like form into another. . . .
>
> The fantastic hypothesis views reality, or Nature, as a deliberate and intelligently behaving system. According to the fantastic hypothesis, we are woven into a tide of self-organizing information, interconnected throughout, whose spectacular final purpose awaits us. For if the natural tendency of the Universe is to foster the integration and cohesion of more and more information, then, as with gravity in the physical realm drawing together atoms and elements, the result of this integrative process in the realm of human consciousness might be to draw some kind of "truthful solution" into being, like an ultimate pattern falling into place. (Powell 2011)

The Psilocybin Solution in the twenty-first century stands in bright counterpoint to the twentieth century's "final" solutions, the counterbalancing light to that deepest darkness of the human spirit, the title capturing the ethical dimension of Powell's message.

CHAPTER 12
A Reasonable Hope

To move beyond the veil of natural language in the course of a psychedelic session is to leave behind the symbolic framework with which one constructs and supports the default world. I enter new worlds, un-languaged as an infant might be, open to wonder. What was moments ago mundane is now miraculous, as Aldous Huxley viewed the folds in his flannel pants with awe. I revel in the sensuous presence of a world-without-names, Eden before it became a botanical garden with labels on flora, fauna, and our feelings of superiority regarding them. Cognition and natural language clearly part company. Cognition is free to apprehend novel linguistic structures that construct realities on different principles—forms of cognition that do not depend on natural language. To know what is going on during a psychonautic voyage when the *what* is mind-bogglingly novel, and when the tools to describe the *unspeakable translinguistic fluidly changing opalescent hyperdimensional shit* . . . has been left behind, is itself a cognitive adventure of such novelty that it belies description in less than extravagant language, a babble of adjectives or a contortionistic reflexivity.

Language in altered states reveals its creative potential in structuring reality, from "primitive" word magic to the ingression of the Logos to create the world, *in the beginning*. The Pentecostal reappearance of the Holy Spirit in the upper room delivered a new linguistic ability—to speak in tongues, in the language-before-words that can be understood by all. The magical properties of the Word, the tapping of the imagination, and the epistemological potency of translinguistic matter postulate forms of language as the creative mechanism for creating reality or worlds. The serpentine form of DNA remains central to the psychedelic linguistic vision: its efficacy as the sacred script by which we are spoken and maintained in existence at every moment at every scalar level. The intertwined serpents of DNA, as a universal symbol, become the tree of knowledge; the Akashic memory store of the biosphere; and, in alchemical extensions of this vision, the Stone itself. But DNA is an evolving Stone, bringing the new Anthropos into view.

While the slipping away of natural language in the psychedelic mind-state can easily map to Hunt's differentiation between the representational and the presentational, it is not ultimately satisfying from the viewpoint of the altered state of consciousness. Correlation of the neurological description with the phenomenological report, while maintaining a parity of realities such that neither reductively trumps the other, requires a special skill of non-attachment to any particular reality, however comfortable, desirable, or fascinating. The neurological description and the phenomenological report may verify or contradict each other, suggesting the need for a metasystem that can structure such approaches to multiple realities and their interactions. Such an imagined metasystem would be in need of constant adjustment, as Lilly suggests in his protocol for integrating new information from altered states. Extreme flexibility in reviewing and revising models would create a space in which the novel can ingress into baseline discourse with some useful clarity.

In the late 1970s, Charles Tart suggested state-specific sciences to get a grasp of psychedelic realities, but no one has yet imagined the program or discussed what the methods might be. New forms of language could well be part of that state-specific science. And new forms of visual language can already be seen, especially in the new art of big-data visualizations, such as those from NOAA[1] on weather, vegetation, atmospheric flows, all based on enormous datasets captured from satellites and other instrumentation. These visual language forms are not only the stunning still images we can now produce at every scale of observation we can reach. The dynamic visions of process in geospatial visualization give us insight into the planet as a whole as a set of intertwingled systems. Our interconnectedness is writ large across the face of the planet.

The authorized research over the last ten years on the use of psilocybin to ease end-of-life anxiety and depression by Charles Grob, Roland Griffiths, and their teams at UCLA and Johns Hopkins uses protocols essentially established by Stan Grof's psychotherapeutic LSD work at Spring Grove and Maryland Psychiatric Research Center in the late '60s and early '70s. This medical/psychiatric/psychotherapeutic model of psychedelic use is the channel for all authorized psychedelic research involving humans at present.

Relief of the problems of the human condition is also, of course, the province of religion and spiritual practices of all kinds, and psychedelics seem to have been used sacramentally since pre-history. The Santo Daime and União do Vegetal churches have moved out of Brazil into the United States, Canada, and Europe, bringing the visionary states with them. In the current medical model in which psychedelic legitimacy is being pursued, there is great promise for the relief of human suffering—the suffering of the dying, the suffering of veterans and others with severe PTSD, the suffering of addicts, and the suffering of persons on the autistic spectrum from anxiety. But it is hard to imagine how all the other uses that psychonauts are making for these substances will be legitimized if the model for use remains limited to doctors, illness, disease, and prescribed drugs. In addition to the underground network of psychedelic therapists, psychonauts are using psychedelics in spiritual practice, as artistic adjuncts, to explore nature, for creative problem-solving, and to experiment with new forms of community. And, goddess forbid, sometimes we use these substances when we want to dance ecstatically, or just have a vacation from the confines of the default world and the same-old self. But this kind of activity invokes the dreaded "recreational" label that sober scientists, making the case for prescription medicines, wish to avoid. The question "When did it become bad to re-create ourselves?" is beyond the scope of this book. These substances are found in plants, animals, and fungi that grow in the wild or can be cultivated. They are part of the human environment, and in our bodies-as-environment as well, in our endogenous DMT. As such they will continue to be explored. The R and D of psychonauts—our methods, creative production, our insights and pratfalls, as well as the alchemical recombinatorics that is churning out ever more psychoactive substances for the high-profit black market—continues at a greater pace and sophistication and quantity than ever before. Local communities exist in most parts of the world, and those local communities are connecting up on the Internet, through festival culture, and academia for technology transfer and community building. There's a psychedelic documentary industry bringing the latest news on ayahuasca culture, ibogaine use in addiction, drug policy reform, and the social history of psychedelics. Psychedelic culture is percolating throughout global society because psychonauts can be found in every walk of life, from CEOs to farmers, nurses and teachers, and librarians. We can be found in force in all the media industries, on the creative/artistic side, where synaesthetic awareness informs our media-surround, as we continue to shift the balance in communication technologies to the visual, the moving, and the immersive. And there are plenty of psychonauts in the programming-engineering end of media as well. The bottom line is we are embedded in the default world, a mycelial network of persons deliberately experimenting with consciousness and its evolution, individually and socially, and applying their findings to their lives.

And we are very much part of the exploratory urge that has driven the curious monkeys on this planet to the moon and the top of Mt. Everest and the bottom of the sea. Terence McKenna called our future, psychedelically in-formed selves "galaxy-roving bodhisattvas, the culmination and quintessence of the highest aspirations of star-coveting humanity." Is the intense longing for outer-space exploration an urge to migrate surging up in the unconscious of our species in response to our growing sense that resources are possibly running out and it's time to get moving again? How many biomes have we depleted (think the extinction of the wooly mammoth at the end of the Pleistocene, ten thousand years ago) in our rush to civilization? How many civilizations have collapsed when the surrounding resources could no longer support a centralized population? So we dream of outer

■ **Figure 119: Earth from space.** Wikimedia Commons.

space (I have since early childhood), design our getaway vehicles, and make the first dramatic forays.

But we clearly do not have the biological or physical knowhow to engineer ourselves to even the nearest possibly habitable planet. Mars? Mars was successfully terraformed in Kim Stanley Robinson's science fiction trilogy *Red, Blue, and Green Mars,* but we have not approached that level of technology. At current writing, the fastest vehicle we have put in space so far would take roughly on the order of 150,000 years to reach what we think might be the nearest habitable planet outside the solar system. And we're just not ready to pack for a 150,000-year voyage at sub-relativistic speeds. It's not only that the amount of rocket fuel exceeds the energy production available. There's the question of life, what forms we need to bring with us to live, and what forms we desire on a one-way ticket to the stars, in a biosphere that has to survive in space, completely self-contained, recycling the same materials for a time period of at least ten times the entire cultural history of humankind. The biospherics necessary for space travel are almost completely unknown in any practical application.

Virgin Galactic, one of fifteen (at this writing) commercial space companies, is getting ready to send a few billionaries and celebrities into suborbital flight for a few minutes at the possible cost of major stratospheric damage. The science of their carbon spew is being argued presently. I think I see Sir Richard's good intention here: if these celebrities and CEOs "get the big picture" as astronaut Edgar Mitchell did, and have the mystical vision of Earth from space (the experience called "the overview effect"), then some good will come of it. I hope he imagines that vision translating into some form of increased care for our stunning home. This biosphere, the only one we have or have located anywhere else, must last long enough to support the enormous human effort to reach the stars, surrounded by a complete biosphere. At the moment there does not appear to be a collective, that is, species-wide awareness of how the biosphere works as a whole, what keeps it healthy (and ourselves as a part of it), and how not to take more than we give. Astronaut Edgar Mitchell came back from the moon and went directly into the study of consciousness with the formation of the Institute for Noetic Sciences. Will such a trip on Virgin Galactic produce those mind- and heart- and life-changing experiences that will raise ecological awareness, for instance, at the same time it may be laying down a Sasquatch-sized carbon footprint?

While I ponder these matters, we are decimating portions of the biosphere of our current and only habitable planet, Spaceship Earth, at a rapid rate. My countering suggestion to Sir Richard would be, if he can't solve the carbon problem, to sell off Virgin Galactic lock, stock, and rocket fuel to preserve the stratosphere (and his legacy as a person trying to do good) and invest in Virgin Ecstatic, the exploration of inner space, the really really *big* frontier, with no carbon footprint for the inter-dimensional transport system. In all seriousness, I hold a reasonable hope that the viewpoint from which we can begin to seek answers to the problems we are still for the most part denying about our unhealthy effects on the biosphere is in the ecstatic awareness of our mutual interconnectedness as life-on-Earth. The ecodelic insight, however attained, is the ground from which we imagine, plan, and implement a more habitable future.

The vision of connectedness, of human beings with each other, and in a reunion with nature, what Richard Doyle calls the ecodelic hypothesis and Simon G. Powell terms the psilocybin solution, is the hope for unity that fuels much psychonautic exploration, constituting an ethical dimension to the work in many forms. Lilly's connection to the dolphin and to interspecies language investigation set the stage for his LSD and ketamine research. Dennis McKenna's view of the pervasive, complex, interwoven communicativeness of Nature informs his work in the life sciences. The utopian technological visions of interconnectivity of Pesce, Pinchbeck, and Leary are linked to a hoped-for transformation in consciousness. Allyson Grey's Secret Writing connects us with a sacred dimension expressed in a vision of fountaining energies that connect every point of consciousness. Jason Tucker, in the act of drawing his serpentine lines, connects with the ingressing anthropomorphs on the other side of the paper as the veil to the world of the Other grows thin. Terence McKenna's vision of a fractal form of time permeating human and cosmic time is a variation on the theme of alchemical interconnectivity and transmutation, *as above, so below*. Jack Cross unpacks the sacred geometry of the alphabet in his linguistic vision. I add my own perception of a myceliation of consciousness connecting all forms at all scales.

This vision and experience of interconnectivity and the interdependence of all systems in nature brings with it a sense of mutual responsibility and caring. Such caring action is the platform of the major behavioral shifts necessary for the continued survival and health of the biosphere, the absolute prerequisite for star travel. How thoroughly do we need to understand the biosphere to miniaturize one, balance it, and set sail for the stars? Presently, most efforts toward space travel are concentrated on the hardware. The International Space Station has some great gear, but all biological processes depend on imports of food, air, and water from Earth, and export of waste material. At any rate, until the gardeners, and the water, air, and soil experts, the waste treatment gurus, nutritionists, ecologists, midwives, psychologists, teachers, and cooks get involved in the planning for how we will breathe, eat, poop, reproduce at the right rates, not have fatal feuds in such tight quarters, and preserve the story of where we came from and where we are going and why, we have not addressed the topic of star travel with any practicality. All those systems need to be kept in dynamic balance for 150,000 years. Until we have mastered these skills, our fantasy of star travel remains a prepubescent dream of running away from home. In this case, home must come with us, as it always does, in one form or another.

Visions of hope for the human future enter consciousness with noetic force in the psychedelic state. They are visions of connectedness, of boundary dissolution and trust. The teaching voice of the Logos, the spirits of the vine, of the mushroom, of the sacred cacti and sage continue to lead psychonauts on to new realizations in the service of growth in consciousness, especially consciousness in the sense of *conscience*. That enlivening of conscience and a shift toward caring and responsibility can be held as the pre-condition of effective change in human social organization at any scale. The old Adam, exiled from Eden, a dirt farmer doomed to die, is posed against the cosmic Anthropos, the new man, the completed or restored endpoint of humanity. The novel symbolic systems that I've studied under the rubric of Xenolinguistics are forms of expression from those worlds beyond the veil of natural language that carry these themes into baseline reality. As such, they pose a reasonable hope, messages from the Other in bottles washed up on the shores of Mind at Large, brought forth by these scribes of the unseen life, ecstatic significations that reverberate across the dimensional abyss.

This possibility of hope in the face of clear and present danger to the biosphere is an opportunity not to be squandered in prohibition on the one hand, or in uninhibited silliness on the other. In my kindest moments I see humankind *vis à vis* psychedelics and their uses as very much in the monkeys-discovering-fire phase. From tasting the first accidental roast pig in the hot coals of a forest fire, it was many burnt feet and fingers later before fire was tamed. From our current first rounds of experimentation with the fires of the mind, the psychedelics, we have a long way to go. Like fire, developing safe use and discovering the myriad applications of this technology takes time, practice, and maturity.

It is from this hope for the future that I take the stand of a cognitive libertarian and a conscientious objector in the War on Drugs. You need not take anyone's word here or elsewhere about psychedelic states and their uses. This is not Big Science; you don't need a Large Hadron Collider to examine inner space. Guts and good sense will do. Psychonautics is small science, citizen science if you will, accessible to all. The territory beckons and can be explored experientially by repeating the basic psychonautic experiment:

- ingest substance with attention to dose, set, and setting
- observe carefully
- report fully
- interpret from your standpoint
- share the knowledge

The Psychedelics and Language website, http://psychedelicsandlanguage.com, is offered as a forum for continued communication.

Notes, Chapter 12

1. NOAA, the National Oceanic and Atmospheric Administration. Their Environmental Visualization Laboratory has a rich collection of these visualizations.

Bibliography

Abbott, Edwin. *Flatland: A Romance of Many Dimensions*. Sioux Falls, South Dakota: NuVision Publications, 2008.

Aberle, David F. *The Peyote Religion among the Navajo*. Chicago: University of Chicago Press, 1982.

Abraham, Ralph, Terence McKenna, and Rupert Sheldrake. *Trialogues at the Edge of the West: Chaos, Creativity, and the Resacralization of the World*. Rochester, Vermont: Bear & Co., 1992.

———. *The Evolutionary Mind: Trialogues at the Edge of the Unthinkable*. Santa Cruz, CA: Dakota Books, 1997.

Abram, David. *The Spell of the Sensuous: Perception and Language in a More-Than-Human World*. New York: Vintage Books, 1996.

Adams, Hazard, and Leroy Searle. *Critical Theory since 1965*. Gainesville, Florida: University of Florida Presses, 1986.

Alhim. "Pathways of Memory Reacquainted: Salvia Divinorum." Erowid.org, www.erowid.org/experiences/exp.php?ID=32006.

Allen, Douglas. *Myth and Religion in Mircea Eliade*. Edited by Robert A. Segal, Theorists of Myth. New York: Routledge, 2002.

Andresen, Jensine, and Robert K. C. Forman, eds. *Cognitive Models and Spiritual Maps*. Bowling Green, Ohio: Imprint Academic, 2000.

Argüelles, Jose A. *The Transformative Vision: Reflections on the Nature and History of Human Expression*. Berkeley: Shambala Press, 1975.

Artaud, Antonin. *The Peyote Dance*. Translated by Helen Weaver. New York: Farrar, Straus, and Giroux, 1976.

Arthur, James. *Mushrooms and Mankind: The Impact of Mushrooms on Human Consciousness and Religion*. Escondido, California: The Book Tree, 2000.

Ascott, Roy. "Global Mind Warming." Facebook, http://www.facebook.com/home.php#/photo.php?pid=2662609&id=554994561&fbid=136360264561.

———. *Telematic Embrace: Visionary Theories of Art, Technology, and Consciousness*. Berkeley: University of California Press, 2003.

———. "When the Jaguar Lies Down with the Lamb: Speculations on the Post-Biological Culture." CAiiA-STAR Symposium (2001).

Aug, R. G., and B. S. Ables. "Hallucinations in Nonpsychotic Children." *Child Psychiatry Hum Dev* 1, no. 3 (1971): 152–67.

Austin, James, H. Zen, and the Brain. *Toward an Understanding of Meditation and Consciousness*. Cambridge: The MIT Press, 2000.

Baars, Bernard J. *In the Theater of Consciousness: The Workspace of the Mind*. Oxford: Oxford University Press, 1997.

Bache, Christopher M. *Dark Night, Early Dawn: Steps to a Deep Ecology of Mind*. Edited by Richard D. Mann, SUNY Series in Transpersonal and Humanistic Psychology. Albany: State University of New York Press, 2000.

Back-Madruga, C., K. B. Boone, L. Chang, C. S. Grob, A. Lee, H. Nations, and R. E. Poland. "Neuropsychological Effects of 3,4-Methylenedioxymethamphetamine (Mdma or Ecstasy) in Recreational Users." *Clin Neuropsychol* 17, no. 4 (2003): 446–59.

Bagner, D. M., M. R. Melinder, and D. M. Barch. "Language Comprehension and Working Memory Language Comprehension and Working Memory Deficits in Patients with Schizophrenia." *Schizophr Res* 60, no. 2-3 (2003): 299–309.

Bailly, D., and M. B. de Chouly de Lenclave. "A Rare and Not Very Studied Disorder: Childhood-Onset Schizophrenia. A Case Report." *Encephale* 30, no. 6 (2004): 540–7.

Bailly, D., M. B. de Chouly de Lenclave, and L. Lauwerier. "Hearing Impairment and Psychopathological Disorders in Children and Adolescents. Review of the Recent Literature." *Encephale* 29, no. 4 Pt 1 (2003): 329–37.

Ballard, C. G., J. T. O'Brien, B. Coope, and G. Wilcock. "Psychotic Symptoms in Dementia and the Rate of Cognitive Decline." *J Am Geriatr Soc* 45, no. 8 (1997): 1031–32.

Balter, Michael. *The Goddess and the Bull: Çatalhöyük: An Archaeological Journey to the Dawn of Civilization*. Walnut Creek, California: Left Coast Press, 2006.

Banchoff, Thomas F. *Beyond the Third Dimension: Geometry, Computer Graphics, and Higher Dimensions*. New York: Scientific American Library, 1996.

Barks, Coleman, and John Moyne. *The Drowned Book: Ecstatic and Earthy Reflections of Bahaud-*

din, the Father of Rumi. New York: HarperCollins, 2004.

Barlow, John Perry. "Being in Nothingness: Virtual Reality and the Pioneers of Cyberspace." Electronic Freedom Foundation, http://www.eff.org/Misc/Publications/John_Perry_Barlow/HTML/being_in_nothingness.html.

Barnard, G. William. *Exploring Unseen Worlds: William James and the Philosophy of Mysticism.* Albany: State University of New York Press, 1997.

Barnard, Mary. *The Mythmakers.* Athens, Ohio: Ohio University Press, 1966.

Barron, Frank. *Creativity and Personal Freedom.* Princeton: D. Van Nostrand Company, Inc., 1968.

Bateson, Gregory. *Steps to an Ecology of Mind: Collected Essays in Anthropology, Psychiatry, Evolution, and Epistemology.* New York: Ballantine Books, 1972.

Baudelaire, Charles. *Artificial Paradise.* Translated by Patricia Roseberry. Harrogate: Broadwater House, 1999.

Beach, Horace. "Listening for the Logos: A Study of Reports of Audible Voices at High Doses of Psilocybin." The California School of Professional Psychology at Alameda, 1996.

Beane, Wendell C., and William G. Doty. *Myths, Rites, Symbols: A Mircea Eliade Reader.* New York: Harper Colophon Books, 1975.

Bednarik, Robert. "Semiotix Course 2006: Cognition and Symbolism in Human Evolution." http://chass.utoronto.ca/epc/srb/cyber/bednarik1.pdf.

Bell, Catherine. *Rituals: Perspectives and Dimensions.* Oxford: Oxford University Press, 1997.

Ben. "Howto: Ego Death." *Shroomery: Magic Mushrooms Demystified,* http://www.shroomery.org/4018/Howto-Ego-Death.

Benedikt, Michael. *Cyberspace: First Steps.* Cambridge: MIT Press, 1993.

Berrios, G. E., and T. R. Dening. "Pseudohallucinations: A Conceptual History." *Psychol Med* 26, no. 4 (1996): 753–63.

Bhati, M. T. "The Brain, Language, and Schizophrenia." *Curr Psychiatry Rep* 7, no. 4 (2005): 297–303.

Black, David. *Acid: The Secret History of LSD.* London: Vision Paperbacks, 1998.

Blood, Benjamin Paul. *Pluriverse: An Essay in the Philosophy of Pluralism.* New York: Arno Press, 1976.

Bobrow, R. S. "Paranormal Phenomena in the Medical Literature Sufficient Smoke to Warrant a Search for Fire." *Med Hypotheses* 60, no. 6 (2003): 864–68.

Boire, Richard Glen. "Center for Cognitive Liberty and Ethics." CCLE.

———. "Mimetics Hostilis: An Assemblage of Law, Psychiatry, and Chemical Artifice." *Configurations: A Journal of Literature, Science, and Technology* 16, no. 2 (2009): 145–65.

Boire, Richard Glen, and Terence K. McKenna. *Sacred Mushrooms & the Law.* Berkeley, CA: Ronin, 2002.

Bolla-Wilson, K., and M. L. Bleecker. "Neuropsychological Impairment Following Inorganic Arsenic Exposure." *J Occup Med* 29, no. 6 (1987): 500–503.

Boon, Marcus. *The Road of Excess: A History of Writers on Drugs.* Cambridge: Harvard University Press, 2002.

Boothroyd, Dave. *Culture on Drugs: Narco-Cultural Studies of High Modernity.* Manchester: Manchester University Press, 2006.

Borges, Jorge Luis. *Labyrinths: Selected Stories & Other Writings.* New York: New Directions Paperbook, 2007.

Briggs, John, and F. David Peat. *The Turbulent Mirror: An Ilustrated Guide to Chaos Theory and the Science of Wholeness.* New York: Harper & Row, Publishers, 1990.

Brown, David J., and Rebecca McClen Novick, eds. *Mavericks of the Mind: Conversations with Terence McKenna, Allen Ginsberg, Timothy Leary, John Lilly, Carolyn Mary Kleefeld, Laura Huxley, Robert Anton Wilson, and Others.* Santa Cruz: MAPS, 2010.

Burroughs, William S., and Allen Ginsberg. *The Yage Letters Redux.* San Francisco: City Lights Publishers, 2006.

Byrd, Don. "The Emergence of the Cyborg and the End of the Classical Tradition: The Crisis of Alfred North Whitehead's Process and Reality." *Configurations: A Journal of Literature, Science, and Technology* 13, no. 1 (2005): 95–116.

Câceres, Abraham D. "In Xoxhitl, in Cuicatl: Hallucinogens and Music in Mesoamerindian Thought." University of Indiana, 1984.

Cachia, A., M. L. Paillere-Martinot, A. Galinowski, D. Januel, R. de Beaurepaire, F. Bellivier, E. Artiges, J. Andoh, D. Bartres-Faz, E. Duchesnay, D. Riviere, M. Plaze, J. F. Mangin, and J. L. Martinot. "Cortical Folding Abnormalities in Schizophrenia Patients with Resistant Auditory Hallucinations." *Neuroimage* 39, no. 3 (2008): 927–35.

Cameron, N. "Abnormalities of Behavior." *Annu Rev Psychol* 1 (1950): 189–206.

Cantu, T. G., and J. S. Korek. "Central Nervous System Reactions to Histamine-2 Receptor Blockers." *Ann Intern Med* 114, no. 12 (1991): 1027–34.

Cardena, Etzel, Steven Jay Lynn, and Stanley Krippner. *Varieties of Anomalous Experience: Examining the Scientific Evidence.* Washington: American Psychological Association, 2000.

Carpenter, Dan. *A Psychonaut's Guide to the Invisible Landscape: The Topography of the Psychedelic Experience.* Rochester, Vermont: Park Street Press, 2006.

Carpenter, W. T., Jr., J. S. Strauss, and J. J. Bartko. "The Diagnosis and Understanding of Schizophrenia. Part I. Use of Signs and Symptoms for the Identification of Schizophrenic Patients." *Schizophr Bull*, no. 11 (1974): 37–49.

Carter, Rita. *Exploring Consciousness*. Berkeley: University of California Press, 2002.

Castenada, Carlos. *Tales of Power.* New York: Simon and Schuster, 1974.

Caves, Sally. "Teonacht." http://www.frontiernet.net/~scaves/teonaht.html.

Ceccherini-Nelli, A., and T. J. Crow. "Disintegration of the Components of Language as the Path to a Revision of Bleuler's and Schneider's Concepts of Schizophrenia. Linguistic Disturbances Compared with First-Rank Symptoms in Acute Psychosis." *Br J Psychiatry* 182 (2003): 233–40.

Chalmers, David, Robert French, and Douglas Hofstader. "High-Level Perception, Representation, and Analogy: A Critique of Artificial-Intelligence Methodology." In *Fluid Concepts and Creative Analogies*, edited by Douglas Hofstader. New York: Basic Books, 1995.

Chalmers, David J. *The Conscious Mind: In Search of a Fundamental Theory.* Edited by Owen Flanagan, Philosophy of Mind series. Oxford: Oxford University Press, 1996.

———. *Philosophy of Mind: Classical and Contemporary Readings*. Oxford: Oxford University Press, 2002.

Champion, Sarah. *Disco Biscuits*. London: Hodder & Stoughton, 1997.

Chatman, Seymour, and Samuel R. Levin. *Essays on the Language of Literature*. Boston: Houghton Mifflin Company, 1967.

Chayefsky, Paddy. *Altered States*. New York: Bantam Books, 1979.

Chevannes, Barry. *Rastafari and Other African-Carribbean Worldviews*. New Brunswick: Rutgers University Press, 1998.

Chris. "A Spiritual Journey: Mushrooms." Erowid.org, www.erowid.org/experiences/exp.php?ID=3781.

Clark, Andy. *Natural Born Cyborgs: Minds, Technologies, and the Future of Human Intelligence.* Oxford: Oxford University Press, 2003.

Cohen, David. *Explaining Linguistic Phenomena.* Washington: Hemisphere Pub. Corp.; distributed by Halsted Press Division, Wiley, New York, 1974.

Collin, Matthew, and John Godfrey. *Altered State: The Story of Ecstasy Culture and Acid House.* London: Serpent's Tail, 1997.

Coulmas, Florian. *The Writing Systems of the World.* Oxford: Blackwell Publishers Ltd., 1996.

Covington, M. A., W. J. Riedel, C. Brown, C. He, E. Morris, S. Weinstein, J. Semple, and J. Brown. "Does Ketamine Mimic Aspects of Schizophrenic Speech?" *J Psychopharmacol* 21, no. 3 (2007): 338–46.

Crick, Francis, and Christof Koch. "116, Consciousness, Neural Basis Of." Elsevier, http://www.klab.caltech.edu/~koch/Elsevier-NCC.html.

Crow, T. J. "Auditory Hallucinations as Primary Disorders of Syntax: An Evolutionary Theory of the Origins of Language." *Cogn Neuropsychiatry* 9, no. 1-2 (2004): 125–45.

Cup, Balloon. "Magnifying (Tunnel of Dots)." Erowid.org, http://www.erowid.org/experiences/exp.php?ID=73649.

Cutting, J., and F. Dunne. "Subjective Experience of Schizophrenia." *Schizophr Bull* 15, no. 2 (1989): 217–31.

Cytowic, Richard E. "Synesthesia: Phenomenology and Neuropsychology, a Review of Current Knowledge." *Psyche, An Interdisciplinary Journal of Research on Consciousness* 2, no. 10 (1995).

D'Imperio, M. E. *The Voynich Manuscript—an Elegant Enigma*. Vol. 27, The Cryptographic Series: Aegean Park Press, 1976.

Dauben, Joseph W. *Georg Cantor: His Mathematics and Philosophy of the Infinite*. Princeton: Princeton University Press, 1990.

Daumal, Rene. *A Night of Serious Drinking*. Woodstock: The Overlook Press, 2003.

David, A. S. "Auditory Hallucinations: Phenomenology, Neuropsychology and Neuroimaging Update." *Acta Psychiatr Scand Suppl* 395 (1999): 95–104.

———. "The Cognitive Neuropsychiatry of Auditory Verbal Hallucinations: An Overview." *Cogn Neuropsychiatry* 9, no. 1-2 (2004): 107–23.

David, A. S., and J. C. Cutting. "Visual Imagery and Visual Semantics in the Cerebral Hemispheres in Schizophrenia." *Schizophr Res* 8, no. 3 (1993): 263–71.

David, A. S., and P. A. Lucas. "Auditory-Verbal Hallucinations and the Phonological Loop: A Cognitive Neuropsychological Study." *Br J Clin Psychol* 32 (Pt 4) (1993): 431–41.

Davidson, Julian M., eds., and Richard J. Davidson. *The Psychobiology of Consciousness*. New York: Plenum Press, 1982.

Davis, Erik. *Beyond Belief: The Cults of Burning Man.* Black Rock City: self-published pamphlet, 2003.

———. *Techgnosis: Myth, Magic and Mysticism in the Age of Information.* New York: Three Rivers Press, 1998.

———. "Terence Mckenna's Last Trip." *Wired Magazine*, http://www.wired.com/wired/archive/8.05/mckenna_pr.html.

———. *The Visionary State: A Journey through California's Spiritual Landscape.* San Francisco: Chronicle Books, 2006.

Davis, Wade. *The Serpent and the Rainbow.* New York: Touchstone, 1985.

de Quincey, Thomas. *Confessions of an English Opium Eater.* New York: Penguin Books, 1979.

de Rios, Marlene Dobkin. *Amazon Healer: The Life and Times of an Urban Shaman.* [location?]Prism Press, 1992.

———. *Hallucinogens: Cross-Cultural Perspectives.* Prism Press, 1984.

de Rios, Marlene Dobkin, and Oscar Janiger. *LSD: Spirituality and the Creative Process.* Rochester, Vermont: Park Street Press, 2003.

Deacon, Terrence. *The Symbolic Species: The Co-Evolution of Language and the Brain.* New York: W. W. Norton & Company, 1997.

Debord, Guy. *Society of the Spectacle.* Translated by Donald Nicholson-Smith. New York: Zone Books, 1998.

deGarcia, Donald J. "Do Psychedelic Drugs Mimic Awakened Kundalini? Hallucinogen Survey Results." http://csp.org/practices/entheogens/docs/kundalini_survey.html.

DeKorne, Jim. *The Hydroponic Hot House.* Port Townsend, Washington: Loompanics Unlimited, 1992.

———. *Psychedelic Shamanism: The Cultivation, Preparation and Shamanic Use of Psychotropic Plants.* Port Townsend, Washington: Breakout Productions, 1994.

Derrida, Jacques. *Of Grammatology.* Translated by Gayatri Chakravorty Spivak. Baltimore: Johns Hopkins University Press, 1974.

———. *Writing and Difference.* Translated by Alan Bass. Chicago: University of Chicago Press, 1978.

Dery, Mark. *Escape Velocity: Cyberculture at the End of the Century.* New York: Grove Press, 1996.

Devereux, Paul. *The Long Trip: A Prehistory of Psychedelia.* New York: Penguin Putnam Inc., 1997.

Dick, Philip K. *Valis.* New York: Vintage Books, 1991.

Doblin, Rick. "Pahnke's 'Good Friday Experiment': A Long-Term Follow-up and Methodological Critique *The Journal of Transpersonal Psychology* 23, no. 1 (1991).

Dowman, Keith, and Robert Beer. *Buddhist Masters of Enchantment: The Lives and Legends of the Mahasiddhas.* Rochester, Vermont: Inner Traditions, 1998.

Doyle, Richard. *The Ecodelic Hypothesis: Plants, Rhetoric, and the Co-Evolution of the Noosphere.* Seattle, Washington: University of Washington Press (in press), 2010.

———. "Introduction: Among the Psychonauts with Dreamworks? Imagining Technoscience after the Transhuman Prohibition." *Configuations: A Journal of Literature, Science, and Technology* 16, no. 2 (2009): 139–44.

Duchan, Judith F., Gail A. Bruder, and Lynne E. Hewitt, eds. *Deixis in Narrative: A Cognitive Science Perspective.* Hillsdale, New Jersey: Lawrence Erlbaum Associates, 1995.

Dulchinos, Donald P. *Pioneer of Inner Space: The Life of Fitz-Hugh Ludlow, Hasheesh Eater.* Brooklyn: Autonomedia, 1998.

Eco, Umberto. *The Aesthetics of Chaosmos: The Middle Ages of James Joyce.* Cambridge, Massachusetts: Harvard University Press, 1989.

———. *Art and Beauty in the Middle Ages.* New Haven; London: Yale University Press, 1986.

———. *The Limits of Interpretation.* Edited by Thomas A. Sebeok, Advances in Semiotics. Bloomington and New York: Indiana University Press, 1994.

———. *Looking for a Logic of Culture.* Lisse, Netherlands: Peter de Ridder Press, 1975.

———. *Misreadings.* 1st ed. San Diego: Harcourt Brace & Co., 1993.

———. *The Search for the Perfect Language, The Making of Europe.* Oxford, UK; Cambridge, Mass., USA: Blackwell, 1995.

———. *A Theory of Semiotics, Advances in Semiotics.* Bloomington: Indiana University Press, 1976.

———. *Travels in Hyperreality: Essays.* 1st ed. San Diego: Harcourt Brace Jovanovich, 1986.

Eco, Umberto, and Stefan Collini. *Interpretation and Overinterpretation.* Cambridge; New York: Cambridge University Press, 1992.

Eco, Umberto, and Costantino Marmo. *On the Medieval Theory of Signs,* Foundations of Semiotics series, v. 21. Amsterdam; Philadelphia: J. Benjamins, 1989.

Elfstone. "Reflections on the Timewave." http://www.fractal-timewave.com/index.html.

Eliade, Mircea. *Myths, Dreams, and Mysteries.* Translated by Philip Mairet. New York: Harper Torchbooks, 1960.

———. *Shamanism: Archaic Techniques of Ecstasy.* Princeton: Princeton University Press, 1964.

Ely, Timothy, Terence K.McKenna, and Artists' Books Collection (Library of Congress). *Synesthesia.* New York: Granary Books, 1992.

Emrys, Sai. "On the Design of an Ideal Language, Revision 8." http://community.livejournal.com/conlangs/14524.html.

Emrys, Sai, and Alex Fink. "Gripping Language." http://000024.org/conlang/gripping.html.

Erowid. "2C-B Basics." Erowid, http://www.erowid.org/chemicals/2cb/2cb_basics.shtml.

Evans-Wentz, W. Y. *The Fairy-Faith in Celtic Countries.* 1st Carol Pub. Group ed., Library of the Mystic Arts. New York: Citadel Press, 1990.

Farmer, Steve, John B. Henderson, and Michael Witzel. "Neurobiology, Layered Texts, and Correlative Cosmologies." *Bull. of the Museum of Far Eastern Antiquities* 72 (2000): 48–90.

Farmer, S. A. "Neurobiology, Stratified Texts, and the Evolution of Thought." Paper presented at the International Conference on Comparative Mythology, Beijing, China, 2006.

———. *Syncretism in the West: Pico's 900 Theses*

(1486). Vol. 167, Medieval & Renaissance Texts & Studies. Tempe, Arizona: Arizona State University, 1998.

Fauconnier, Giles, and Eve Sweetser. *Spaces Worlds and Grammar.* Chicago: University of Chicago Press, 1996.

Fischer, Roland. "Cartography of Conscious States: Integration of East and West." In *Expanding Dimensions of Consciousness,* edited by Arthur A. and Ralph Tarter Sugarman. New York: Springer Publishing Company, 1978.

———. "A Cartography of the Ecstatic and Meditative States." *Science* 174, no. 4012 (1971).

———. "The Making of Reality." *J. of Altered States of Consciousness* 3, no. 4 (1977): 371–89.

Fischer, Roland, Karen Thatcher, Thomas Kappeler, and Philip Wisecup. "Personality Trait Dependent Performance under Psilocybin." *Diseases of the Nervous System* 31, no. 3 (1970): 181–92.

Fischer, Roland, and Colin Martindale. "The Effects of Psilocybin on Primary Process Content in Language." *Confinia psychiat.* 20 (1977): 195–202.

Forte, Robert, R. Gordon Wasson, David Steindl-Rast, Jack Kornfield, Dale Pendell, Robert Jesse, Albert Hofmann, Thomas Riedlinger, Thomas Robeerts, Rick Strassman, and Eric Sterling. *Entheogens and the Future of Religion.* San Francisco: Council on Spiritual Practices, 1997.

Frith, C. "The Role of the Prefrontal Cortex in Self-Consciousness: The Case of Auditory Hallucinations." *Philos Trans R Soc Lond B Biol Sci* 351, no. 1346 (1996): 1505–12.

Frith, C. D. "Consciousness, Information Processing and Schizophrenia." *Br J Psychiatry* 134 (1979): 225–35.

Gebser, Jean. *The Ever-Present Origin.* Translated by Noel with Algis Mickunas Barstad. Athens, Ohio: The Ohio University Press, 1984.

Giddens, Gary. *Visions of Jazz: The First Century.* New York: Oxford University Press, 1998.

Glickman, N. "Do You Hear Voices? Problems in Assessment of Mental Status in Deaf Persons with Severe Language Deprivation." *J Deaf Stud Deaf Educ* 12, no. 2 (2007): 127–47.

Godart, Louis. *The Phaistos Disc: The Enigma of an Aegean Script.* Translated by Alexandra Doumas: Itanos Editions, 1995.

Golas, Thaddeus. *The Lazy Man's Guide to Enlightenment.* New York: Bantam Books, 1981.

Goldman, Robert, and Stephen Papson. *Sign Wars: The Cluttered Landscape of Advertising.* New York: The Guilford Press, 1996.

Goodman, Felicitas D. *Speaking in Tongues: A Cross-Cultural Study of Glossolalia.* Chicago: University of Chicago Press, 1972.

Goswami, Amit. *The Self-Aware Universe: How Consciousness Creates the Material World.* New York: Jeremy P. Tarcher, 1993.

Gottlieb, Adam. *Psilocybin Production.* Berkeley: Ronin Publishing, Inc., 1997.

Gowan, John Curtis. *Development of the Psychedelic Individual: A Psychological Analysis of the Psychedelic State and Its Attendant Psychic Powers.* Privately published, 1974.

———. *Trance, Art and Creativity: A Psychological Analysis of the Relationship between the Individual Ego and the Numinous Element in Three Modes: Prototaxic, Parataxic, and Syntaxic.* Buffalo: Creative Education Foundation, 1975.

Gracie, and Zarkov. "Gracie's 'Visible Language' Contact Experience." *The Vaults of Erowid,* http://www.erowid.org/cgibin/search/htsearch.php?method=and&restrict=&format=long&config=htdig&exclude=&words=Gracie.

———. "A High-Dose 2C-B Trip." *Erowid,* http://www.erowid.org/cgi-bin/search/htsearch.php?exclude=&words=Graciie+and+Zarkov&Search.x=0&Search.y=0.

Greenberg, Alan J., Ellen L. Bassuk, and Stephen C. Schoonover. *The Practitioner's Guide to Psychoactive Drugs.* 3rd ed. New York: Plenum Medical Book Company, 1991.

Grey, Alex. *The Mission of Art.* Boston: Shambhala, 1998.

Grey, Allyson. "Biography." CoSM, www.allysongrey.com/.

———. "Interview." CoSM, www.allysongrey.com/interview.html.

Griffiths, R. A. "Mystical-Type Experiences Occasioned by Psilocybin Mediate the Attribution of Personal Meaning and Spiritual Significance 14 Months Later." *Journal of Psychopharmacology* 22, no. 6 (2008): 621–32.

Grinspoon, Lester, and James Bakalar. *Psychedelic Reflections.* New York: Human Sciences, 1983.

Grof, Stanislav. *Ancient Wisdom and Modern Science.* Albany: State University of New York Press, 1984.

———. *Beyond the Brain: Birth, Death and Transcendence in Psychotherapy.* Edited by Richard D. Mann and Jeanne B. Mann, SUNY Series in Transpersonal and Humanistic Psychology. Albany: State University of New York Press, 1985.

———. "Grof Holotropic Breathwork." http://www.holotropic.com/about.shtml.

———. *Psychology of the Future: Lessons from Modern Consciousness Research.* Edited by Richard D. Mann, SUNY Series in Transpersonal and Humanistic Psychology. Albany: State University of New York Press, 2000.

Grof, Stanislav, and Christina Grof. *Beyond Death: The Gates of Consciousness.* London: Thames and Hudson, 1980.

Gromala, Diane J. "Toward a Phenomenological Theory of the Visceral in the Interactive Arts." University of Plymouth, 2006.

Guardian, the. "Government Drug Adviser David Nutt Sacked." *Guardian News and Media Limited,* www.guardian.co.uk/politics/2009/oct/30/drugs-adviser-david-nutt-sacked.

Hajicek-Dobberstein, S. "Soma Siddhas and Alchemical Enlightenment: Psychedelic Mushrooms in Buddhist Tradition." *J Ethnopharmacol* 48, no. 2 (1995): 99–118.

Halifax, Joan. *Shamanic Voices: A Survey of Visionary Narratives.* New York: E. P. Dutton, 1979.

Hammond, Norm. "Solstice Markers At 'House of Two Suns'." *Archaeoastronomy: The Journal of Astronomy in Culture* XVII, no. 2002-2003 (2003): 23–30.

Hancock, Graham. *Supernatural: Meetings with the Ancient Teachers of Mankind.* [location?]Doubleday Canada, 2005.

Harner, Michael. *The Way of the Shaman: A Guide to Power and Healing.* New York: Bantam Books, 1986.

Harner, Michael J. *Hallucinogens and Shamanism.* London: Oxford University Press, 1973.

Harpignies, J. P. *Visionary Plant Consciousness: The Shamanic Teachings of the Plant World.* Rochester, Vermont: Park Street Press, 2007.

Harraway, Donna J. *Simians, Cyborgs, and Women: The Reinvention of Nature.* London: Routledge, 1991.

Harrison, John. *Synaesthesia: The Strangest Thing.* Oxford: Oxford University Press, 2001.

Harvey, Graham. *Shamanism: A Reader.* London; New York: Routledge, 2003.

Hayes, Charles. *Tripping: An Anthology of True-Life Psychedelic Adventures.* New York: Penguin Putnam, 2000.

Hayes, Curtis W., Jacob Ornstein, and William W. Gage. *The ABC's of Languages and Linguistics: A Practical Primer to Language Science.* 2nd ed. Lincolnwood, Illinois: National Textbook Company, 1997.

Hayles, N. Katherine. "The Transformation of Narrative and the Materiality of Hypertext." *Narrative* 9, no. 1 (2001): 21–39.

———. *Writing Machines.* Cambridge: MIT Press, 2002.

Heinrich, Clark. *Magic Mushrooms in Religion and Alchemy.* Rochester, Vermont: Park Street Press, 2002.

Hemmingsen, R. "Consciousness Functions in Psychoses. Concepts, Empirism and Hypotheses." *Ugeskr Laeger* 153, no. 16 (1991): 1104–09.

Hemphill, R. E. "Auditory Hallucinations in Polyglots." *S Afr Med J* 45, no. 48 (1971): 1391–94.

Henderson, Linda. *The Fourth Dimension and Non-Euclidean Geometry in Modern Art.* Princeton: Princeton University Press, 1983.

Henriksen, A. L., C. St. Dennis, S. M. Setter, and J. T. Tran. "Dementia with Lewy Bodies: Therapeutic Opportunities and Pitfalls." *Consult Pharm* 21, no. 7 (2006): 563–75.

Hewes, Gordon W. "Origin and Evolution of Language and Speech." Paper presented at the Origin and Evolution of Language and Speech, New York, 1976.

hiab-x. "Bad Trip and Umpsquamadic Peels (LSD)." Erowid.org, www.erowid.org/experiences/exp.php?ID=15901.

Higgs, John. *I Have America Surrounded: The Life of Timothy Leary.* Fort Lee: Barricade Books, Inc., 2006.

Hinton, C. Howard. *Fourth Dimension.* Montana: Kessinger Publishing, 1904.

Hirano, S., Y. Hirano, T. Maekawa, C. Obayashi, N. Oribe, T. Kuroki, S. Kanba, and T. Onitsuka. "Abnormal Neural Oscillatory Activity to Speech Sounds in Schizophrenia: A Magnetoencephalography Study." *J Neurosci* 28, no. 19 (2008): 4897–903.

Ho, Mae-Wan. *The Rainbow and the Worm: The Physics of Organisms.* New Jersey: World Scientific, 1998.

Hobson, J. Allan. *The Dream Drugstore: Chemically Altered States of Consciousness.* Cambridge: The MIT Press, 2001.

Hobson, P., and J. Meara. "Risk and Incidence of Dementia in a Cohort of Older Subjects with Parkinson's Disease in the United Kingdom." *Mov Disord* 19, no. 9 (2004): 1043–49.

Hoenig, J. "'Audible Thoughts' and 'Speech Defects' in Schizophrenia." *Br J Psychiatry* 169, no. 3 (1996): 380.

Hoffman, Daniel D. *Visual Intelligence: How We Create What We See.* New York: W. W. Norton and Company, Inc., 1998.

Hoffman, R. E. "The Duphar Lecture: On the Etiology of Alien, Nonself Attributes of Schizophrenic 'Voices'." *Psychopathology* 24, no. 6 (1991): 347–55.

———. "A Social Deafferentation Hypothesis for Induction of Active Schizophrenia." *Schizophr Bull* 33, no. 5 (2007): 1066–70.

Hoffman, R. E., M. Hampson, K. Wu, A. W. Anderson, J. C. Gore, R. J. Buchanan, R. T. Constable, K. A. Hawkins, N. Sahay, and J. H. Krystal. "Probing the Pathophysiology of Auditory/Verbal Hallucinations by Combining Functional Magnetic Resonance Imaging and Transcranial Magnetic Stimulation." *Cereb Cortex* 17, no. 11 (2007): 2733–43.

Hoffman, R. E., and T. H. McGlashan. "Parallel Distributed Processing and the Emergence of Schizophrenic Symptoms." *Schizophr Bull* 19, no. 1 (1993): 119–40.

Hoffman, R. E., and S. L. Satel. "Language Therapy for Schizophrenic Patients with Persistent 'Voices'." *Br J Psychiatry* 162 (1993): 755–58.

Hoffman, R. E., and M. Varanko. "'Seeing Voices':

Fused Visual/Auditory Verbal Hallucinations Reported by Three Persons with Schizophrenia-Spectrum Disorder." *Acta Psychiatr Scand* 114, no. 4 (2006): 290–92; discussion 92.

Hofmann, Albert. *LSD: My Problem Child.* New York: Tarcher, 1983.

Holland, John H. *Emergence: From Chaos to Order.* Reading, Massachusetts: Helix Books, Addison-Wesley, 1998.

Holmes, David A. *The Bioluminescent Brain.* [location?] The Library of Consciousness, 2005.

Holroyd, S., and M. L. Shepherd. "Alzheimer's Disease: A Review for the Ophthalmologist." *Surv Ophthalmol* 45, no. 6 (2001): 516–24.

Holtzman, Steven R. *Digital Mantras: The Languages of Abstract and Virtual Worlds.* Cambridge: The MIT Press, 1996.

Honda, T., H. Suzuki, K. Iwai, Y. Fujiwara, H. Kawahara, and S. Kuroda. "Autochthonous Experience, Heightened Awareness, and Perception Distortion in Patients with Schizophrenia: A Symptomatological Study." *Psychiatry Clin Neurosci* 58, no. 5 (2004): 473–79.

Honig, L. S., and R. Mayeux. "Natural History of Alzheimer's Disease." *Aging* (Milano) 13, no. 3 (2001): 171–82.

Horgan, John. *Rational Mysticism: Spirituality Meets Science in the Search for Enlightenment.* Boston: Houghton Mifflin Company, 2003.

Howard. "The Universe Is a Fractal." Erowid.org, www.erowid.org/experiences/exp.php?ID=69232.

Huang, Al. *The Numerology of the I Ching: A Sourcebook of Symbols, Structures, and Traditional Wisdom.* Rochester, Vermont: Inner Traditions, 2000.

Hubbard, V. S. Ramachandran, and E. M. "Synaesthesia—A Window into Perception, Thought, and Language." 2001.

Hughes, James. *Altered States: Creativity under the Influence.* New York: The Ivy Press, 1999.

Hunt, Harry T. "The Linguistic Network of Signifiers and Imaginal Polysemy: An Essay in the Co-Dependent Origination of Symbolic Forms." *Journal of Mind and Behavior* 16, no. 4 (1995): 405–20.

———. *On the Nature of Consciousness: Cognitive, Phenomenological, and Transpersonal Perspectives.* New Haven: Yale University Press, 1995.

Husserl, Edmund. *Cartesian Meditations: An Introduction to Phenomenology.* Translated by Dorion Cairns. The Hague: Martinus Nijhoff, 1973.

Huxley, Aldous. *The Devils of Loudun.* New York: Harper Perennial Modern Classics, 2009.

———. *The Doors of Perception and Heaven and Hell.* Harmondsworth: Penguin Books, 1974.

———. *Island.* New York: Harper & Row, Publishers, 1962.

———. *Moksha: Writings on Psychedelics and the Visionary Experience.* Los Angeles: J. P. Tarcher, Inc., 1977.

Huxley, Laura Archera. *This Timeless Moment.* Millbrae, California: Celestial Arts, 1968.

———. *This Timeless Moment: A Personal View of Aldous Huxley.* Berkeley, California: Celestial Arts, 2000.

James, William. *Essays in Radical Empiricism.* Lincoln, Nebraska: University of Nebraska Press, 1996.

———. *Essays in Radical Empiricism.* Mineola: Dover Publications, 2003.

———. *Principles of Psychology.* Edited by Robert Maynard Hutchins. Vol. 53, Great Books of the Western World. Chicago: Encyclopedia Britannica, 1952.

———. *The Varieties of Religious Experience: A Study in Human Nature.* Centenary Edition. New York: Longmans, Green, and Co., 2002.

Jansen, Karl L. R. *Ketamine: Dreams and Realities.* Sarasota: MAPS, 2004.

Jaskolski, Helmut. *The Labyrinth: Symbol of Fear, Rebirth, and Liberation.* Boston: Shambala, 1997.

Jeffrey, Francis, and John C. Lilly. *John Lilly, So Far . . .* Los Angeles: Jeremy P. Tarcher, Inc., 1990.

Jenkins, John Major. *Maya Cosmogenesis 2012: The True Meaning of the Maya Calendar End-Date.* Santa Fe, New Mexico: Bear & Co., 1998.

Johnson, Mark. *The Body in the Mind: The Bodily Basis of Meaning, Imagination, and Reason.* Chicago: The University of Chicago Press, 1990.

Johnson, Steven. *Interface Culture: How New Technology Transforms the Way We Create and Communicate.* San Francisco: HarperEdge, 1997.

Jonsson, Benct Philip. 5/13/2009 2009. [any additional info?]

Josephson, Brian. "Possible Connections between Psychic Phenomena and Quantum Mechanics." *New Horizons*, January (1975): 224–26.

Joyce, James. *Portrait of the Artist as a Young Man.* New York: W. W. Norton & Company, 2007.

JT. "LSD and Ego Dissolution." http://csp.org/nicholas/A5.html.

Jung, Carl G. *Flying Saucers: A Modern Myth of Things Seen in the Skies.* Princeton, New Jersey: Princeton University Press, 1978.

———. *Psychology and Alchemy.* Translated by R. F. C. Hull. Edited by Michael Fordham, Herbert Read, and Gerhard Adler. 20 vols. Vol. 12, Bollingen Series, the Collected Works of C. G. Jung. London: Routledge and Kegan Paul, 1953.

Justin. "Lysergic Bioassay iii - Cosmic Transducer: Lsa." Erowid.org, www.erowid.org/experiences/exp.php?ID=55485.

Kauffman, L. H., and F. J. Varela. "Form Dynamics." *J. Social and Bio. Struct.* 3 (1980): 171–206.

Kelly, Kit. *The Little Book of Ketamine.* Berkeley: Ronin Publishing, 1999.

Kenkel, N. C. and D. J. Walker. "Fractals in the Biological Sciences." *Coenoses* 11 (1996): 77–100.

Kerns, J. G., H. Berenbaum, D. M. Barch, M. T. Banich, and N. Stolar. "Word Production in Schizophrenia and Its Relationship to Positive Symptoms." *Psychiatry Res* 87, no. 1 (1999): 29–37.

Keyes, James. *Only Two Can Play This Game*. New York: The Julian Press, 1972.

Kircher, T. T., and D. T. Leube. "Self-Consciousness, Self-Agency, and Schizophrenia." *Conscious Cogn* 12, no. 4 (2003): 656–69.

Klages, W., and I. Klages. "On the Psychology and Psychopathology of the Sense of Smell." *Arch Psychiatr Nervenkr* 205 (1964): 37–48.

Klein, R. H. "A Computer Analysis of the Schreber Memoirs." *J Nerv Ment Dis* 162, no. 6 (1976): 373–84.

Kluver, Heinrich. *Mescal and the Mechanism of Hallucinations*. Chicago: University of Chicago Press, 1966.

Knight, R. A., D. S. Elliott, J. D. Roff, and C. G. Watson. "Concurrent and Predictive Validity of Components of Disordered Thinking in Schizophrenia." *Schizophr Bull* 12, no. 3 (1986): 427–46.

Kobayashi, R., and T. Murata. "Behavioral Characteristics of 187 Young Adults with Autism." *Psychiatry Clin Neurosci* 52, no. 4 (1998): 383–90.

Kofman, Sarah. *Nietzsche and Metaphor*. Translated by Duncan Large. Stanford: Stanford University Press, 1993.

Kontsevoi, V. A., and T. A. Druzhinina. "Clinico-Psychopathologic Picture of Schizophrenia Following a Course of Attacks with Verbal Hallucinations." *Zh Nevropatol Psikhiatr Im S S Korsakova* 73, no. 6 (1973): 902–09.

Kranz, H. "Cow Walking in a Catholic Manner. A Wood-Carving by a Schizophrenic Patient Corresponding to a Medieval Stone Relief." *Med Welt* 25, no. 24 (1974): 1087–91.

Krassner, Paul. *Magic Mushrooms and Other Highs: From Toad Slime to Ecstasy*. Berkeley: Ten Speed Press, 2004.

———. *Pot Stories for the Soul*. New York: Trans-High Corporation, 1999.

Kreuter, Holly. *Drama in the Desert: The Sights and Sounds of Burning Man*. San Francisco: Raised Barn Press, 2002.

Krippner, Stanley. "The Effects of Psychedelic Experience on Language Functioning." In *Psychedelics: The Uses and Implications of Hallucinogenic Drugs,* edited by Bernard Aaronson and Humphrey Osmond. New York: Doubleday & Company, 1970.

Krippner, Stanley, and Alberto Villoldo. *The Realms of Healing*. Berkeley: Celestial Arts, 1986.

Kristeva, Julia. *Language the Unknown: An Initiation into Linguistics*. Translated by Anne M. Menke, European Perspectives. New York: Columbia University Press, 1989.

———. *Revolution in Poetic Language*. New York: Columbia University Press, 1984.

Kuperberg, G., and S. Heckers. "Schizophrenia and Cognitive Function." *Curr Opin Neurobiol* 10, no. 2 (2000): 205–10.

LadyBee. "The Outsider Art of Burning Man." *Leonardo* 36, no. 5 (2003): 343–48.

Laing, R. D. *The Politics of Experience*. New York: Ballantine Books, 1967.

Lakoff, George, and Mark Johnson. *Metaphors We Live By*. Chicago: University of Chicago Press, 1980.

———. *Philosophy in the Flesh: The Embodied Mind and Its Challenge to Western Thought*. New York: Basic Books, 1999.

Langan, Christopher Michael. "The Cognitive-Theoretic Model of the Universe: A New Kind of Reality Theory." *Progress in Complexity, Information, and Design* 1.2 and 1.3, April--September (2002).

Langdon, R., S. R. Jones, E. Connaughton, and C. Fernyhough. "The Phenomenology of Inner Speech: Comparison of Schizophrenia Patients with Auditory Verbal Hallucinations and Healthy Controls." *Psychol Med* 39, no. 4 (2009): 655–63.

Lanham, Richard A. *The Economics of Attention: Style and Substance in the Age of Information*. Chicago: University of Chicago Press, 2006.

———. *The Electronic Word: Democracy, Technology, and the Arts*. Chicago: University of Chicago Press, 1993.

———. *A Handlist of Rhetorical Terms*. Berkeley: University of California Press, 1991.

Larsen, Deena. "Language Dancing in a Maze: Ternary Logic, Language, and Mind-States in Glide." At DAC conference, Melbourne, Australia, 2003.

Larsen, Steven. *The Mythic Imagination: The Quest for Meaning through Personal Mythology*. Rochester, Vermont: Inner Traditions International, 1996.

———. *The Shaman's Doorway: Opening Imagination to Power and Myth*. Rochester, Vermont: Inner Traditions, 1998.

Laughlin, Charles. "Glossary of Technical Terms Used in Biogenetic Structuralism." www.biogeneticstruc-turalism.com/glossary.htm.

———. "Profile in Research: Roland Fischer." www.biogeneticstructuralism.com/nnn/winter91.htm.

Laughlin, Charles D., John McManus, and Eugene G. d'Aquili. *Brain, Symbol, & Experience: Toward a Neurophenomenology of Human Consciousness*. Edited by Francisco J. Varela Jeremy W. Hayward, Ken Wilbur, New Science Library. Boston: Shambhala, 1990.

Leary, Timothy. *Change Your Brain*. Berkeley: Ronin Publishing, 2002.

———. *Chaos & Cyberculture*. Berkeley: Ronin Publishing, Inc., 1994.

———. *Design for Dying*. San Francisco: HarperEdge, 1997.

———. *Flashbacks: An Autobiography*. Los Angeles: Jeremy P. Tarcher, Inc, 1990.

———. *The Intelligence Agents.* Culver City: Peace Press, Inc., 1979.

———. *Musings on Human Metamorphosis.* Berkeley: Ronin Publishing, 2003.

———. *Starseed.* San Francisco: Levels Press, 1973.

———. *Surfing the Conscious Nets.* [location?]Last Gasp, 1995.

———. *Your Brain Is God.* Berkeley: Ronin Publishing, 2001.

Leary, Timothy, Richard Alpert, and Ralph Metzner. *The Psychedelic Experience: A Manual Based on the Tibetan Book of the Dead.* New Hyde Park: University Books, 1964.

Leary, Timothy, and Robert Anton Wilson. *The Game of Life.* Phoenix: New Falcon Publications, 1993.

Lechte, John. *Fifty Key Contemporary Thinkers: From Structuralism to Postmodernity.* New York: Routledge, 1994.

Lee, Martin A. and Bruce Shlain. *Acid Dreams: The Complete Social History of LSD: The CIA, the Sixties, and Beyond.* New York: Grove Press, 1992.

LeVine, W. R., and R. L. Conrad. "The Classification of Schizophrenic Neologisms." *Psychiatry* 42, no. 2 (1979): 177–81.

Lewis-Williams, J. D., and T. A. Dowson. "The Signs of All Times." *Current Anthropology* 29, no. 2 (1988): 201–24.

Lieberman, P. B. " 'Objective' Methods and 'Subjective' Experiences." *Schizophr Bull* 15, no. 2 (1989): 267–75.

Lilly, John C. *The Center of the Cyclone: An Autobiography of Inner Space.* New York: Bantam Books, 1979.

———. *The Deep Self.* New York: Warner Books, 1977a.

———. *Programming and Metaprogramming in the Human Biocomputer.* New York: The Julian Press, Inc., 1972.

———. *The Scientist: A Novel Autobiography.* Philadelphia: J. B. Lippincott Company, 1978.

———. *Simulations of God: The Science of Belief.* New York: Bantam Books, 1976.

Lilly, John C., and Antonietta Lilly. *The Dyadic Cyclone.* New York: Pocket Books, 1977b.

Loras, O. "The Universe of Prometheus Bound: The Existential Language of Hallucinations." *Ann Med Psychol* (Paris) 116, no. 4 (1958): 624–49.

Lorimer, David. *Thinking Beyond the Brain: A Wider Science of Consciousness.* Edinburgh: Floris Books, 2001.

Ludlow, Fitz-Hugh. *The Hasheesh Eater: Being Passages from the Life of a Pythagorean (Subterranean Lives).* New Brunswick, New Jersey: Rutgers University Press, 2006.

Luna, Luis Eduardo, and Pablo Amaringo. *Ayahuasca Visions: The Religious Iconography of a Peruvian Shaman.* Berkeley: North Atlantic Books, 1999.

Lyttle, Thomas. *Psychedelics Reimagined.* Brooklyn: Autonomedia, 1999.

Macey, David. *The Lives of Michel Foucault.* New York: Vintage, 1995.

Man, Bong. "Take the Third Toke!" Erowid.org, http://www.erowid.org/cgi-bin/search/htsearch.php?exclude=&words=dmt&Search.x=0&Search.y=0.

Mandelbrot, Benoit B. *The Fractal Geometry of Nature.* New York: W. H. Freeman and Company, 1983.

MAPS. "R & D Medicines: Psychedelic Research around the World." MAPS, www.maps.org/research.

Marent, Thomas. *Rainforest.* New York: DK Publishing, 2006.

Markoff, John. *What the Dormouse Said: How the Sixties Counterculture Shaped the Personal Computer Industry.* New York: Puffin Books, 2005.

Marks, Lawrence E. "Synesthesia." In *Varieties of Anomalous Experience: Examining the Scientific Evidence*, edited by Etzel Cardena, Steven Jay Lynn and Stanley Krippner, 121–50. Washington, DC: American Psychological Association, 2000.

Martindale, C., and R. Fischer. "The Effects of Psilocybin on Primary Process Content in Language." *Confin Psychiatr* 20, no. 4 (1977): 195–202.

Masters, R.E.L., and Jean Houston. *Mind Games: The Guide to Inner Space.* New York: Dell Publishing Company, 1971.

———. *The Varieties of Psychedelic Experience: The Classic Guide to the Effects of LSD on the Human Psyche.* New York: Dell Publishing Company, 1966.

Maturana, Humberto. "Neurophysiology of Cognition." In *Cognition, a Multiple View,* edited by P. L. Garvin. New York: Spartan, 1970.

McCaffery, Steve, and Jed Rasula. *Imagining Language: An Anthology.* Cambridge: The MIT Press, 1998.

McCulloch, W. S. "Of I and It." *Perspect Biol Med* 12, no. 4 (1969): 547–60.

McGuire, P. K., D. A. Silbersweig, I. Wright, R. M. Murray, R. S. Frackowiak, and C. D. Frith. "The Neural Correlates of Inner Speech and Auditory Verbal Imagery in Schizophrenia: Relationship to Auditory Verbal Hallucinations." *Br J Psychiatry* 169, no. 2 (1996): 148–59.

McKenna, Dennis. *The Brotherhood of the Screaming Abyss.* St. Cloud, Minnesota: North Star Press, 2012.

McKenna, Dennis. 2009. [[**Missing info??]]

McKenna, Dennis, J. C. Callaway, and Charles S. Grob. "The Scientific Investigation of Ayahuasca: A Review of Past and Current Research." *The Heffter Review of Psychedelic Research* 1 (1998): 65–76.

McKenna, Terence. *Alien Dreamtime.* San Francisco, 1993. Multi-media event.

———. "Appreciating Imagination Part 1." In *The Psychedelic Salon*, edited by Lorenzo Hagerty, 1994.

———. *The Archaic Revival: Speculations on Psychedelic Mushrooms, the Amazon, Virtual Reality, UFOs, Evolution, Shamanism, the Rebirth of the Goddess, and the End of History.* 1st ed. San Francisco, California: HarperSanFrancisco, 1991.

———. "The Camden Centre Talk." http://deoxy.org/t_camden.htm.

———. "The Definitive UFO Tape." In *The Psychedelic Salon*, edited by Lorenzo Hagerty, 1983.

———. *The Definitive UFO Tape.* Berkeley, California: Dolphin Tapes, 1983.

———. *Food of the Gods: The Search for the Original Tree of Knowledge: A Radical History of Plants, Drugs, and Human Evolution.* New York: Bantam Books, 1992.

———. "In the Valley of Novelty." In *The Psychedelic Salon*, edited by Lorenzo Hagerty, 1998.

———. "Mushrooms, Elves and Magic." www.mav-ericksofthemind.com/ter-int.htm.

———. "Ordinary Language, Visible Language & Virtual Reality." http://deoxy.org/t_langvr.htm.

———. *Psilocybin and the Sands of Time.* Berkeley, California: Dolphin Tapes, 1986. Audio tape.

———. "Sacred Antidotes: An Interview With Terence McKenna." *Tricycle: The Buddhist Review* 6, no. 1 (1996): 94–97.

———. "Skepticism and the Balkanization of Epistemology." In *The Psychedelic Salon*, edited by Lorenzo Hagerty, 1998.

———. "Terence McKenna on the Art Bell Show." [[**DATE?]]

———. "Terence McKenna—How to Take Psychedelics Pt. 1." edited by LSDfunk, 2009.

———. "Terence McKenna—How to Take Psychedelics Pt. 2." edited by LSDfunk, 2009.

———. "Time and Mind." http://deoxy.org/time-mind.htm.

———. *True Hallucinations: Being an Account of the Author's Extraordinary Adventures in the Devil's Paradise.* 1st ed. San Francisco: HarperSanFrancisco, 1993.

———. "Tryptamine Hallucinogens and Consciousness." In Lilly/Goswami Conference on Consciousness and Quantum Physics. Esalen, 1983.

———. "Understanding and the Imagination in the Light of Nature." [[**MORE INFO?]]

McKenna, Terence, and Dennis J. McKenna. *The Invisible Landscape: Mind, Hallucinogens, and the I Ching.* 1st HarperCollins ed. San Francisco, Calif.: HarperSanFrancisco, 1993a.

McKenna, Terence, and Mark Pesce. "Technopagans at the End of History." In *The Psychedelic Salon*, edited by Lorenzo Hagerty, 1998.

McKenna, Terence, and Ralph Abraham. "Dynamics of Hyperspace." www.scribd.com/doc/13362891/TerenceMcKenna-and-Ralph-Abraham-Dynamics-of-Hyperspace?autodown=pdf.

McKenna, Terence, R. Gordon Wasson, and Thomas J. Riedlinger. *The Sacred Mushroom Seeker: Tributes to R. Gordon Wasson.* Rochester, Vermont: Park Street Press, 1997.

McKenna, Terence, Rupert Sheldrake, and Ralph Abraham. *Chaos, Creativity, and Cosmic Consciousness.* Rochester, Vermont: Park Street Press, 2001.

McLuhan, Marshall. *Understanding Media: The Extensions of Man.* New York: New American Library, 1964.

McLuhan, Stephanie, and David Staines, eds. *Understanding Me: Lectures and Interviews.* Cambridge: MIT Press, 2004.

McVay, Douglas A. *Drug War Facts.* 4th edition ed: Common Sense for Drug Policy, 2004.

MediLexicon. "Medical Dictionary-'Hypernoia'." MediLexicon International Ltd., www.medilexicon.com/medicaldictionary.php?t=42461.

MedTerms. "Definition of Hallucination." MedicineNet.com, www.medterms.com/script/main/art.asp?articlekey=24171.

Melechi, Antonio. *Psychedelia Britannica: Hallucinogenic Drugs in Britain.* London: Turnaround, 1997.

Mercante, Marcelo S. "Images of Healing: Spontaneous Mental Imagery and Healing Process of the Barquinha, a Brazilian Ayahuasca Religious System." Saybrook Graduate School, 2006.

Merkur, Dan. *The Ecstatic Imagination: Psychedelic Experiences and the Psychoanalysis of Self-Actualization.* Albany: State University of New York Press, 1998.

Merleau-Ponty, Maurice. *Consciousness and the Acquisition of Language.* Translated by Hugh J. Silverman. Edited by James M. Edie, Northwestern University Studies in Phenomenology & Existential Philosophy. Evanston: Northwestern University Press, 1973.

———. *The Phenomenology of Perception.* New York: Routledge, 2002.

———. *The Primacy of Perception and Other Essays.* Translated by multiple translators. Edited by John Wild, Northwestern University Studies in Phenomenology & Existential Philosophy. Evanston: Northwestern University Press, 1964.

———. *Sense and Non-Sense.* Translated by Hubert L. Dreyfus and Patricia Allen Dreyfus. Edited by John Wild, Northwestern University Studies in Phenomenology and Existential Philosophy. Evanston: Northwestern University Press, 1964.

———. *Signs.* Translated by Richard C. McCleary. Edited by John Wild, Northwestern University Studies in Phenomenology and Existential Philosophy. Evanston: Northwestern University Press, 1964.

———. *The Visible and the Invisible.* Translated by

Alphonso Lingis. Edited by John Wild, Northwestern University Studies in Phenomenology and Existential Philosophy. Evanston: Northwestern University Press, 1968.

Messaris, Paul. *Visual "Literacy": Image, Mind, and Reality.* Boulder: Westview Press, Inc., 1994.

Metzner, Ralph. *Ayahuasca: Human Consciousness and the Spirits of Nature.* New York: Thunder's Mouth Press, 1999.

———. *Green Psychology: Transforming Our Relationship to the Earth.* Rochester, Vermont: Park Street Press, 1999.

———. *Maps of Consciousness.* New York: Collier Books, 1971.

———. *Sacred Mushrooms of Visions: Teonanacatl.* Rochester, Vermont: Park Street Press, 2005.

———. *The Unfolding Self: Varieties of Transformative Experience.* Novato, CA: Origin Press, 1998.

Meyer, Peter. "Apparent Communication with Discarnate Entities Induced by Dimethyltryptamine (DMT)." www.serendipity.li/dmt/dmtart00.html.

———. "Timewave Zero and the Fractal Time Software." www.fractal-timewave.com/index.html.

Michaux, Henri. *Miserable Miracle (Mescaline).* Translated by Louise Varese. San Francisco: City Lights Books, 1956.

Miller, M. D., R. L. Johnson, and L. H. Richmond. "Auditory Hallucinations and Descriptive Language Skills." *J Psychiatr Res* 39 (1965): 43–56.

Miro. "Enter the Mist." Erowid.org, www.erowid.org/experiences/exp.php?ID=17069.

Moore, Marcia, and Howard Alltounian. *Journeys into the Bright World.* Rockport: Para Research, Inc., 1978.

Moritz, S., and F. Laroi. "Differences and Similarities in the Sensory and Cognitive Signatures of Voice-Hearing, Intrusions and Thoughts." *Schizophr Res* 102, no. 1-3 (2008): 96–107.

Moscowitz, Dennis. "Rikchiks." http://suberic.net/~dmm/rikchik/intro.html.

Mullis, Kary B. *Dancing Naked in the Mind Field.* London: Bloomsbury Publishing, 2000.

Munn, Henry. "The Mushrooms of Language." In *Hallucinogens and Shamanism,* edited by Michael J. Harner, London: Oxford University Press, 1973.

———. "Writing in the Imagination of an Oral Poet." In *A Book of the Book,* edited by Jerome Rothenberg, New York: Granary Books, 2000: 251–56.

Murray, Janet H. *Hamlet on the Holodeck: The Future of Narrative in Cyberspace.* Cambridge: The MIT Press, 1997.

Narby, Jeremy. "The Cosmic Serpent, DNA, and the Origins of Knowledge: Q & A with Jeremy Narby" http://deoxy.org/narbystew.htm.

———. *The Cosmic Serpent: DNA and the Origins of Knowledge.* New York: Jeremy P. Tarcher, 1999.

———. *Intelligence in Nature.* New York: Jeremy P. Tarcher, 2005.

Narby, Jeremy, and Francis Huxley. *Shamans through Time: 50 Years on the Path to Knowledge.* New York: Jeremy P. Tarcher, 2001.

Narby, Jeremy, Jan Kounen, and Vincent Ravelec. *The Psychotropic Miind: The World According to Ayahuasca, Iboga, and Shamanism.* Rochester, Vermont: Park Street Press, 2008.

Natale, M., C. C. Dahlberg, and J. Jaffe. "Effect of Psychotomimetics (LSD and Dextroamphetamine) on the Use of Primary- and Secondary-Process Language." *J Consult Clin Psychol* 46, no. 2 (1978): 352–53.

Natale, M., M. Kowitt, C. C. Dahlberg, and J. Jaffe. "Effect of Psychotomimetics (LSD and Dextroamphetamine) on the Use of Figurative Language During Psychoanalysis." *J Consult Clin Psychol* 46, no. 6 (1978): 1579–80.

Needham, Joseph, and Ling Wang. *Science and Civilization in China: History of Scientific Thought.* 7 vols. Vol. 2. Cambridge: Cambridge University Press, 1991.

Nelson, Theodor H. *Computer Lib/Dream Machines* (Rev. Ed.). Redmond, Washington: Tempus Books of Microsoft Press, 1987.

———. "Ted Nelson Autobiography." Ted Nelson, http://archives.obs-us.com/obs/english/papers/ted/tedbio12.htm.

Newland, Constance. *Myself and I.* Toronto: Signet Books, 1962.

Nezahualcoyotl. "The Painted Book." In *A Book of the Book,* edited by Jerome Rothenberg. New York: Granary Press, 2000: 249–50.

Nichols, David E. "Hallucinogens." *Pharmacol. Ther.* 101, no. 2 (2004): 131–81.

Nicolescu, Basarab. "Interview with Basarab Nicolescu." Ad Astra 1, no. 1 (2002).

———. *Manifesto of Transdisciplinarity.* Translated by Karen Claire-Voss. Edited by David Appelbaum, SUNY Series in Western Esoteric Traditions. Albany: State University of New York Press, 2002.

———. *Science, Meaning, and Evolution: The Cosmology of Jacob Boehme.* New York: Parabola Books, 1991.

Nicotra, Jodie. "William James in the Borderlands: Psychedelic Science and the 'Accidental Fences' of Self." *Configurations: A Journal of Literature, Science, and Technology* 16, no. 2 (2009): 199–213.

Noffke, Will. "A Conversation over Saucers." *ReVision: A Journal of Consciousness* 11, no. Winter (1989): 23–28.

norman. "Night Like No Other (Monsters)." Erowid.org, www.erowid.org/experiences/exp.php?ID=23345.

O'Connor, D. W., D. Ames, B. Gardner, and M. King. "Psychosocial Treatments of Psychological Symptoms in Dementia: A Systematic Review of Reports Meeting Quality Standards." *Int Psychogeriatr* 21, no. 2 (2009): 241–51.

O'Donnell, James Joseph. *Avatars of the Word: From Papyrus to Cyberspace.* Cambridge, Massachusetts: Harvard University Press, 1998.

Osmond, Humphrey, and Bernard Aaronson. *Psychedelics: The Uses and Implications of Hallucinogenic Drugs.* Garden City: Anchor Books, 1970.

Oss, O. T., and O. N. Oeric. *Psilocybin: Magic Mushroom Grower's Guide.* [location?]Quick American Publishing, 1986.

Ott, Jonathan. *The Age of Entheogens and the Angel's Dictionary.* Kennewick, Washington: Natural Products Company, 1995.

Oxman, T. E., S. D. Rosenberg, P. P. Schnurr, G. J. Tucker, and G. Gala. "The Language of Altered States." *J Nerv Ment Dis* 176, no. 7 (1988): 401–08.

Pahnke, Walter N. "Drugs and Mysticism." *The International Journal of Parapsychology* VIII, no. 2 (1966): 295–313.

———. "Drugs and Mysticism: An Analysis of the Relationship between Psychedelic Drugs and the Mystical Consciousness." Harvard University, 1963.

———. "The Psychedelic Mystical Experience in the Human Encounteer with Death." *Psychedelic Review* 11 (1971).

Palmer, Gary B. *Toward a Theory of Cultural Linguistics.* Austin: University of Texas Press, 1996.

Pellerin, Cheryl, Robert Crumb, and Gilbert Shelton. *Trips: How Hallucinogens Work in Your Brain.* New York: Seven Stories Press, 1998.

Pesce, Mark. "Bios and Logos." In *The Psychedelic Salon,* edited by Lorenzo Hagerty, 2002.

———. "Psychedelics and the Creation of Virtual Reality." MAPS, www.maps.org/news-letters/v10n3/10304pes.html.

Pickering, Andrew. *The Cybernetic Brain.* Chicago: University of Chicago Press, 2011.

Pickover, Clifford A. *Sex, Drugs, Einstein, & Elves.* Petaluma: Smart Publications, 2005.

Pinchbeck, Daniel. *2012: The Return of Quetzalcoatl.* New York: Jeremy P. Tarcher, 2006.

———. *Breaking Open the Head: A Psychedelic Journey into the Heart of Contemporary Shamanism.* New York: Broadway Books, 2002.

Pinker, Steven. *The Language Instinct: How the Mind Creates Language.* New York: HarperPerennial, 1994.

Plasmamorphing. "Alien Contact." Erowid.org, www.erowid.org/cgi-bin/search/htsearch.php?method=and&restrict=&format=long&config=htdig&exclude=&words=alien.

Plato. *Euthyphro, Apology, Crito, Meno, Gpgias, Menexenus.* Translated by R. E. Allen. Vol. 1, The Dialogues of Plato. New Haven: Yale University Press, 1984.

Polari de Alverga, Alex. *Forest of Visions: Ayahuasca, Amazonian Spirituality, and the Santo Daime Tradition.* Translated by Rosana Workman. Rochester, Vermont: Park Street Press, 1999.

Pollack, Robert. *Signs of Life: The Language and Meanings of DNA.* Boston: Houghton Mifflin, 1994.

Pollan, Michael. *The Botany of Desire: A Plant's Eye View of the World.* New York: Random House, 2001.

Polyani, Michael. *Personal Knowledge: Towards a Post-Critical Philosophy.* London: Routledge, 1962.

Pomarol-Clotet, E., G. D. Honey, G. K. Murray, P. R. Corlett, A. R. Absalom, M. Lee, P. J. McKenna, E. T. Bullmore, and P. C. Fletcher. "Psychological Effects of Ketamine in Healthy Volunteers. Phenomenological Study." *Br J Psychiatry* 189 (2006): 173–79.

Pope, H. G., Jr., M. B. Poliakoff, M. P. Parker, M. Boynes, and J. I. Hudson. "Is Dissociative Amnesia a Culture-Bound Syndrome? Findings from a Survey of Historical Literature." *Psychol Med* 37, no. 2 (2007): 225–33.

Porush, David. "The Anthropic Cosmology Principle and Literary Theory." Paper presented at the Society for Literature, Science and the Arts, Boston, Massachusetts, 1993.

———. "Telepathy: Alphabetic Consciousness and the Age of Cyborg Illiteracy." In *Virtual Futures,* edited by Joan Broadhurst and Eric Cassidy Dixon. London and New York: Routledge, 1998: 44–64.

Powell, Simon G. "God's Flesh: Sacred Mushrooms and the Quest for Higher Knowledge." Unpublished manuscript, 2007: 210.

———. *The Psilocybin Solution.* Rochester, Vermont: Inner Traditions, 2011.

———. *Sacred Ground: Psilocybin Mushrooms and the Rebirth of Nature.* London: Psychoactive Media Production, 2008.

Pribham, Karl. "Commentary on 'Synaesthesia' by Ramachandran and Hubbard." *Journal of Consciousness Studies* 10, no. 3 (2003): 75–76.

Price, David H. "Gregory Bateson and the OSS: World War II and Bateson's Assessment of Applied Anthropology." *Human Organization* 57, no. 4 (1998): 379–84.

Pursglove, Paul David. *Zen in the Art of Close Encounters: Crazy Wisdom and UFOs.* Berkeley: The New Being Project, 1995.

Ramachandran, V. S., and E. M. Hubbard. "Synaesthesia—A Window into Perception, Thought, and Language." *Journal of Consciousness Studies* 8, no. 12 (2001): 3–34.

rapture, green. "Sonic Alien Contact." Erowid.org, www.erowid.org/cgi-bin/search/htsearch.php?method=and&restrict=&format=long&config=htdig&exclude=&words=green+rapture.

Ray, Thomas. "The Chemical Architecture of the Human Mind: Probing Receptor Space with Psychedelics." Paper presented at Toward a Science of Consciousness, Tucson, Arizona, 2004.

———. "Psychedelics and the Human Receptorome." PLoS ONE (2010).

Renwick. "Overview: Ketamine." Erowid.org, www.erowid.org/experiences/exp.php?ID=19628.

Ricouer, Paul. *The Conflict of Interpretations, Studies in Phenomenology and Existential Philosophy.* Evanston: Northwestern University Press, 1974.

Rimbaud, Arthur. *Arthur Rimbaud: Complete Works.* New York: Harper Perennial Modern Classics, 2008.

Rivas, E., F. Rivas, M. Pineda, Q. Pineda, and E. Rebollo. "Hallucinations as a Metaphor and Metonymy." *Arch Neurobiol* (Madr) 43, no. 2 (1980): 101–06.

Rivers, Catfish. "Possible Loss of Potency? But Active!: 4-Acetoxy-Mipt." Erowid.org, www.erowid.org/experiences/exp.php?ID=44625.

Robbins, M. "The Language of Schizophrenia and the World of Delusion." *Int J Psychoanal* 83, Part 2 (2002): 383–405.

Roberts, Thomas B. *Psychedelic Horizons.* Exeter: Imprint Academic, 2006.

———. *Psychoactive Sacramentals: Essays on Entheogens and Religion.* San Francisco: Council on Spiritual Practices, 2001.

Romme, M. A., and A. D. Escher. "Hearing Voices." *Schizophr Bull* 15, no. 2 (1989): 209–16.

Roney-Dougal, Serena. *Where Science and Magic Meet.* Longmead: Element Books Limited, 1991.

Rothenberg, Jerome. *Technicians of the Sacred.* Berkeley: University of California Press, 1985.

Rucker, Rudy. *The Fourth Dimension: Toward a Geometry of Higher Reality.* Boston: Houghton Mifflin Company, 1984.

Rucker, Rudolf, and B. Rucker, eds. *Speculations on the Fourth Dimension: Selected Writings of Charles H. Hinton.* New York: Dover Publications, Inc., 1980.

Russell, Bertrand. "On the Nature of Acquaintance, Part I." *The Monist* 24, no. 1 (1914): 1–16.

Rysdyk, Evelyn C. *Modern Shamanic Living: New Explorations of an Ancient Path.* York Beach, Maine: Samuel Weiser, Inc., 1999.

Sand, Nick. "Reflections on Imprisonment and Liberation as Aspects of Consciousness." In *The Psychedelic Salon*, edited by Lorenzo Hagerty, 2001.

Sarlin, M. B. "The Use of Dreams in Psychotherapy with Deaf Patients." *J Am Acad Psychoanal* 12, no. 1 (1984): 75–88.

Saunders, Nicholas, and Anja Dashwood. "Barquinha." www.entheology.org/edoto/anmviewer.asp?a=127.

Saussure, Ferdinand de. *Course in General Linguistics.* Translated by Wade Baskin. New York: Philosophical Library, 1959.

Schaechter, F. "The Language of the Voices." *Med J Aust* 2 (1964): 870–71.

Schafer, Georg, and Nan Cuz. In *The Kingdom of Mescal: A Fairy-Tale for Adults.* Berkeley: Shambala Publications, Inc., 1970.

Schmidt, P. "Psychosis and Grammatical Reality. Preliminary to an Axiomatic System." *Ann Med Psychol* (Paris) 139, no. 5 (1981): 497–511.

Schultes, Richard Evans, Albert Hofmann, and Christian Rätsch. *Plants of the Gods: Their Sacred, Healing, and Hallucinogenic Powers.* Rochester, Vermont: Healing Arts Press, 1992.

Sells, Michael A. *Mystical Languages of Unsaying.* Chicago: University of Chicago Press, 1994.

Sewell, R. A., Halpren, J. H., Pope, H. G., Jr. "Response of Cluster Headache to Psilocybin and LSD." Neurology 66, no. 12 (2006): 1920–22.

Shanon, Benny. *The Antipodes of the Mind: Charting the Phenomenology of the Ayahusca Experience.* Oxford: Oxford University Press, 2002.

Shear, Jonathan, ed. *Explaining Consciousness—The Hard Problem.* Cambridge: The MIT Press, 1998.

Sheldrake, Rupert, Terence K. McKenna, and Ralph Abraham. *The Evolutionary Mind: Conversations on Science, Imagination and Spirit.* Rev. ed. Rhinebeck, New York: Monkfish Book Pub. Co., 2005.

———. *The Evolutionary Mind: Trialogues at the Edge of the Unthinkable.* 1st ed. Santa Cruz, CA: Trialogue Press, 1998.

Shulgin, Alexander, and Ann Shulgin. *PIHKAL: A Chemical Lovestory.* Berkeley: Transform Press, 1991.

———. *TIHKAL: The Continuation.* Berkeley: Transform Press, 1997.

Siegal, Ethan. "Starts with a Bang!" Science blogs.

Singh, Simon. *Fermat's Last Theorem.* London: Harper Perennial, 2005.

Sirius, R. U. "Counterculture and the Tech Revolution." *10 Zen Monkeys*, www.10zenmonkeys.com/2006/11/19/counterculture-and-the-tech-revolution/.

Skullman. "T'was the Night." Erowid.org, www.erowid.org/experiences/exp.php?ID=73726.

Skutnabb-Kangas, Tove. "Why Should Linguistic Diversity Be Maintained and Supported in Europe?" Strasbourg: University of Roskilde, 2002.

Slattery, Diana, William Brubaker, Charles R. Mathis, and Robert E. Dunie. "From Interface to Interspace: LiveGlide and the 3rd Dimension." In Digital Arts Conference. Melbourne, 2003.

Slattery, Diana. "The Glide Project." http://web.archive.org/web/20130122085556/http://www.academy.rpi.edu/glide/.

———. "The Noetic Connection: Synesthesia, Psychedelics, and Language." In International Conference on Computer Graphics and Interactive Techniques, 124–27. Los Angeles: ACM, 2004.

Slattery, Diana Reed. "The Glide Model: Communicating Intention through Gestural Language." Paper presented at the SETI Workshop on the Art and Science of Interstellar Message Composition, Paris, March 2003.

———. *The Maze Game.* Kingston, New York: Deep Listening Publications, 2003.

———. "The Noetic Connection: Synaesthesia, Psychedelics, and Language." Paper presented at the Siggraph, Los Angeles, California, 2004.

———. "Psychedelics: My Problem Discourse." *Configurations: A Journal of Literature, Science, and Technology* 16, no. 2 (2009): 283–96.

———. "Writing toward the 4th Dimension: The Glide Model of Multidimensional Writing." In *Sensorial Net.* Fortaleza, Brazil, 2003.

Smith, Huston. *Cleansing the Doors of Perception: The Religious Significance of Entheogenic Plants and Chemicals.* New York: Jeremy P. Tarcher, 2000.

Snow, C. P. *The Two Cultures and the Scientific Revolution.* Cambridge: Cambridge University Press, 1963.

Sotomayor, Sylvia. "An Introduction to Kelen." Presentation at the Language Creation Society, Cambridge, 2009.

Southworth, Franklin C., and C. J. Daswani. *Foundations of Linguistics.* New York: The Free Press, 1974.

Spacetime, Continuum, Terence K. McKenna, and Stephen Kent. *Alien Dreamtime.* S.l.: Astralwerks: distributed by Caroline Records, 1993. Sound recording.

Spinella, Marcello. *The Psychopharmacology of Herbal Medicine: Plant Drugs That Alter Mind, Brain, and Behavior.* Cambridge: MIT Press, 2001.

Stafford, Peter. *Psychedelics Encyclopedia.* Berkeley: And/Or Press, 1977.

Stafford, Peter, and Bonnie Golightly. *LSD: The Problem-Solving Psychedelic.* New York: Award Books, 1967.

Stamets, Paul. *Mycelium Running: How Mushrooms Can Help Save the World.* Berkeley: Ten Speed Press, 2005.

Steiner, George. *After Babel: Aspects of Language and Translation.* Oxford: Oxford University Press, 1998.

Steiner, Rudolph. *The Fourth Dimension: Sacred Geometry, Alchemy, and Mathematics.* Great Barrington: Anthroposophic Press, 2001.

Stephane, M., P. Thuras, H. Nasrallah, and A. P. Georgopoulos. "The Internal Structure of the Phenomenology of Auditory Verbal Hallucinations." *Schizophr Res* 61, no. 2-3 (2003): 185–93.

Stevens, Jay. *Storming Heaven: LSD and the American Dream.* New York: Grove Press, 1998.

Stolaroff, Myron J. *The Secret Chief: Conversations with a Pioneer of the Underground Psychedelic Therapy Movement.* Sarasota: MAPS, 1997.

Stone, Allucquère Roseanne. *The War of Desire and Technology at the Close of the Mechanical Age.* Cambridge: The MIT Press, 1998.

Strassman, Rick. *DMT: The Spirit Molecule.* Rochester, Vermont: Park Street Press, 2001.

Strassman, Rick, Slawek Wojtowicz, Luis Eduardo Luna, and Ede Frecska. *Inner Paths to Outer Space.* Rochester, Vermont: Park Street Press, 2008.

Strik, W., T. Dierks, D. Hubl, and H. Horn. "Hallucinations, Thought Disorders, and the Language Domain in Schizophrenia." *Clin EEG Neurosci* 39, no. 2 (2008): 91–94.

Strogatz, Steven. *Sync: How Order Emerges from Chaos in the Universe, Nature, and Daily Life.* New York: Hyperion Books, 2003.

Sugarman, Arthur A., ed., and Ralph E. Tarter. *Expanding Dimensions of Consciousness.* New York: Springer Publishing Company, 1978.

Sutin, Lawrence. In *Pursuit of Valis: Selections from the Exegesis*—Philip K. Dick. Novato: Underwood-Miller, 1991.

———. *The Shifting Realities of Philip K. Dick: Selected Literary and Philosophical Writings.* New York: Vintage Books, 1995.

Sweetser, Eve. *From Etymology to Pragmatics.* Edited by C. J. Filmore, B. Comrie et al. Vol. 34, Cambridge Studies in Linguistics. Cambridge: Cambridge University Press, 1990.

Szasz, T. S. "Schizophrenia: The Sacred Symbol of Psychiatry." *Br J Psychiatry* 129 (1976): 308–16.

Tart, Charles T. *Altered States of Consciousness.* Garden City: Anchor Books, 1972.

———. *Living the Mindful Life: A Handbook for Living in the Present Moment.* Boston: Shambhala, 1994.

———. *On Being Stoned: A Psychological Study of Marijuana Intoxication.* Palo Alto: Science and Behavior Books, 1971.

———. "A Systems Approach to Altered States of Consciousness." In *The Psychobiology of Consciousness*, edited by Julian M. and Richard J. Davidson. New York: Plenum Press, 1980: 489.

Tart, Charles T., ed. *Transpersonal Psychologies.* New York: Harper Colophon Books, 1977.

Tart, Charles T. *Open Mind, Discriminating Mind: Reflections on Human Possibilities.* San Francisco: Harper & Row, Publishers, 1989.

Teafaerie, The. "To Believe or Not to Believe." *Erowid.*

Teresa, St. *The Life of St. Teresa of Avila by Herself.* Translated by J. M. Cohen. New York: Penguin Classics, 1988.

Ternaux, Jean-Pierre. "Synesthesia: A Multimodal Combination of Senses." *Leonardo* 36, no. 4 (2003).

Thomas, P. F., and I. Leudar. "Auditory Hallucinations in Schizophrenia." *Lancet* 342, no. 8882 (1993): 1301.

Thompson, Evan. *Between Ourselves: Second-Person Issues in the Study of Consciousness.* Thorverton: Imprint Academic, 2001.

Tolkien, J. R. R. *The Monsters and the Critics and Other Essays*. New York: Houghton Mifflin, 1983.

Townsley, Graham. "'Twisted Language,' A Technique for Knowing." In *Shamans through Time*, edited by Jeremy and Francis Huxley, 263–71. New York: Jeremy P. Tarcher, 2001.

Tucker, Jason WA. Personal communication, 2010.

———. "The Evolution of Transformation." *Reality Sandwich* (2008), www.realitysandwich.com/node/832.

Turnbull, David. *Maps Are Territories: Science Is An Atlas*. Chicago: The University of Chicago Press, 1989.

———. *Masons, Tricksters, and Cartographers*. London: Routledge, 2000.

Turner, D. M. *The Essential Psychedelic Guide*. San Francisco: Panther Press, 1994.

Turner, Mark. *Reading Minds: The Study of English in the Age of Cognitive Science*. Princeton: Princeton University Press, 1991.

Ueno, B. "An Analysis of the Process of Language Deformation in the Beginning Stages of Schizophrenia." *Seishin Shinkeigaku Zasshi* 96, no. 8 (1994): 609–27.

Varela, Francisco J. "A Calculus for Self-Reference." *Int. J. General Systems* 2 (1974): 5–24.

———. "Neurophenomenology: A Methodological Remedy for the Hard Problem." *Journal of Consciousness Studies* 3, no. 4 (1966): 330–50.

———. *Principles of Biological Autonomy*. New York: Elsevier North Holland, Inc., 1979.

Varela, Francisco J., and Jeremy W. Hayward. *Gentle Bridges: Conversation with the Dalai Lama on the Sciences of Mind*. Boston: Shambhala Publications, Inc., 1992.

Varela, Francisco J., and Jonathan Shear. *The View from Within: First-Person Approaches to the Study of Consciousness*. Bowling Green: Imprint Academic, 1999.

Varela, Francisco J., ed., and the Dalai Lama. *Sleeping, Dreaming, and Dying: An Exploration of Consciousness with the Dalai Lama*. Boston: Wisdom Publications, 1997.

Varela, Francisco J., Evan Thompson, and Eleanor Rosch. *The Embodied Mind: Cognitive Science and Human Experience*. Cambridge: The MIT Press, 1996.

Vollenweider, Franz. "Brain Mechanisms of Consciousness." Paper presented at the conference, Toward a Science of Consciousness, Tucson, Arizona, 2004.

Vollenweider, Franz, Tom Ray, and Olivia Carter. *Hallucinogens and Consciousness*. Tuscon: Conference Recording Services, Inc., 2004. Conference recording.

von Foerster, Heinz. *Understanding Understanding: Essays of Cybernetics and Cognition*. New York: Springer-Verlag, 2003.

von Petzinger, Genevieve. "Making the Abstract Concrete: The Place of Geometric Signs in French Upper Paleolithic Art." Masters, University of Victoria, 2009.

Wallace, B. Alan. *The Taboo of Subjectivity: Toward a New Science of Consciousness*. New York: Oxford University Press, 2000.

Walsh, Roger, and Charles S. Grob. *Higher Wisdom: Eminent Elders Explore the Continuing Impact of Psychedelics*. Edited by Richard D. Mann, SUNY Series in Transpersonal and Humanistic Psychology. Albany: State University of New York Press, 2005.

Wasson, R. Gordon, Stella Kramrisch, Jonathan Ott, and Carl A. P. Ruck. *Persephone's Quest: Entheogens and the Origins of Religion*. New Haven: Yale University Press, 1986.

Watts, Alan. *In My Own Way: An Autobiography. 1915–1965*. New York: Pantheon Books, 1972.

———. *The Joyous Cosmology: Adventures in the Chemistry of Consciousness*. New York: Vintage Books, 1962.

Weiger, L. *Chinese Characters*. Translated by S. J. L. Davrout. 2nd ed. New York: Dover Publications, Inc., 1965.

Weil, Andrew. *The Natural Mind*. New York: Houghton Mifflin Company, 1973.

Werner, Heinz, and Bernard Kaplan. *Symbol Formation: An Organismic-Developmental Approach to the Psychology of Language*. Hillsdale, New Jersey: Lawrence Erlbaum Associates, Publishers, 1984.

Wilson, Robert Anton. *Coincidance*. Tempe, Arizona: New Falcon Publications, 1988.

———. *Cosmic Trigger: The Final Secret of the Illuminati*. New York: Pocket Books, 1977.

———. *Email to the Universe and Other Alterations of Consciousness*. Tempe: New Falcon Publications, 2005.

———. *Prometheus Rising*. Tempe: New Falcon Publications, 1994.

———. *Quantum Psychology: How Brain Software Programs You and Your World*. Tempe, Arizona: New Falcon Publications, 1990.

Winkelman, Michael. "A Perspective on Psychedelics from Evolutionary Psychology." Paper presented at the World Psychedelic Forum, Basel, Switzerland, March 21–24, 2008.

———. "Psychointegration: The Physiological Effects of Entheogens." http://www.public.asu.edu/~atmxw/psychointegration.pdf.

———. *Shamanism: The Neural Ecology of Consciousness and Healing*. Westport, Connecticut: Bergin & Garvey, 2000.

———. "Trance States: A Theoretical Model and Cross-Cultural Analysis." *Ethos: Journal of the Society for Psychological Anthropology* 14, no. 2 (1996).

Winkelman, Michael J., and Thomas B. Roberts, eds. *Psychedelic Medicine: New Evidence for Hallucinogenic Substances as Treatments*. Praeger, 2007.

Women, 150 Mayan. *Incantations by Mayan Women*. San Cristóbal, Chiapas, Mexico: Taller Lenateros, 2007.

Wood, Denis. *The Power of Maps*. New York: The Guilford Press, 1992.

Wooley, Benjamin. *Virtual Worlds: A Journey in Hype and Hypermedia*. London: Penguin Books, 1993.

Wyss, F. E. "'Audible Thoughts' and 'Speech Defects' in Schizophrenia." *Br J Psychiatry* 169, no. 3 (1996): 379–80.

Xi, Fu. *The Yi King*. Translated by James Legge. Vol. 16, Sacred Books of the East. Oxford: The Clarendon Press, 1899.

Youngblood, Gene. *Expanded Cinema*. Toronto: Clarke, Irwin & Company Limited, 1970.

Zaehner, R. C. *Mysticism Sacred and Profane*. Galaxy Books ed. New York and Oxford: Oxford University Press, 1961.

About the Author

Photo by Anderson Behling

Diana Reed Slattery was born in time to compile a full 60s resume: civil rights photojournalism, peace marching, cults, and communes. Social justice, self-exploration, and LSD went hand in hand. She went on to co-found an ecologically oriented K-12 school with working farm, dairy, livestock, and forestry that held the first renewable energy conference in Oregon. She later continued her career by founding, funding, and managing a series of not-for-profit organizations. In 1999, in an altered state of consciousness, she acquired a strange, alien script, Glide, beginning a ten-year psychonautic investigation of linguistic phenomena in the psychedelic sphere. Out of this solo—and secret—adventure came a novel, *The Maze Game,* a million words of session reports, software to work with the language, and a PhD in xenolinguistics. Slattery lives in California, and has presented her work at numerous art, technology, consciousness, and psychedelic conferences over the past fifteen years.